Plural Medicine, Tra  Modernity, 1800–2000

Research into 'colonial' or 'imperial' medicine has made considerable progress in recent years, while the study of 'indigenous' or 'folk' medicine in colonised societies has received much less attention. This book redresses the balance by bringing together current critical research into medical pluralism over the last two centuries. It includes a rich international selection of historical, anthropological and sociological case studies ranging from New Zealand to Africa, China, South Asia, Europe and the USA.

Contributions focus on the exchanges and overlaps between various strands of different medical theories. Chapters tackle different aspects of current debates on medical pluralism, including nationalism, globalisation and spirituality. Topics include:

- the underlying dynamics that lead to the perceived marginalisation of 'indigenous' medicine in non-Western countries, and of 'heterodox' or 'alternative' medicine in the West
- the problematic nature of dichotomous categorisations, such as 'traditional' and 'modern' medicine
- the scope and limitations of medical pluralism within different geographical and cultural settings and historical periods
- the ideological and economic factors that contribute to the ways in which different medical systems are imagined as 'rational and scientific' or 'irrational and unscientific'.

Essential reading for scholars of the history of medicine, this work will also interest historians, social anthropologists, sociologists, and scholars of colonial and post-colonial studies.

Waltraud Ernst is currently Lecturer in the Department of History, University of Southampton. She obtained her PhD in History in 1987 at the School of Oriental and African Studies, London, and has since published widely on the history of colonial psychiatry. She is President of the International Association for the Study of Traditional Asian Medicine (IASTAM). She is the author of *Mad Tales from the Raj* (Routledge, 1991) and co-editor of *Race, Science and Medicine* (Routledge, 1999).

Routledge Studies in the Social History of Medicine
Edited by Bernard Harris, Joseph Melling and Anne Borsay
Department of Sociology and Social Policy, University of Southampton, UK
University of Exeter
University of Wales at Lampeter

The Society of the Social History of Medicine was founded in 1969, and exists to promote research into all aspects of the field, without regard to limitations of either time or place. In addition to this book series, the Society also organises a regular programme of conferences, and publishes an internationally recognised journal, *Social History of Medicine*. The Society offers a range of benefits, including reduced-price admission to conferences and discounts on SSHM books, to its members. Individuals wishing to learn more about the Society are invited to contact the Series Editors through the Publisher.

The Society took the decision to launch 'Studies in the social history of medicine', in association with Routledge in 1989, to provide an outlet for some of the latest research in the field. Since that time, the series has expanded significantly under a number of series editors, and now includes both edited collections and monographs. Individuals wishing to submit proposals are invited to contact the Series Editors in the first instance.

1 **Nutrition in Britain**
   Science, scientists and politics in the twentieth century
   Edited by David F. Smith

2 **Migrants, Minorities and Health**
   Historical and contemporary studies
   Edited by Lara Marks and Michael Worboys

3 **From Idiocy to Mental Deficiency**
   Historical perspectives on people with learning disabilities
   Edited by David Wright and Anne Digby

4 **Midwives, Society and Childbirth**
   Debates and controversies in the modern period
   Edited by Hilary Marland and Anne Marie Rafferty

5 **Illness and Healing Alternatives in Western Europe**
   Edited by Marijke Gijswit-Hofstra, Hilary Marland and Hans de Waardt

Plural Medicine, Tradition and Modernity, 1800–2000

Edited by Waltraud Ernst

LONDON AND NEW YORK

First published 2002
by Routledge
2 Park Square, Milton Park, Abingdon, Oxfordshire OX14 4RN

Simultaneously published in the USA and Canada
by Routledge
711 Third Avenue, New York, NY 10017
First issued in paperback 2014

Routledge is an imprint of the Taylor and Francis Group, an informa company

Typeset in Baskerville by
HWA Text and Data Management, Tunbridge Wells

British Library Cataloguing in Publication Data
A catalogue record for this book is available from the British Library

Library of Congress Cataloging in Publication Data
Plural medicine, tradition and modernity, 1800–2000 / edited by
Waltraud Ernst.
     p.   cm.
  Includes bibliographical references and index.
  1. Medical care–Cross-cultural studies. 2. Medical care–Comparative
method. 3. Pluralism–Health aspects. 4. Medicine, State–
Cross-cultural studies. 5. Medicine, State–Comparative method.
  I. Ernst, Waltraud, 1955–

RA394 .P584 2002
362.1–dc21   2001048501

ISBN 978-0-415-23122-0 (hbk)
ISBN 978-0-415-75832-1 (pbk)

Contents

Figures

Contributors

David Arnold is Professor of South Asian History at the School of Oriental and African Studies, London, UK. His publications include *Colonizing the Body: State Medicine and Epidemic Disease in Nineteenth-Century India* (Berkeley, 1993), *Science, Technology and Medicine in Colonial India* (Cambridge, 2000), and *Gandhi* (Harlow, 2001). His current research is on science in mid-Victorian India.

Maarten Bode has trained as a clinical psychologist. In 1994 he completed his MA thesis (in medical anthropology) which dealt with the practice of an Ayurvedic physician in Kathmandu and the role of Ayurveda in the health services of Nepal. He is currently working on his PhD thesis on 'Ayurvedic and Unani bioceuticals: an anthropological inquiry into the modernisation of traditional medical knowledge'. Since 1996 he has made five trips to India to gather data for his thesis. He is affiliated with the Medical Anthropology Unit of the University of Amsterdam, The Netherlands, where he contributes to the Amsterdam Masters in Medical Anthropology (AMMA), an international course in medical anthropology. He also teaches a course on Ayurveda at the India Institute, Amsterdam. He is married and has a daughter of sixteen.

James Bradley is a Research Fellow at the Wellcome Unit for the History of Medicine, University of Glasgow, UK. His recent work includes articles on hydropathy and tattooing. He is currently working on a monograph charting the rise and fall of the water cure in Britain.

Walter Bruchhausen graduated in medicine, theology and medical ethics at the Universities of Würzburg, Bonn and Glasgow. After surgical training in Germany and medical work in Rwanda he joined the working group on medical anthropology at the Institute of Medical History, University of Bonn, Germany, and became a research fellow and lecturer in medical ethics, anthropology and history. He is currently working on a research project, 'Past and present medical pluralism in South-Eastern Tanzania'.

Anne Digby is Professor of Social History at Oxford Brookes University, UK, and has published widely in the social history of medicine. Currently she is working with Helen Sweet on medical pluralism in the Cape, focusing on colonial, missionary and indigenous medicine.

Waltraud Ernst is Lecturer in the Department of History, University of Southampton, UK. She is currently President of the International Association for the Study of Traditional Asian Medicine and editor of *Asian Medicine* and *Wellcome History*. Her publications include *Mad Tales from the Raj: The Treatment of the European Insane in British India, 1800–1858* (Routledge, 1991) and *Race, Science and Medicine* (Routledge 1999; co-edited with B. Harris). She is currently working on a monograph, *Colonising the Mind*.

Michael Hardey is a Lecturer in Sociology at the University of Southampton, UK. His publications include *The Social Context of Health* (Open University Press, 1998) and a number of papers about the role of the internet, such as 'Doctor in the house' (in *Sociology of Health and Illness*), 'Narratives of health' (in *Health: An Interdisciplinary Journal*) and 'The reconfiguration of patients into producers of health information' (in *Communication and Society*). He is currently writing a book on e-health.

Patricia Laing gained her PhD in anthropology in the mid-1970s. Her thesis considered the language and cultural experiences of Samoan children settling in Aotearoa New Zealand. This work set the scene for her ongoing interest in the health and wellbeing of Maori and Pacific peoples in migrant and colonial circumstances. She has undertaken research into the relationship between Maori and Pacific health practices and Western medicine, being funded by the Health Research Council of New Zealand and the Department of Health. She worked in the Department of Health Research Unit and at Victoria University of Wellington teaching in the Social Work Programme. Currently she is Senior Advisor in Research and Evaluation for the Department of Child, Youth and Family Services where she is leading an extensive and in-depth study of recurrent child maltreatment.

Claudia Liebeskind is Assistant Professor of History at Auburn University, Alabama, USA. She is the author of *Piety on Its Knees: Three Sufi Traditions in South Asia in Modern Times* (Oxford University Press, 1998). She is currently writing a book on the history of Unani medicine in modern India.

Kate Reed is currently a Lecturer in Sociology at the University of Kent at Canterbury, UK. Her research interests include gender studies, globalisation, health and illness, race and ethnicity, and social theory.

Ria Reis is an anthropologist and senior staff member of the Medical Anthropology Unit (University of Amsterdam, The Netherlands). She is Director of the Master's Programme in Medical Anthropology at the same University. Her doctoral research focused on medical pluralism and epilepsy in Swaziland. She is also Secretary General of the foundation Epilepsy Care in Developing Countries (Epicadec).

Volker Roelcke is Associate Professor for the History of Medicine and Science at the University of Lübeck, Germany. He has published on German psychiatry during the nineteenth and twentieth centuries, medicine during the time of

National Socialism, the history of 'diseases of civilisation', and concepts of medical anthropology. His current research is on the history of psychiatric genetics, ca. 1920–1960.

Sumit Sarkar is Professor of History at Delhi University, India. His published work includes *The Swadeshi Movement in Bengal, 1903–1908* (Delhi, 1973), *Modern India, 1885–1947* (second edition, Basingstoke, 1989), and *Writing Social History* (Delhi, 1997). He continues to work on nationalism and popular movements in nineteenth- and twentieth-century Bengal.

Volker Scheid is a Wellcome Trust Research Fellow in the History of Medicine at the School of Oriental and African Studies (SOAS), University of London, UK, as well as a practitioner and teacher of Chinese medicine for twenty years. His academic research focuses on diversity, continuity and change in the development of Chinese medicine from the nineteenth century to the present. He is the author of *Contemporary Chinese Medicine: Plurality and Synthesis* (Duke University Press, 2002).

Helen Sweet is Research Assistant to Anne Digby in the Humanities Research Centre at Oxford Brookes University, UK, working on medical pluralism in the Cape. Her particular research interests are in the social history of nursing and medicine, and in oral history. She is founder and convenor of the UK History of Nursing Research Colloquium and takes an active part in promoting history of nursing both nationally and internationally.

Ned Vankevich is Associate Professor of Communication at Trinity Western University in British Columbia, Canada. His scholarly research areas include media studies and health communication, and he is currently exploring the implications of psychoneuroimmunology and emerging medical epistemologies.

1 Plural medicine, tradition and modernity

Historical and contemporary perspectives: views from below and from above

Waltraud Ernst

In current writing on the history and development of medicine 'pluralism' figures prominently. Cant and Sharma, for example, entitled their recent book *A New Medical Pluralism?* and asked whether the perceived increase in the popularity of alternative medicines meant that we were witnessing a new form of medical pluralism.[1] The idea of pluralism seems to capture particularly well medical developments at a time when the world is supposed to be in its 'post-modern' and 'post-colonial' stage, and when references to cultural diversity and the variety of local practices abound.[2] Even the similarly ubiquitous term, 'globalisation', which implies, in the view of some, the undermining of variety and pluralism, has come to be seen by many instead as the apotheosis of a plurality of local practices, as encapsulated in the slogan 'think globally and act locally'.[3] Emphasis is on the wide range of medical approaches patients turn to and the multitude of existing and newly emerging professional interest groups and formal as well as informal medical institutions – from high-tech cardiac wards staffed by specialist nurses and doctors, to health clubs, traditional Chinese medicine centres, internet discussion groups and chat rooms filled by occasional as well as habitual web surfers, and spiritual or psychotherapeutic healing sessions attended by what Sharma called 'earnest seekers', 'stable' and 'eclectic users'.[4]

However, pluralism is new neither as a favoured concept within the history and philosophy of science (or within philosophy in general), nor as a phenomenon characteristic of medicine. In regard to the latter, we have learned from historical analyses such as Porter's *The Popularization of Medicine, 1650–1850* that 'the terrain of healing has always been characterized by great diversity', with learned or scientific medicine existing alongside popular or folk traditions, irregular or alternative medicine, as well as 'quackery'.[5] The variety of medical practices has also for long been a major focus within social anthropology. Arthur Kleinman and Charles Leslie, founding figures of medical anthropology in the USA, highlighted the existence of different strands of folk medicine alongside 'learned' Asian medicine as well as the varied, culturally specific medical traditions that co-exist alongside (or compete with) 'Western' medicine.[6]

One of the early classics of medical anthropology published in 1976, *Asian Medical Systems*, is based on the contention that 'Asian medical systems are intrinsically dynamic, and, like the cultures and societies in which they are embedded, are continually evolving'.[7] In a number of essays the 'culture of plural medical systems' is very much at the centre of analysis.[8] Patients' perspectives and what have become known among social historians of medicine as 'views from below' were not neglected either, as practices such as 'healer hopping' – namely patients' strategies of consulting a number of healers in their pursuit of cure and better health care – were investigated in as much detail as other cultures' medical literature and their practitioners' variedly applied treatment regimes. Unlike in much of the medical historical and sociological writing of the same period, within the context of medical anthropology patients were perceived as active subjects rather than merely passive objects, subjugated by the prevalent medical discourse and suffering the treatments imposed on them by domineering medical experts.

Perhaps most importantly though, from the perspective of medical anthropology, Western medicine's claim to epistemological and therapeutic superiority was being challenged by contrasting it with the successful treatment outcomes and the high levels of patient satisfaction of a variety of non-Western medical systems. It was shown that Western medicine was not always the universally preferred (or easily accessible) treatment option in all areas of the globe, and that a number of profoundly effective and highly sophisticated 'traditional' systems of healing not only predated the arrival of modern Western medicine in non-Western cultures, but also adapted successfully to the changing circumstances of a modern world.

Medical historians have only slowly come to avail themselves of the conceptual and empirical insights of anthropological scholarship in non-European cultures. Up until the 1990s or so a strand of 'social historians' of medicine, newly formed during the 1970s and 1980s, had been too busy throwing off what they perceived as the shackles of 'Whig' history, breaking away from the traditional, narrow historiographic focus on the medical profession, on medical institutions, and medical ideas. With social history of medicine came a focus on medical alternatives or 'heterodoxies', folk medicines, 'quackery', as well as on 'the patient's view'.[9] On the whole, however, this new historiographic approach remained, much like its Whig predecessor, for a time essentially Euro- and Americo-centric in scope and in outlook. Critical publications on the history of colonial medicine, and the persistent vigour and challenge of fashionable subaltern and post-colonial theories eventually caused social historians of medicine, too, to draw on anthropological perspectives and to consider the development of non-Western medical paradigms and indigenous medicine worthy subjects of historical analysis.[10]

Despite the current trend towards anthropologically informed histories and inter-disciplinarity, typically only lip-service is paid to the recognition of non-Western perspectives as valid medical systems epistemologically, if not therapeutically, on a par with Western medicines. But at least recently published textbooks and encyclopaedias of medical history now contain (albeit short) chapters on 'Eastern' or 'non-Western' traditions alongside 'the Western tradition', and university courses on history of medicine in Britain include modules on non-Western medical perspectives.[11] The cross-fertilisation between medical anthropology and medical history certainly constitutes a welcome development.

At least potentially it enables previously marginalised non-Western ideas and practices to be valued, if not yet always on their own terms, then at least alongside Western medicine, as part of a plurality of traditions – within both Western and non-Western cultures. This book is a contribution to the growing field of studies that cut across academic methodologies and theoretical concerns and, most importantly, aim at breaking away from an exclusively Western and biomedically centred perspective. The essays on medical ideas and practices in India and Africa reveal the extent to which different medical traditions, including Western medicine, have prevailed and continue to exist alongside and, at times, in competition with, each other. In other chapters a similar situation is shown to have been prevalent also in nineteenth-century England, and modern-day China, Britain, Northern America, and New Zealand.

Despite the fecundity of inter-disciplinary and pluralist perspectives a number of conceptual (and perceptual) problems still persist. First of all, the conundrum of dichotomously arranged categories that tend to unduly restrict phenomena to criteria relevant to their binary opposites remains as yet unresolved. Debates about dichotomies and the move towards pluralism are, of course, not characteristic only of medical history and anthropology. Medical sociologists, cultural theorists, philosophers and literary studies scholars, too, are variously engaged in breaking away from the restrictions of deterministic monisms or dualisms and simplistic concepts and perceptions based on seemingly clear-cut binary constellations.[12] They all attempt to fathom the extent to which pluralist perspectives allow more sophisticated analyses.

Despite critical awareness, terms like 'indigenous medicine', 'folk medicine' and 'healer', for example, even if used in their plural forms, are still redolent of those features that they have for long been thought of as lacking in comparison to their binary opposites (namely 'Western medicine', 'learned medicine' and 'medical expert'). So much have they become seen as synonymous with 'unscientific', 'superstition' and 'quack' that even when they are not explicitly denigrated, their scientific status, the validity of their knowledge base and the integrity of their practitioners is almost automatically impugned. 'Western medicine', in contrast, is not usually required to justify its status as a 'scientific' procedure – it is implicitly thought of as such, even if, as explored in Bradley's essay on hydropathy and orthodoxy, the basis on which the claim to scientificity is established may not be as solidly 'objective' and 'scientific' as it appears to Western imagination.[13]

We may well have come to see pure, perfect and pristinely delineated medical 'systems' and categories as inherently 'ideological constructs' that need to be used with caution.[14] Their legacy, however, still lingers on even as we turn attention to medical 'encounters' or 'exchanges' or 'interactions' between … – well, one medical 'system' or category and another. The language of pluralism still tends to reflect the very same static and discrete meanings and perceptions that many writers, including the contributors to this book, aim to challenge and expose as products of restricted and restrictive imaginations and ideologies. Even terms such as 'hybridity' and 'syncrecy', 'the global' and 'the local', fashioned and put forward as solutions, tend instead to further highlight and illustrate the very problem of dichotomising a reality that is multi-faceted, forever in flux and never purely delineated, as these terms, too, are built on the assumption of pre-existing discrete (however vaguely defined) entities.

An emphasis on medical pluralism alone thus can, of course, not offer a straight-forward solution to dichotomous polarisation. Its apparent capacity to challenge Euro-centrism, cultural myopia and prejudice may, however, make it conceptually preferable to the earlier focus on 'Western medical superiority', 'power' and 'domination' that did as much to reify these as to expose them. The current weari-ness with the 1960s and 1970s focus on issues of power, domination and hegemony and the wish to embrace a – seemingly – less deterministic perspective make pluralism appear as a more positive term that is congruent with and supportive of what is widely perceived as desirable social and political developments, such as the emergence of modern multi-cultural societies in former colonies and in Western countries with significant immigrant populations. As is shown in the essays on the options offered to and chosen by 'consumers' of healthcare in Britain, India and New Zealand, medical pluralism is indeed an important feature of multi-cultural societies all over the globe.

However, the emphasis on pluralism also harbours certain dangers. To begin with, it may well give further credence to one of the persistent ideological ploys of Western biomedicine: that medicine is located outside the realms of power, domination and hegemonic strife. An exclusive focus on medical pluralism in the domains of medical ideas and professional institutions, and in regard to patients' freedom of choice colludes with the image of the medical market place and the sphere of healing as a 'liberal heaven', in which patients of all social and cultural backgrounds are supposed to have free choice and easy access to their favoured medical treatment; where medical professionals and itinerant healers of all stripes are said to ply their trade alongside, and in mutual respect for, each other; and where biomedicine could not only be simply one of a number of different modes of healing but also abstains from undue claims of epistemological superiority and greater efficacy and efficiency.

It is important here to differentiate carefully between the desirability of medical pluralism and the extent to which it has been realised in a 'globalised' medical world that is still powerfully dominated by American and European pharmaceutical firms, and by the promulgation of Western images of a healthy life-style and of biomedicine as the ultimate point of reference for the assessment of health problems and treatment outcomes. Analyses that focus on pluralism therefore still need to be situated squarely within the wider social and political context, being also sensitive to issues of power and medical hegemony. The essays in this book are written with this contention in mind. As shown in the chapters by Arnold and Sarkar, Scheid, Liebeskind, and Reis, patients' and practitioners' choices of and preferences for particular approaches are not simply individual decisions, but are also closely related to the struggle and search for national(ist) identity and the assertion of, and resistance to, cultural and political hegemony. An analytic focus on medical discourses in addition to reflections on patients' views from below and practitioners' virtuosity are therefore called for. As pointed out by Cant and Sharma, 'The biomedical power which social scientists have wished to critique is no illusion. Historically speaking it has grown from … biomedicine's political alliance with the state and … its espousal of scientific method as the basis for its authoritative claims to knowledge and expertise'.[15]

Another potential flaw of pluralist perspectives has been discussed particularly well by philosophers of science who argue that although pluralism is rightly envisaged to encapsulate tolerance towards different cultural and scientific frameworks and practices, it still requires to be constrained in some way on moral grounds (and, for some, on ontological grounds as well). Acceptance of differing views may on the whole be desirable, but on occasion particular approaches ought not to be tolerated (as in the case of Nazi medical experiments). This need to impose restrictions on medical practices and procedures on morally justified grounds posits again the very problem that medical pluralism may have been hoped to have dispensed with, namely the question of who is to assume the authority to decide on restrictions of pluralism and, therefore, issues of power, hegemony and domination.

The resulting problem is illustrated well by discussions in the United Kingdom and the United States about government intervention and professional regulation of the pluralist, alternative medicine market and the policing of health-related internet sites. Vankevich explores this issue further in his essay on the limits of pluralism. When the ethics, efficiency and effectiveness of alternative approaches are to be assessed, authorities steer precariously between the Scylla of imposing the well-tried and supposedly superior, scientific criteria of biomedicine on a whole range of healing practices, and the Charybdis of leaving the public exposed to potentially unprofessional, unethical and fraudulent, or simply ineffective, practices. In a similar vein patients' and alternative practitioners' interest groups, too, make at times incompatible demands when canvassing consumers' rights to free choice and access to a range of treatments, while simultaneously reasserting government's and scientific experts' obligation to protect the public from potentially harmful practices.

Far from constituting a *counter*-paradigm to those much favoured up until recently (such as power discourses, medical systems and hegemony), a critical and informed pluralist perspective could therefore be conceived of as bringing both diversity *and* power issues into view. Importantly, power needs to be looked at not only in regard to Western biomedicine, the usual 'bad guy' in revisionist histories of the Foucaultian as well as the post-colonial genre. Traditional and non-Western systems of healing that have more commonly been seen mainly as victims of Western domination and arrogance are on their part not immune or averse to professional power play, shrewd global marketing and personal networking either. This point is explored in the chapters on Chinese medicine (Scheid), homoeopathy (Arnold and Sarkar), Unani (Liebeskind), and Ayurveda (Bode), in which the romanticised vision of non-Western systems of healing, as aloof from the profane domains of politics and profiteering, and true only to their ancient origins, spiritual values and holistic philosophy, is challenged.

It also is important to keep in mind that supposedly never-changing medical traditions such as Ayurveda (Hindu medicine), Unani (Islamic medicine), and Chinese medicine are not only made up of a number of different schools and diverse strands, but that they have also, over time, adapted in a variety of ways to changing local circumstances and global trends, and even shown themselves more recently as particularly adept in becoming active players in the medical market place – in their country of origin as much as in the West. Ayurvedic medical centres, for example, flourish not only in their expected strongholds (such as Varanasi in India), but also in cosmopolitan conurbations such as Mumbai, New Delhi and Calcutta, as well as in New York and London where Ayurvedic doctors can now be consulted and 'traditional Ayurvedic' remedies easily purchased in any 'Body Shop'.

This phenomenon could well be lamented and construed as crass Western-style commercialisation of traditional medicine, as some sort of McDonaldization[16] of traditional medicine that ought to be differentiated from the 'real' thing, the pure and original Ayurveda based on an age-old tradition that has been clearly codified in the ancient Vedic texts and practised the same way ever since. A significant number of traditionalist Ayurvedic practitioners as well as some New Age Western protagonists of the 'real' Traditional Ayurveda do indeed perceive these recent developments in such terms. However, they could also be seen as testimony to the fact that any one 'tradition' or 'medical system' is inherently heterogeneous (i.e. 'plural') and represented by different groups of people with diverse views on how practice ought to be adapted (or not) to changing circumstances – a potential for profiteering and commercialisation notwithstanding.

Moreover, just because a medical corpus can trace its origins back to some ancient text does not mean that it has to be inherently static and homogeneous. In the case of Ayurveda, for example, it has been shown that scriptural injunctions such as 'the wise must … adhere to tradition, without arguing' (in *Susruta Samhita*[17]), do not necessarily imply homogeneity of approaches and consensus on diagnostics and treatment.[18] Not only have a number of different interpretations of Ayurvedic doctrine prevailed in any one period, but they have adapted variously to changing social and environmental realities, at times even running counter to particular, simultaneously held prohibitions (such as the consumption of meat alongside vegetarianism in India).[19] 'Medical traditions' are intrinsically 'plural' – both in terms of the variety of ways in which any one tradition has been interpreted and codified by different learned authorities, and in terms of the great variety of their practical applications.

The further point that different paradigms, even if based on seemingly contradictory positions, can be successfully held together by one individual is illustrated by an anecdote about the Mysore-born and Western-trained poet A.K. Ramanujan who succeeded in combining realms that appeared to some of his contemporaries as irreconcilable. Pondering on whether there was such a thing as 'an Indian way of thinking', he recollected memories about his father:

> He was a mathematician, an astronomer. But he was also a Sanskrit scholar, an expert astrologer … [who] had just been converted by Russell to the 'scientific attitude'. I (and my generation) was troubled by his holding together in one brain both astronomy and astrology; I looked for consistency in him, a constituency he didn't seem to care about, or even think about. When I asked

him what the discovery of Pluto and Neptune did to his archaic nine-planet astrology, he said, 'You make the necessary corrections, that's all'. Or, in answer to how he could read the *Gita* religiously, having bathed and painted on his forehead the red and white feet of Vishnu, and later talk appreciatively about Bertrand Russell and even Ingersoll, he said, 'The *Gita* is part of one's hygiene. Besides, don't you know, the brain has two lobes?'.[20]

The question then arises of how a seemingly clearly bounded 'tradition' or 'medical system', whether of the 'Western' or the 'traditional' variety, comes into existence. In a broad and straightforward sense a plausible answer would be that 'traditions' are the result of negotiation among the main protagonists at any one time, namely authors of medical treatises, promulgators of medical lore, practitioners, state authorities, cultural communities, patients, and the public. An important, yet more elusive, dimension in this process of negotiation, and at times contestation, is the way in which traditions are 'envisioned', 'imagined', if not 'invented'.[21] Examples of this process are discussed in Bradley's chapter on the emergence of medical 'orthodoxy' in mid nineteenth-century Britain and in Reis' essay on 'traditional healing' in Swaziland.

Another example of how cultural representations have a bearing on the ways in which a particular medical system is perceived and defined is the current inversion of the meaning of 'traditional medicine'. At least since the period of the Enlightenment, Asian and African 'traditions' and 'customs', for example, had by many Europeans (and, increasingly, by Western-educated Asians and Africans, too) been associated with a variety of negative terms, such 'inferior', 'backward', 'uncivilised', 'barbaric', 'crude' and 'primitive'.[22] Yet more recently the term 'traditional medicine' has acquired further, largely positive, connotations by virtue of commercial marketing strategies that present Ayurvedic or traditional Chinese medicine, for example, as wholesome, spiritual, holistic, authentic, humane, and as something people in the West as well as in the East would be well advised to make use of in order to live in harmony with the modern world. Bode and Reis explore this further in regard to Ayurvedic and Swazi medicine.

It is, however, not merely the ways in which traditional medicine has come to be represented and envisioned that have changed to conveying the opposite of what it was imagined to be during earlier periods. The very stuff of which Ayurveda, for example, is supposed to be made has changed, too. The particular procedures and specific remedies that are selected from the wide-ranging repertoire of traditional Indian medicine and offered for wholesome consumption by modern man and woman have only a tenuous link with the whole package and complex sequence of medical and health-related practices from which they are isolated. Ayurvedic treatments, for example, have in the West been adapted to pander to, and to elicit, Western images of relaxation and gentleness by purging them of those components (such as purgatives, emetics and errhines) that had a central place in their practice in India, yet would be considered as too 'interventionist', 'violent' and off-putting to sensitive Western consumers. Zimmermann described the modern emphasis on the gentle elements in Ayurveda, arguing that it 'changes the tradition significantly'.[23] Modern Ayurvedic medicine has been truly re-invented. It is now imagined as based on ancient tradition and as offering 'an alternative to the harshness of biomedicine'.[24] In 'contemporary practice in South Asia, as well as in Ayurvedic therapies exported to the West, practitioners avoid using emetics or drastic purgatives. All violence has disappeared from medications aiming to cleanse the patient's humoral system. Neither red (the red of bloodletting), nor black (the black of chemical oxides), but green – the green of herbs freshly gathered, a symbol of nonviolence: this is the new motto of Ayurveda's flower children.'[25]

It would be plausible but naïve to conclude that 'traditional medicine', in this case Ayurveda, is simply being misconstrued by profiteering business people or ignorant Westerners. First of all, as shown in the chapter by Bode, in India itself 'traditional' has become for some largely a designer product, with positive connotations that conjure up relief from the stresses and strains of life, and with pills available straight off the shelf, in a truly 'modern', nicely packaged and easily swallowed shape. Secondly, how would we decide *which* Ayurveda was more 'authentic', more 'original', more 'traditional'? Would it be appropriate to assume that rather than the practices and procedures focused on in modern-day Ayurveda, those mentioned in the ancient Vedic texts, for example, were the truly authentic and traditional ones? And, if so, which one of these, out of an array of different textual traditions, would we choose as the definite source? Even if there was such a thing as an original blueprint of *the* Ayurvedic doctrine, would it make sense to elevate the written tradition above Ayurvedic doctors' real-life, and usually more 'messy' and idiosyncratic, practical adaptations and modifications of the theoretical corpus? And what about patients' active role in the pursuit of better health and consumers' decision in favour of medical approaches that appeal to them on account of their perceived authenticity and anticipated benefit? Does it matter that current representations of 'traditional medicine' are at times but faintly linked with any one of the various brands of Ayurveda practised in India centuries ago? Ultimately, we are faced with the questions of what is supposed to count as authenti-cally 'traditional', and what, if anything, is 'traditional' about 'traditional medicine'.

Scheid has recently tackled these questions in regard to the case of Chinese medicine.[26] He suggests that traditional Chinese medicine (TCM) is thought of in the West as well as in China as the continuation of an ancient, original and authentic tradition practised widely and successfully over the centuries. Yet what has been referred to as TCM in recent times is merely the revived medicine of the former elite of pre-revolutionary China. This medicine has been promoted in the People's Republic since the late 1950s by the Communist government and undergone modernisation along Western principles of standardisation and scientificity. Like modern Ayurveda and Swazi indigenous healing, TCM, too, can therefore be conceived of as an 'invented tradition',[27] largely grown out of nationalistic endeav-our and the pressing need for health services for the masses.

In this collection of essays as well as in the wider literature, the term 'plural medicine' is used in basically two different ways. In its long familiar version it denotes 'plurality' in the sense of a variety of medical approaches existing alongside each other, at times in competition and at times in collaboration with or complementary to each other. In its second, more complex, version the term refers to the plural or multi-dimensional qualities inherent in medical practices and experiences, as these draw on and are open to different approaches, are 'bastardised' or hybridised, syncretic, and versatile. Analyses of plural medicine in the wider sense of the term, focus on what could be described as practitioners' 'virtuosity' in moving between different doctrines or medical approaches and patients' 'versatility' as they draw on a number of different strands of medical practices – in India as much as in Leicester, Swaziland and in cyberspace.

As some of the essays in this volume show, plural medicine is not new, nor, arguably, is it on the rise – even if the extension of pharmaceutical marketing and the fast-and-easy internet have accelerated the pace with which medical practices – 'modern' and 'traditional' – have become globalised. What needs explaining therefore is the increased focus on it. It is suggested here that recent debates on 'national identity' and the meaning of 'tradition' in the (post-)modern and post-colonial age have led to an increased interest in pluralism, as questions about the nature of modern multi-cultural or 'syncretic' societies in the west and of former colonial countries, that aim at becoming part of 'modern' world society without losing track of their 'traditional', cultural roots, have moved centre-stage. Any exploration of plural medicine, therefore, needs to be aware of issues of tradition and modernity, of national identity and globalisation.

The essays in this book assess the many interpretations and practical applications of any one medical system as well as the variety, or plurality, of medical approaches that co-exist or compete with each other at any one time and place. Some explore the phenomenon of plural medicine and medical pluralism through the eyes of the patients (Laing, Reed, Hardey, Reis). Others assume the practitioners' (or students') perspectives (Scheid, Bradley, Reis, Digby and Sweet) or investigate the processes by which particular medical approaches become imagined and repre-sented as 'scientific', 'alternative', 'orthodox', or 'traditional' (Bradley, Bruchhausen and Roelcke, Liebeskind, Arnold and Sarkar, Vankevich). Although the analysis of medicine(s) as systems of knowledge and discourses of power is not lost sight of, it is the pliability of a medical corpus and the virtuosity of its practitioners in adapting to changing social and cultural conditions, that are very much to the fore.

Of course, a collection of essays on plural medicine could not possibly explore all and every aspect in an encyclopaedic way. Instead detailed examples from diverse settings are presented, intended to reveal some of the issues involved in discussions on the nature and the manifestations of plural medicine. It is hoped that specific case studies will enable readers to recognise and relate particular phenomena to what they may have come across and be aware of from other cultural or historical settings.

The individual chapters have been arranged in chronological order, with the first five, historical, essays focusing on the tensions and the cross-fertilisation between 'orthodox' Western biomedicine and 'other' medical approaches within the context of different cultural settings during the course of the nineteenth and early twentieth centuries. Here the geographic perspective is wide-ranging (from India, to Britain, and to Africa) and the major conceptual focus is on medicine(s) as knowledge and discourse. Although clearly located within the discipline of history, some of the issues raised in these essays resonate and link up with modern concerns. The chapters by Bruchhausen and Roelcke (on German East Africa) and Digby and Sweet (on South Africa), for example, highlight the continuity of the past in the present on the level of academic discourse as well as in regard to professional tactics, and Arnold and Sarkar observe that an '[e]levation of immunity from modern/Western discourses into the sole criterion for valorisation might at times be seriously anachronistic' (p. 54).

The remaining chapters assess present-day issues in locations as far afield as Swaziland, China, India, Britain, New Zealand, and the virtual world of the internet. Despite a diversity of disciplinary backgrounds (ranging from anthropology, to science studies, medical sociology and media studies), the focus is here on how ideas about seemingly polarised entities, such as 'tradition' and 'modernity', 'heterodoxy' and 'orthodoxy', influence medical practice, medical marketing and patients' health-related behaviour within diverse cultural, economic and political contexts as well as on the world wide web.

The first essay focuses on the interactions between 'hydropathy' and 'orthodoxy' in mid-nineteenth-century Victorian Britain. Bradley shows how hydropathy emerged as a newly consolidated 'heterodoxy' out of the water cure procedures that were very much part of the Hippocratic corpus, the repertoire of 'folk' medicine, as well as mid-nineteenth-century 'mainstream' medical practice. More importantly though he argues that 'heterodoxy' was as much defined and delimited by 'orthodoxy' as 'orthodoxy' took shape and defined itself in contrast to 'heterodoxy'. Bradley's aim is to 'resist the urge to divide the world into centres and peripheries' (p. 19), and to 'decentre' an assumedly monolithic orthodoxy that was, just like its heterodox counterpart, 'evolving, mutating and ever so slightly amorphous' (p. 21). He inverts the contention of many medical historians that 'medical heresies', such as hydropathy, were the shadow of orthodoxy, by suggesting that 'orthodoxy was constructed as a shadow of heterodoxy' (p. 32).

Arnold and Sarkar focus on homoeopathy, another 'heterodoxy' that was popular in nineteenth-century Britain, and which spread to India as well. Homoeopathy was readily accepted on the Indian subcontinent on account of the cheapness of its remedies and its self-help appeal. It enabled educated Indians who were excluded from pursuing successful careers in the almost entirely British-dominated Indian Medical Service to engage in what was thought of by many as a modern, rational medical system. Homoeopathy transcended not only 'the conventional boundaries between "Western" and "indigenous" medicine' (p. 49), but also 'India's seemingly entrenched ethnic and cultural boundaries' (p. 42). Rather than necessarily defining its practitioners as 'Indian', Ayurvedic or Unani, and long before the supposedly unique age of 'globalisation', it enabled them to see themselves as part of a wider international community – a community, that was imagined as 'Western' and 'modern', without being colonial.

In their conceptually wide-ranging essay, Arnold and Sarkar critique also some of the assumptions that underpin both conventional histories and 'subaltern' and 'post-colonial' writing on Western and indigenous medicine in (post)-colonial countries. They show that the usual story of homoeopathy as a Western heterodoxy that was appropriated by the colonised and accepted as 'an almost indigenous form of medicine close to the people' (p. 43) is anchored in a series of problematic polarities in which 'the apparently opposing elements are implicitly assumed to be homologous and inseparable' (p. 41). The history of homoeopathy in Bengal, they argue, 'cannot be made to fit a sharp Western/indigenous divide' nor should its 'popular' or 'subaltern' dimension (p. 53–4) be over-emphasised and construed as a kind of 'indigenous cultural nationalist reaction to the domination of Western colonial discourse' (p. 51). The Western/indigenous divide is shown to be particularly problematic as it continues a prominent nineteenth-century pre-occupation: it tends to 'excessively prioritise the question of origins' and to focus on nationalist strife (p. 54). By so doing it makes, 'in effect, the rejection of ideas of Western origin the sole criterion for authentic autonomy' (p. 54).

In her essay on Islamic (Unani) medical practitioners in India, Liebeskind too touches on nationalist ambitions and anti-colonial strife insofar as these constituted the context within which claims to the scientificity of indigenous medicine in the five decades leading up to India's Independence in 1947 were put forward. Her specific focus is on a detailed study of the defence of Unani as rational and scientific knowledge by three eminent practitioners. In spite (or rather because) of the commonalities of Unani and pre-modern Western medicine – in terms of their shared Greek philosophical origins and humoral frameworks – Islamic medicine was considered by the majority of Western-educated doctors in India as unscientific, irrational, and as an outdated relic of the sort of practices the West strove to distance itself from in the wake of the Enlightenment and the rise of modern science.

In their response Unani practitioners pursued revivalist strategies that ranged from the attempt to synthesise the best features of indigenous and modern Western medicine to the fundamentalist approach of reviving and accentuating features then considered to be 'pure' and 'traditional'. Representatives of both camps agreed however on two major issues: first, that Unani was essentially scientific and rational, and, second, that biomedicine itself failed to live up to the scientific criteria of its own rhetoric. By basing both their defence and attack on criteria favoured by Western bioscience, they implicitly accepted biomedicine as the benchmark. Much of the discussion about Unani's claim to scientificity and biomedicine's failure to live up to its own standards drew on the classic Aristotelian framework of natural philosophy and realism (which Islamic medicine shared with pre-modern Western medicine). It consequently mirrored the wider philosophical debates during much of the twentieth century in Europe that critically engaged with and still continue to challenge logical empiricism and positivism.

The three hakims or practitioners of Islamic medicine discussed by Liebeskind may well have used the very same criteria that were part of the hegemonic discourse of Western scientific knowledge. However, as Liebeskind concludes, 'looking at biomedicine from the outside from an inferior position in the power-game but one grounded in a strong sense of the history and achievements of their medicine, [the hakims] unpicked its rhetoric and positivism, value-neutrality and universality and highlighted its construction in Europe by Europeans' (p. 71).

The construction of scientific knowledge and of its imagined counterpart, 'indigenous medicine', is also at the centre of the chapter on 'African medicine' by Bruchhausen and Roelcke. The authors investigate how modern images of 'traditional' or 'indigenous' African medicine are redolent with earlier formative discourses of the colonial period. In regard to German discourses on East African healing practices they show that what is nowadays conceived of as authentically and intrinsically 'African', may in fact have been the creation if not invention of Europe. Traditional African medicine, Bruchhausen and Roelcke argue, is 'the result of political and scientific developments, ethnographic and psychological approaches, administrative activities and, last but not least, controversies about orthodox and heterodox medicine in Europe' (p. 76). The translation of a complex array of heterogeneous medical ideas and practices extant in the territories of German East Africa into one single, allegedly homogeneous and authentically 'African medical tradition' occurred between 1884 and 1918, when German doctors, missionaries and ethnographers busied themselves with the collection and categorisation of cultural artefacts and customs. Although originally construed as a unifying label, 'traditional African medicine' provides indigenous populations with a wide range of easily accessible treatment options available to them alongside Western biomedicine.

In her essay on traditional healing in modern-day Swaziland, Reis explores how patients suffering from epilepsy as well as healers make use of a number of different strands of both Western and traditional Swazi medicine. As patients are engaged in 'healer hopping', picking the treatment of their choice, and practitioners are shown to draw on a wide range of traditional, biomedical, as well as Western alternative, even 'new age', methods, the intrinsically plural character of both 'Western medicine' and 'traditional Swazi-medicine' is revealed and their supposedly clearly bounded nature is called into question. At the same time, however, Reis discerns a process of perceptual re-dichotomisation that finds its expression in public representations of Western medicine and herbalism as mainly 'technical procedures', in contrast to a traditional Swazi medicine that is grounded in respect for the sanctity of the ancestors and the Swazi King. According to Reis, these contrasting representations are based on the different degrees of moral legitimacy, spiritual propriety and national authenticity attributed to the various approaches. Even if easily embraced by both patients and practitioners, Western biomedicine is seen to be devoid of one particular aspect that is vital to Swazi people's self-identity, both on an individual level and in terms of national identity. Unlike divinatory healing, biomedicine is not inspired by respect for ancestral authority and loyalty to the King, and therefore is not by itself nor in combination with other, traditional medical techniques (such as herbalism) imbued with spiritual and political legitimacy.

Consequently, the 'biomedical *vs.* traditional medicine' dichotomy that is usually taken to be the unquestioned analytical starting point for both its apologists and for its critics does not adequately capture the situation in Swaziland – neither in regard to patients' treatment choices and practitioners' preferred approaches nor in regard to public and politically endorsed perceptions of what is to count as authentic Swazi medical practice. First, both patients and healers move easily between and across the divide between Western and traditional medicine. Second, rather than traditional healing being simply subject to incorporation into a Western, biomedically dominated national health system, 'Swazi healing easily incorporates biomedicine into the traditional idiom of illness and healing' (p. 107). Third, the one dichotomisation that is most clearly manifest in public representations of medicine in Swaziland derives its impetus from the perceived centrality of ancestral (and royal) legitimacy, and thus of divinatory healing. The latter is thought to be superior by far to both Western biomedicine and traditional herbal medicine.

Digby and Sweet's study shows how biomedically trained nurses in South Africa moved easily across the allegedly strict boundaries between Western missionary medicine and traditional modes of healing. Since the early days of the mission hospital in South Africa biomedically trained African nurses successfully managed to reconcile their role as 'standard bearers of Western medicine' with their allegiance and sympathy for indigenous practices. Western-trained doctors in mission hospitals depended on nurses' skills in translating indigenous symptoms into the categories of Western medicine and making Western medical intervention and treatment methods culturally acceptable to patients. Western missionary societies therefore expected African nurses to facilitate the replacement of indigenous beliefs and healing practices with Christianity and Western medicine. This they did, reliably, within the confines of Western institutions and a biomedically dominated atmosphere. However, the further nurses' workplaces were removed from the centres of institutionalised Western medicine, the more versatile and plural their approaches became. Digby and Sweet suggest that in remote areas community nurses acted as mediators or 'culture brokers', advising patients of the whole range of medical options available to them – both Western and indigenous. In order to fulfil this role successfully, it was vital for nurses to be accepted by, and willing to co-operate with, leading traditional community representatives and indigenous healers in the different localities.

Scheid's chapter critiques the continued reliance on the discourse of modernisation which proceeds from a juxtaposition of 'tradition' and 'modernity'. Like Arnold and Sarkar, Bruchhausen and Roelcke, and Reis, he highlights the restrictiveness of this perspective and the ideological, Europe-centred bias that goes along with the application of this set of oppositional terms and prevents a more sophisticated understanding of medical practices. In a formal sense and at the level of medical discourses, the case of Chinese medicine shows a plurality of different practices co-existing at any one time: modern traditional Chinese medicine and modern biomedicine in China, and modern traditional Chinese medicine in the United Kingdom or the United States. The disjunction between the modern and the traditional may therefore serve well as a useful heuristic device, even if narrowly conceived. However, it would be misleading to assume that individual practitioners would fit easily into one of these seemingly discrete heuristic categories.

Scheid illustrates this point in his case study of Professor Rong who is at the centre of a variety of intersecting networks of practices, and moves easily between them. His work would not be adequately characterised by labels such as 'modern' or 'traditional'. Being part of a number of medical, social, and political networks, Rong makes, for example, use of inherited cultural tools in the pursuit of contemporary goals. As Rong's case shows, medical practice is multiply determined and locally emergent – this holds true in the case of Chinese medicine as much as, arguably, in regard to other practices as well. Scheid suggests that rather than merely focusing on the variety and plurality of medical practices, it may be more appropriate to conceive of medical practice as intrinsically plural and, on account of medical practitioners' virtuosity, as infinitely more complex than reference to the dichotomising discourse of tradition/modernity suggests.

The conceptual boundaries around different healing discourses are crossed, too, in Laing's chapter on constructions of Maori healing. Laing's reflections draw on both her expertise as a medical anthropologist and health researcher, and on her personal health beliefs and healing strategies in response to a medical diagnosis of breast cancer. She provides an engaging and self-reflective account of the various medical and spiritual approaches she drew on. Laing's illness narrative shows her reluctance to let herself be constrained by biomedical notions and role prescriptions of how cancer 'patients' ought to behave, on the one hand, and by ideas about Europeans' alleged 'materialist', non-spiritual nature, on the other.

Laing traces what she perceives to be the misleading and politically motivated juxtaposition of Maori people as 'spiritual' and 'superstitious' with Europeans as 'rational' and 'materialistic' to nineteenth- and twentieth-century anthropological characterisations of Maori people by Europeans. She shows how these fuelled the ideologically and politically fraught debates preceding and following the passing of the *tohunga* (Maori healers) Suppression Act of 1907. Laing argues that what had originally been intended by European and Westernised Maori as an essentially negative attribution (spiritual = superstitious = inferior Maori healing) has more recently been inverted by some Maori groups to convey positive connotations (spiritual = non-materialist = superior Maori healing).

In her own quest for spiritual and bodily health Laing cuts across such simplistic and restrictive equations, making use instead of a plurality of approaches that range from new age goddess cults to Maori ideas of *mana wahine* (women's authority), Christian-based anthroposophy to Eastern philosophy. All of these become fused in what Laing conceives of as a feminist perspective on women's health.

In her chapter on British South Asian mothers, Reed argues that while the categorisation of medical approaches into 'Western', 'Indian' and 'alternative' may be appropriate and revealingly indicative of ideological strategies at the level of medical discourses, the conceptually strict boundaries around these collapse once people's health beliefs and behaviours are the focus of research. On the basis of in-depth interviews with British-born South Asian women in Leicester, Reed examines the ways in which her respondents drew on a variety of different medical approaches that were available to them in both Leicester and India. The women were members of a number of social networks, both in Leicester and other locations in Britain as well as in their parents' countries of origin. They made use of the different medical systems connected with all of these in a syncretic way, 'mixing and matching them and creating something new in the process' (p. 173). Rather than interpreting 'diasporic' women's use of Indian health products and health services in India as an indication of the search for authenticity, she suggests that a more pragmatic reading may be more appropriate.

While Reed shows us that British-born Indian women make syncretic use of a range of medical approaches and medicines from both Britain and India, Bode looks at the equally syncretic ways in which Ayurvedic and Unani pharmaceuticals are marketed in India. Both Ayurveda and Unani medicine are usually characterised as representative of 'tradition' and as inextricably linked with 'nature'. Yet, as Bode shows, in the marketing of its products, tradition is being linked up with the 'modern' and the 'scientific'. This is most poignantly expressed in the advertising image of a Hindu *rishi* (seer) meditating in a test-tube. As one of the representatives of the three pharmaceutical firms studied by Bode put it: science has been added to culture. Indian consumers easily recognise particular images of Indian culture, traditional values and nature used in advertisements. These are promoted alongside those of Western culture, science and efficiency, creating not merely something 'modern', but something new and contemporary. Bode concludes that as 'traditional and modern medical forms are creatively rearranged in the Indian context', medical pluralism exists *within*, rather than between medical systems.

Hardey explores the new space of the internet, where health-related advice is freely available, the sale and purchase of medicines and potions flourishes, and medical pluralism is all too evident. Rather than investigating cyberspace marketing techniques, Hardey focuses on the consumers' perspective, exploring the health-related behaviour and motivation of a number of chat-room participants in the UK and of personal web-site owners in the UK and USA. He finds that patients in search of medicine and health information value the internet on account of the free and easy access it offers to members of the public. It also plays an enabling role. Although internet access itself is not available to people of all social classes, those who are connected to it can turn from passive patients to active consumers. They do not have to rely exclusively on their doctor as the sole and only source of medical expertise.

Yet, patients are at the same time aware of the need to be wary and selective in regard to the usefulness, efficacy and quality of the products and information offered. Despite its status as a paragon of 'modernity', the internet is subject to the very same issues that exercised members of the public and orthodox and heterodox practitioners long before the advent of modernity. Hardey's chapter title, 'Health for sale', which is borrowed from Roy Porter's historical account of quackery in England, gives an indication of the contentious issues modern patients and practitioners are still struggling with. The internet constitutes yet another marketplace where tricksters as well as experts, genuine practitioners and any member of the public can spread information or ply their trade. As such it is also subject to discussions about the need to impose controls and restrictions on pluralism.

Whilst Hardey's study focuses on the freedom of choice enjoyed by internet-literate patients in the UK, Vankevich explores how medical practitioners in the United States attempt to goad them back to the narrow confines of the biomedically defined 'sick-role'. Taking the internet-based campaigns of Dr Stephen Barrett and his *Quackwatch* web-site as a starting point, Vankevich shows that the age-old idea of 'quackery' still has currency in the modern world and in cyberspace. In fact, the use of an antiquarian term such as 'quack' within the very modern space of the internet further highlights the prevalent dichotomising discourse that aims to discredit the 'old-fashioned', 'traditional', 'folksy' and heterodox by contrasting it with the 'modern', 'scientific' and orthodox.

Drawing on the familiar juxtaposition of 'science' and 'quackery', Barrett warns web-surfers of the inefficacy and dangers of alternative medicines and of the ulterior motives and uninformed/unscientific methods of alternative practitioners. From Barrett's perspective, the lay public ought to confine itself to seeking advice and treatment from biomedically-trained practitioners, rather than making use of what the plural health and medicine market has on offer. As Vankevich points out, the regulation of the medical cyber-market with a view to preventing fraudulent and potentially harmful practices may be well justified. However, Barrett's approach is to reject and label as 'quackery' each and every approach that is not part of science-based medicine. Quite apart from minimising or even ignoring the patient's involvement in any healing process, Barrett's equation of good medicine with science reasserts the latter as the one and only criterion for how medicine is to be practised and therefore eschews medical pluralism.

As Hardey's and Vankevich's studies show, today's internet-based discussion groups and alternative practitioners are both strong protagonists in the plural medicine field and victims of the hegemonic discourse of Western science-based medicine – just like the hydropaths in nineteenth-century England, the homoeopaths and Unani practitioners in nineteenth- and early twentieth-century India, and the indigenous healers in German East Africa.

Acknowledgements

I would like to thank The Wellcome Trust for their support of the conference on 'Plural Medicine' that was held at Southampton in September 1998. The research leading up to the conference was part of a wider project on 'A comparative historical sociology of mental health and healing in British India and New Zealand' funded by The Wellcome Trust.

Notes

1 S. Cant and U. Sharma, *A New Medical Pluralism?*, London, UCL Press, 1999, p. 1.
2 A. Giddens, *The Consequences of Modernity*, Cambridge, Polity Press, 1990. B. Ashcroft, G. Griffiths and H. Tiffin, *The Post-Colonial Studies Reader*, London, Routledge, 1995. E. Boehmer, *Colonial and Postcolonial Literature: Migrant Metaphors*, Oxford, University Press, 1995. P. Childs and P. Williams, *An Introduction to Post-Colonial Theory*, London and New York, Prentice Hall/Harvester Wheatsheaf, 1997. P. Chatterjee, *The Nation and its Fragments: Colonial and Postcolonial Histories*, Princeton, University Press, 1993. On writing on pluralism see: R. Bauboeck, A. Heller and

A.R. Zolberg (eds), *The Challenge of Diversity: Integration and Pluralism in Societies of Immigration*, Aldershot, Avebury, 1996. E. Rooney, *Seductive Reasoning: Pluralism as the Problematic of Contemporary Literary Theory*, Ithaca, Cornell University Press, 1989. D.Th. Goldberg (ed.), *Multiculturalism: A Critical Reader*, Oxford, Blackwell, 1994. P. Hirst, *From Statism to Pluralism: Democracy, Civil Society and Global Politics*, London, UCL Press, 1997.

3 M. Albrow, *Globalization: Myths and Realities*, London, Roehampton Institute, 1994. A.D. King (ed.), *Culture, Globalization and the World System*, London, Macmillan, 1991. E. Kofman and G. Youngs, *Globalization: Theory and Practice*, London, Pinter, 1996. R. Robertson, *Globalization: Social Theory and Global Culture*, London, Sage, 1992. T. Spybey, *Globalization and World Society*, Cambridge, Polity, 1996. M. Featherstone (ed.), *Global Culture*, London, Sage, 1990. J. Friedman, *Cultural Identity and Global Process*, London, Sage, 1994. H. Bhabha, *The Location of Culture*, London, Routledge, 1994.

4 U. Sharma, *Complementary Medicine Today. Practitioners and Patients*, London and New York, Routledge, 1992, pp. 42–3.

5 R. Porter (ed.), *The Popularization of Medicine, 1650–1850*, London, Routledge, 1992, p. 1. See also R. Cooter (ed.), *Studies in the History of Alternative Medicine*, Houndsmill, Macmillan, 1988.

6 A. Kleinman, *Patients and Healers in the Context of Culture*, Berkeley, University of California Press, 1980. C. Leslie and A. Young (eds), *Paths to Medical Knowledge*, Berkeley, University of California Press, 1992.

7 C. Leslie (ed.) *Asian Medical Systems. A Comparative Study*, Berkeley, University of California Press, 1976. Quote, referring to *Asian Medical Systems*, from C. Leslie and A. Young (eds), *Paths to Medical Knowledge*, Berkeley, University of California Press, 1992, p. 6.

8 Leslie, *Asian Medical Systems*, pp. 184–271. C. Leslie, 'The ambiguities of medical revivalism in modern India', pp. 356–67. W.T. Jones, 'World-views and Asian medical systems: some suggestions for further study', pp. 383–400.

9 See for historiographic reviews D. Porter, 'The mission of social history of medicine: an historical overview', *Social History of Medicine*, 8 (1995): 345–60. L. Jordanova, 'The Social Construction of Medical Knowledge', *Social History of Medicine*, 8 (1995): 361–82.

10 D. Arnold (ed.), *Imperial Medicine and Indigenous Societies*, Manchester, Manchester University Press, 1988. R. MacLeod and L. Milton (eds), *Disease, Medicine and Empire: Perspectives on Western Medicine and the Experience of European Expansion*, London, Routledge, 1988. R. Guha, *Subaltern Studies*, Delhi, Oxford University Press, 1982. W. Ernst, *Mad Tales From the Raj*, London, Routledge, 1991. M. Vaughan, *Curing their Ills: Colonial Power and African Illness*, Oxford, Polity Press, 1991. D. Arnold, *Colonizing the Body. State Medicine and Epidemic Disease in Nineteenth-Century India*, Berkeley, University of California Press, 1993.

11 Look, for example, at the but cursory references to non-European systems of healing even in Porter's popular publications: R. Porter (ed.), *Cambridge Illustrated History of Medicine*, Cambridge, Cambridge University Press, 1996. R. Porter, *The Greatest Benefit to Mankind. A Medical History of Humanity from Antiquity to the Present*, London, Harper Collins, 1997. For evidence of a less Euro-centric perspective see: W.F Bynum and R. Porter (eds), *Companion Encyclopedia of the History of Medicine*, London, Routledge, 1993.

12 J. Dupre, *The Disorder of Things: Metaphysical Foundations of the Disunity of Science*, Cambridge, MA: Harvard University Press, 1993. C. Geertz, *Available Light: Anthropological Reflections on Philosophical Topics*, Princeton, Princeton University Press, 2000. E. Frankel Paul, F.D. Miller and J. Paul (eds), *Cultural Pluralism and Moral Knowledge*, Cambridge, Cambridge University Press, 1994. S. Clarke, 'Pluralism unconstrained', *International Studies in the Philosophy of Science*, 11 (1997): 143–6. See also note 2 for further literature.

13 See also B. Good, 'How medicine constructs its objects', in B. Good, *Medicine, Rationality and Experience*, Cambridge, Cambridge University Press, 1990. B. Barnes, 'On the conventional character of knowledge', in K.D. Knorr-Cetina and M. Mulkay (eds), *Science Observed*, London, Sage, 1983. A. Pickering (ed.), *Science as Practice and Culture*, Chicago, London, 1993. P. Wright and A. Treacher (eds), *The Problem of Medical Knowledge*, Edinburgh, Edinburgh University Press, 1982.

14 Porter, *Popularization...*, p. 8.

15 Cant and Sharma, *New Medical Pluralism*, p. 11.

16   G. Ritzer, *The McDonaldization of Society*, Thousand Oaks, Pine Forks, 1993.
17   Quoted from F. Zimmermann, *The Jungle and the Aroma of the Meats. An Ecological Theme in Hindu Medicine*, Delhi, Motilal Banarsidass, 1999 (Editions Du Seuil, 1982), p. 158.
18   D. Wujastyk, *The Roots of Ayurveda: Selections from Sanskrit Medical Writings*, New Delhi, Penguin, 1998. K. Zysk, *Asceticism and Healing in Ancient India: Medicine in the Buddhist Monastery*, Oxford, Oxford University Press, 1991. A.L. Basham, 'The practice of medicine in ancient and medieval India', in Leslie, *Asian Medical Systems*, pp. 18–43. F. Dunn, 'Traditional Asian medicine and cosmopolitan medicine as adaptive systems', in Leslie, *Asian Medical Systems*, pp. 133–58. Leslie, 'The Ambiguities…'. C. Leslie, 'Interpretations of illness: syncretism in modern Ayurveda', in Leslie and Young, *Paths to Medical Knowledge*, pp. 177–208. See similar arguments in regard to Chinese Medicine: C. Croizier, 'The ideology of medical revivalism in modern China', in Leslie, *Asian Medical Systems*, pp. 341–55. Y. Otsuka, 'Chinese traditional medicine in Japan', in Leslie, *Asian Medical Systems*, pp. 322–40. M. Topley, 'Chinese traditional etiology and methods of cure in Hong Kong', in Leslie, *Asian Medical Systems*, pp. 243–70. M. Porkert, 'The intellectual and social impulses behind the evolution of traditional Chinese medicine', in Leslie, *Asian Medical Systems*, pp. 63–80. P.U. Unschuld 'Epistemological issues and changing legitimation: traditional Chinese medicine in the twentieth century', in Leslie and Young, *Paths to Medical Knowledge*, pp. 44–61.
19   On meat consumption and vegetarianism see Zimmermann, *The Jungle and the Aroma of Meats*.
20   A.K. Ramanujan, *The Collected Poems of A.K. Ramanujan*, Oxford, Oxford University Press, 1996. See also A. Chaudhuri, 'The twin-lobed brahmin', in *The Times Higher*, 1 March 1996, p. 31.
21   E. Hobsbawm and T. Ranger (eds), *The Invention of Tradition*, Cambridge, Cambridge University Press, 1983. B. Anderson, *Imagined Communities*, London, Verso, 1991. W. Ernst, 'Idioms of madness and colonial boundaries', *Comparative Studies in Society and History*, 39 (1997): 153–81. R.B. Inden, *Imagining India*, Oxford, Blackwell, 1990.
22   See, for examples, Bruchhausen and Roelcke in Chapter 5.
23   F. Zimmermann, 'Gentle purge: the flower power of Ayurveda', p. 210, in C. Leslie and A. Young (eds), *Paths to Asian Medical Knowledge*, Berkeley, University of California Press, 1992, pp. 209–23.
24   Zimmermann, 'Flower power', p. 209.
25   Zimmermann, 'Flower power', p. 210.
26   V. Scheid, *Contemporary Chinese Medicine: Synthesis and Plurality*, Durham, NC, Duke University Press, 2001. E. Hsu, *The Transmission of Chinese Medicine*, Cambridge, Cambridge University Press, 1999. For earlier literature on the same issue see note 18.
27   E. Hobsbawm and T. Ranger (eds), *The Invention of Tradition*, Cambridge, Cambridge University Press, 1983.

2 Medicine on the margins?

Hydropathy and orthodoxy in Britain, 1840–60

James Bradley

'The past is a foreign country', runs the oft-quoted opening line of L.P. Hartley's *The Go-Between*. 'They do things differently there'.[1] This message has only been partially received by historians of British nineteenth-century heterodox medicine. The all-too schematic historiography, much of which is contained in two collections of essays produced more than a decade ago, strives to label those practices and practitioners existing outside the realms of the dominant form of medicine as 'alternative', 'fringe', 'marginal', or one of many other descriptions that emphasise the otherness of heterodox systems.[2] As Matthew Ramsey has recently commented, this usage tends to posit 'a dichotomy between two domains, seen from the perspective of one of them'[3] – a problem for those interested in plural medicine who should resist the urge to divide the world into centres and peripheries. To be sure, historians of the medical fringe have gone to great lengths to emphasise the blurring of boundaries, and the exchange-and-mart of ideas and practices between the official and unofficial.[4] But still nineteenth-century 'unorthodoxy' is prescribed in these accounts by a language that dwells upon the notion of the alternative. To be alternative is to be other. Thus the discursive centrality of official medicine is reinforced, while unofficial medicine is pushed to the intellectual margins. Few fail to avoid the trap of constructing a dichotomy relying upon the notion that the world consists, or has consisted, of insiders and outsiders. Of those that have, Cooter's often cogent and always sophisticated analysis stands out.[5] But even he is unable, at times, to avoid the pitfall of privileging orthodoxy. He suggests, for example, that heterodox practitioners frequently buffed up their theories with the veneer of scientific positivism to legitimate their practice – an argument that undermines the coherence at the heart of many heterodox practices, and underrates the extent to which scientific positivism was a 'veneer' that glossed the surface of orthodox medical thought.[6]

If the past is a 'foreign country', it might be as well for historians to engage with that past like social anthropologists approaching another culture. Since Charles Leslie first published his methodological suggestions for analysing non-Western medical systems in 1976, anthropologists have generally accepted that Western orthodoxy should not be the centre against which non-Western medical systems are judged,[7] thus providing the intellectual space for examining Asian medical systems on their own terms. The anthropological analysis of plural medicines could now proceed without the burden of discussing whether they were efficacious, or more or less superior to their Western counterpart.

While it is debatable whether we can describe heterodox medical systems in Victorian Britain as examples of plural medicine, the decentred orthodoxy of cultural anthropology offers historians a vital gain. Specifically, it allows us to shimmy around (rather than leap over) the twin problems of incommensurability and presentism. Here, 'incommensurability' is deployed in a Kuhnian sense, as an acknowledgement that between the mid-nineteenth and the late-twentieth centuries what amounts to a paradigmatic shift occurred in the field of medicine, and that performance and language shifted accordingly.[8] This situation presents the historian with the problem of translating across the divide. 'Presentism', refers to the practice of applying early-twenty-first-century concepts to the mid-nineteenth-century world – in other words, ignoring incommensurability.

Of course, any project that denies it is not, to some degree, presentist in orientation is guilty of naïvety. Whatever our desires, we cannot create a virtual time-machine that removes ourselves from the present. Our concerns, our interests, our vision will always be socially constructed, or at the very least socially directed. Consequently, we must pay particular attention to the language of the period in question, attempting to uncover the words used to identify particular social situations within mid-nineteenth-century medicine (for example, 'orthodox'), prising out the processes by which these words gained their meanings. Descriptive labels, like 'alternative', that derive from our own twenty-first-century understanding of social reality, should be avoided as far as possible.

The relativism implicit in this perspective permits a symmetrical treatment of competing nineteenth-century medical systems and negates the encroachment of our presentist notions upon the field of study. It also allows us to resist attacks by those who charge relativism with undermining the notion of truth. Historians of medicine recognise that the manner in which truth is established varies over time and place.[9] It is not the historian's task to explain the success of one system or the failure of others in teleological terms characterised by present-day notions of efficacy. Instead, the non-presentist account focuses on how an emergent truth was shaped, contested, established and (often) discarded. Because orthodoxy is treated here like any other social institution (as open to epistemological analysis as, say, hydropathy), it is inevitably decentred. Indeed, nineteenth-century orthodox thought and practice were as fractured as any other system and their eventual, albeit partial, hegemony was not the result of cautious inductive reason ironing out, one-by-one, the troublesome creases of unscience and unreason.

Decentring orthodoxy does not, of course, mean ignoring it. The major problem facing the historian of nineteenth-century heterodoxies is that orthodoxy possesses a patchy historiographical existence. There is no full description of reform-age orthodoxy that encompasses diagnosis, pathology, physiology, therapeutics and the many other components of medicine. Thus we do not fully understand the orthodoxy that confronted heterodoxies. This chapter will, therefore, use hydropathy as a case study to explore the interactions between orthodoxy and a single heterodoxy and will provide a first step to understanding the nature of mid-nineteenth-century orthodoxy. The water cure provides an ideal platform for this task as it was placed both inside and outside the boundaries of orthodox thought and practice. Not only does its adoption and adaption demonstrate how blurred the boundaries were between heterodoxy and orthodoxy, it also shows that orthodoxy, rather than being a monolithic object – a given, against which all other systems should be judged – was itself evolving, mutating and ever so slightly amorphous.

From practice to principles: adapting Priessnitz

During the nineteenth century, hydropathy, or the cold water cure, alongside homoeopathy and mesmerism, was one of the major Western heterodox medical systems. It was the invention of Vincent Priessnitz. The story of his discovery is revealing. A 'genius' (to lay hydropathic believers), an 'untutored genius' (to medically-qualified hydropathic believers), but a Silesian 'peasant' to supporters and detractors alike, it was said he enacted a self-cure for broken ribs by tightly bandaging himself in wet sheets and drinking large quantities of water. His inspiration had come from watching a wounded deer curing itself with spring water. He developed his system empirically; that is, he incrementally tinkered with different means and methods until he had perfected the regime. At first he experimented upon the local livestock and then his willing neighbours, until the cure worked.[10]

There is a whiff of myth about this story, not least because there existed a local tradition of using water as a remedial agent.[11] Furthermore, this account gives the very real sense of a divinely ordered nature revealing itself through providence. Priessnitz's impact was, however, anything but mythical. From the mid-1820s, he established Gräfenburg, in the Silesian Alps, as the first and most famous hydropathic centre. Reverberations were felt throughout Europe. The chronically sick travelled to be ministered to by the Silesian. Qualified medical practitioners, some sceptical, others willing to believe, also made the journey, returning to their respective countries with miraculous or cynical tidings according to taste. Despite resistance from local practitioners, Priessnitz's practice thrived until, by the 1840s, he was personally treating hundreds of patients a year – many of them staying for months, and a few for years, at a time.[12]

Priessnitz saw his system as a negation of orthodox therapy: it was intended to make medicine redundant. Hydropathy was based upon the application of cold water, either generally, locally or internally. The water could be administered through a variety of means: baths and douches; wet bandages; sweating blankets; friction from rubbing a partially wrung sheet over the body; and famously, the tightly packed wet-sheet swaddling the entire body. These direct methods were combined with a regimen that involved abstinence from stimulants, a diet of plain wholesome food, and regular exercise in the mountain-surrounds of Gräfenberg. Priessnitz, himself, held to a basic or 'folkish' conception of humoralism.[13] He perceived disease as a result of 'bad matter' infecting the blood (the bad matter was often, in his opinion, the result of drug treatment by allopathic practitioners).[14]

It was the job of the hydropathist to remove that matter by bombarding the skin and mucous membrane with water. The water acted firstly to stimulate the system through the medium of the *vis medicatrix naturæ* – the body's natural capacity to heal itself – to a point of 'crisis'. Suppurating pustules breaking out upon the patient's skin were denoted the 'visible crisis' – the sign that the body was purging itself of the 'morbific material'.[15] It was also intended that the patient be hardened against future disease (not unlike the eighteenth-century cool regime promoted by, among others, the balneologist John Floyer and the founder of Methodism, John Wesley).[16]

Priessnitz's ideas were imported into Britain through a variety of channels, most visibly Captain Claridge's mission of the 1840s (he travelled the length and the breadth of the British Isles proselytising on behalf of the cure).[17] The system itself proved highly versatile in its appeal to orthodox and unorthodox practitioners, and a broad cross-section of patients. On the one hand, as in North America,[18] it found a bedrock of support among radicals and sectarians, a genuine example of Ramsey's 'counterhegemonic' medicine. Mary Gove Nicholls, the First Concordians,[19] John Smedley in Matlock who defected from an evangelical established church to become a lay preacher for the United Free Methodist Church,[20] Alexander Munro and John Kirk in Scotland of the small breakaway sect the Evangelical Union,[21] are some of the abundant examples illustrating hydropathy's function as a 'democratic epistemology'.[22] In these instances, the cure was portrayed as a providential gift, a system where water, spirituality and purity were bound together.[23] Conversion to hydropathy was, therefore, akin to religious conversion – a baptismal rite.

On the other hand, there were orthodoxly qualified hydropathists who attempted to make hydropathy an analogue of orthodox medicine. Thus, before and after Claridge, a number of qualified physicians visited Gräfenberg, and then busied themselves by explaining the benefits of Priessnitzian hydropathy. The more astute of them were able to see the commercial potential of creating cure-centres – hydropathic institutions – along the lines of Gräfenberg, for it created opportunity on the edge of orthodoxy at a time when medical livings were depressed. Indeed, in this respect, it is hard to differentiate hydropathy from other practices located on the margins of orthodox medicine, for example spa practice and specialist hospitals. Many hydropathic institutions were opened during the 1840s and persisted stubbornly through the reform era. The locations chosen for these were often the result of careful deliberation. James Manby Gully and James Wilson, for example, scoured the south of England for the correct combination of pure water, good air and fine climate, before settling at Malvern. Many others were founded in watering places or seaside resorts (for example, Cheltenham, Ben Rhydding near Ilkley Wells, Glenburn, Ramsgate), while others were opened near the major urban centres (Sudbrook Park near London, Umberslade Hall near Birmingham).[24]

The majority of hydropathic institutions were run, and the bulk of the theoretical literature produced, by the orthodoxly qualified. They, as a group, shared a number of beliefs and experiences: a faith in the water cure, however described; a similar set of social experiences in the financial and social insecurity of the medical profession;[25] and an almost overwhelming belief in orthodox models of pathology and physiology (whether based on neo-humoralist chemical physiology or morbid anatomy). But what they did not share as a group were religious, political or therapeutic beliefs. Some, it is true, like William MacLeod, had radical or dissenting roots similar to the lay hydropaths. Others, like Edward Johnson, exhibited few of these signs. But virtually all of them, from whatever background they came, upheld orthodox medicine's conceptions of disease and the body. Indeed, to a man, they believed that hydropathy, skilfully deployed, could replicate the effects of the orthodox *materia medica*. The water cure, thus represented, was equivalent to orthodox practice as it refused to deny medicine's curative power. Rather it accepted the allopathic case, with the important reservation that drugs had harmful side-effects, whereas water had none.

In reality, though, it is hard to place medically qualified hydropathists on either side of the drugs/no-drugs dichotomy. Some, like Gully, professed to have abandoned drugging.[26] Others, Edward Johnson and Graham for example, believed hydropathy should augment allopathy.[27] Still others, notably MacLeod, blended orthodox prescription with an eclectic range of unorthodox therapies – homoeopathy, Ling gymnastics and the 'compressed air bath', to name a few of his favoured methods.[28]

This bifurcation of hydropaths into the opposition of medically educated *versus* medically ignorant is, however, overly schematic. Many unqualified hydropathists bowed to the authority of their qualified brethren and therefore used orthodox ideas to explain Priessnitz's success. This represented an acceptance of orthodox medicine's theoretical priority. Their published work is a testament to this. Smedley, for example, relied heavily upon Gully's account of the therapeutic rationale of hydropathy. He borrowed from the work of Marshall Hall on the nervous system and W.B. Carpenter's popular, but nevertheless highly technical, physiology.[29]

The difference, however, between the accounts of qualified and non-qualified lay in style and organisation. Comparing the qualified Johnson's *Hydropathy* with Smedley's *Practical Hydropathy* is instructive. Johnson organised his work methodically and systematically. The first section was basically an account of Priessnitz's system as he had observed it. The second and third sections used Justus Liebig's newly-delineated chemical physiology and Billing's modification of the *materia medica* to demonstrate how disease functioned and what the aims of the physician were in combating ill health.[30] These were then made congruent with the water cure, and if it was not for the hydropathic subject matter, the monograph would appear supremely orthodox in its use of scientific authority to present its case.

Smedley's *Practical Hydropathy* had a similar structure, working its way from a personal account to physiological theory and then to therapy. Nevertheless, where Johnson's description of his conversion was supported by a rhetoric of scientific observation (he came, he saw, he observed), Smedley's relied upon the tropes of evangelicalism. The effectiveness of hydropathy was, for him, a revelation, and his journey from chronic illness to robust health a pilgrim's progress. The remainder of Smedley's manual is a somewhat incoherent, cut-and-paste account of orthodox medicine and hydropathic cure, interspersed with random appeals to the divine.

While Johnson was not immune to such appeals, such insertions never dominated the text. Orthodox and unorthodox practitioners may therefore be differentiated by the amount of emphasis they placed upon divinity and providence, as well as the skill with which medical and scientific writing was deployed as an authority to mobilise support for this new therapeutic system.

As this suggests, adopting the water cure was not a simple matter of taking Priessnitz's system unaltered. Indeed, Priessnitz constructed, at one and the same time, a considerable obstacle and an immense opportunity for the potential water doctor: he failed to leave a written account of his system. There were three paths that could be taken to enlightenment. First, a putative practitioner might travel to Gräfenberg and observe Priessnitz in action. The Silesian was prepared to tolerate observers, although he remained suspicious of orthodoxly qualified practitioners. This route was taken by Wilson and Johnson, amongst others.[31] Second, the rationale of hydropathy could be obtained second-hand, either by reading one or more of the copious works produced on the subject or discussing the treatment with an individual who had taken the first route. Gully, for example, was converted to the water cure through conversations with his long-standing friend Wilson.[32] Third, a potential practitioner could visit as a patient (often in desperation) one of the many other hydropathics that were opened in Britain and Europe during the 1840s. Thus, Herbert Mayo, former chief surgeon at the Middlesex Hospital, became a hydropathic practitioner following treatment for a debilitating chronic condition at Marienberg.[33] Smedley took up hydropathy's cause after his cure at Ben Rhydding.[34] Nevertheless, for all routes the mode of hydropathy adopted was a translation, linguistically and theoretically of Priessnitz's original system, and was therefore structured by previously held medical beliefs and the social settings in which the practitioner found himself at the time of conversion. The end result was a syncretic system that enfolded Priessnitzian hydropathy within the individual practitioner's own experiences.

This dynamic is most clearly discernible in the accounts of qualified hydropathic practitioners. The written work they produced prior to adopting hydropathy is remarkably consistent with their theoretical and practical translations of Priessnitz's system. Before adopting hydropathy, T.J. Graham had authored the highly successful *Domestic Medicine*,[35] Gully had written two well-received, and technically detailed books – *Treatment of Neuropathy* and *The Simple Treatment of Disease*,[36] and Johnson had produced *Letters to Brother John*.[37] Comparing these works with those produced after their discovery of hydropathy, Gully remained a convinced follower of Broussais, loyal to the latter's uniquely reductive conception of localised disease, Johnson's emphasis on the humoral pathology of the fluids, particularly the chemical composition of the blood, endured, while Graham abided by the orthodox belief in the localised disease of mainstream pathology.[38]

More importantly, there were identifiable continuities in their respective therapeutic perspectives. All remained adamant that: orthodox practice relied too heavily on drugging; successful cure was a function of the healing power of nature; and effective therapy should be weighted towards dietetic and hygienic measures – a programme of preventative medicine that had diet, environment and bathing as the key elements of cure rather than the active interventions more commonly associated with orthodoxy.[39] These views did not cause them to join the ranks of the water doctors: although links between hygienic medicine and the water cure should not be discounted, most practitioners who adhered to hygienic methods remained firmly in the orthodox camp. The powerfully developed sense of theory and practice displayed by the medically qualified hydropathists did, however, structure the way in which they received the water cure, providing the mental scaffolding around which individual adaptations of Priessnitz could be built. As Johnson commented after his visit to Gräfenberg, Priessnitz appeared to be '*reducing to practice* all the great *principles*' he had described in an earlier, pre-hydropathic, publication.[40] Yet, at the root of these adaptations of Priessnitz, there lay something deeper relating to the social meaning of therapeutics. To draw out the implications of this, we must explore the reactions of the medical profession.

Hydropathy and the medical profession

In retrospect, the lack of overall patient or bed numbers indicates the problems of empirically measuring hydropathy's impact upon the British public. Nevertheless, *in lieu* of what an economic historian would regard as 'hard' evidence, the success of key early works, particularly those of Claridge, Gully, Wilson and Johnson, reveals that the water cure struck a resonant chord with the valetudinarians of early Victorian society. The speed at which hydropathic institutions were opened, and the longevity of many of these, suggests that the demand for hydropathic services remained boyant throughout this period. Diseased savants, sick poets and poorly novelists were particularly drawn to hydropathy – Tennyson, Darwin, Jerrold and Reade are examples.[41] The cure even permeated the mid-Victorian periodical, providing satirical material for publications like *Punch* and *Blackwood's*.[42]

As this suggests, hydropathy in its classic guise was a distinctive cure-system for the better sorts of Victorian society. This is not to say that the cold-water cure excluded the lower classes. Attempts were made to spread the hydropathic creed throughout society. Self-help manuals encouraged hydropathic practices in the home, although given the difficulties of obtaining an effective supply of clean water in the slumlands of the cities, as well as the prohibitive cost of the multitude of baths and douches, this was hardly realistic. Some water doctors, usually unqualified, held dispensaries in major cities, designed to serve a wide clientele. Furthermore, for a short period in the late 1840s there was a failed attempt to set up a hydropathic hospital in London. But notwithstanding these small efforts hydropathy was geared towards a wealthy clientele.

Many patients who undertook the water cure produced verbose accounts of their experiences. The majority of these were unsolicited propaganda for Priessnitz's system. For every critical piece, like a review in *Blackwood's* critical of hydropathy's excesses[43], there were a spiralling number of extended, enthusiastic, even joyous lay accounts, including: Bulwyer Lytton's *Confessions of a Water Cure Patient*; R.J. Lane's *Life at the Water Cure*; and Blackie's *Water Cure in Scotland*. Gully even appeared as Dr Gullson in a sympathetic walk-on role in Charles Reade's novel *It's Never too Late to Mend*.[44]

The reaction of the medical profession was more complex and reflected to a large degree the pattern of adaptation described above. In other words, practitioners who favoured hygienic/regimented treatment were most likely to see benefits in the system. Thus, aside from those practitioners who adopted the system, the profession's reaction could be placed upon a spectrum spanning outright rejection at one pole, to unbridled enthusiasm at the other. Where the lines were drawn reveals more about the nature of orthodoxy than the medical legitimacy of the water cure.

The sternest critics of hydropathy were to be found in the medical press, particularly *The Lancet*, and the forerunner of the *British Medical Journal* – the *Provincial Medical and Surgical Journal* (*PMSJ*). They aimed a wide variety of accusations at hydropathy. First, while it was clear that in certain circumstances, particularly stubborn chronic conditions that required an alteration in the patient's regimen, hydropathy had a role to play, critics were adamant that it had no claims to being an entire medical system. As medical practitioners were well acquainted with these and other uses for water and baths, due to the role water-based therapies played in both the Hippocratic corpus and contemporary medical procedures, they did not think it appropriate to be told of the effectiveness of water by 'peasants' and 'impostors'. Hydropathy was, therefore, considered a mere pretension, an old and well-known method masquerading as a novelty.[45] Second, they accused qualified practitioners of advertising their wares by 'puffing' their own establishments and cures.[46] Hydropathy was seen to breach the behavioural ethics that *The Lancet*, in particular, was striving to impose on the profession. Third, the critics maintained that hydropathy was potentially dangerous, particularly in the hands of the medically unqualified. Many letters were published showing that patients had been harmed or, worse still, killed while undertaking the cure.[47] To emphasise this *The Lancet* published detailed accounts of the coroners' proceedings following the deaths of patients under hydropathic treatment.[48]

Finally, and most importantly, the water cure was attacked on the level of epistemology. How, they asked, could an effective therapeutic system be invented by an illiterate peasant 'ignorant of the nature and symptoms of disease'?[49] In other words, therapeutic innovation inevitably flowed from pathological and physiological knowledge; not from the observations of an unlearned man. This critique, therefore, represented an attack upon what was considered quackish empiricism and a defence of Pierre Louis's empirical programme:

> We have said on other occasions, that among the moderns, LOUIS is the model that should be looked for in the physician. What a wide and deep chasm of ignorance and darkness yawns between this able and accurate man and those who are at once his detractors, and the abettors of the quack-cheat, PRIESSNITZ![50]

Put simply, scientific truth could not be derived from false premises.

There were, however, a number of qualified practitioners who went some distance towards accepting hydropathy's claims. The chemical analyst, Charles

Scudamore, a long-time sufferer from rheumatism, found much relief at the hands of Priessnitz, and wrote a short book describing his experiences at Gräfenberg.[51] Erasmus Wilson, proto-dermatologist, also found much to welcome. The first edition of his *Practical Treatise on Healthy Skin* dedicated an entire chapter to hydropathy, using as its main authority a work by James Wilson.[52] For Erasmus Wilson, the water cure was easily integrated into his programme for hygienic medicine, with its emphasis on the cleansing of the skin for the prevention of disease. He was more than happy to recommend the cure, praising James Wilson for his 'candid analysis of Priessnitz' and suggesting the need for '*hygienic sanatoriums*' modelled upon the hydropathic institution.[53]

The radical Edinburgh physician and phrenologist, Andrew Combe, saw similar benefits deriving from Priessnitz's system, as well as the active part that the water cure might play in combating disease.[54] Most importantly, John Forbes, erstwhile translator of Laennec and editor of the *British and Foreign Medical Review*, opened his arms to hydropathy – it appears to have left him genuinely enthused. The work of Johnson and Gully, in particular, had persuaded him that not only did the water cure leave full play to the natural power of healing, it was also a potent and active therapy in its own right.[55] He believed it was proven that the skilful application of water could produce all the effects of the *materia medica*:

> It is scarcely too much to say that he [Priessnitz] has modified the application of water, and some very few other means, in a manner so ingenious as to render them no imperfect *nominal* substitute, at least, for most of the drugs in the pharmacopœia. He has his stimulant, his sedative, his tonic, his reducing agent, his purgative, his astringent, his diuretic, his styptic, his febrifuge, his diaphoretic, his alterative, his counter-irritant.[56]

Some were less willing to endorse hydropathy wholeheartedly. For Edwin Lee, spa doctor and medical writer, hydropathy was undoubtedly effective in a limited number of cases, but hardly had the power of his chosen, and less contested, therapeutic preference – spa treatment mixed with climatology. Unlike spa therapy, hydropathy was too time-consuming and too heroic.[57] Taking the waters at a spa achieved the same ends as hydropathy, but did so more efficiently, particularly as the baths relied upon higher temperatures combined with the action of the minerals contained in the water.[58] He did, however, admit that there were some instances where hydropathy was preferable, particularly when the regimen accompanying spa treatment had failed to impose itself upon the patient.[59] He then recommended that anyone requiring hydropathic treatment should consult Gully, Wilson or Johnson.[60]

Mind the therapeutic gap: interpreting the practice of medicine

There is a social dimension implicit within these different positions. To understand this we need a clearer conception of the meaning of therapeutics. The practice of medicine was divided into three interconnected parts: pathology (the study of disease, including etiology, prognosis, and the actual processes of disease); therapeutics (the cure of disease); and hygiene (the prevention of disease). The interaction of these parts is crucial to understanding the nature of both orthodox medicine and hydropathy. With the possible exception of diagnosis, no area in the historiography of British nineteenth-century medicine is as poorly represented as therapeutics. And yet, as has been demonstrated in the North American context, the therapeutic encounter is where knowledge and belief are made concrete in practice. It is hardly surprising that therapeutics were invested with a 'symbolic power' intimately connected to the self-identity of the medical practitioner.[61] For therapy provided the link that physically and mentally bound the patient and the practitioner. It also defined the social role and status of the practitioner.

Orthodox medicine as a field was fragmented, both as a body of knowledge and means of practice. The diverse professional reaction to hydropathy was a symptom of the divisions that afflicted orthodoxy before and after the Medical Act of 1858. On the level of medical theory there was, however, something approaching unanimity. To be sure, the new localised pathology of morbid anatomy, a translation of Paris hospital medicine informed by the Cullenian tradition, vied with a revivified humoral pathology, which received impetus from Justus Liebig's chemical physiology.[62] The conflict, which derived from the opposition of functional and local models of disease, turned upon the issue of proximate causation. A chicken-and-egg dispute was its outcome – did local disease precede general disease, or *vice versa*? Yet, it was merely a debate about first causes, and did not threaten the consensus that existed over the remote causes of disease. It was generally admitted that there were zymotic, predispositional and constitutional factors in etiology, which together or apart accounted for an individual's susceptibility to specific disease conditions.[63]

The division between proximate and remote causes was of great significance. Proximate causation found its focus either in morbid anatomy or chemical analysis, while remote causes with their emphasis on mind, body and environment ensured that the sick person remained highly visible in the medical cosmology. Consequently, the majority of practitioners *still* conceived the body in holistic terms. The various organs (including the brain), nervous system and fluids were intimately combined into a systemic whole. Health and disease represented the body system in equilibrium or disequilibrium, where the malfunction of one part might affect many others, or a generalised imbalance might manifest itself locally in a single organ.[64] The body moved through a hostile world, always vulnerable to attack. Continued good health resulted from the avoidance of any factor – social, mental, environmental – that might upset the precarious balance. Repulsing ill health was, however, another matter, for the art of therapeutics laid bare the deep divisions of reform-age medicine.

Some practitioners clung outright to the established 'revulsive' regime – *medicina perturbatrix* – administering bleedings and high doses of heavy metal in an assault designed to repel disease from the body. Others rejected this mode in favour of 'expectancy' or hygienic measures, both of which, in an effort to stimulate the natural power of healing, emphasised the non-invasive management of the patient's constitution. Acceptance or rejection of a particular therapeutic perspective was more likely to be determined by the social and political outlook of a practitioner than specific pathological or physiological principles. Indeed, different therapeutic rationales often led to the employment of identical therapeutic regimes – a reductive and scientific practitioner like John Hughes Bennett might deploy similar therapeutic techniques to sceptical physicians, whose methods were often described, albeit rhetorically, as nihilistic.[65] The situation, in its starkest form, can be described as the 'therapeutic gap' – the speculative space between physiology and pathology, on the one side, and the practice of medicine, on the other. The filling of the abhorred vacuum reveals much about the fractured nature of orthodoxy.

The Lancet was highly articulate in expressing its own perceptions of the alliance forged between orthodox knowledge and practice. At its most basic, this consisted in accepting Pierre Louis's statistical epidemiology as the best way of generating scientific knowledge about the effectiveness of different therapies. At the same time, it wholeheartedly denied the implications of Louis's findings – that many 'traditional' therapies like bloodletting had no impact upon the course of a disease. Indeed, time and again, *The Lancet* thundered against those therapeutic sceptics who argued that the role of the practitioner was to manage illness without active intervention, letting nature take its course. Responding to two sceptical correspondents, it stated that by adopting the inductive programme, therapy had been immeasurably improved:[66]

> we … assert that modern physicians, when thoroughly acquainted, practically as well as theoretically, with the medical learning of the day, are immeasurably superior 'in their practice' to the physicians of former times …. We bleed, we purge, we narcotise, like our predecessors, it is true, but being better acquainted with the history of disease than they were, we know better *when* to bleed, *when* to purge, *when* to narcotise, than they did …[67]

The Lancet's rhetoric was not a mirror held up to the profession. It did not state an objective reality. The preferred reader for both *The Lancet* and the *PMSJ* was the general practitioner, the largest but least powerful group within the profession.[68] During this period general practitioners perceived themselves as the victims of poor market circumstances. They competed against a vast army of irregulars.[69] Their appointment to official positions was controlled by lay authorities like the Poor Law Guardians, to whom they remained beholden. In short, they were prevented from attaining the respect that they thought they were due. Their practice was predicated upon action, not least because the main means of attaining an income was through the frequent prescription of medicine as well as physical interventions like bleeding. Their patients were mainly drawn from the less wealthy. Any attempt to undermine the rationale behind their therapy or their practice not only represented a direct attack upon their income, but also a full-frontal assault upon the behaviour that most clearly identified them as general practitioners. Hydropathy threatened both.

Many of the orthodox practitioners who defended the water cure were able to deploy a different, less active approach to therapeutics. They placed more emphasis upon harnessing the *vis medicatrix* – body's natural capacity to heal itself – and less upon assaulting disease head on. Thus, aside from his positive intervention into the debate over hydropathy, Forbes explained the conjoint success of non-Western healing systems, ancient orthodoxy and modern heterodoxy in these terms. This provided the basis for his half-hearted defence of homoeopathy. The homoeopaths' delusions were considered by him as ineffective, but by prescribing an inert remedy the practitioner allowed the *vis medicatrix* full play.[70]

Men who supported Forbes' sceptical position were most often drawn either from the élite of the profession (proto-Harley Street), or from those that had managed to attain financial security independent of general practice. They were likely to support passive intervention in disease, providing the backbone of the movement promoting hygienic medicine, both as a political programme and as a mode of treatment. This implied a radical concern with improving the conditions of the working classes[71] while servicing a high status clientele that demanded a therapeutic encounter founded in 'bedside' or 'biographical' medicine.[72] Here, emphasis on the *vis medicatrix* resulted in the graded control of the patient's regimen and diet through discussion, advice and surveillance.

It was an ideal aspired to by many practitioners, but few could afford to put it into practice. It required access to patients who had time and money, and who therefore did not always require the 'quick fix'. It was, in the barest terms, easy for the Physician Extraordinary to the Queen, or a surgeon at the Middlesex Hospital, to practise a form of medicine based upon consultation and advice, but not so for a general practitioner slaving away in a poor rural or urban district. Hydropathy, therefore, offered some physicians a venue for cure advice that had obvious continuities with their own favoured remedial regimes.[73]

The case of Edwin Lee, described above, falls to some extent into the camp of non-interventionist practitioners – or at least, he aspired to this condition. Although he believed that he had been marginalised by London's medical élite, failing to achieve a hospital appointment,[74] he successfully avoided having to practise as a General Practitioner. Instead he advised patients on spa treatment and climatology, which he combined with authoring an abundance of works on a jumble of medical and social subjects. This allowed him to further his interests by a different, non-institutional route. His chosen therapy was underpinned by the élite belief in passive intervention.[75] Nevertheless, hydropathy still constituted a commercial threat to his own therapeutic practice as it pitched for a share of his clientele.

Evidence suggests that, like Lee, many medically qualified hydropathic practitioners rejected outright or aspired to reject the mill of general practice. Many – Gully, Wilson and Macleod are examples – had the financial means and backing necessary to develop or buy out hydropathic institutions, which were capital intensive ventures as they required the lease or purchase of large buildings and the installation of an array of baths and douches. Gully appeared to 'specialise' in treating nervous diseases, and worked from a West End address in Sackville Street, Picadilly.[76] Wilson had served as a personal physician travelling around the continent with an aristocratic patron, until he defected to investigate the water cure before returning in 1842 to a temporary address a few doors down from Gully.[77] If we take him at his word, he was 'fortunate ... to have a sufficient income to travel on the continent with my family as long as I please, when health or information are the plea; and enough, when I return to live in *dear*, dear England in comfort without practising my profession, if I could endure idleness'.[78]

Johnson had been a general practitioner in the poverty-stricken London district of Southwark. He had built up a successful practice through twenty years of hard work. The 20,000 prescriptions he claimed to write a year, combined with the success of his populist medical writing, had eventually provided him with enough resources to establish a more up-market practice in New Burlington Street, a West End location just around the corner from Gully. His old clientele south of the Thames was separated from his new West End patients by a deep social chasm. No longer did he need to dash off prescription after prescription. Now he could accompany three of his patients to Gräfenberg.[79]

Nevertheless, with the exception of Herbert Mayo, none of the medically qualified practitioners had attained a hospital staff position beyond that of house physician or surgeon, and they were not favourably placed to develop a career among the élite.[80] Their therapeutic rationale was, however, geared towards their social aspirations and hydropathy provided them with a vehicle to move up on. The medically qualified hydropathists, therefore, bore marked similarities to those like Forbes and Erasmus Wilson that supported, rather than practised hydropathy, and spa practitioners like Lee, excluded from the élite but aspirant to their status. The hydropathists were engaged in a practice that was only marginally removed from what was then considered orthodox. Adherence to hygienic medicine marked them as men who rejected the modalities of the general practitioner in favour of a therapeutic relationship that promised autonomy while permitting access to a middle-class, and therefore potentially wealthy, clientele. The water cure, practised within a hydropathic institution, allowed practitioners to maintain status while increasing income.[81]

The importance of the therapeutic gap, then, lies here – while there was a degree of unanimity about pathology and physiology, there were a multitude of ways of practising medicine. These tended to be aligned with the social forces that structured the profession. In other words, the therapy employed to effect a cure was a function of the social position of the practitioner in combination with that of the patient. In short, medical method was the product of social forces. And, in consequence, so was the making of a medical living.

To be 'a charlatan'?: hydropathy and the construction of orthodoxy

Just as orthodox practice was fragmented, so too was hydropathy. There were few attempts to unite hydropathists as a group – there was, for example, no society of hydropathy. Efforts to establish and maintain a publication, *The Water Cure Journal*, foundered after two years (1847–9), amid dissension and disorganisation. During its time, the journal had seen a bevy of editors (among them Gully, MacLeod, and G. Garrett), arguments over connections with unqualified hydropathic practitioners, and a dispute about the column inches dedicated to homoeopathy.[82]

While the field remained institutionally and intellectually disjointed, lacking a coherent mouthpiece and divided by adherence of individual hydropathists to varying degrees of therapeutic orthodoxy, there existed a pressing need for them to differentiate themselves from other medical practitioners, thus rhetorically orientating themselves towards their specific market niche. Thus all would have described themselves as hydropathists and their practice as hydropathy. However orthodox their styles of thought, however undifferentiated their practice was from that of other medical men, the adoption of the label 'hydropath' implied either scepticism towards or rejection of what was considered the mainstream. As Gully commented in a letter to the early twentieth-century historian of hydropathy, Richard Metcalfe: 'I began to think it was necessary to be a charlatan in order to deal successfully with disease which the higher places of our calling could not deal with'.[83]

Yet, as has been illustrated here, hydropathy as practised by medically qualified practitioners (and the unqualified practitioners who bowed to the authority of orthodox medicine's models of disease and the body), was orthodox in theory and, taking into consideration the variation in practice and its proximity to spa treatment and hygienic medicine, almost orthodox in practice. However, the reactions of the campaigning medical press and Gully's ironic self-description of 'charlatan' illustrate that even if practised by the medically qualified, most of whom had not rejected orthodox models of disease and the body, the water cure was not considered orthodox at the level of representation. In this respect, representation is everything. It is not so much that medicalised hydropathy was the embodiment of a counter-hegemonic blow aimed at orthodoxy, as that it was perceived, by supporters and detractors alike, to be so. And it is this turn that directs us to two inter-related facts about orthodoxy: firstly that it was an ideal founded more upon specific modes of behaviour, or action, and rather less upon an approved set of theoretical beliefs; and secondly, it was an ideological construction.

The case of hydropathy shows that rather than heterodoxy being defined by the authority of orthodox medicine, orthodox medicine also defined itself in relation to heterodox practices. In this sense, orthodoxy was constructed as a shadow of heterodoxy.[84] The implications of this argument are vital for the way we view orthodoxy and its historiography. If we take the view of most medical historians, recently restated by De Blécourt and Usborne, that 'alternative medicine' is defined 'in opposition to academic medicine and is thus dependant on the particular temporal and spatial occurrence of the latter', we uncritically accept and reify orthodox medicine's rhetorical claim to authority.[85] Orthodoxy is presented as a given against which all other systems are judged. Yet, during an era of reform, that spanned the first sixty years of the nineteenth century, it was far from obvious that what would emerge as 'orthodoxy' was on the verge of a decisive victory. Nor was it apparent that orthodox medicine had absolute medical authority over anyone or anything. Despite the strides that had been made in theory, many medical practitioners were still at the mercy of their patients, who often did not accept the complete authority of orthodox medicine.[86] Still lacking a state-guarded monopoly to ward off unorthodox competitors this remained the case until the passage of the Medical Act in 1858. Even then, with its limited powers, this legislation was merely the first way-station on the road to the authority that many historians anachronistically assume it possessed.

We need a deeper conception of what orthodoxy actually was. Rather than being a monolithic object, it should be treated as a dynamic process continually in the process of becoming. Rather than being simply a collection of social relations and institutions, orthodoxy was also an evolving ideology. It was a struggle for power, not a signifier of power obtained. In this respect, an analysis of the etymology of medical 'orthodoxy' is enlightening. During the 1840s and 1850s, 'orthodoxy' does not appear to have been a common description. A more likely designation was 'legitimate' or 'scientific' medicine.[87] To be 'legitimate' was to be underwritten by law, the true inheritor of the fruits of a formally defined social institution. Marriage, of course, was the prime example of a legitimate institution. The reformist press, however, was primarily concerned with legitimacy as a symbol for scientific knowledge soundly propagated. By demonstrating a witty connection between the two types of legitimacy, a characteristically intemperate *Lancet* leader of 1846 indicates what was at stake. Here hydropathy, mesmerism and homoeopathy were described, in Milton's words, as the '"Brood and folly without father bred"'.[88]

Notably the issue of legitimacy was linked to the idea of 'orthodoxy'. 'We have been charged with orthodoxy', commented the leader writer. 'We accept the accusation; it is consistent with the soundest professional politics'. Significantly, 'orthodoxy' was initially a critical designation used by opponents of the medical profession to denigrate the practice and practitioners of 'legitimate medicine'. It is here we must remind ourselves that 'orthodox' was, essentially, a religious term with, in this historical setting, a cogent set of contemporary associations deriving from the disputes between the Oxford Movement and the evangelicals over what constituted correct (legitimate) doctrine. While 'orthodoxy' might represent 'straight or correct teaching', it also served as an evangelical critique of the 'catholic' doxology of the Tractarians. Clearly, Wakley and his followers revelled in the tensions of the word. It is as if they were saying 'we are exactly as you heretics describe us'.[89] 'Legitimate' and 'orthodox' were, therefore, rhetorical constructs signifying the correctness of emergent 'scientific medicine', rarely used outside of discussions of heterodoxy. They served as signposts to natural authority set against dissent. Yet their use was, if anything, representative of a complete lack of confidence. As concrete as these terms might appear, resounding with the assumption of power and its trappings, they were in reality symptoms of how much boundary-making needed to be done.

One of the problems here is the relationship between the construction of orthodoxy and the process of professionalisation. The latter has generally been conceived in terms of a set of political and legalistic landmarks that constitute the making of the medical profession – the Apothecaries Act (1815), Hander *v.* Henson (1830) and the battle for the Medical Act (1858). We should, however, pay attention also to the *ideological* making of the profession. In this respect, it would pay historians to examine professionalisation as akin to nation-building. Benedict Anderson's *Imagined*

Communities thesis is particularly instructive. This puts forward the idea that a nation is an imagined community, forged through the distribution and acceptance of particular ideas and myths:

> It is *imagined* because the members of even the smallest nation will never know most of their fellow-members, meet them, or even hear of them, yet in the mind of each lives the image of their communion.[90]

Just as the nation is an imagined community so is a profession, and it required the construction of a commonly held identity to bind it together. That identity was built under the banner of 'orthodoxy'. The emergent medical profession's most cogent imaginings occurred in the medical press, the site, above all others, where practitioners, mostly unknown to one another, scattered the length and breadth of the British Isles, could unite as a virtual community.[91] Both before and after the Medical Act of 1858, community imagining was, it could be argued, an important function of the medical press, and bore the hallmark of Massimo d'Azeglio's celebrated comment on the Risorgimento – 'we have made Italy, now we have to make Italians',[92] which could be translated into 'we have made the medical profession, now we have to make medical practitioners'.

The rhetoric of the medical press was a principal component of the mould that was shaping the medical profession. Part of that rhetoric was defining acceptable behaviour and practice. Often this was best expressed in prescribing what practitioners should and should not do – in particular, imposing their version of how the therapeutic gap was to be bridged. Hydropathy, as portrayed by the medical press was a rhetorical construct that bore little relationship to the actual theories and practices connected with it. Ironically, its peasant origins and the threat it posed to general practitioners ensured its placement on the margins or outside the boundaries of legitimate medicine and acted as a fable of deviation against which the mainstream could be defined. Although legitimate medicine affected the course and development of hydropathy, it could not block it. It could not proscribe it. Aside from suasion, which appears not to have carried much weight with the water cure's clientele, its weapons were few and its options fewer. In these terms Gully may have been a charlatan, albeit a medically educated charlatan, but it did not prevent him from being successful and respected outside the realms of professionalising medicine. At the same time, hydropathy, as practised by medically qualified practitioners could barely be described as heterodox – paramedical might be a better, if somewhat anachronistic description. Yet, it was in the social, and therefore pecuniary, interests of hydropathists to differentiate themselves from other forms of cure. It was, then, almost by mutual agreement that hydropathy found itself placed beyond the borders of orthodoxy.

Acknowledgement

I would like to thank the Wellcome Trust for the generous support of this research. I am also grateful to Marguerite Dupree and Malcolm Nicholson for their help and advice.

Notes

1 The most monumental usage of this quote was D. Lowenthal, *The Past is a Foreign Country*, Cambridge, Cambridge University Press, 1985.

2 W.F. Bynum and R. Porter (eds), *Medical Fringe and Medical Orthodoxy 1750–1850*, London, Croom Helm, 1987; R. Cooter (ed.), *Studies in the History of Alternative Medicine*, Basingstoke, Macmillan, 1988. More recently there has been W. de Blécourt and C. Usborne (eds), 'Alternative medicine in Europe since 1800', *Medical History*, 1999, 43. There are very few monographs on single heterodox practices within the British context, one example being P.A. Nicholls, *Homœopathy and the Medical Profession*, London, Croom Helm, 1988. The historiography of British hydropathy is particularly thin.

3 M. Ramsey, 'Alternative medicine in modern France', *Medical History*, 1999, 43, p. 287. A similar point was made by R. Porter, 'Quacks: an unconscionable time dying', in S. Budd and U. Sharma (eds), *The Healing Bond. The Patient-Practitioner Relationship and Therapeutic Responsibility*, London, Routledge, 1994, pp. 63–4.

4 W.F. Bynum and R. Porter, 'Introduction', in Bynum and Porter (eds), *Medical Fringe*, p. 1 and esp. p. 3; R. Cooter, 'Introduction: the alternations of past and present', in R. Cooter (ed.), *Studies*, p. xii-xiii. Also see P.S. Brown, 'Social Context and medical theory in the demarcation of nineteenth-century boundaries', in Bynum and Porter (eds), *Medical Fringe*, particularly his description of hydropathy, pp. 224–7.

5 See, in particular, Cooter, 'Alternative medicine, alternative cosmology', in Cooter (ed.), *Studies*, pp. 63–78.

6 Cooter, 'Introduction', p. xi; also Cooter, 'Alternative medicine, alternative cosmology', p. 73.

7 Charles Leslie and Allan Young, 'Introduction', in C. Leslie and A. Young (eds), *Paths to Asian Medical Knowledge*, Berkeley, University of California Press, 1992, pp. 4–6.

8 T.S. Kuhn, *The Structure of Scientific Revolutions*, 2nd edn, Chicago, University of Chicago Press, 1970 (1st edn 1962).

9 Summarised by David Harley from his article, 'Rhetoric and the social construction of sickness and medicine', in *Social History of Medicine*, 1999, 12, 3, pp. 407–35. Harley's definition is drawn from Barry Barnes and David Bloor, particularly B. Barnes and D. Bloor, 'Relativism, rationalism and the sociology of knowledge', in M. Hollis and S. Lukes (eds), *Rationality and Relativism*, Oxford, Blackwell, 1982, pp. 21–47.

10 This story is replicated many times. The best distillation of it is in T.D. Luke and Norman Hay Forbes, *Natural Therapy. A Manual of Physiotherapeutics and Climatology*, Bristol, John Wright, 1913, pp. 1–9.

11 Friedhelm Kircheld and Wade Boyle, *Nature Doctors. Pioneers in Naturopathic Medicine*, Portland, Oregon, Medicina Biologica, 1994, p. 13.

12 R.T. Claridge, *Hydropathy; or, The Cold Water Cure, as Practised by Vincent Priessnietz, at Graefenberg, Silesia, Austria*, London, James Madden, 1842, pp. 11–17.

13 This synthesis was derived from Charles Scudamore, *A Medical Visit to Gräfenberg, in April and May 1843; For the Purpose of Investigating the Merits of the Water-Cure Treatment*, London, John Churchill, 1843, pp. 7–26. This configuration of humanism should not be confused with the emergent neo-humoralism that located many diseases in the changes that occurred in the chemical properties of the fluids.

14 Ibid., p. 5. Also see, James Wilson, *A Practical Treatise on the Cure of Diseases by Water, Air, Exercise, and Diet*, 3rd edn, London, John Churchill, 1842, p. 42 (1st edn 1842).

15 Scudamore, *A Medical Visit*, p. 27.

16 Virginia Smith, 'Cleanliness: the development of idea and practice in Britain, 1770–1850', Unpublished PhD thesis, University of London, 1985, esp. p. 101.

17 See R.T. Claridge, *Hydropathy; or, the Cold Water Cure, as Practised by Vincent Priessnitz, at Græfenberg, Silesia, Austria*, London, James Madden and Co., 1842.

18 See Susan E. Cayleff, *Wash and Be Healed. The Water Cure Movement and Women's Health*, Philadelphia, Temple University Press, 1987; Ronald L. Numbers, *Prophetess of Health: Ellen G. White and the Origins of Seventh-day Adventist Health Reform*, revised edn, Knoxville, University of Tennessee Press, 1992 (1st edn 1976).

19 Cooter, 'Alternative medicine, alternative cosmology', pp. 66–8.

20 Kelvin Rees, 'Water as a commodity: hydropathy in Matlock', in Cooter, *Studies*, p. 34.

21 I am grateful to Marguerite Dupree for tracing these connections.

22 Logie Barrow, 'Why were most medical heretics at their most confident around the 1840s? (The other side of mid-Victorian medicine)', in Roger French and Andrew Wear (eds), *British Medicine in an Age of Reform*, London, Routledge, 1991.

23 Porter, 'Quacks', p. 77.

24 Janet Browne, 'Spas and sensibilities: Darwin at Malvern', in Roy Porter (ed.), *The Medical History of Waters and Spas, Medical History*, Supplement No. 10, London, Wellcome Institute, 1990, fn. 4, p. 102, lists 26 hydropathic institutions 'in existence before 1850'. The list is not entirely accurate. For example, it includes Cluny Hill, founded in the mid-1860s, while excluding Sir Arthur Clarke's Dublin establishment.

25 The term 'medical profession' is here used somewhat loosely. The idea that the medical profession existed in the 1840s might disappoint sociological purists as many of the preconditions that indicate the formation of a profession – particularly legal protection by the state – were some way off. Nevertheless, qualified practitioners consistently referred to themselves as belonging to a profession. These conceptions were based around a number of factors: the classical heritage of medical practice; qualification with a recognised medical qualification; adherence to a broad, but well-defined corpus of knowledge and practices; and, finally, a belief in a set of ethics, albeit emergent ones, about the behaviour expected of a medical practitioner. In the final analysis, the fact that the term 'medical profession' was uncontested and universally used requires us to pay attention to this mode of institutional self-representation.

26 Gully made this explicit in most of his works, but perhaps most tellingly with Wilson in James Wilson and James M. Gully, *The Dangers of the Water Cure*, London, Cunningham and Mortimer, 1843, p. viii: it was an 'egregious error … to carry on a system of drug medication simultaneously with the treatment by water'. Thus they are not against drug medication *per se*, but against its use simultaneously with hydropathy.

27 Edward Johnson, *Hydropathy. The Theory, Principles and Practice of the Water Cure Shewn to be in Accordance with Medical Science and the Teachings of Common Sense*, London, Simpkin, Marshall & Co., 1843, p. xiv; Thomas J. Graham, *A Few Pages on Hydropathy or the Cold Water System*, London, W.E. Painter, 1843, p. 4.

28 See, for example, William MacLeod, *A Theory of the Treatment of Disease Adopted at Ben Rhydding*, London, John Churchill, 1868.

29 John Smedley, *Practical Hydropathy*, London, John Kendrick, 1858. See in particular the short bibliography ('valuable works of reference quoted in this work') at the end of the book (p. 520). Another example of a non-qualified practitioner accepting the theoretical claims of orthodox medicine while decrying its therapeutic excesses can be seen in Joseph Constantine, *A Handy Book on Hydropathy, Practical and Domestic*, London, Whittaker and Co., 1860.

30 Archibald Billing, *First Principles of Medicine*, London, Thomas and George Underwood, 1831, p. 44, shows he had reduced the effects of the *materia medica* into four classes: stimulant, sedative, narcotic and tonic.

31 See Wilson, *A Practical Treatise*, pp. 34–73; Johnson, *Hydropathy*, pp. vi–vii.

32 Richard Metcalfe, *The Rise and Progress of Hydropathy in England and Scotland*, London, Simpkin, Marshall, Hamilton, Kent and Co., 1906, pp. 58–9, quoting a personal letter from Gully.

33 Herbert Mayo, *The Cold Water Cure, its Use and Misuse Examined*, London, Henry Renshaw, 1845, pp. iii–v.

34 Smedley, *Practical Hydropathy*, p. xii. Notably, both Mayo and Smedley became convinced from their own experiences as patients that the cold water system required modification to make it less spartan.

35 Thomas J. Graham, *Modern Domestic Medicine*, 7th edn, London, Simpkin and Marshall, 1837 (1st edn 1826).

36 James M. Gully, *An Exposition of the Symptoms, Essential Nature and Treatment of Neuropathy, or Nervousness*, London, John Churchill, 1837, and *The Simple Treatment of Disease Deduced from the Methods of Expectancy and Revulsion*, London, John Churchill, 1842.

37 Edward Johnson, *Letters to Brother John. Life, Health, and Disease*, London, Saunders and Otley, 1837.

38 Compare: Gully, *Simple Treatment*, p. 25, with *The Water Cure in Chronic Disease*, London, John Churchill, 1846, p. 11; Johnson, with *Hydropathy*, p. 217; T.J. Graham, *Modern Domestic Medicine*, p. x, esp, note 2, and Thomas J. Graham, *A Few Pages on Hydropathy or the Cold Water System*, London, W.E. Painter, 1843, p. 11.

39 Gully, *Simple Treatment*, p. 116 and *Exposition*, p. 29; Johnson, *Letters*, Letters VIII and IX, pp. 214–84; Graham, *Domestic Medicine*, p. 97, pp. 138–86. Also see Thomas J. Graham, *Sure Methods of Improving Health, and Prolonging Life; or a Treatise on the Art of Living Long and Comfortably by Regulating the Diet and Regimen*, London, Simpkin and Marshall, 1828.

40 Johnson, *Hydropathy*, p. v.

41 See Browne, 'Spas and sensibilities', pp. 104–5.

42 'Life at the cold brandy-and-water cure (*From the MS. of a late Patient.*)', *Punch*, 1846, 11, pp. 243–4; 'The water cure', *Blackwood's Magazine*, 1846, LX, pp. 376–88.

43 'Moist man', *Three Weeks in the Wet Sheets, Being the Diary and Doings of a Moist Visitor to Malvern*, 3rd edn, London, Hamilton, Adams and Co., 1856 (1st edn 1851).

44 Edward Bulwyer Lytton, *Confessions of a Water Cure Patient*, London, Henry Colborne, 1845; R.J. Lane, *Life at the Water Cure*, London, Longman, 1846; J.S. Blackie, *The Water Cure in Scotland: Five Letters from Dunoon*, Aberdeen, George Davidson, 1849; Charles Reade, *It's Never Too Late to Mend, A Matter-of-Fact Romance*, 3rd edn, London, Walter Scott Ltd, no date (1st edn 1856), pp. 171–98.

45 *Lancet*, 1842–3, 1, p. 687; *PMSJ*, 1843–4, 7, pp. 52–4.

46 *Lancet*, 1841–2, 2, pp. 429–30, 489–91; *Lancet*, 1843–4, 1, p. 610; *PMJ*, 1843, 6, pp. 393–5.

47 The Worcester practitioner Charles Hastings, founder of the Provincial Medical and Surgical Association (later the BMA), was geographically well placed to observe the workings of the water cure in Malvern. He wrote a series of letters to the *PMJ* about the dangers of hydropathy. See, *PMJ*, 1842–3, 5, pp. 73, 149 and 328, and *PMJ*, 1843, 6, pp. 345–7. For another of the numerous examples see *Lancet*, 1843–4, 1, p. 610 for account of Sir Francis Burdett's death following hydropathic treatment. Also see *Lancet*, 1842–3, 1, pp. 241–4 and *Lancet*, 1849, 1, p. 62.

48 Most celebrated was the Ellis case with the coronary reported in *Lancet*, 1846, 1, pp. 666–7. Ellis was sent to trial but, to *The Lancet*'s disgust, was acquitted, p. 711. Also see reports in *Lancet*, 1847, 1, p. 157; *Lancet*, 1849, 2, pp. 243–4. Juries appeared unwilling to convict hydropathists.

49 *Lancet*, 1843–4, 1, 612.

50 *Lancet*, 1846, 2, p. 537.

51 Scudamore, *Medical Visit*.

52 Erasmus Wilson, *A Practical Treatise on Healthy Skin: with Rules for the Medical and Domestic Treatment of Cutaneous Diseases*, London, John Churchill, 1845.

53 Ibid., Ch. 10, pp. 185–210.

54 Andrew Combe, *The Principles of Physiology Applied to the Preservation of Health*, 15th edn, Edinburgh, Maclachlan and Stewart, 1860, pp. 69, 203, 261–3. This edition was revised and updated after Combe's death. Originally published in 1838, it is likely the comments on hydropathy crept in during the late 1840s. The comments of the editor of the 15th edition, James Coxe M.D., implies that the sections on hydropathy had been untouched by him. I have not, as yet, seen an earlier edition.

55 *British and Foreign Medical Review*, 1846, 21, p. 254.

56 *British and Foreign Medical Review*, 1846, 18, p. 437.

57 Edwin Lee, *Hydropathy and Homœopathy Impartially Appreciated*, London, John Churchill, 1847, pp. 38–40.

58 Ibid., pp. 48.

59 Ibid., pp. 50–1.

60 Ibid., p. 53.

61 For America see John Harley Warner, *The Therapeutic Perspective: Medical Practice, Knowledge, and Identity 1820–1885*, Cambridge, MA., Harvard University Press, 1986, p. 6.

62 Margaret Pelling, *Cholera, Fever and English Medicine, 1825–1865*, Oxford, Oxford University Press, 1978, pp. 16 and 145.

63 Christopher Hamlin, 'Predisposing causes and public health in early nineteenth-century medical thought', in *Social History of Medicine*, 1992, 5, pp. 50–3. 'Zymotic' can roughly be translated as 'infectious'.

64 Charles Rosenberg, 'The therapeutic revolution: medicine, meaning, and social change in nineteenth-century America', in M.J. Vogel and C.E. Rosenberg (eds), *The Therapeutic Revolution: Essays in the Social History of Medicine*, Philadelphia, Philadelphia University Press, pp. 3–25, argues this case. However, his remarks appear to apply to American, not British, bodies.

65 See, for example, John Harley Warner, 'Therapeutic explanation and the Edinburgh bloodletting controversy: two perspectives on the medical meaning of science in the mid-nineteenth century', in *Medical History*, 1980, 24.

66 *Lancet*, 1844, 1, pp. 155–7, 278, 474–5.

67 Ibid., pp. 163–4.

68 As there has been no proper analysis of the readership or circulation of these publications, this remark has been formulated in terms of the preferred reader, in other words the idealised reader as conceived by the editors, revealed in editorial comments, correspondence etc.

69 See, in particular, Anne Digby, *Making a Medical Living. Doctors and Patients in the English Market for Medicine, 1720–1911*, Cambridge, Cambridge University Press, 1994, and Irvine Loudan, *Medical Care and the General Practitioner 1750–1850*, Oxford, Clarendon Press, 1986.

70 'Homœopathy, allopathy and "young physic"', *British and Foreign Medical Review*, 1846, 21, esp. pp. 253–4, which puts forward his thesis against active intervention and its relationship to the success of heterodox medicines.

71 Combe, *Principles of Physiology*, pp. 1–7; Erasmus Wilson, *Practical Treatise*, pp. 157–84.

72 N.D. Jewson, 'The disappearance of the sick-man from medical cosmology, 1770–1870', *Sociology*, 11976, 10; and John V. Pickstone, 'Ways of Knowing: towards a historical sociology of science, technology and medicine', *British Journal for the History of Science*, 1993, 22, pp. 435–6.

73 It should be noted some therapeutic sceptics were also sceptical about the water cure, although they used it as an illustration of the *vis medicatrix*. See Charles Mackin, 'The Principles and Practice of Medicine', in *Lancet*, 1844, 1, pp. 473–5.

74 Edwin Lee, *The St. George's Hospital Medical Staff*, London, John Churchill, 1859, p. 36.

75 Lee, *Hydropathy and Homœopathy*, pp. 21–2.

76 Gully gives his address as 37 Sackville Street (located off Picadilly Circus) in *Exposition*.

77 Metcalfe, *The Rise and Progress of Hydropathy*, pp. 59–61. Wilson's *Practical Treatise on the Cure of Diseases*, p. xxi, gives his address as 18 Sackville Street.

78 *Lancet*, 1841–2, 2, p. 453.

79 Johnson, *Hydropathy*, pp. xiii–iv. Despite the geographical proximity of Gully and Wilson to Johnson, there is no evidence that they were personally acquainted.

80 Mayo had been elected to the surgeon's position at the Middlesex in 1827. He held this post until 1842. He also held the first chair of Physiology at King's College during the 1830s. He retired from his surgeoncy due to ill health, and was advised by medical friends to try hydropathy.

81 James Bradley, Marguerite Dupree and Alastair Durie, 'Opportunity on the edge of orthodoxy: medically qualified hydropathists in the era of reform, 1840–60', forthcoming, explores the social and financial opportunities provided by the hydropathic institution.

82 *The Water Cure Journal*, 1848, 18, p. 2.

83 Metcalfe, *The Rise and Progress of Hydropathy*, p. 75. Significantly, I believe we should understand 'higher places of our calling' to refer to élite physicians and the conditions that they treated among their élite clientele.

84 Robin Price, 'Hydropathy in England, 1840–1870', in *Medical History*, 1981, 25, p. 280, describes 'medical heresies' as 'the shadow of orthodoxy'. I suggest this is putting the cart before the horse.

85 Willem De Blécourt and Cornelie Usborne, 'Preface: situating "alternative medicine" in the modern period', in *Medical History*, 1999, 43, p. 284.

86 That men of a scientific or intellectual character, like Darwin and Blackie, were prepared to resort to hydropathy indicates this.

87 For example, *Lancet*, 1846, 2, pp. 567–8 which uses the term 'legitimate medicine' three times.

88 Ibid., p. 568. Quote from Milton's *Il Penseroso*, line 2.

89 *Lancet*, 1846, 2, pp. 567–8.

90 Benedict Anderson, *Imagined Communities*, revised edition, London, Verso, 1991, p. 6 (1st edn 1983).

91 A point that seems to have been largely missed by the contributors to W.F. Bynum, Stephen Lock and Roy Porter, *Medical Journals and Medical Knowledge*, London, Routledge, 1992.

92 Quoted in E.J. Hobsbawm, *Nations and Nationalism since 1870*, Cambridge, Cambridge University Press, 1991, p. 44.

3 In search of rational remedies

Homoeopathy in nineteenth-century Bengal

David Arnold and Sumit Sarkar

Despite extensive discussion in recent years of many aspects of the medical history of modern India, including both indigenous and orthodox Western medicine, there has been surprisingly little discussion of homoeopathy in colonial India. The principal exceptions are two articles published in the early 1980s by Surinder M. Bhardwaj. Following ideas of medical 'pluralism' advanced by Charles Leslie and his associates,[1] Bhardwaj described the rise of homoeopathy in India beginning with its introduction as a 'Western medical system' in the early nineteenth century, through its adoption by the 'modern, newly emergent and Western-influenced Indian élite', especially in Bengal, its subsequent 'naturalisation' and harmonisation with Hinduism and the Ayurvedic system of medicine, its dispersal throughout India (to the extent that by 1961 there were at least 27,000 practising homoeopaths in the country), and its formal recognition as a medical system by the Government of India after Independence in 1947.[2] Reiterating his main theme, Bhardwaj concluded that:

> By the end of the nineteenth century homoeopathy seems to have been naturalised in India … Through the latter half of the nineteenth century, Bengal served as the domicile of homoeopathy … Bengali physicians espoused homoeopathy with remarkable, even religious[,] zeal soon after its introduction by a few European laymen, physicians and missionaries. The almost religious attachment to Hahnemannian law ['like cures like'] by the homoeopaths, and the repudiation of the same 'law' by the Indian allopaths[,] resulted in the recognition of the 'new art of healing'. Homoeopathy was gradually but surely Indianised.[3]

There are many points of Bhardwaj's discussion that can happily be accepted, not least the importance of Bengal in the establishment and dissemination of homoeopathy in nineteenth-century India. However, we need to look more critically (in the light of the historical and cultural evidence) at his claim that homoeopathy, while originating as a 'Western medical system', came to be 'naturalised' in India and more especially his observation that 'Bengali physicians made serious efforts to harmonise the fundamental principles of homoeopathy with those of Hinduism, thus creating broad cultural receptivity for this medicine of European origins'.[4] It is certainly possible that the widespread adoption of homoeopathy in India was ultimately (in the twentieth century) facilitated through an accommodation with Hinduism and with Ayurveda (the two are not necessarily identical), but this need not account for its initial appeal, especially to the Bengali middle classes, nor should the apparent recognition of homoeopathy as a medical 'system' alongside Ayurveda or the Unani (i.e., 'Ionian' or Greek) medicine identified with Muslim physicians be accepted without qualification.

Beyond these issues of immediate South Asian regional and historical significance, questions need to be raised about what has become the standard frame of reference in discussing heterodox medical traditions and 'alternative' sciences in general. Serious and sympathetic consideration of such 'alternatives', for long suppressed or despised, has clearly demanded a certain distancing from the more extreme claims of modern, Western, scientific rationality to exclusive ownership of the entire domain of worthwhile knowledge. Yet one must also recognise the problems posed by the emergence in recent scholarship of certain counter-orthodoxies. These posit a series of polarities, in which the apparently opposing elements are implicitly assumed to be homologous and inseparable – hence, Western and indigenous, modern and traditional, universal and local, dominant and popular, elite and subaltern. An important theme of this volume as a whole is to question such excessively homogenised polarities, which, in the case of medical history as elsewhere, tend to reproduce in inverted form some of the most problematic features of 'Orientalist' thinking.

The rise of homoeopathy in Bengal

At first sight, homoeopathy, despite its self-evidently Western origins, might appear to fit the currently dominant framework of historical analysis rather well. Here, it would seem, was an instance of the appropriation by the colonised of a heterodox strand within dominant discursive practices – a move presumably motivated by the impulses of an emergent cultural nationalism. It is possible to suggest that part of the appeal of homoeopathy was precisely that, apart from a few stray Englishmen (notably some missionaries on the lookout for ways of dispensing cheap medicines in remote places[5]), the early practitioners in India of the theories of Samuel Hahnemann of Saxony (1755–1843) were Europeans from countries other than Britain and having no direct connection with colonial governance. They included Dr J.M. Honigberger from Transylvania (who, although not a committed homoeopath, treated Ranjit Singh, the ruler of Punjab, with homoeopathic remedies shortly before the latter's death in 1839), C. Fabre Tonnerre from France (founder of the first, short-lived, Native Homoeopathic Hospital in Calcutta in 1852), and Dr Leopold Salzer from Vienna, resident in Calcutta for much of the late nineteenth century. Early Indian patrons of homoeopathy included the Rajas of Tanjore and Pudukottai, who established hospitals for homoeopathy in south India, though apparently under the direction of a retired Madras surgeon, Dr Samuel Brooking.[6]

In fact, while homoeopathy was intensely criticised by many orthodox Western practitioners,[7] it seems to have enjoyed a certain vogue among other sections of the European community, including the army and judiciary, in the mid-nineteenth century. Writing in 1852, F.C. Skipwith claimed that, while in certain respects homoeopathy remained 'comparatively unknown' in India, 'the system' had been 'extensively practised by amateurs, in the civil and military services, and by other gentlemen' and 'the success that has attended their practice, both upon Europeans and natives' had been such as to 'astonish themselves and all who have witnessed it'. There was, he added, 'scarcely a large district in India, in which such an amateur has not for years been diffusing benefits around him'.[8] The ability of homoeopathy to transcend India's seemingly entrenched ethnic and cultural boundaries was further underscored by the case of the Parsi social reformer Behramji M. Malabari. First introduced to homoeopathy by the wife of a British military officer, in 1878 Malabari was saved from death by a Hindu homoeopath, Dr Thakurdas. He subsequently took lessons in homoeopathy and sought to popularise it in Bombay.[9]

It is clear, nonetheless, that homoeopathy established itself most quickly in Bengal, especially in Calcutta, and from there spread outwards across India, particularly along the Ganges valley and through Bengalis resident in other provinces. Among the earliest Indian practitioners of homoeopathy was Rajendra Datta (1818–89), who studied for some years at the Calcutta Medical College without completing a degree, set up a charitable dispensary for allopathic medicine, and later (by the 1860s) became a celebrated homoeopath, who treated and 'converted' some of the leading figures of the period including Iswarchandra Vidyasagar and Radhakanta Deb.[10] It is unclear where Datta gained his presumably self-taught knowledge of homoeopathy, but he seems to have become dissatisfied with the effectiveness of allopathic treatments. He in turn encouraged others to take up homoeopathy: his 'disciples' included a British judge, J.H.B. Ironside in Varanasi, and Mahendralal Sircar (1833–1904), who qualified as a doctor at the Calcutta Medical College in 1863, but who four years later announced his conversion to homoeopathy.

Although this chapter focuses on Mahendralal and on Bengal, it should be noted in passing that other Bengalis also played a major part in the spread of homoeopathy elsewhere in India: for instance, Lokenath Maitra, with Ironside's support, set up the first homoeopathic hospital at Varanasi in 1867, and in 1899 C.C. Ghosh and S.B. Mukherjee started the *Indian Homoeopathician* in Lucknow.[11] In 1852 there were only three homoeopathic hospitals in the country, one in Calcutta ('just opened') and two in south India.[12] By the time of Mahendralal's death in 1904 Calcutta alone had four schools of homoeopathic medicine, with about two dozen regular practitioners in the city and its suburbs. It appears by that date also to have penetrated into at least some parts of rural Bengal.[13] In addition to an extensive English-language literature on homoeopathy, there were numerous tracts, manuals and journals produced in Bengali. This was far from accidental: Mahendralal was among those members of the Bengali intelligentsia who believed in promoting Western scientific knowledge through translation and original writing in the vernacular, thereby enriching Bengali language and literature in the process.[14]

The wide dissemination of homoeopathy was undoubtedly aided by the ability of individuals to instruct themselves in homoeopathy through English and vernacular manuals, and subsequently through correspondence courses, without needing to acquire formal training. As well as being directly influenced by Rajendra Datta, Mahendralal Sircar's conversion to homoeopathy was reputedly stimulated by reading Samuel Morgan's *Philosophy of Homoeopathy*: he himself paid tribute to Hahnemann's *Organon* (first published in 1810), in which he 'found a master mind dealing with his subject in the most thorough and scientific manner'. It revealed Hahnemann, compared to other medical authorities, as 'a giant among pigmies'.[15]

The progress of homoeopathy in colonial India and its acceptance as an almost indigenous form of medicine close to the people was also bound up with its cheapness in terms of both fees and the cost of medicines. From the point of view of the would-be practitioners, too, entry into homoeopathy was relatively easy and inexpensive. Students of official or 'allopathic' medicine who had failed to complete their courses or obtain degrees often turned to homoeopathy as an occupation (as in the case of Rajendra Datta). One of the major attractions of homoeopathy has always been its 'do-it-yourself' appeal, the easy entrance through Hahnemann's *Organon* and *Materia Medica Pura*, in sharp contrast to the increasingly formidable and esoteric corpus of official modern medicine. In this respect, as in the actual language of its dissemination, homoeopathy was particularly open to processes of vernacularisation. It became indigenised largely through a world of autodidacts, practitioners who had little or no formal training, and self-medication for common maladies like colds or mild stomach complaints, homoeopathic remedies for which have become very widely known in middle- and lower middle-class Indian households.

The barriers between fully trained doctor and 'quack', specialised practitioner and lay patient, becoming increasingly formidable with the development of allopathic medical science, were made more permeable through homoeopathy. Mahendralal himself came to be seen by many other Bengalis, in an age in which the 'improving' ideology of Samuel Smiles was as potent as the healing principles of Samuel Hahnemann, as 'an ideal to us of self-help'.[16] Cheapness apart, this idea of self-help (rather than accommodation with Hinduism and Ayurveda as Bhardwaj argues) helps to explain homoeopathy's rapid and successful adoption. One also needs to remember that official Western medicine spread only slowly in India, due in part to the smallness of the medical service, its remoteness from the mass of the population, and the inadequacy of state investment in public health.[17]

The appeal of homoeopathy in nineteenth-century Bengal was thus in part that it by-passed the colonial medical establishment, dominated by the (then almost entirely British) Indian Medical Service (IMS), and the political, racial and cultural authority it represented. Perhaps it helped that Hahnemann was German and not British; it was certainly important that members of the British civil and military establishment in India could be followers of homoeopathy as well as Indians (in a way that was not possible with the more racially and culturally exclusive world of Ayurvedic and Unani medicine). Rather than necessarily defining them as Indian and Hindu, homoeopathy opened up a way for them to feel part of a modern, progressive international community through contacts with homoeopaths in Britain, the United States, France and Germany. As Bhardwaj himself put it: 'From the viewpoint of many Indians, homoeopathy was Western and modern without being colonial. That cognition was virtually the antithesis of allopathy which marched into India as a representative of the West with its scientific air as well as its colonial regalia.'[18]

Although homoeopathy was vehemently denounced as quackery by the colonial medical establishment, particularly through the semi-official, Calcutta-based *Indian Medical Gazette*, there is ample evidence to suggest an eclectic mixing of allopathic and homoeopathic practice in the city in the late nineteenth century. An editorial in the *Gazette* in 1882 noted that Calcutta possessed homoeopaths of all descriptions – 'qualified, unqualified and amateur. Some of the qualified members of the sect do a large business, and one of them [Mahendralal?] charges and receives Rs. 16 a visit'. The editor, Kenneth McLeod, IMS, confessed he knew little of 'this sphere of practice' but suspected that 'a good deal of quacking goes on'. Some, he believed, practised homoeopathy 'from conviction', its 'refinements and illusions' commending themselves to the 'imaginative and unpractical minds' of Bengalis, for the 'mystery of homoeopathy rather commends itself to the native mind, and the medicines ... are tasteless and cheaper'. Other Indians, he believed, practised it because it paid better than 'so-called orthodox medicine', and no doubt at a time when private medical practice in Calcutta was still largely confined to Europeans, practising homoeopathy often gave Indians access to higher fees and better status than if they had remained lowly subordinates in the provincial medical service. There were also said to be 'a few qualified men who profess both allopathy and homoeopathy, and practice [sic] either according to the whim of themselves or their patients'. McLeod thought these cases 'exceptional', however, and consoled himself with the thought that most Bengali practitioners preferred the 'realities and imperfections of rational medicine to the delusions and pretended finality of infinitesimals'.[19]

McLeod was hardly an impartial observer, nor particularly well-informed about homoeopathy, but S.C. Ghose, writing around 1910, also noted the existence of what Hahnemann himself would have termed 'mongrel homoeopaths'.[20] 'There are many eminent allopaths in the field at the present moment who secretly keep cholera boxes full of homoeopathic medicines, and use them at the time of emergency', but they did not have 'the courage to avow it openly'.[21] Even among self-declared homoeopaths, Ghose noted a tripartite division between those who had degrees from the Calcutta Medical College but had switched to homoeopathy, those who had acquired their knowledge of homoeopathy in the United States before returning to India and, lowliest of all, those whose only qualification were from homoeopathic institutions in India.[22]

While many practitioners of orthodox Western medicine in nineteenth-century India regarded homoeopathy as anathema and a kind of simple-minded superstition, there were conversely a number of apparent connections and similarities between homoeopathy and Ayurvedic medicine. It could even be suggested that a certain link, however tenuous, was implicit in the origins of homoeopathy itself.

Living at a time when the Orientalist 'discovery' of India had made its mark on the West, Hahnemann was credited with having 'sifted all medical theories' and was said to have regarded all earlier medical ideas as 'tributary' to his own, including 'the fragmentary medical lore of the older India'.[23] More immediately, one of homoeopathy's most significant contributions to the developing discourse of 'medical systems' in India was the introduction in the 1840s and 1850s of the term 'allopathy' to represent, largely negatively, orthodox Western medicine and thereby to contrast it with all other diagnostic ideas and therapeutic practices, whatever their source and character.[24] The term has remained powerfully entrenched in India's medical literature – and its medical history – to this day.

There were other respects, too, in which homoeopathy and Ayurveda might appear to share common ground: these included the need to individualise by studying the specific characteristics, temperamental as well as physical, of each patient. A common critical stance towards orthodox Western medicine also made homoeopathy and Ayurveda potential allies. For example, attempts were being made (though significantly not until the 1890s) to discover 'Vedantic' foundations for the homoeopathic doctrine of infinitesimal dosages, while the aversion to human dissection and the avoidance of animal products and alcohol-based remedies in Indian homoeopathy fitted well with high-caste Hindu dietary aversions and pollution taboos and invited a joint exploration of India's rich vegetable *materia medica*.[25]

But the links and parallels between homoeopathy and Ayurveda can be easily overstated. In some ways homoeopathy, despite its indisputable origin in the West, consorted rather better with high-caste Hindu orthodox or revivalist inclinations than Ayurveda, which has, in fact, had a somewhat heterodox reputation, with some ancient texts recommending consuming beef during illness and projecting a materialist view on life. In their basic methodology, too, allopathy and Ayurveda lie closer to each other than either does to homoeopathy, for neither would accept the homoeopathic doctrine of 'like cures like' nor share its belief in the efficacy of 'infinitesimal' doses. The extensive use in Ayurveda of complex, compound medicines, requiring a sophisticated knowledge of medicinal drugs and their interactions, was also far removed from the belief in simple, single medicines favoured by Hahnemann and his followers. In this divergence we can begin to see some of the difficulties in Bhardwaj's interpretation of the 'naturalising' of homoeopathy and its 'harmonisation' with Ayurveda, and, more generally, in the tendency to present needlessly sharp dichotomies between 'indigenous' and 'Western'.

For its nineteenth-century supporters, and despite the jibes of unbelievers like McLeod, homoeopathy appeared to be rational – and humane – in a way Western medicine was not. This is especially the case if one examines the views of Mahendralal Sircar, whose 'espousal of homoeopathy', Bhardwaj sees as 'perhaps the most significant landmark' in the propagation of homoeopathy in nineteenth-century Bengal.[26] Homoeopathy, in Mahendralal's words, had created 'the only system of medicine in the world which pretends to have a rational basis'. Although the 'law' of *similia similibus curantur* ('like cures like') was, in his view, 'imperfectly expressed' and could not be taken uncritically as 'the ultimate of therapeutical science', it was, nonetheless, 'the best guide-law yet discovered for the selection of remedies'. It offered a rationale for why certain medicines worked, while Western medicine, by contrast, not only seemed to lack any rationale beyond its own empiricism but particularly in the treatment of such widely prevalent diseases as cholera and malaria employed techniques that were both violent and ineffective.[27]

Before 'the immortal Hahnemann', chance, not science, was the 'discoverer of the most potent drugs' in daily use.[28] Homoeopathy, Mahendralal maintained, had 'proved itself infinitely more successful than the orthodox system'. It had 'banished for ever from the therapeutic quiver, blistering, leeching, bleeding, cauterising, etc.,' and thereby 'disarmed medicine of its horrid barbarities' which had previously been used in the 'name of the healing art'. Essentially, homoeopathy for Mahendralal was about finding effective, and therefore rational, remedies: it signalled the possibility of reforming medicine by using gentler, more sympathetic drugs, particularly when used in infinitesimal quantities, and especially those derived from India's own 'rich mine' of *materia medica*. Commending the publication of Kanny Lal De's *Indigenous Drugs of India*, Mahendralal remarked that Indians should take up the 'mantle of Hahnemann' and investigate the nature and properties of Indian drugs, which were potentially a 'very valuable treasure indeed'.[29]

Here, too, there might be a patriotic as well as pragmatic link with Ayurveda. Indeed, Mahendralal's *Calcutta Medical Journal*, founded in 1868, carried on its masthead a *sloka* (verse) from the *Caraka Samhita* (a treatise of classical Indian medicine):

> That alone is the right medicine which can remove disease;
> He alone is the true physician who can restore health

though it was chosen for its seemingly rationalist, secular connotations rather than as an expression of religious faith. 'The publication of ancient Sanskrit works on medicine ought to be looked upon by our community as a national undertaking', Mahendralal declared. It was a matter of great shame that that 'which constitutes the chief glory and greatness of our country' should be 'buried in oblivion'. 'It is our imperative duty', he added later that year, 'to utilise the truths contained in these ancient writings'.[30] In encouraging the location and (with the aid of Vidyasagar among others) the translation into English of neglected Sanskrit texts, Mahendralal can be considered something of a pioneer of the Ayurvedic revival, a movement more commonly associated with the 1890s than with the 1860s.

And yet Mahendralal's attitudes to Ayurveda were deeply ambivalent and even increasingly hostile the more he understood of its form and content. In deploring the ignorance of their own traditions among present-day *kavirajs* and *hakims* (practitioners of Ayurvedic and Unani medicine respectively), Mahendralal remarked that there could be no simple attempt to revive the ancient doctrines of Caraka, Sushruta, Galen and Avicenna. This would no more succeed than an attempt to 'infuse life into the fossil remains of animals that have long since made their exit from the stage of existence'. It was 'our imperative duty to utilise the truths contained in these ancient writings, but this would be impossible without a thorough knowledge of medicine in the present day'. The old systems were 'too immersed in error' to be receptive to modern medical discoveries.[31] The following year Mahendralal published an article on the 'Desirability of cultivation of the sciences by natives of India', in which his firm and uncompromising belief in the supreme importance of rationality was coupled with condemnation of 'the despotism of traditional opinion' that Hinduism represented. The Hindu religion was 'a chaotic mass of crude and undigested and unfounded opinions on all subjects, enunciated and enforced in the most dogmatic way imaginable'. Rather than attempting to return to the past, modern Hindus needed to acquire a more scientific outlook and shed their 'inherent indolence and apathy'.[32] Mahendralal valued India's ancient medical tradition as part of its rich and distinctive heritage, but he did not regard it as a self-sufficient basis for modern, rational practice, nor as a suitable foundation for India's national science.

Homoeopathy and India's medical 'systems'

It is important to recognise the epidemiological as well as the cultural context in which homoeopathy arose. In mid- and late-nineteenth-century Bengal homoeopathy was particularly deployed in the treatment of those diseases – principally cholera and malaria – that had become widespread in the province during the course of the century and which were seen as contributing to the 'ruin' of the countryside and the 'devitalising' of its people, but against which Western medicine seemed ineffective. Rajendra Datta's success as a homoeopath was particularly attributed to his use of arsenic albumen to treat the many cases of malaria that had arisen with the eruption of 'Burdwan fever' in Bengal in the 1850s.[33] As in many other parts of the world, including Europe, the advent of cholera (and the failure to treat it successfully by allopathic means) was a great stimulus to the adoption of homoeopathy, but the disease had a special relevance for Bengal. Mahendralal, whose mother died of the disease while he was still young,[34] pointed out that cholera, though it had become world wide, had its origins in Bengal and hence it was a disease 'which it behoves Indian physicians to study with particular care'.[35] A large proportion of the homoeopathic tracts in nineteenth-century Bengal were about preventing or treating cholera, including Mahendralal's own *Sketch of the Treatment of Cholera*, first published in 1870.[36] Not untypically, he began that work by acknowledging that homoeopathy alone could not provide an adequate solution for the treatment of this 'dire disease', but, in keeping with his criticism of rigid and supposedly self-contained 'systems' of medicine, he believed the intelligent physician could learn from the practices and experiences of the 'Old School' (allopathy) as well as from the 'New' (homoeopathy).

> The great difference between the Old and the New Schools of Medicine consists in the one generally ignoring the vital or dynamic laws, and the other the mechanical and chemical laws, which all combine in maintaining life. This we look upon as a serious and mischievous error, and unless each school will make ample concessions, unless each will condescend to learn from either,

we cannot expect their re-union, nay we cannot expect a perfect therapeutical science; on the contrary, there will be a perpetual war of school against school, system against system, to the great detriment of the profession and misfortune of the human race.[37]

Mahendralal accordingly drew his understanding of cholera from a wide range of sources, from Sushruta and Caraka ('the oldest of our medical authors ... who flourished probably before Hippocrates') to Patrick Manson's recent *Manual* of tropical diseases. When it came to treating the disease, Mahendralal found Hahnemann's own suggestions, dating from the 1830s, and using camphor and copper, rather antiquated and unhelpful. He proposed instead a variety of remedies (including such Indian drugs as aconitum and nux vomica and, more idiosyn-cratically, cobra venom) appropriate for each of the five stages of the disease.[38]

Although chronic illnesses were not altogether ignored, cholera, malaria and, in the 1890s, plague (on which Sircar also wrote) seem to have been among the principal diseases treated by Bengali homoeopaths in the mid to late nineteenth century, reflecting their immense epidemiological, political and social importance and the apparent ineffectiveness of orthodox Western medical and sanitary measures against them. Conversely, the discovery of the cholera bacillus by Robert Koch in 1884 threw homoeopathy into confusion. It was widely maintained that bacteriological explanations for this and other diseases were inadequate, Mahendralal himself maintaining shortly before his death that the comma bacillus could not alone explain all cases of cholera. Like many allopathic sceptics, he continued to believe that the onset of the disease must involve 'a variety of causes'.[39] In the twentieth century the locus of homoeopathy shifted away from the treatment of major epidemic diseases, like malaria and cholera, to relatively minor ailments and chronic complaints, where it was widely believed in Bengal (and perhaps in India generally) that allopathic drugs were ineffective, even harmful.

Although Mahendralal and others often referred to homoeopathy as a system, in some ways its appeal was as an anti-system – a set of ideas and practices that could contest the dominance, intolerance and complacency of allopathic medicine. Homoeopathy was regarded not as a kind of 'alternative' or 'complementary' medicine but rather as a means of supplanting the old orthodoxy, for reforming medicine as a whole and synethesising under its own aegis therapeutic wisdom drawn from a variety of sources.[40] In the Indian context, homoeopaths felt free to borrow from Ayurveda as an ancient system of medical observation and therapeutics and as a storehouse of indigenous *materia medica*, but without having to accept it as divine revelation or with its accompanying religious associations. Homoeopathy's appeal was that it was modern and rational and did not entail acceptance of 'other worlds of knowledge', whether Western, colonial, Indian or Hindu. As far as Mahendralal was concerned, the focus was accordingly on remedies, not systems. 'The question', he remarked in the preface to his cholera book, was 'not one of "the system versus the life of our patient", but of "cure versus disease"'.[41]

Homoeopathy thus sought to transcend conventional boundaries between 'Western' and 'indigenous' medicine by seeing itself as superior to both, or at least as providing a rational meeting ground for the best in both. But it should be noted that however homoeopathy was conceived by Mahendralal and other founding figures in India, there were undoubtedly pressures for it to 'belong', by winning recognition, in a pluralistic medical environment, as one among several 'systems' of thought and practice. In the early nineteenth century the notion of 'systems' was widely prevalent in the discussion of both Western and non-Western science, with Ayurveda often described interchangeably as a 'science' and a 'system'.[42] Despite European condemnation of Ayurveda and Unani (as well as the various forms of folk practice) in India in the nineteenth century, the term 'system' kept alive the pluralistic idea that there could be different ways of understanding, health, disease and therapeutics: these might, in Western eyes, be antiquated, even dangerous, but it was accepted they could still be internally consistent and sanctioned by ancient usage and textual authority. While Western writers and practitioners sought increasingly to reserve the term 'science' for themselves, they were less concerned about a looser use of the term 'system'. From the 1890s proponents of a revitalised Ayurveda took up for themselves the pluralistic terminology of 'systems', though they at times used 'science' as well. This helped to place Ayurveda and Western medicine on a seemingly equal footing without expecting one to be subsumed in the other. It also created the discursive space and political opportunity for the inclusion of other non-orthodox 'systems' – including Unani medicine and, almost inevitably, homoeopathy.

Homoeopathy was being described as a 'system' in India as early as the 1850s. Skipwith described it as 'a system of specifics' and went on to remark: 'Surely there is something highly scientific in a system which ... requires a physician to adapt his remedy so exactly to the disease of his patient, and in choosing it under all circumstances according to a certain determinate law'.[43] By the 1930s, as homoeopaths became more organised, they began to press the government for full recognition of their 'system' alongside Ayurveda and Unani medicine.[44] On the other hand, homoeopathy was not given any significant consideration in the several investigations into 'indigenous medicine' in the 1920s and 1930s, including the important Madras committee in 1923, where proponents of Ayurvedic medicine were anxious to establish the credentials of their own 'system' as a 'complete, original and self-reliant science'.[45] By the mid-1940s, homoeopathy had made little progress in trying to gain equal status with Ayurveda and other 'indigenous systems'. K.C.K.E. Raja, representing the official viewpoint, dismissively described homoeopathy as more a system of therapeutics than of medicine as such. Lacking in physiology, anatomy, pathology, obstetrics and surgery, homoeopathy could not, 'by itself, constitute a complete system of medical practice'.[46]

The homoeopath and the saint

Having strayed into the 1940s, let us now return to Mahendralal Sircar. His reputation as the virtual father of Bengali homoeopathy requires some explanation, for he had as his predecessor (and continuing mentor) the highly successful Rajendra Datta. One reason could be that Mahendralal entered homoeopathy explicitly as a rebel, breaking sharply with white-dominated medical officialdom in a way that Datta did not. Unusually, he came from a humble, intermediate caste background (he was a Sadgop),[47] and was noted, in later life, for having not only 'simple habits and ... unostentatious ways' but also 'rough manners'.[48] Mahendralal (unlike Rajendra) completed his course at the Calcutta Medical College. He became only the second MD to qualify from Bengal, in 1863, and a luminary of the Calcutta branch of the British Medical Association, serving as its assistant secretary from 1863 to 1867.[49] In 1863 Mahendralal began a vigorous denunciation of homoeo-paths, calling them, in the approved language of the time, 'quacks and charlatans'.[50] Then, in February 1867, he announced his dramatic conversion to heterodox homoeopathy in a paper presented to the Calcutta branch of the Association and was promptly expelled and ostracised, losing many of his patients in the process.[51] 'I am a peasant's son', he is reported to have remarked, 'I will survive: but one must stick to what one believes to be the truth'.[52]

What might be called his proto-nationalist linkages continued into the years of Mahendralal's subsequent success: he founded the Indian Association for the Cultivation of Science in 1876, a project supported by burgeoning nationalist politicians like Surendranath Banerji, who started the Indian Association in the same year. He has been hailed as 'the doyen of the scientific spirit in our country, one who dedicated his life to sciencetising [sic] a traditional society'.[53] In 1888 he was President of the Bengal Provincial Conference, at which he denounced the exploitation of tea-garden labourers in Assam by European planters.[54] It might then appear logical to try to locate Mahendralal's prominence in the *Ramakrishna-Kathamrita*, an influential hagiographical text of the period, in a broadly similar, proto-nationalist context. The *Kathamrita*, compiled by 'M' (Mahendranath Gupta) claims to represent the conversations of the Hindu saint Ramakrishna Paramhansa with his disciples and various visitors between 1882 and his death in 1886.[55] Among the latter was Mahendralal Sircar, who for a time treated Ramakrishna for the throat cancer that eventually killed him. Ramakrishna was not only the most influential Hindu religious teacher in Calcutta in the 1880s: his most famous disciple, Swami Vivekananda, also became an undoubted source of inspiration for twentieth-century Indian nationalism and its Hindu variant.

A glance at the *Kathamrita*, however, would quickly dispel any such proto-nationalism assumption, for Mahendralal is throughout projected in that text, not as any kind of cultural and/or political nationalist, but as the rationalist, sceptical foil to Ramakrishna, the symbol of religious, often highly emotional and ecstatic, faith and devotion (*bhakti*). He is a foil, nonetheless, who, despite his inclinations, cannot help but be deeply impressed by Ramakrishna, and who in the end implicitly submits – at least to the extent of lapsing into silence at crucial points in the dialogue.

The whole effect is, in fact, the product of very careful and deliberate authorial strategies, for the *Kathamrita* achieves its appearance of unmediated authenticity only through a high degree of self-conscious construction. A reader is likely to get the impression that Mahendralal was one of Ramakrishna's principal interlocutors, for he appears continuously through about a fifth of the first volume and more intermittently in the remaining four. It is only by looking carefully at the dates and arranging the entries in chronological order, breaking up the volume divisions (helped by the notes appended to the final volume by Mahendranath's sons, not by the diarist-author himself) that one realises, with a certain sense of shock, that the sessions where the homoeopath was present number only twelve out of the 186 covered by Mahendranath's account.

Moreover, all but one of these recorded meetings took place within a very short spell of less than three weeks (18 October to 6 November 1885), the time when Mahendralal was treating the saint for throat cancer. This treatment clearly failed and, perhaps significantly, in the last recorded meeting (22 April 1886),[56] Mahendralal was accompanied by his senior in homoeopathy, Rajendra Datta. It should be noted, too, that there is no evidence in the *Kathamrita* of any conscious preference for homoeopathy on the part of either Ramakrishna or his disciples, who were clearly trying all possible medical options. Several Ayurvedic *kavirajs* were applied to, as well as practitioners of orthodox Western medicine like Bhagaban Rudra (though there is a reference to the latter being very expensive).[57]

Mahendralal the homoeopath is thus associated unequivocally with modernity in this text and not with any kind of indigenous cultural nationalist reaction to the domination of Western colonial discourse. His location in the *Kathamrita* is, in fact, very similar to that of the social reformer and educationalist Iswarchandra Vidyasagar. It is also relevant to note that Rajendra Datta was a figure of perhaps even more unequivocal, indeed iconoclastic, modernity and 'Westernism', for his affinities were with the Derozians, the group repeatedly reviled by social conservatives and cultural nationalists throughout the nineteenth century and beyond as denationalised 'Anglicists'.[58] And while Mahendralal was undoubtedly interested in, and impressed by, Ramakrishna, his 'silence' (highlighted in several passages of the text) may, like that of Vidyasagar, not have amounted to much more than politeness in front of a dying patient.

There is no evidence at all that Mahendralal's rationalist world-view (which helped attract him to homoeopathy in the first place) was ever affected by his encounters with Ramakrishna. In 1889, three years after the saint's death, he came out strongly, for instance, in support of the Age of Consent Bill which was trying to raise the minimum age for cohabitation in marriage from ten to twelve in the teeth of ferocious orthodox and cultural-nationalist opposition.[59] The Brahmo reformer Sibnath Sastri in 1903 published a highly appreciative autobiographical notice of Mahendralal in his *Ramtanu Lahiri o Tatkalin Bangasamaj*.[60] This, not unexpectedly, said nothing about his meetings with Ramakrishna, but rightly emphasised Mahendralal's ever-questioning spirit and curiosity about new ideas and experiences. And yet the rapid 'indigenisation' of the homoeopathy propagated by Rajendra and Mahendralal remains undeniable, as well as the probable role in its appeal of an element of anti-foreign resentment. What is in need of modification, therefore, is the widespread assumption that equates all worthwhile anti-colonial impulses with rejection in cultural-nationalist ways of modern, Western 'rationality' and makes, in effect, the rejection of ideas of Western origin the sole criterion for authentic autonomy.

A closer look at the precise terms of the Ramakrishna–Mahendralal dialogue can help to substantiate this point from a different angle. Using some passages from this dialogue, Partha Chatterjee has sought to explain the appeal of Ramakrishna to the educated middle class of Calcutta primarily in terms of a deepening sense of disaffection with what he has called 'the prison-house of Reason'. The discourse of Reason was inevitably oppressive for the 'colonised middle-class mind', Chatterjee argues, because of the 'invariable implication it carried of the historical necessity of colonial rule and its condemnation of indigenous culture as the store-house of unreason.'[61] Rationality here has been assumed to be equivalent to 'Western' and 'colonial'. Such attitudes were certainly present, and can be seen at work, for instance, in the assertion of Swami Saradananda's biography of Ramakrishna that Mahendralal failed to fully understand the saint because of 'the influence of Western education'.[62]

The *Kathamrita* passages on the Ramakrishna–Mahendralal encounter demand a more complex reading. Three themes stand out, and we also meet them again, directly or indirectly, in the conversation with Vidyasagar in another part of the text. First, there is what can be plausibly considered a reason/faith polarity, but which is more precisely definable as the contrast between learned folly and unlearned wisdom which is almost ubiquitous in the conversations of Ramakrishna (a rustic, poor Brahman with virtually no formal education) with his overwhelmingly English-educated disciples. 'Many think they cannot have knowledge and learning without reading books. But hearing is better than reading, and seeing is better than hearing.' 'Mere reading does not make one learned (*pandit*).'[63] The orality/literacy contrast here, it should be noted in passing, should not be construed too quickly as some kind of valorisation of the popular or subaltern – for Ramakrishna, despite his poor origins, was a Brahman, and much of Brahmanical high culture has been preserved, propagated, and kept from women and lower castes primarily through oral means. More directly relevant for the present argument is that the arrogance of mere book-learning which Ramakrishna condemned had as its target *both* traditional and modern-Western formal knowledge: reason and devotion here cannot be collapsed into a simple Western/indigenous polarity, as Chatterjee's analysis tends to do. The English-educated, Ramakrishna told Mahendralal, would not believe someone who says that he has seen a house collapse, until they read about it in a newspaper. But he also declared, 'Pandits know a lot – the Vedas, the Puranas, the Tantras. But of what avail is mere book-learning?' There is no need to read the entire *Gita*, for devotion (*bhakti*) is more vital than learning, old or new.[64]

A second recurrent theme is Ramakrishna's rejection of what might be called social activism, organised efforts at ameliorating the conditions of the world. 'Your good works would get reduced by themselves as you become more devout', Ramakrishna had told Vidyasagar, the great reformer and philanthropist, for 'men cannot improve the conditions of the world. He is doing it Himself'.[65] On going to Mahendralal Sircar's house for the first time to invite him to visit Ramakrishna, 'M' related to the doctor one of the saint's favourite stories that carried a similar moral: how the philanthropist Sambhu Mallik had foolishly spent all his energies on building hospitals, dispensaries and schools, instead of seeking divinity through devotion.[66] Like formal book-learning, obviously much stimulated by the coming of print under colonialism, social activism and reformist endeavours had acquired enhanced importance in nineteenth-century educated middle-class life. But, once again, it will be noticed that Ramakrishna is taking on, and subordinating to *bhakti*, not social reform (not even the widow remarriage campaign which had made Vidyasagar both famous and notorious), but philanthropy of the kinds that, in one form or another, must have preceded colonial rule.

Mahendralal's brief excursion into Ramakrishna's intimate circle coincided with a debate taking place among some of his devotees about whether the saint was an *avatar*, an incarnation of divinity. The rationalist and sceptical doctor was clearly shocked. He had the highest respect for Ramakrishna as a human being, but felt that such talk would ruin a good man by making him into a cult figure. In such debates Mahendralal, interestingly, asserted the principle of human equality, which made erecting any mortal into God abhorrent to him. Implicit here was a confrontation between a view of equal rights, and the crucial high-Hindu principle of *adhikari-bheda*, or hierarchical powers and claims, which Ramakrishna repeatedly reaffirmed. The equality versus *adhikari-bheda* dichotomy had figured very prominently, too, in the encounter with Vidyasagar, which preceded talk about Ramakrishna's *avatar* status.[67] Here, in the stress on equal rights that was common to Vidyasagar and Mahendralal, one could legitimately affirm the influence of modern-Western 'post-Enlightenment' discourse. But it needs to be added that the specific debate on *avatar*-hood in which Mahendralal was intervening has had a long internal history within Hindu culture, one that long predates any Western impact. Many orthodox Bengali Vaishnavites (worshippers of the god Vishnu in his various incarnations, principally Krishna and Rama) would be shocked by the *avatar* claim, which could potentially take away the special position of Caitanya, the inspirational figure behind the sixteenth-century devotional movement in Bengal, while incarnation does not enter at all into the other major Hindu traditions of devotion – to Siva or the Mother-Goddess.

Taken as a whole, it is this internal nature of the *Kathamrita* discussions and debates that strikes one as significant. Colonial domination, whether cultural or political, actually figures very little within it in a direct manner.[68]

Conclusion

One might in conclusion suggest a few more general observations. One is quite obvious: homoeopathy, with its combination of purely modern, Western origins, its early emphasis on 'rational' therapeutics, and its rapid assimilation into Indian society, cannot be made to fit a sharp Western/indigenous divide. Second, there appears to be a need to question more generally such a frame for studying the whole theme of 'alternative' medicine – at least to the extent of problematising the easy slippage so common today from 'alternative' to 'indigenous' and 'subaltern'. Alternatives to orthodox medicine can be interesting and significant without fitting either of these categories. Thus, despite the important dimensions of cheapness and permeability of specialist/lay divides, the 'popular' or 'subaltern' character of homoeopathy in India should not be exaggerated: even today it seems more of a metropolitan or small-town, rather than genuinely rural, phenomenon.[69] Even more 'authentically' indigenous forms also need not be 'popular' in the sense of being somehow removed from the taint of power relations. Ayurvedic knowledge is grounded in Sanskrit texts of the kind Mahendralal was seeking to gain access to and have translated in the late 1860s, and the revitalised Ayurveda movement was itself engaged in conflict with folk medicine in the late nineteenth and early twentieth centuries in an attempt to establish its own superiority and to gain authority over what it, too, saw as a kind of 'quackery'.[70]

It should be noted that while Ayurvedic medicine has undergone its own process of popularisation and internationalisation since the 1890s, official Western medicine in India has also been exposed to a process of vernacularisation through the spread of print culture, though not on the same scale as homoeopathy and only in its more elementary forms. Vernacular texts on allopathy also became fairly common in Bengal from the late nineteenth century, and the censuses and other official documents indicate the presence of a large number of 'quacks', including practitioners of allopathic medicine who did not hold proper degrees. A smattering of knowledge about standard remedies had become fairly widespread, at times dangerously so, as with the recent rise of self-medication through the better-known antibiotics. The key problem with frameworks grounded in Western/indigenous divides is that they tend to excessively prioritise the question of origins. Elevation of immunity from modern/Western discourses into the sole criterion for valorisation might at times be seriously anachronistic. Need we assume automatically that the colonised have always been primarily concerned with questions of cultural nationalism?

Notes

1   Charles Leslie (ed.), *Asian Medical Systems: A Comparative Study*, Berkeley, University of California Press, 1976.
2   Surinder M. Bhardwaj, 'Homoeopathy in India', in Giri Raj Gupta (ed.), *The Social and Cultural Context of Medicine in India*, Delhi, Vikas, 1981, pp. 31–54; Bhardwaj, 'Medical pluralism and homoeopathy: A geographic perspective', *Social Science and Medicine*, 14 B (1980): 209–16.
3   Bhardwaj, 'Homoeopathy', pp. 50–1.
4   Bhardwaj, 'Medical pluralism', p. 214.
5   Sarat Chandra Ghose, *Life of Dr Mahendra Lal Sircar* (first published *c*.1910), 2nd edition, Calcutta, Hahnemann Publishing Co., 1935, pp. 32–3, mentions, for instance, Dr Mullens of the London Missionary Society at Bhowanipur.
6   Bhardwaj, 'Homoeopathy', pp. 33–6.
7   As by Charles Morehead, a leading figure in the Bombay Medical Service and Principal of Grant Medical College, who denounced it in the late 1840s, along with mesmerism and hydrotherapy, as purely 'speculative': Hermann A. Haines, *Memorial of the Life and Times of Charles Morehead*, London, W.H. Allen, n.d., p. 37.
8   [F.C. Skipwith], 'Homoeopathy and its introduction into India', *Calcutta Review*, 17 (1852): 52.
9   Dayaram Gidumal, *The Life and Life-Work of Behramji M. Malabari*, Bombay, Education Society's Press, 1888, pp. lxxiv, 286–7.
10 S.C. Sengupta and Anjali Basu, *Sansad Bangali Caritabhidhan*, Calcutta, Sahitya Sansad, 1976, p. 459.

11 Bhardwaj, 'Medical pluralism', p. 214.

12 [Skipwith], 'Homoeopathy', pp. 19, 43.

13 Ghose, *Mahendra Lal*, pp. 81–8.

14 *Calcutta Journal of Medicine* [hereafter *CJM*], 1, (1868): 190–1. For some Bengali works on homoeopathy, see *Author Catalogue of Printed Books in Bengali Language*, vol. 3, Calcutta, National Library, 1959, pp. 55, 58, 61, 62.

15 Ghose, *Mahendra Lal*, p. 7; Mahendralal Sircar, 'A retrospect', *CJM*, 2 (1869): 400.

16 Sivanath [Sibnath] Sastri, 'Men I have seen – VI: Personal reminiscences of Dr Mahendralal Sircar', *Modern Review*, April (1911): 324.

17 For the various factors involved, see David Arnold, *Colonizing the Body: State Medicine and Epidemic Disease in Nineteenth-Century India*, Berkeley, University of California Press, 1993; Mark Harrison, *Public Health in British India: Anglo-Indian Preventive Medicine, 1859–1914*, Cambridge, Cambridge University Press, 1994; Anil Kumar, *Medicine and the Raj: British Medical Policy in India, 1835–1911*, Delhi, Sage, 1998.

18 Bhardwaj, 'Medical pluralism', p. 214.

19 K. McLeod, 'Medical practice in Calcutta', *Indian Medical Gazette*, 1 August 1882, pp. 215–16.

20 Norman Gevitz, 'Unorthodox medical theories', in W.F. Bynum and R. Porter (eds), *Companion Encyclopedia of the History of Medicine*, I, London, Routledge, 1993, p. 611.

21 Ghose, *Mahendra Lal*, p. 80.

22 Ghose, *Mahendra Lal*, p. 94.

23 [Skipwith], 'Homoeopathy', p. 21.

24 The term 'allopathic' was sufficiently new (and troublesome) in 1852 for the editor of the *Calcutta Review* to seek to explain it without wishing to appear to endorse its use: ibid., p. 25.

25 Bhardwaj, 'Homoeopathy', pp. 44–8. Similarly, one recent account of homoeopathy by a London-based, India-born, practitioner suggests that homoeopathy has more in common with holistic Eastern medical traditions than with allopathy and includes, without further explanation, a chapter on the Ayurvedic theory of *tridosha* (the three elements): C.H. Sharma, *A Manual of Homoeopathy and Natural Medicine*, New York, E.P. Dutton, 1976, p. 1 and chapter 9.

26 Bhardwaj, 'Homoeopathy', p. 41.

27 The critique of violent purges, bloodletting, fierce mercurials and 'antiphlogistic remedies' in general was not confined to homoeopaths, but their use of 'safe', 'gentle' and 'simple' remedies undoubtedly contributed to their appeal and perceived efficacy: see Charles Morehead, *Clinical Researches on Disease in India*, vol. 1, London, Longman, Brown, Green and Longman, 1856, pp. 40, 174–9, 199–218; cf. [Skipwith], 'Homoeopathy', pp. 37–9.

28 Mahendralal, 'Our creed', *CJM*, 1 (1868): 2–3.

29 Untitled review by Mahendralal of *The Indigenous Drugs of India* by K.L. Dey, *CJM*, 1 (1868): 25.

30 'Charaka', *CJM*, 1 (1868): 115; 'Colleges of hakims and kavirajs', *CJM*, 1 (1868): 118–19.

31 'Colleges of hakims and kavirajs', p. 116.

32 'On the desirability of cultivation of the sciences by the natives of India', *CJM*, 2 (1869): 287–8.

33 Ghose, *Mahendra Lal*, p. 35. For the importance of this disease, see David Arnold, '"An Ancient Race Outworn": Malaria and race in colonial India, 1860–1930', in Waltraud Ernst and Bernard Harris (eds), *Race, Science and Medicine, 1700–1960*, London, Routledge, 1999, pp. 123–43. Note, too, the several articles by Mahendralal on malaria in the early issues of *CJM*.

34 Ghose, *Mahendra Lal*, p. 2.

35 Mahendralal Sircar, *A Sketch of the Treatment of Cholera* (first published 1870), 2nd edn, Calcutta, P. Sircar, 1904, p. 1.

36 E.g., Radha Kanta Ghosh, *Cholera and Its Treatment on Homeopathic Principles*, Calcutta, Berigny, 1887 (previously published as a Bengali pamphlet in 1876); D.N. Ray, *A Treatise on Cholera and Kindred Diseases*, Calcutta, Elm Press, 1906, which notes (pp. 111–13) the reputation homoeopathy had acquired for the more successful treatment of the disease than by allopaths, with less patient distress and fewer deaths; L. Salzer, *Lectures on Cholera and Its Homoeopathic Treatment*, Calcutta, C. Ringer, 1910.

37 Sircar, *Sketch*, p. v.

38 Sircar, *Sketch*, pp. 5, 39, 66–71.

39 Sircar, *Sketch*, p. 21.

40 For North American parallels, see John Harley Warner, 'Orthodoxy and otherness: Homoeopathy and regular medicine in nineteenth-century America', in Robert Jutte, Guenter B. Risse, and John Woodward (eds), *Culture, Knowledge and Healing: Historical Perspectives of Homeopathic Medicine in Europe and North America*, Sheffield, European Association for the History of Medicine and Health Publications, 1998, pp. 5–29.

41 Sircar, *Sketch*, p. iv; see also Bhardwaj, 'Homoeopathy', pp. 40–1.

42 E.g., J.F. Royle, *An Essay on the Antiquity of Hindoo Medicine*, London, W.H. Allen, 1837, pp. 5–6, 75, 156–61; T.A. Wise, *Commentary on the Hindu System of Medicine* (first published 1845), London, Trubner, 1860, pp. i–iii.

43 [Skipwith], 'Homoeopathy', pp. 24–5.

44 For some examples from Madras, a part of India where homoeopathy was increasingly establishing itself in the early twentieth century, see the correspondence in Local Self-Government (Public Health), 100–01, 17 January 1930, Tamil Nadu Archives, Chennai; LSG (PH), 351, 14 February 1933, TNA; and at the all-India level, Education, Health and Lands (Health), 54–14/40, 1940, National Archives of India, Delhi.

45 Pandit C.T. Arumugam Pillai, in *Report of the Committee on the Indigenous System of Medicine*, Madras, Government Press, 1923, p. 48.

46 *Report of the Committee on Indigenous Systems of Medicine, II*, Appendices, New Delhi, Ministry of Health, 1948, p. 294. Bhardwaj notes the tendency for supporters of the 'indigenous systems' to dissociate themselves from homoeopathy, but, following his 'naturalisation' thesis, he sees this as a development only of the post-Independence era: 'Homoeopathy', p. 42, n. 13.

47 Sadgops were an off-shoot of the originally pastoral Gop *jati* or caste of southwest Bengal, who turned to agriculture and were climbing up the social scale from the sixteenth century onwards. Despite such upward mobility, a Sadgop would be rare among the *bhadralok* (the overwhelmingly upper-caste literati) of nineteenth- and even twentieth-century Bengal. Hiteshranjan Sanyal, 'Continuities in social mobility in traditional and modern societies in India: Two case-studies of caste mobility in Bengal' in his *Social Mobility in Bengal*, Calcutta, Papyrus, 1981, pp. 82–112.

48 Sastri, 'Men I have seen', pp. 324, 326.

49 Kumar, *Medicine and the Raj*, p. 35.

50 *Indian Scientists: Biographical Sketches*, Madras, G.A. Natesan, 1929, pp. 15–16.

51 The branch itself apparently broke up over the issue: Terence J. Johnson and Marjorie Caygill, 'The British Medical Association and its overseas branches: A short history', *Journal of Imperial and Commonwealth History*, 1 (1973): 310.

52 Anilchandra Ghosh, *Vigyane Bangali*, Dhaka, n.p., 1931, pp. 12–13 and passim. Ghosh probably took this passage from the first account of Mahendralal's life, the biographical notice in Sibnath Sastri, *Ramtanu Lahiri o Tatkalin Bangasamaj*, first published 1903, Calcutta, New Age publishers, 1955, pp. 259–67.

53 Chittabrata Palit, 'Mahendra Lal Sircar, 1833–1904: The quest for national science', in Deepak Kumar (ed.), *Science and Empire: Essays in Indian Context (1700–1947)*, Delhi, Anamika Prakashan, 1991, p. 159.

54 Palit, 'Mahendra Lal', pp. 154–8; Deepak Kumar, *Science and the Raj, 1857–1905*, Delhi, Oxford University Press, 1995, pp. 198–201; Sengupta and Basu, *Sansad Bangali Caritabhidhan*, pp. 401–2.

55 'M', *Ramakrishna-Kathamrita*, 5 volumes, Calcutta, Sri Mar Thakurbari (1901, 1904, 1908, 1910, 1932). There have been many editions and reprints, of which that used here was published in 1980–1. Mahendranath, we are told, noted down the conversations every day in a diary, and the very precisely dated text (compared by some admirers to Boswell's journal) does succeed in conveying a sense of great authenticity as an apparently verbatim record of actual conversations.

56 *Kathamrita*, II. 27, p. 231–2.

57 *Kathamrita*, IV. 26 (31 August 1885); V. 18 (20 September 1885); I. 15 (22 October 1885). The 31 August entry mentions that Dr Rudra's usual fee was as high as Rs 25, but the disciples were hoping to reduce it to Rs 4 or 5. Mahendralal, by contrast, charged no fees at all after the first

visit. Rudra was surely over-charging. According to McLeod in 1882, 'the fee usually paid to a qualified native medical man is Rs 2 per visit. Some demand and receive Rs 4, and a very few Rs 8. A small operation or night visit entitles to a double fee'. 'Medical practice in Calcutta', p. 215. Perhaps Rudra did not want to treat the saint or was trusting to the exceptional devotion of Ramakrishna's disciples.

58 Sengupta and Basu, *Sansad Bangali Caritabhidan*, p. 459. For the Derozians, the generation of Hindu College students inspired by their charismatic and iconoclastic teacher, Henry Louis Vivian Derozio, see Susobhan Sarkar, 'Derozio and Young Bengal' in Atul Gupta (ed.), *Studies in the Bengal Renaissance*, Calcutta, National Council of Education, 1958, and Sumit Sarkar, 'The complexities of Young Bengal', in his *A Critique of Colonial India*, Calcutta, Papyrus, 1985, pp. 18–36.

59 Charles H. Heimsath, *Indian Nationalism and Hindu Social Reform*, Princeton, Princeton University Press, 1964, p. 167.

60 Ghosh in *Vigyane Bangali* is also silent about this episode.

61 Partha Chatterjee, *The Nation and Its Fragments: Colonial and Post-Colonial Histories*, Princeton, Princeton University Press, 1993, p. 55 and passim.

62 Swami Saradananda, *Sri Sri Ramakrishna-Leelapranga*, volume V, Calcutta, Udbodhan, 1919, p. 300.

63 *Kathamrita*, I. 15, p. 216 (22 October 1885); I. 17, p. 239 (26 October 1885). There are similar passages involving Vidyasagar, e.g., 'Mere learning is nothing': III. 1, p. 10 (5 August 1882). For a more detailed study of this and other aspects of the *Kathamrita*, see Sumit Sarkar, 'Kaliyuga, chakri, and bhakti: Ramakrishna and his Times', *Economic and Political Weekly*, 18 July 1992, XXVII, reprinted with minor changes in Sumit Sarkar, *Writing Social History*, Delhi, Oxford University Press, 1997, chapter 8.

64 *Kathamrita*, I. 15, p. 219 (22 October 1885); III. 21, pp. 230–1 (30 October 1885).

65 *Kathamrita*, III. 1, p. 15 (5 August 1882).

66 *Kathamrita*, III. 20, p. 215 (18 October 1885).

67 For this, see Sarkar, *Writing Social History*, chapters 7 and 8.

68 With the important exception of *chakri*, or office-work in predominantly British government and mercantile institutions: Sarkar, *Writing Social History*, chapter 8.

69 Bhardwaj, 'Homoeopathy', p. 51.

70 K.N. Panikkar, 'Indigenous medicine and cultural hegemony: A study of the revitalization movement in Keralam', *Studies in History*, 8 (1992): 283–308.

4 Arguing science

Unani *tibb*, hakims and biomedicine in India, 1900–50

Claudia Liebeskind

'It is a great injustice', declared Hakim 'Abd al Latif in 1950, 'that without studying a science (*'ilm*) and without knowing anything about it, somebody should decide whether it is scientific (*sa'intifik*) or unscientific (*ansa'intifik*).'[1] So complained a member of one of India's leading medical families about the official attitude which, since the late nineteenth century, had developed towards the indigenous medical systems, Ayurveda and Unani *tibb* (medicine). The hakim felt betrayed by the government of the day. 'It appears that the English government has gone, but its policies,' contended the hakim, 'have not disappeared ... Those Englishmen who look like Indians put forward the same old and stale excuse that the indigenous medicines are unscientific (*ansa'intifik*).'[2]

Opposition to indigenous medical systems[3] from the advocates of the medical tradition originating in Europe was nothing new; it was a by-product of the rapid developments within Western medicine which, in the second half of the nineteenth century, had transformed it into what we now call biomedicine.[4] Variously referred to in British India as 'allopathy', the 'modern', 'English' or 'Western system of medicine', we will use the term 'biomedicine' throughout the text. This medical transformation brought different theoretical and practical aspects to the fore, exemplified, for instance, by the shift from a miasmatic to a germ-based theory of disease causation. In consequence the points of contact and contention between the medical systems were altered and advocates of biomedicine shifted the battle-lines as to what constituted a 'proper' medical system on to the territory of a domain called 'science'.[5]

Modern science and the processes of its manufacture go back to conceptual transformations in the sixteenth and seventeenth centuries. During that period the foundation on which natural philosophical knowledge rested began to move from universals constructed from commonplace experience to particular events such as artificially contrived unique experiences. The concern in natural philosophy moved from knowledge of causes to knowledge of matters of fact.[6] Experimentally produced matters of fact that were discovered and supposedly value-neutral were detached from theories that were humanly constructed.[7] This was grounded in the Baconian enterprise to differentiate between ancient commonalities and 'deracinated particulars'.[8] Through the reordering of the scientific disciplines the meaning of knowledge-building tools such as experience and observation was redefined.[9] This period has generally been termed 'the scientific revolution',[10] although recent scholarship has underscored the fact that while the sixteenth and seventeenth centuries saw novel developments these were embedded in continuities and that the acceptance of these procedures and their findings was not inevitable.[11]

While the new understanding of knowledge and science was being created, or even constructed, its proponents had to contend with the views of advocates of Aristotelian-scholastic philosophy which contested the claims and value of the new knowledge and the procedures of its production. This contest between different intellectual traditions had occurred within the same civilisational setting, Europe.[12] In the nineteenth and twentieth centuries, European expansion meant that the sites of conflict were extended to the non-Western world.[13] The intellectual traditions of Europe interacted with intellectual traditions that had their own notions of knowledge and science. In South Asia practitioners of the European medical tradition drew clear distinctions between themselves and practitioners of indigenous medical systems. In the case of Unani, or Greek, medicine, however, they were faced by practitioners of a medical tradition which shared a common ancestry with Western medicine. This ancestry was not finally rejected in the West until the nineteenth century.

Unani medicine, alongside Ayurveda (Hindu medicine) and Siddha (South Indian medicine), had been part of the Indian medical repertory for many centuries. Unani medicine as practised in the subcontinent was based on the work of Ibn Sina (980–1037). He had systematised the medicine of Hippocrates and Galen as it had been transmitted and further developed by the Arabs. In his *Qanun*, Ibn Sina had integrated Greek humoral medicine into an Islamic framework that has been translated, abridged and commented on in India down to the present day.[14] The practitioners of the indigenous medicines had interacted amongst themselves but also with the forms of Western medicine brought, since the seventeenth century, to the subcontinent by various European trading powers. Changes in the power relationship between Indians and Europeans in the eighteenth century combined with the changes in the European medical tradition in the nineteenth century to provide for an environment in which the colonial power championed biomedicine almost exclusively and withheld legitimation from the indigenous medical systems. This situation changed only after 1919 when the Montagu-Chelmsford reforms transferred responsibility for medical provision from the central government to the provincial governments[15] and Indians took control of the provincial legislative assemblies for the first time.

Although political expediency after 1919 altered the official attitude towards the indigenous medical systems (the fact that Indians were in charge of the provincial medical departments did not mean that they were in favour of indigenous medicines), the biomedical establishment, both the colonial Indian Medical Service (IMS) and biomedical associations, continued to declare its hostility towards them openly. Their antagonism culminated in attempts in the late 1940s to reserve the title 'modern scientific medicine' for what had previously been labelled 'allopathic' or 'Western' medicine.[16] Further pressure was exerted through the shifting expectations of the increasingly Westernised indigenous élite that patronised indigenous medicines but came to judge them against Western biomedical specifications.

In the face of this changing outlook and sustained criticism, practitioners of Indian medicines were not slow to act and react. Here I want to look at the strategies pursued by hakims, practitioners of Unani medicine, in the period between 1900 and 1950 as they argued for the scientific standing of Unani *tibb*. This was part of the wider attempts made by Muslims since the middle of the nineteenth century to make the Islamic sciences, both revealed and rational, compatible with nature and the shifting definition of scientific truths as postulated by the colonial power.[17] I shall analyse six texts written by three different hakims, initially situating the authors in their social and cultural space and mapping the political occasions in which the texts originated. I shall then point to the particular as well as the shared modes of argument they employed in defending Unani medicine as a science. Lastly I shall examine the critique of biomedicine which they produced both implicitly and explicitly. Hakims in India offered both resistance to and criticism of biomedicine in a way that stands in contrast to how hakims in West Asia behaved: there they appeared to have capitulated wholesale in the face of biomedical rhetoric and knowledge.[18]

Authors and occasions

There has never been a disciplined and homogeneous community of practitioners of Unani medicine. Equally there has never been one homogeneous and unified version of Unani *tibb*, but a plethora of practices and interpretations within the broad and holistic church of *tibb*. Being a hakim, at one end of the scale, implied having a rudimentary grasp of some theoretical concepts and a solid repertory of drugs to be dispensed to patients. At the other end of the scale being a hakim, literally a sage, was part of the cultural make-up of a gentleman belonging to Perso-Islamic society. Those hakims who were influential in determining the officially sanctioned shapes and contents of Unani medicine in the twentieth century belonged to élite families with court-ties which had been involved in the dissemination and practice of *tibb* for centuries. Two of the three hakims whose writings I shall analyse here, Hakims Ajmal Khan (1863–1927) and 'Abd al Latif (1900–70), came from such families; the third, Hakim Kabir al Din (1894–1976), was an early product of the new institutionalised setting of Unani medicine which, allowing for greater access to Unani education, democratised its study.

Hakim Ajmal Khan was the scion of what has come to be regarded as India's premier *tibbi* family, the Sharifs of Delhi. Crucially influenced in his childhood by the remnants of the cosmopolitan Persianate culture of pre-1857 Delhi, he received a traditional education from the leading *ulama*, learned Muslim scholars, of Delhi. His political outlook moved from being heavily influenced by Sir Saiyid Ahmad Khan and his Aligarh/Muslim League style of politics aimed at the protection of the Muslim élite through close cooperation with the British colonial state to his championing of Hindu–Muslim unity and deep involvement with the Indian National Congress in the 1920s in opposition to the colonial power.[19]

His family had been teaching and practising *tibb* for centuries. His elder brother, under the influence of the Aligarh movement, was the first to institutionalise Unani education in northern India in the 1880s.[20] Ajmal Khan continued running the Madrassa Tibbia[21] (college) reinventing it in 1916 as the Ayurvedic and Unani Tibbia College, Delhi. There students received instruction in biomedical topics alongside either Ayurveda or Unani *tibb*. The threat towards Ayurveda and Unani medicine and their practitioners, which Ajmal Khan perceived in the (bio-) Medical Registration Acts which had been under discussion since the early 1880s, and which were enacted in the 1910s, had made him realise the need for cooperation between the advocates of the two systems. In 1910 he organised the first annual meeting of the All-India Ayurvedic and Unani Tibbi Conference, Delhi, which acted both as a pressure group negotiating with government and as an organisation designed to discipline its members and standardise their understanding of Ayurveda and Unani *tibb*. In spite of organising the two indigenous medicines in the same medical association and educational institution, Ajmal Khan did not envisage the future of Ayurveda and Unani *tibb* to lie in their eventual fusion.[22] His concern was to supplement both Ayurveda and Unani *tibb* with biomedical topics and subjects in order to advance them.

In 1916 he succeeded in getting the Imperial Legislative Assembly to pass a resolution looking into ways of 'placing the ancient and indigenous systems on a scientific basis',[23] but felt betrayed when, in 1918, the inquiry dismissed such a possibility.

> The opinion unanimously expressed by local Government is that it is practically impossible to place the indigenous systems of medicine on a scientific basis. The systems are a survival of a state of medical knowledge that once prevailed in Europe, but has been superseded by a series of scientific investigations and discoveries extending over several centuries. They ignore the instruments of scientific investigation that have made modern medicine and surgery possible, and the theories on which they are based are demonstrably unsound.[24]

In opposition to these findings Hakim Ajmal Khan set out his view on the scientific nature of *tibb* in three texts which I shall analyse in the next section: a speech given in Karachi in February 1919 to the ninth annual meeting of the All-India Ayurvedic and Unani Tibbi Conference, Delhi; and two pamphlets written in English, *Memorandum of the Ayurvedic and Unani Tibbi Conference on Indigenous Systems of Medicine*, 1919, and *The Ayurvedic and Unani Systems of Medicine*, 1918.[25] While the speech was directed to indigenous practitioners in the first instance, the two pamphlets were aimed at the colonial establishment. At about the same time Ajmal Khan became more involved with nationalist politics emerging as one of its leaders in the 1920s.[26]

The second hakim, Kabir al Din, was a product of the Madrassa Tibbia (medical college)[27] of Hakim Ajmal Khan. Born in Shaikhpura, *zilla* (district) Monghyr in Bihar, he was educated first at home, then at Canning College in Lucknow and finally after studying with Mawlana Ahmad Hasan in Kanpur passed the Mawlawi examination.[28] In 1909 he joined the Madrassa Tibbia and received his *sanad* (certificate) in 1911; later on he also passed the highest Unani medical class of Lahore Islamia College receiving the title 'Zubdat al Hukama' (The Best of the Hakims). For most of his life he was employed by, or managed, Unani Medical Colleges throughout India.[29] He is better known, though, for the many medical books he produced. His command of English, Arabic, Persian and Urdu allowed him to play the key role in this area. The new Unani medical institutions experienced a dearth of textbooks, and Hakim Kabir al Din and the office he organised in 1916 translated source texts and published new books for *tibbi* colleges.[30] Kabir al Din favoured an 'integrated' vision of *tibb*: he was concerned to make available to hakims knowledge about biomedicine and biomedical technology.

In the 1920s provincial governments became involved in the management of the indigenous medicines, initially with the aim of supervising its education either through state-run schools and colleges or through regulated exams and qualifications. The Government of Madras convened the 'Uthman Committee in 1921 to inquire into indigenous medical systems. The replies of Hakim Kabir al Din to this committee's questionnaire were published in a booklet entitled *Tibb-i Qadim wa Jadid ki 'Ilmi Jang* (*The Scientific ('ilmi) War between Old and New Medicine*), 1922, one of the two texts by him I shall scrutinise in the next section.[31] It was the first time that a local government had initiated an inquiry headed by non-officials and the outcome was the creation of the School of Indian Medicine, Madras, covering Unani, Ayurveda and Siddha, in 1924.[32]

The second text by Kabir al Din, *Burhan* (*Demonstrated Proof*), 1935–37,[33] was a collection of articles written in reply to an accusation from an Indian member of the IMS that *tibb* was unscientific, and originally published in the *tibbi* journal *Al Tabib* from Lahore. For the hakim personally 1935 was a decisive year; he left his previous employment at the Ayurvedic and Unani Tibbia College, Delhi, and with two colleagues set up his own educational institution, Jami'a Tibbia.[34] For Unani medicine and its practitioners the 1930s were largely a period of frustration. In spite of government involvement there was no change in the position of hakims and their medical system. Biomedicine was still the official favourite in British India. In 1937 Hakim Kabir al Din left British India for the princely state of Hyderabad to work in the Nizamia Tibbia College and remained there until independence in 1947.

The third hakim under discussion, 'Abd al Latif 'Falsafi', belonged to the most prominent medical family of Lucknow, Uttar Pradesh, the 'Azizis. Educated at home, at Nadwat al Ulama and in Rampur by Mawlana Fazl Haqq Rampuri, he received his medical training from his family at Takmil al Tibb,[35] a medical institution that his father had founded in 1902. Aged 27 he was appointed as a teacher at the newly established Tibbia College within Aligarh Muslim University where he rose to become Principal. He participated in many committees related to indigenous medicines and health instituted by central as well as provincial governments and was on the boards of management of a number of *tibbi* institutions.[36] The medical tradition he inherited from his family was one concerned to keep *tibb* as 'pure' as possible; throughout his life he worked for the abolition of 'integrated' or mixed curricula in which biomedical topics were taught alongside *tibb*. This mixing, he felt, stifled the vitality of *tibb*, robbed it of its unique character and produced hakims ignorant of their own medicine.[37]

In 1950 he wrote the book *Tibb Awr Sa'ins (Medicine and Science (sa'ins))* from which I quoted at the beginning of this chapter. In 1948 the report of the Chopra Committee on the Indigenous Systems of Medicine had been made public, its main recommendation was that a synthesis between biomedicine and the indigenous systems was necessary, possible, and practicable even if time-consuming and difficult.[38] The central Ministry of Health was less keen to follow this route and after a long delay answered with counter-proposals and the suggestion for another committee.[39] Practitioners of Ayurveda and Unani *tibb* all over India were disappointed with their government's attitude. 'This is nothing but paving the way for gradual under-nourishment and ultimate ruin of the Indigenous systems ...'.[40] For Hakim 'Abd al Latif it was the continuation of policy instituted by the British.

> With the excuse to advance it [the indigenous medicines], they mixed it with modern sciences (*'ulum-i jadida*) in such a manner that slowly, slowly the mixture would be increased until the indigenous medicines were killed off by the hands of the *tabibs* [hakims] and Indians themselves.[41]

The hakim set out his views in *Tibb Awr Sa'ins* in return.

These six texts, *The Ayurvedic and Unani Systems of Medicine*, *Memorandum* and the speech by Hakim Ajmal Khan; *Tibb-i Qadim wa Jadid ki 'Ilmi Jang* and *Burhan* by Hakim Kabir al Din; and *Tibb Awr Sa'ins* by Hakim 'Abd al Latif, were written for different occasions as well as constituencies. Some were aimed at the colonial establishment, others at fellow hakims. The authors came from distinct *tibbi* cultures and in the next part I shall show that they grounded their defence of Unani medicine in their distinctive understanding of the medical tradition.

Defence of *tibb* as science

In their strategies of proving the scientific standing of Unani medicine, hakims responded to a series of statements made and threats posed by the biomedical and colonial establishment. Unani *tibb* was accused of not being a medical 'system', of being wrong, dogmatic, old, inflexible; of being only popular because it was cheap and its clients ignorant. Hakims faced also two dangers: that in reforming *tibb* they would turn it into a copy of biomedicine and the two medicines would become one; and that the drugs they considered part of their medicine would be divorced from it and official patronage would be given only to the former.[42] It was their concern to counter these points in their arguments.

The three hakims started from the premise that Unani *tibb* was a science. They set about defining science in separate ways. Hakim Ajmal Khan's definition was based on the notion of knowledge.

> Science means that portion of human knowledge, based on well-defined principles and laws, which possesses a method and a regulated system and clearly shows the inter-relation existing between its component parts.[43]

In as far as Unani *tibb* represented such 'classified and systematised human knowledge' it was a science.[44] This is the Islamic understanding of knowledge as science; in Arabic, Persian and Urdu the same word *'ilm* (pl. *'ulum*) is used to denote both. Islam traditionally considered knowledge as something sacred based on the concepts of unity and hierarchy. Knowledge was not considered to be random, but hierarchically classified and could be acquired through revelation and its subsequent transmission or through God-given intelligence.[45] Hakim Ajmal Khan saw science as the 'accumulated knowledge of centuries' relying on 'experiences of ages past' which, while it did not claim perfection, was striving towards it.[46]

Hakim 'Abd al Latif worded his definition slightly differently.

> Science means that thing whose foundations are based on the rules of science (*sa'ins*). Or that thing which is made according to the rules of science (*sa'ins*). The Arabic world for science (*sa'ins*) is *hikmat*. *Hikmat* is defined thus: it is that science/knowledge (*'ilm*) through which we can understand the real condition of the existing things/nature to the extent of human capabilities.[47]

He drew heavily on the Aristotelian division of the sciences and demonstrated the scientific standing of tibb by showing that, indeed, its foundation depended on different fields of science and that its basic rules were scientific.[48] The foundations of Uniani medicine he examined were physics, botany, zoology and chemistry while indicating that metaphysics, mathematics, geometry, asyrnomy and music also played a role.[49] He then demonstrated how various components of *tibb*, from elements and humours to anatomy and *materia medica* were scientific in themselves and contained modern understandings of medicine.[50] While his exposition of why *tibb* was scientific was done largely by drawing on concepts and principles inherent in it, Hakim 'Abd al Latif bowed, too, to the power of biomedicine and modern science, and aimed to show that modern discoveries were foreshadowed already in the texts of the ancients. In comparing Ajmal Khan's definition of science with that of 'Abd al Latif, it becomes clear that while the former saw science as a *way* of obtaining knowledge, the latter viewed science as a particular *form* of knowledge in itself.

The definition proffered by Hakim Kabir al Din was constructed differently from the above two. Postulating, in *'Ilmi Jang*, biomedicine as the 'system of medicine which they [doctors and scientists] call scientific (*sa'intifik*)', he stated that 'modern medicine is in reality an advanced version of Unani *tibb*, the shape and form of which has changed according to the necessities of time'. But if 'modern medicine is only a changed version of old medicine then how should a sensible person understand this statement that *Unani* tibb *is a savage and unscientific (ansa'intifik) form of medicine?*'[51] Kabir al Din reasoned that if biomedicine was a science then Unani medicine had to be one too. Throughout *'Ilmi Jang* he was concerned to highlight the similarities between the two medicines, looking in detail at causation of disease, diagnosis and treatment.

In *Burhan*, in contrast, he questioned the axiom that biomedicine was a science. Pointing to the fact that doctors had claimed the term science for biomedicine thirty or forty years earlier when their stock of knowledge had been much smaller, and still laid claim to it at the present time when their knowledge and theories had changed, sometimes even come to oppose the earlier ones, Kabir al Din asked:

> From which time and day onwards was modern medicine a science (*sa'ins*)? ... either the modern medicine of [that] period ... was a science (*sa'ins*) or that of today is. And if both periods are supposed to be science (*sa'ins*), then we should agree that old [Unani] medicine is also a science (*sa'ins*) although some of its problems have lost their basis through research in different periods.[52]

Hakim Kabir al Din contended that both old and new medicine were sciences which had been compiled or classified by human beings and were subject to their intellectual limitations.[53] While Hakims Ajmal Khan and 'Abd al Latif indicated the scientific quality of *tibb* through presenting its internal consistency, Hakim Kabir al Din took biomedicine as his scientific yardstick showing that either *tibb* measured up to its criteria and rhetoric or otherwise biomedicine fell short of them itself.

All the hakims had to take a stance on the central issue that distinguished Unani from biomedicine: humoral versus germ theory of disease causation. And all did so from within their intellectual traditions. Hakim 'Abd al Latif was concerned to point to the description of germs in the old Greek theories,[54] following the widespread strategy of re-interpreting old texts in the light of new discoveries. Like Hakim Kabir al Din he also outlined the resemblance of the two theories.[55] Kabir al Din elaborated on this similarity. Identifying the cause of illness as in both cases due to poisonous or corrupt material developing in the body, he contended that whether this corrupt matter (*fasid mawad*) came through disturbed humours or through special germs, the difference was only one of interpretation and language.[56] Applying a paradigmatic model he contrasted the hakim examining a patient on the basis that special matter (*makhsus mada*) had developed in the body with the doctor who examined the same patient within the framework of germ theory, he declared that the difference depended only on access to the microscope.[57] He also stressed a more pragmatic approach, identical with that of Ajmal Khan, who had said that 'whatever the value of a particular theory regarding the origin of a certain disorder', what mattered was that the actual treatment was effective and there Unani medicine had accumulated considerable experience.[58] Ajmal Khan chose to stress the values of observation, diagnosis and prognosis, and treatment over that of purely theoretical considerations.[59]

Apart from reflecting distinct intellectual traditions, these arguments were presented on occasions of very different kinds. Ajmal Khan was addressing the colonial establishment with the aim of receiving government support for the indigenous medical systems at a time when that had just been denied. His interest lay in emphasising the usefulness of indigenous medicine however this was achieved. Kabir al Din in *'Ilmi Jang* was addressing a government inquiry and thus underlined the similarity between *tibb* and biomedicine, which he took as the benchmark. In *Burhan*, when directing his remarks towards other practitioners he became much more iconoclastic in his rhetoric. 'Abd al Latif spoke to fellow hakims at a time when hakims felt pressurised not only by advocates of biomedicine but also by practitioners of Ayurveda who were claiming *tibb* as part of their own medical system.[60] It appears to have been important for him to stress the Greek roots of his medical system and therefore to locate the origins of germ theory in Greece in pre-Galenic times, thus claiming it for Unani medicine alone.

Another issue to confront was the methods that practitioners of the two medical systems employed for making science. Advocates of biomedicine claimed to be the only ones who produced their findings through experiments and research. Unani medicine, in their view, was based only on empiricism and unsubstantiated theories.[61] Both Hakims Kabir al Din and 'Abd al Latif went out of their way to disprove this pronouncement. Hakim 'Abd al Latif, trained in Aristotelian philosophy including metaphysics, questioned whether everything could be observed through experiments. How could they, the experts, understand 'the things which are beyond the circle of their senses' through either observation or mind and reason?[62] Things had causal properties that were hidden from direct observation, in addition to which God, in an Islamic understanding of the world, could intervene at any time to alter the behaviour of objects.[63]

Furthermore, mistakes could also be made in observation and experiment and not only in mental reasoning.[64] Indeed, 'Abd al Latif whose honorific was 'philosopher' (*falsafi*) and who was skilled in logic, felt that it was more likely that mistakes were made in the observation of things than in intellectual reasoning.[65] He rebuked sharply those who rejected the arts of logic and metaphysics. 'If someone calls the arts of logic (*mantiq*) or metaphysics (*hikmat-i ilahiyat*) unscientific (*ansa'intifik*), then that is only because their workings are outside of the laboratory.'[66] Hakim 'Abd al Latif's outlook was grounded in the classic Islamic cosmology in which the universe was not divided between natural and supernatural realms but was a unified hierarchy. For knowledge-claims consequently there was no natural/ supernatural divide which contained opposing systems of verification; knowledge-claims were joined in a single epistemology.[67]

Hakim Kabir al Din's refutation of the accusation that *tibb* was based only on intellectual reasoning followed another path. He showed that biomedical knowledge as a whole was not based on observation either. Premising his argument on the statement that Western medicine had throughout claimed to be a science,[68] he then questioned how it could have been a science when it was still in the process of development and not all its problems and theories had been researched. If, then, Western medicine was based on a mixture of observed and unobserved knowledge, what was the difference between it and Unani medicine, which also consisted of observed and unobserved knowledge.[69] If biomedicine as a medical science was itself not grounded purely in observation, what reason was there for *tibb* to be dismissed as unscientific if not all of its claims were based on observation. Kabir al Din found that yet again biomedicine did not live up to its own rhetoric.

The hakims recognised, too, that Unani *tibb* as a 'system' appeared less complete than biomedicine. Apart from noting gaps in anatomy and surgery in Unani medical education and practice which were to be remedied by incorporating the biomedical versions of these, Hakims Ajmal Khan and Kabir al Din recorded that what differentiated the two medicines was the use of scientific instruments in surgery and diagnosis. While conceding that instruments like the microscope allowed for a more detailed investigation regarding disease causation,[70] Kabir al Din, in 1922, countered that such detail had not always produced the expected results, and pointed to the biomedical failure to deal with the past influenza epidemic.[71] He also opposed the notion that biomedical technology eradicated mistakes in diagnosis; biomedical technology could be imprecise and lead to distorted findings.[72] He did not, however, want to reject them or their usage.[73] One of his agendas in publishing was to produce tracts in Urdu on biomedical technology like the thermometer and stethoscope to popularise their use among hakims. Hakim 'Abd al Latif was more concerned with the limitations of this obsession with technology as it obscured the bigger picture and prevented people from including logic and metaphysics in their thinking.[74] But the adoption of scientific instruments by hakims was not to imply that the difference between the two medicines would be eradicated and they would become one.[75] Biomedical technology, like the subjects of anatomy and surgery, was regarded as a neutral tool that could be integrated into Unani medicine if necessary.

Basing his argument on the idea of one underlying reality Hakim 'Abd al Latif pointed to the mental conditioning of a person to explain why those trained in the Western sciences regarded *tibb* as unscientific. He saw language, culture, the arts and sciences as influenced by religion, community, mental discipline and upbringing.[76] Someone who had been educated in one system of learning and had become familiar with its arts and sciences would be unable to follow or understand concepts and ideas based on another structure. '[P]roblems of the English type are difficult to follow for those educated as *mawlwis* [and] *pandits* in Arabic and Hindi. And equally the problems of Arabic or Hindi style are very hard for those educated in English or born outside this country.'[77] He saw this as a law of nature according to which misunderstandings and conflicts between people were common. That was why one and the same truth/reality expressed in two different languages and framed in their different theoretical contexts, could be represented by two statements, east and west, isolated from one another.[78] While reality was conceived of as one, there were no neutral tools with which to translate it. The conversion into thoughts and speech determined the way a problem or fact was integrated and understood. It was therefore difficult to find somebody to judge what was truth and what was not since the decision depended on the mental framework of a person outside of which he could not step. In writing about *tibb* and science Hakim 'Abd al Latif knew that he was equally imprisoned by mental discipline, customs, habits and nature, realising that he could appraise the issue only from within his own knowledge-structures.[79]

Disputing the claims of biomedicine

In the process of validating *tibb* as a science the hakims questioned the claims of biomedicine and the values which accompanied it. Their criticism struck at a number of issues. The main contention they challenged was that there could only be one universally applicable, culturally neutral medical system in the world.[80] For once they themselves had been exponents of a medical tradition that through its holistic premise and adaptation to local circumstances could claim to be a universally valid system within the Islamic world which was distinct from bio-medicine. The point most widely agreed on by hakims and their supporters was that Unani *tibb* was better suited to the Indian body, temperament, country and climate. This was so because of the accumulated experience of the hakims but also because of the *materia medica* they used. In pointing out that 'the results of observations made in cold climates and the treatment provided for specific and chronic cases often prove wide of the mark in tropical climates', they referred to their *materia medica* which was not only better suited to 'tropical habits' but also readily available in the country and thus cheaper and fresher.[81] Both Hakims Kabir al Din and Ajmal Khan regarded their drugs and knowledge about them not as free-standing but as firmly grounded in their medicine.[82]

Western drugs were seen as too strong or pure and too poisonous; they brought about 'quick results' but could also cause much harm. Unani *tibb* eschewed fast action in favour of a slow improvement of the patient that brought about fewer side-effects.[83] Kabir al Din contrasted the 'Easternness' of *tibb* with the 'Western grace' which was firmly attached to biomedicine in spite of all the drugs, inventions and other useful things from foreign countries it was absorbing into its system.[84]

Biomedicine appeared to the hakims to be too fickle in its views too. Hakim Ajmal Khan referred to 'the crop of conflicting theories that seem to be the pride of the Western systems'.[85] This was especially so, as biomedicine claimed to be completely based on observation, as its pronouncements were to be a true account of nature. 'If all the problems of modern medicine have been tested through research and observation, then why do its scientific (*sa'intifik*) theories keep changing everyday?'[86] While Kabir al Din acknowledged that a lively scientific discussion and a rapid change in the problems and contents of the sciences were a sign of their flourishing,[87] he mocked the doctors practising in India.

> In the port of Bombay a big bundle of new books arrives … and from that moment onwards the doctors have changed their faith and creed. They have no need for research or thinking and contemplation [of their own], nor have they time to think about what the earlier books had written and why it has been changed.[88]

If the Sahib Bahadur (esteemed master) of Europe said something then all believed it. And if he changed his mind, then that was accepted without question too. 'If the indigenous *tabibs* (practitioners of Unani medicine) had had such type of faith and belief in the statements of the former hakims then we would have called them ignorant, prejudiced and short sighted.'[89] However, as fluid theories were a hallmark of biomedicine, the hakims demonstrated that theories within Unani medicine had changed over time too. Listing, for instance, the opposing ideas of Hippocrates, Galen, Ibn Sina, Razi and Mulla Nafis, Kabir al Din underlined that different opinions had been dominant at various times.[90]

At the heart of all these arguments was a different understanding of science and knowledge from that employed by Europeans about Western science in the nineteenth and twentieth centuries. For all the hakims science was accumulated knowledge based on experience and observation. Knowledge was added in order to advance it; it was a catalogue of pieces of information acquired through experience and observation, the classic Aristotelian framework for natural philosophy but within an Islamic context. Facts and theories were derived from such accumulated universal experiences that were acquired in daily life. The basic principles of *tibb* were given and were not for the hakim to prove or disprove. As Ibn Sina had stated:

> The physician must follow the fundamental principles, for they are taken for granted in the secondary sciences [of which medicine was one]. It is only in the primary sciences, called Metaphysics, that they can be reasoned out.[91]

Based on this world view, the strategy of the hakims for turning *tibb* into a similar science was to incorporate into it those pieces of information or those technological devises and techniques which appeared to be missing, for instance, anatomy, surgery, the microscope, the laboratory. It was for the hakims a simple matter of the acquisition of new knowledge rather than a cognitive shift from founding knowledge on experience to experiment (for which the same term '*tajriba*' is used in Urdu and Persian making a distinction between them impossible), from grounding facts in universals and commonality to discrete singular events and from proving theories through Aristotelian-scholastic rhetoric to marshalling matters of fact in their defence.

As these two intellectual traditions disputed the scientific standing of each other's knowledge-practices, the criticism that emerged was two-way albeit tempered by the unequal power relationship between the two. The hakims found that the knowledge produced by biomedical doctors lacked certainty. Their own knowledge was based on the authoritative texts of the ancients, and on accumulated but not singular or historically situated experiences. Nature, in its regularity, could be observed through the senses. But since objects had hidden properties, discrete events could neither be understood through observation alone nor offer secure foundations for knowledge. As biomedical knowledge possessed less certitude, hakims also disputed the notion that it was moving towards an ever closer, ever truer account of nature.

Power, knowledge and science

There was, therefore, a clash between ideas of what constituted science and knowledge and what were the proper authorities to consult in the quest to interpret nature. The Western science that the hakims encountered was grounded in the idea of progressiveness, of moving towards a better understanding of and closer fit with nature. The hakims themselves regarded the knowledge of the past as more true because it was closer in time to when it had been revealed by God. The further that knowledge moved away from revelation the greater the possibility that it would be corrupted during its transmission.[92] Therefore Hakim 'Abd al Latif tried to prove that *tibb* was a science through re-interpreting the texts of the ancients to suit modern discoveries. Thus Hakims Ajmal Khan and Kabir al Din, also, tried to combine the two notions of science by stating that no progressive science could call itself perfect or complete. But they still strove to complete or perfect *tibb* through the integration into it of instruments and subjects from biomedicine. Hence all wondered how biomedicine was a science if it kept on changing and developing. Hakims were grappling with the mutability of biomedical knowledge and the shifting content of science.

In their defence of *tibb* as science hakims shared modes of argument with those of other indigenous medical practitioners. They worked from within the 'ideology of decline' that stated that once Unani medicine had been great but had come to stagnate and needed to be revived to regain its former height. This ideology had been inculcated into all practitioners of indigenous medicine by British orientalists in the nineteenth century and provided the ideological framework for the medical revivalism of that century.[93] In its sentiment it mirrored the nationalist ideology which was forming at the same time.[94] The 'culture of medical decline' generated two polar revivalist strategies: that of integrating *tibb* with biomedicine and producing a system superior to both and that of keeping *tibb* pure and reviving it from within. Representatives of the two traditions were concerned to prove the scientific standing of *tibb* and did so by both drawing on a pool of culturally shared symbols, but also by using methods distinct to Unani *tibb*.

What was disputed was who had the authority to decide what was a science. In the *Memorandum* of 1919 Hakim Ajmal Khan went to the heart of this predicament when he commented that 'if the expression "Medical Science" is taken to imply "the system of medicine prevalent in the West at present" then the application of the definition to the indigenous systems may be doubted.'[95] The monopoly of power which biomedicine commanded forced other medical systems to prove themselves in its light. This was clearly visible in the many quotes from European scientists, doctors and encyclopaedias that the hakims interspersed in their writings in their attempts to use Western scientific authorities to prove *tibb* to be a science.[96] It was also illustrated by the fact that, regardless of whether hakims were concerned to reform their medical system from within, as was Hakim 'Abd al Latif, or without, as were Hakims Ajmal Khan and Kabir al Din, the benchmark for what they wanted to achieve was provided by biomedicine.

It was because of the hakims' intense engagement with biomedicine that they criticised some of its statements and those related to science more generally. Some of their arguments advanced points which were discussed at the time within the Western philosophical establishment and were later to be put forward by those involved in science studies, albeit from a different perspective. There was the refusal to accept biomedicine as the only true and universal medical system since Unani *tibb* provided better treatment for Indians through its centuries-long adaptation to country and climate. There was the refusal to see biomedicine as providing an ever truer account of nature since its theories, but also the knowledge produced through direct observation kept changing rapidly. Hakim Kabir al Din pointed to recent changes in anatomical knowledge and questioned the supposed congruence of biomedicine and nature.[97]

There was also the point made by both Hakims Kabir al Din and 'Abd al Latif that language acted as a filter which distorted what was seen and could thus produce two different or opposing statements. Hakim and doctor saw different things when they examined a patient. Hakim 'Abd al Latif, in 1950, explained how different intellectual conditioning created people belonging to different intellectual communities unable to accept each other's knowledge and science as valid. He foreshadowed Thomas Kuhn's theory of incommensurability between people belonging to different scientific paradigms and language communities.[98]

Hakims looking at biomedicine from the outside from an inferior position in the power-game but one grounded in a strong sense of the history and achievements of their medicine, unpicked its rhetoric of positivism, value-neutrality and universality and highlighted its construction in Europe by Europeans. Comparing the reliance on human observation and experiment in biomedical knowledge-production with the authority accorded to the texts of the ancients in Unani medicine, they felt that their knowledge was much more certain.

Acknowledgements

Earlier versions of this paper were presented at the Autumn Conference, Society for the Social History of Medicine, University of Southampton, September 1998, and the Research Seminar, Medical Science and Technology in Asian Cultures, Wellcome Institute for the History of Medicine, November 1998. I would like to thank Dr Sabiha Anwar, Lucknow, for help with the translation of the texts. I am grateful to Peregrine Horden, Rob Iliffe and Andrew Warwick for advice on science studies literature and to Francis Robinson for commenting on the whole paper. This article was written as part of a larger research project on the 'Practice of Unani Medicine in India, 1850 to 1950' funded by the Wellcome Trust (grant no. 043041).

Notes

1 'Abd al Latif, *Tibb Awr Sa'ins*, Aligarh, National Printers Committee, 1950, p. 2.
2 Ibid, pp. 4, 6.
3 The term 'medical system' is used here in the sense in which it was employed in the South Asian colonial context where officials and practitioners talked of the 'Western system of medicine' and the 'indigeneous' or 'Indian systems of medicine'. Unani medical knowledge had been 'systematised', classified and structured at various stages of its development, for instance by Galen and Ibn Sina (980–1037 CE). While Unani medical knowledge was internally consistent, its country-wide 'systematisation' or standardisation became only possible through the infra-

structure provided by the state in the twentieth century. Crucial to efforts to standardise *tibb* were the foundation of the Central Council for Research in Indian Medicine and Homoeopathy (1969) and the Central Council for Research in Unani Medicine (1978). For a discussion of 'medical systems' in the Asian context see C. Leslie (ed.), *Asian Medical Systems: A Comparative Study*, Delhi, Motilal Banarsidass Publishers, 1998 (1st Indian edition), pp. 9–11.

4   The term 'biomedicine' gained wider currency only in the post-World War II period.

5   What Habermas has called 'scientism', the ideology that science is no longer one form of possible knowledge, but that knowledge has to be identified with science. See: J. Habermas, *Knowledge and Human Interests*, Cambridge, Polity Press, 1986, p. 4.

6   S. Shapin and S. Schaffer, *Leviathan and the Air-Pump: Hobbes, Boyle, and the Experimental Life*, Princeton, Princeton University Press, 1985, pp. 110–54.

7   Ibid, pp. 22–79.

8   M. Poovey, *A History of the Modern Fact: Problems of Knowledge in the Sciences of Wealth and Society*, Chicago and London, University of Chicago Press, 1998, p. 10.

9   P. Dear, *Discipline & Experience: The Mathematical Way in the Scientific Revolution*, Chicago and London, University of Chicago Press, 1995, pp. 11–62.

10   For a counter-argument see: S. Shapin, *The Scientific Revolution*, London and Chicago, University of Chicago Press, 1996; for a deconstruction of the term 'the scientific revolution' see especially pp. 1–4.

11   See, for instance, Dear, *Discipline and Experience* and Shapin and Schaffer, *Leviathan and the Air-Pump*.

12   Disputes continued to occur within the same culture or country, of course. See, for instance, the conflict over the meaning, methods and contents of science in the debate between evolutionists and creationists in nineteenth- and twentieth-century North America and Europe. E. Barker, 'In the beginning: the battle of creationist science against evolution', R. Wallis (ed.), *On the Margins of Science: The Social Construction of Rejected Knowledge*, Keele, Monographs of the Sociological Review 27, 1979, pp. 179–200; R.L. Numbers, 'The creationists', in D.C. Lindberg and R.L. Numbers (eds), *God and Nature: Historical Essays on the Encounter between Christianity and Science*, Berkeley, Los Angeles, London, University of California Press, 1986, pp. 391–423; R.L. Numbers, *The Creationists: The Evolution of Scientific Creationism*, Berkeley, Los Angeles, London, University of California Press, 1993. I would like to thank Rob Iliffe for suggesting the comparison between the issue of science in Unani *tibb* and that in creationism.

13   Literature on this area is growing quite fast. See, for instance, D. Kumar, *Science and Empire: Essays in Indian Context 1700–1947*, Delhi, Anamika Prakashan, and National Institute of Science, Technology, and Development, 1991; and also his: *Science and the Raj, 1857–1905*, Delhi, Oxford University Press, 1995; S. Goonatilake, *Aborted Discovery: Science and Creativity in the Third World*, London, Zed Books, 1984; L. Brockway, *Science and Colonial Expansion: The Role of the British Royal Botanical Gardens*, New York, Academic Press, 1979; and for an overview: S. Harding, *Is Science Multicultural? Postcolonialisms, Feminisms, and Epistemologies*, Bloomington and Indianapolis, Indiana University Press, 1998.

14   See A. Hameed and A. Bari, 'Impact of Ibn Sina's medical works in India', *Studies in History of Medicine*, 8, 1 & 2 (1984): 1–12.

15   The exception to this rule was policy to do with epidemics that required India-wide coordination.

16   *A Note on Chopra Committee's Report on Indigenous Medicine* by Dr. K.C.K.E. Raja, Director General of Health Services (1949), p. 1, in 'Report of Government of India Committee on Indigenous Systems of Medicine (Chopra Committee)', File 1105/1949, Medical (B) Department, Uttar Pradesh State Archives [UPSA].

17   J. Majeed, 'Nature, hyperbole and the colonial state: some Muslim appropriations of European modernity in late nineteenth-century Urdu literature', in J. Cooper, R.L. Nettler, M. Mahmoud (eds), *Islam and Modernity: Muslim Intellectuals Respond*, London and New York, I.B. Tauris, 1997, p. 25.

18   B. Good, *The Heart of What's the Matter. The Structure of Medical Discourse in a Provincial Iranian Town*, PhD thesis, Department of Anthropology, University of Chicago, 1977; B. Good and M.-J. DelVecchio Good, 'The comparative study of Greco-Islamic medicine: the integration of

medical knowledge into local symbolic contexts', in C. Leslie and A. Young (eds), *Paths to Asian Medical Knowledge*, Berkeley, Oxford, University of California Press, 1992, pp. 257–71.

19 B.D. Metcalf, 'Nationalist Muslims in British India: The Case of Hakim Ajmal Khan', *Modern Asian Studies*, 19, 1 (1985): 1–28.

20 Systematised educational institutions were being set up in the second half of the nineteenth century. See: B.D. Metcalf, 'The madrasa at Deoband: a model for religious education in modern India', *Modern Asian Studies*, 12, 1 (1978): 111–34; and D. Lelyveld, *Aligarh's First Generation: Muslim Solidarity in British India*, Princeton, Princeton University Press, 1978.

21 The name translates as 'College of Medicine'.

22 Although opponents claimed the contrary. See Z. Rahman, *Tazkira Khandan-i 'Azizi*, Aligarh, Litho Colour Printers, 1978, pp. 249, 255.

23 Home/Medical proceedings, July 1916, A, 38–50, National Archives of India [NAI]. The mover of the resolution, Khan Bahadur Mir Asad Ali Khan, was concerned to point out that: 'By a scientific basis is meant that the ancient systems which through long neglect and consequent deterioration became rusty, should be so improved as to possess the advantages of the modern system, and brought up to date in the light of recent scientific researches. It must not, however, be understood that the ancient systems are unscientific.' They could be said to be 'less scientific'. Summaries of Proceedings of Indian Legislative Council on 15 March 1916, in ibid.

24 Home/Medical proceedings, July 1919, A, 26–51, progs 41, p 127, NAI.

25 *Presidential Address*, 1919 Karachi session of All-India Ayurvedic and Unani Tibbi Conference, Delhi, in Appendix to Notes, p. 24, Home/Medical proceedings, July 1919, A, 26–51, NAI; *Memorandum* of the Ayurvedic and Unani Tibbi Conference on indigenous systems of medicine, printed and published by the Standing Committee of the Conference, 1919; *The Ayurvedic and Unani Systems of Medicine*, published by Board of Trustees of the Ayurvedic and Unani Tibbi College, Delhi, National Printing Works, Delhi, 1918.

The *Memorandum* borrows heavily from the earlier pamphlet *Ayurvedic and Unani Systems of Medicine*. Hakim Ajmal Khan was the leading figure behind both the Standing Committee of the Conference and the Board of Trustees of the Tibbi College and although he signed only the *Memorandum*, his authorship of *Ayurvedic and Unani Systems of Medicine* is undisputed.

26 This was symbolised, for instance, by the opening of the Ayurvedic and Unani Tibbia College by M.K. Gandhi in 1921, while the Viceroy, Lord Hardinge, had laid the foundation stone in 1916.

27 The Mawlawi exam was a stage in the *Dars-I Nizami*, the *madrassa* curriculum developed by Firangi Mahal, Lucknow's premier family of scholars and teachers. It came to be endorsed by the University of Lucknow in the period after World War I.

28 The Mawlawi Examination is an educational qualification in Arabic issued by a number of universities in India.

29 T. Siddiqi, 'Zubdat al-Hukama' 'Allama Hakim Kabiruddin', *Studies in History of Medicine*, 5, 1 (1981): 87–9; Z. Rahman, *Dilli Awr Tibb-i Unani*, Delhi, Urdu Academy, 1995, pp. 319–22.

30 Unani medicine came to be taught in the vernacular rather than in Arabic in the first half of the twentieth century.

31 Kabir al Din, *Tibb-i Qadim wa Jadid ki 'Ilmi Jang*, Delhi, 1935 (3rd edn).

32 G.J. Hausman, 'Siddhars, alchemy and the abyss of tradition: 'traditional' tamil medical knowledge in 'modern' practice', unpublished PhD thesis, University of Michigan, 1996, pp. 203–52.

33 Kabir al Din, *Burhan*, Delhi, Daftar al Masih 1937.

34 The name translates as 'Collection of Medicine'.

35 The name translates as 'Perfection of Medicine'.

36 Rahman, *Khandan-i 'Azizi*, pp. 402–4, 408.

37 Ibid, p. 405.

38 *Report of the Committee on Indigenous Systems of Medicine*, Vols. 1 and 2, published by the Ministry of Health, Government of India, 1948; and 'Report of Government of India Committee on Indigenous Systems of Medicine (Chopra Committee)', File 1105/1949, Medical (B) Department, UPSA.

74   *Claudia Liebeskind*

39   Letter from Undersecretary to the Government of India, Ministry of Health, 9 November 1949, F.28–I/49–M.I., p. 2, File 1105/1949, Medical (B) Department, UPSA.

40   *Reflections on the Chopra Committee on the Indigenous Systems of Medicine and the Subversive Decisions of the Government*, (by Ayurveda Sevak Sangha, Contai, Midnapur, W. Bengal) p. vi, File 1105/49, Medical (B) Department, UPSA.

41   Latif, *Tibb Awr Sa'ins*, p. 6.

42   Since 1895 one or other committee on both the central and provincial levels had been convened to inquire into the usefulness of indigenous drugs and how to exploit them. Apart from committees the Government of India had delegated this task to individual doctors and to the New Tropical School of Medicine in Calcutta. In 1920 the Board of Scientific Advice suggested to the Department of Agriculture and Revenue that they should establish a Drugs Manufacture Committee. See Home/Medical proceedings, December 1895, A, 15–18; May 1914, A, 25–28; July 1920, A, 89–91, NAI; and Hausman, 'Abyss of Tradition', pp. 146–91.

43   Khan, *Presidential Address*. For a longer version see: Khan, *Memorandum*, p. 7.

44   Khan, *Presidential Address*. This comes close to the definition of 'science' used in dictionaries of the period. See also Numbers, *Scientific Creationism*, pp. 50–3.

45   S.H. Nasr, *Islamic Science*, Westerham, World of Islam Festival, 1976, pp. 3–17. See also O. Barkar, *Classification of Knowledge in Islam*, Cambridge, Islamic Texts Society, 1998.

46   Khan, *Ayurvedic and Unani Systems of Medicine*, p. 7; *Memorandum*, p. 7.

47   Latif, *Tibb Awr Sa'ins*, p. 8.

48   Ibid, pp. 42, 55.

49   Ibid, pp. 13–37.

50   Ibid, pp. 55–76.

51   Emphasis in original. Din, *'Ilmi Jang*, pp. 3, 6.

52   Din, *Burhan*, pp. 32, 42–3.

53   Ibid, p. 33.

54   Which, according to him, had been advanced in the period between Aristotle and Galen. See Latif, *Tibb Awr Sa'ins*, p. 60.

55   Ibid, p. 59; Din, *'Ilmi Jang*, pp. 6–10.

56   Din, *'Ilmi Jang*, pp. 6, 8.

57   Ibid, p. 8. Realising the importance of germs as contributors to illnesses, Hakim Kabir al Din asked: '[i]f our *tibb* is called savage today because of its ignorance of the presence of germs, then … if tomorrow the presence of germs is proven in a new illness through new research, will you also call today's [modern] medicine savage?' Ibid, p. 13.

58   Khan, *Memorandum*, p. 7, and *Presidential Address*; Din, *'Ilmi Jang*, p. 8.

59   Khan, *The Ayurvedic and Unani Systems*, p. 7; Khan, *Memorandum*, p. 7; Khan, *Presidential Address*.

60   After 1947 hakims and Unani *tibb* suffered from the after-effects of partition. In the state administration of Uttar Pradesh, for instance, all the indigenous medicines were grouped together under the label 'Ayurveda'.

61   Din, *Burhan*, pp. 14–21; Home/Medical proceedings, July 1919, A, 26–51, NAI, for responses from the different provinces of British India.

62   Latif, *Tibb Awr Sa'ins*, p. 41.

63   For similar views in Europe see: P. Dear, 'Miracles, experiments, and the ordinary course of nature', *Isis*, 81 (1990): 663–83; L. Daston, 'Marvellous facts and miraculous evidence in early modern Europe', *Critical Inquiry*, 18 (1991): 93–124.

64   Latif, *Tibb Awr Sa'ins*, p. 42.

65   Ibid, pp. 78–81.

66   Ibid, p. 13.

67   B. Good and M.-J. DelVecchio Good, 'The comparative study of Greco-Islamic medicine: the integration of medical knowledge into local symbolic contexts', in C. Leslie and A. Young (eds), *Paths to Asian Medical Knowledge*, Berkeley, Los Angeles, Oxford, University of California Press, 1992, p. 260.

68   Din, *Burhan*, p. 33.

69   Ibid, p. 34. The style of the argument he employed rested on Aristotelian-scholastic rhetoric.

70 Din, *'Ilmi Jang*, pp. 8–10.

71 Ibid, p. 9. Viruses had then not been discovered.

72 Ibid, p. 17. If used in an undisciplined manner they could lead to distorted findings, see Latif, *Tibb Awr Sa'ins*, p. 78; and also G. Gooday, '"Nature" in the laboratory: domestication and discipline with the microscope in Victorian life science', *British Journal of the History of Science*, 24 (1991): 307–41.

73 Din, *'Ilmi Jang*, p. 18.

74 Latif, *Tibb Awr Sa'ins*, p. 13.

75 Din, *'Ilmi Jang*, p. 18.

76 Latif, *Tibb Awr Sa'ins*, p. 2.

77 Ibid, p. 3.

78 Ibid, p. 4.

79 Ibid, p. 7.

80 As J. Hullah, Officiating Departmental Secretary to the Government of India, Home Department, had elaborated in 1918: '[T]he cardinal fact [is] that there is, and can be, only one system of medicine, that is, the sum total of human knowledge of the subject, acquired by scientific research and discovery. It is neither of the east nor of the west; it is world-wide in its origin and growth and should be world-wide in its application'. Notes, Home/Medical proceedings, July 1919, A, 26–51, NAI.

81 Khan, *Memorandum*, p. 10; Din, *'Ilmi Jang*, pp. 30–4, 47–8. This is a point that was made very widely and very often by all practitioners of the indigenous medicines.

82 Khan, *Presidential Address*; Din, *'Ilmi Jang*, p. 18.

83 Din, *'Ilmi Jang*, pp. 33–4.

84 Ibid, p. 18.

85 Khan, *The Ayurvedic and Unani Systems*, p. 7.

86 Din, *Burhan*, p. 33.

87 Ibid, p. 35.

88 Ibid, p. 37.

89 Ibid, pp. 44–5.

90 Ibid, pp. 35–6; Din, *'Ilmi Jang*, p. 19; Latif, *Tibb Awr Sa'ins*, pp. 14–36, 38–41.

91 Ibn Sina, *Al-Qanun fi'l-Tibb*, Book I, English translation, Jamia Hamdard, New Delhi, 1993, p. 4. Compare to Aristotle's dictum that no science demonstrates its own principles.

92 F. Robinson, 'Knowledge, its transmission and the making of Muslim societies', in F. Robinson (ed.), *Cambridge Illustrated History of the Islamic World*, Cambridge, Cambridge University Press, 1996, pp. 208–49.

93 C. Leslie, 'The professionalizing ideology of medical revivalism', in M. Singer (ed.), *Entrepreneurship and Modernization of Occupational Cultures in South Asia*, North Carolina, Duke University: Monograph and Occasional Papers Series: Monograph 12, 1973, pp. 222–30.

94 For the impact of the orientalist vision on history-writing and understandings of the past more generally, see P. Chatterjee, *The Nation and Its Fragments: Colonial and Postcolonial Histories*, Princeton, Princeton University Press, 1993, esp. pp. 76–115.

95 Khan, *Memorandum*, p. 7. For a similar view see Latif, *Tibb Awr Sa'ins*, p. 76.

96 Din, *Burhan*, pp. 37–8, 39–40, 60, etc.; Latif, *Tibb Awr Sa'ins*, pp. 82–7.

97 Din, *Burhan*, pp. 37–8, 39–44.

98 T.S. Kuhn, *The Structure of Scientific Revolutions*, Chicago and London, University of Chicago Press, 1996 (3rd edn), pp. 111–35, 144–59, 198–204. See also B. Good, *Medicine, Rationality and Experience: An Anthropological Perspective*, Cambridge, Cambridge University Press, 1990.

5 Categorising 'African medicine'

The German discourse on East African healing practices, 1885–1918

Walter Bruchhausen and Volker Roelcke

As various contributions in this volume demonstrate, pluralism is a characteristic of medical practices in most societies, in India as well as in Southern Africa, in the USA and in New Zealand. Frequently, plurality in medicine is accompanied by the development of stereotypical images of the competing practitioners and groups, or medical traditions. These images are part of the public discourse, and may also be constitutive for the self-image of practitioners and their clientele. Yet little is known about how such images of 'other' medicine emerge. On what conceptual resources do the relevant descriptions draw? From where do they take their points of reference, their metaphors and their terminology? This chapter intends to investigate these questions with regard to the German encounter with the medical traditions of East Africa.

The German experience of colonialism, from 1891 to 1916, was short in comparison to that of the Dutch, British, French, Spanish and Portuguese, but it flourished during the very same period when modern scientific medicine emerged as a dominating force. The German administration brought this new type of medicine to East Africa where mainly indigenous modes of healing were used by the local populations. Nowadays, the practice of 'African medicine' is regarded by many as a valuable legacy of the past, as something that remains intrinsically 'African' and 'traditional', and therefore warrants preservation. A speaker from the Medical Faculty in Dar es Salaam, for example, recently confirmed in a talk: 'I feel there is a cultural heritage, something which shows our identity. A heritage of authentic traditional medicine which will be an alternative to Western scientific medicine in the same way as traditional Chinese medicine, Ayurveda, and homoeopathy.'[1] Other contributions in this volume deal with the assumed authenticity of traditional Chinese medicine and homoeopathy. Concerning traditional African medicine, as the quoted Tanzanian professor would also admit and probably lament, many of the categories and paradigms that are used to explain its specifically 'African' and 'traditional' nature are in fact 'European'. They are the result of political and scientific developments, ethnographic and psychological approaches, administrative activities and, last but not least, controversies about orthodox and heterodox medicine in Europe. It will be argued here that 'African medicine' as represented at specialist meetings as well as in publications aimed at the wider public is understood mainly in reference to European ideas, practices and institutions.[2] This (re-)definition of African healing practices in Western terms emerged in the territories of modern mainland Tanzania, Rwanda and Burundi during German colonial rule, from the Berlin Conference of 1884–5 up to World War I.

Colonial policy and indigenous medicine

Europeans have not always been hostile to other peoples' healing methods. Studies of colonial medicine in South America and Asia show that Europeans frequently relied on local medicine – if sometimes out of necessity.[3] This was also the case in Africa before 1850. Local pharmaceuticals became part of medical practices of Europeans, as in the case of remote Boer communities. African practitioners were consulted even in places close to European medical institutions, as by the Portuguese of Mozambique.[4] Until the mid-nineteenth century, displacement of indigenous medicine was not necessarily the intention of European doctors travelling in Africa. Livingstone's often-quoted recommendation to his colleague Dr. John Kirk in 1860 was to respect the local healers and to let them have their patients:

> They possess medical men among themselves who are generally the most observant people to be met with. It is desirable to be at all times on good terms with them. In order to do this, slight complaints, except among the very poor ought to be referred to their care, and severe cases before being undertaken should be enquired into of the doctor himself and no disparaging remark ever made on the previous treatment in the presence of the patient.[5]

However, political and military conflicts concerning the new African colonies, both in Europe and in Africa, increasing numbers of Europeans in Africa,[6] and professional as well as scientific developments in European medicine, led to a change in this accommodating attitude.[7] The study of anthropological writing,[8] of travel reports,[9] as well as of novels[10] demonstrates that, by the late nineteenth century, the representation of the 'African negro' in popular and academic literature had become much more negative than in earlier (and, arguably, later[11]) periods.[12] Africans were represented as 'cruel', 'stupid' and 'uncivilised'. Such stereotypical images were taken to justify the hardships that Europeans as well as Africans had to endure in the name of progress and civilisation. Alternatively, they were taken as proof of Africans' unworthiness of European attention. The assessment of indigenous medicine by Germans tended to fluctuate between these two approaches.[13]

Perceptions of 'African medicine' in Germany were particularly negative in the first decade of German colonial activity, following the partition of Africa by the Berlin conference of 1884–5. The medical doctor Max Buchner (1846–1921), first interim Imperial Commissioner in Cameroon and, after his return, vociferous sceptic of colonialism,[14] accused natives and their healers[15] of irrational thinking, noxious therapies and fraudulent practice in a generalising article on 'The Medicine of the Negroes' published in 1886 in one of the major medical journals in

Germany.[16] He saw 'the negro's' lack of interest in systematic causal explanation as being founded on a 'simple, most natural philosophy'. In Buchner's view there was not much to be expected from medicinal herbs used by Africans. He did concede though that 'the negro's ... talent barely places him lower than the average crude European'.

Wilhelm Steuber (1862–1941), one of the first military medical officers (1889–93) and later director of the health services in German East Africa (1901–3), had a similarly low opinion of African native medicine, using 'medical profession' and 'medical care' in relation to local medicine in quotation marks only.[17] He, too, compared native healers, whom he labelled as 'sorcerers' and 'fetish priests' (without quotation marks) to what were, in Germany, considered to be 'quacks'. Although Steuber intended to displace African healing by science and named his job 'medical cultivation',[18] he had no qualms about making use of Africans' alleged gullibility when he prescribed what would be considered by scientific medicine as mere 'placebos': effervescent powder and cognac.[19] Steuber called traditional healers 'riffraff' and 'parasites' and held them responsible for the high infant mortality rates. His attacks on African healers were not restricted to verbal abuse. During a vaccination campaign Steuber not only pulled down the insignia ('feathers, skins and the other rags') of a mganga[20] who opposed the European doctor's visit, but also beat him and his assistants ('the black scoundrels') with the hippo whip.[21]

Remarks such as those by Buchner and Steuber were primarily the result of their personal preconceptions. They cannot necessarily be taken as representative of a general attitude amongst German doctors. Yet there exist hardly any other writings on indigenous medicine before 1895 from which people at home could come to an alternative assessment of the situation in the colonies. [22] In fact, the scarcity of other sources is indicative of a lack of intellectual interest and material incentives for systematic research into indigenous medicine on the part of German doctors and the German governments in Dar es Salaam and Berlin alike. A notable exception is Dr Alexander Becker, Senior Staff Surgeon and Chief Medical Officer of the troops in East Africa (1891–1900).[23] He demonstrated an official interest in indigenous healing, even in practices then shunned by modern scientific medicine, such as the invocation of the devil in the treatment of lunatics.

On the whole, however, interest in indigenous medical practice remained generally low throughout the imperial period. This contrasts with the importance attributed to the study of native law which was applied by German district officers in collaboration with local authorities at the so called shauri.[24] In contrast to African medicine, studies on African law figure highly in ethnographies.

Official research into poisons, drugs and native life

One area of research in African medicine was of considerable interest to the Imperial Health Office, however: the investigation of local poisons and remedies. Before the era of Salvarsan and the Sulpha drugs, preparations of plants still constituted a major part of European pharmacopoeia: a keen interest in potential new drugs could only be expected. A case in point is that of Professor Ludwig

Brieger (1849–1919), the Director of the Department for Hydrotherapy at the Royal University Hospital in Berlin, the Charité. Brieger had collections of medicinal plants and of poisons and their antidotes sent from the colonies. He also procured additional research funding for his assistant, Dr. Max Krause, from the Colonial Department of the Foreign Office.[25] The research aims were, of course, wholly Euro-centric. Brieger and Krause hoped to find remedies against poisoned arrows and snake bites, and new drugs against the diseases from which Europeans suffered in the colonies. Despite disappointing results, Brieger and Krause and, with them, scientists from the Imperial Health Office, still managed to attract further funding. They stressed that:

> Experience shows that the primitive people (Naturvölker) distinguish poisonous and non-poisonous plants with a high degree of certainty; they detect the therapeutic effects of both and know how to use them. We owe many important drugs of our pharmacopoeia to the medicine men of the primitive peoples; remember the China bark, the Coca leaves, Strychnos, Ipecuanha, Serega etc.[26]

Pharmacological research remained 'medically' interesting – quite in contrast to indigenous medical practices and cosmologies which were seen to belong to the sphere of the 'ethnologically' interesting and obscure, yet biomedically irrelevant.

As with any colonial government, the type of knowledge considered worth having was that which facilitated administrative control, had economic potential and guaranteed the health and safety of government agents and military personnel. The situation of the African population and engagement with their medical practices had no high priority. When military doctors stationed in East Africa were occasionally granted special leave it was for scientific exploration and general ethnography.[27] The restructuring of colonial bureaucracy in Berlin[28] and the appointment of Bernhard Dernburg (1865–1937), who has been described as an 'enlightened' colonial administrator, as head of the German colonial administration in 1907, are often seen as turning points in German colonial policy.[29] The welfare of the African population ascended in the list of official priorities – mainly because it was seen to be a prerequisite for economic development. Locally this shift in policy increasingly led to quarrels between the administration and white settlers.

However, even during the allegedly more 'enlightened' period of colonial administration, financial support tended to be provided for research that was expected to have direct economic spin-offs. The anthropologist Fritz Graebner (1877–1934), for example, was unsuccessful in his recommendation to have ethnologists appointed to the Colonial Office in 1908.[30] Two years later, the French politician Lucien Herbert approached the German Government with a proposal for an 'international ethnographic bureau' and a related conference.[31] The intention was to bring together research results gathered by the various European researchers in the colonies and to protect their peoples' traditional way of life and their rights – for 'economic, scientific and humanitarian reasons'.[32] The proposal was rejected, one of the objections being the dislike of co-operation with rival colonial powers.

In the same year, the Colonial Institute in Hamburg, founded in 1908 for research and the training of colonial agents,[33] started a publication series that included ethnology and the history of culture and languages. However, this series rarely featured African medical and health-related practices, as at that time ethnology in Germany was dominated by linguistic studies.

Ethnography, medical matters and medical practitioners

Despite the essential contributions of medical doctors to the early development of general ethnology,[34] ethnographic interest in indigenous medical matters was largely restricted to epidemiology and pharmacology. What reference there is to medical practices concerns mainly their presentation and the rituals surrounding them, rather than their content and meaning. There prevailed a preference for the collection and display of cultural artefacts.[35] Their exotic appearance secured a prominent place for medical objects in illustrations of publications on Africa (e.g. the dress of a medicine man or a medicine puppet on the inner cover of ethnographic books[36]). Health-related behaviour and medical ideas received, in contrast, scant attention.[37]

Quite in contrast to the scarcity of ethnographic and ethnological work[38] on indigenous medicine produced by physicians, Christian missionaries studied indigenous religion which included questions of sickness and healing in considerable depth.[39] Knowing the natives' customs, beliefs and morals was considered vital for the missionary endeavour. Missionaries' studies were not only indispensable for the proselytising mission and the development of Christian communities, but also greatly advanced German anthropological knowledge in general.

Few of the Germans in Africa possessed basic training in ethnographic methods from the courses run in Berlin and Hamburg.[40] Yet curiosity in Germany demanded accounts on the natives in the colonies. Thus even the bacteriologist Robert Koch was invited by the Berlin Anthropological Society to deliver a lecture on his highly impressionistic and sporadic observations of 'the natives' during his research on sleeping sickness in East Africa.[41] Colonial doctors, military officers, civil servants and missionaries, with more time than Koch on his expedition, studied the ethnic groups they encountered more thoroughly.[42] As a result of this interest, some of them became members of the first German anthropological society.[43]

The personal objectives and careers of those doctors who did engage in general ethnography were varied. For some, like Friedrich Fülleborn (1866–1933) and Otto Peiper, the studies they published during their service in German colonies remained the only ethnological work in a long list of publications that consisted mainly of articles on tropical medicine or hygiene.[44] For Otto Dempwolff (1871–1938) ethnographic work was the basis for an academic career in linguistics.[45] For most doctors though, ethnographic studies were the only publications relating to the colonies that they produced. Some doctors' routine health reports on the districts for which they were responsible also included ethnographic details. Here questions on medically relevant life-events and the general living conditions of European and indigenous inhabitants alike (such as housing and clothing) led some to digress into colourful descriptions of 'native customs'.[46]

Throughout the second half of the nineteenth century ethnology in Germany was strongly influenced by the paradigm of evolution. Darwinian thinking fell on fertile ground in circles where the idea of continuous progress had been inherited from the Enlightenment.[47] Kurt Sprengel (1766–1833) had published a historiography of medicine in which, as early as 1792, he held that African and other foreign healing practices were relics of the prehistory of medicine.[48] Foreign cultures continued to be classified as stages in the assumed linear development of humankind and as living remnants of a primitive stage in the development of modern medicine. As such, they were considered worth studying. Max Bartels (1843–1904), for example, subtitled his book *Die Medicin der Naturvölker* (*The Medicine of the Primitive Peoples*) as 'ethnological contributions to the prehistory of medicine', and proclaimed the existence of similar practices and ideas in 'primitive peoples' throughout the world.[49] His account of the 'medical skills of primitive peoples' was later selected for the introductory chapter of the major German handbook on the history of medicine (published in 1902).[50] According to Bartels and other authors in the tradition of evolutionary thinking, the ideas and practices observed in Africa were not 'local' but more or less 'universal' and typical of a particular stage of evolution.

Evolutionary thinking was, of course, not the only factor that influenced ethnological theory. According to the diffusionist school of thought, similar elements in different cultures were not necessarily the result of a 'natural' progress, but due to dissemination of practices by commerce, war or migration. In this approach the ethnographic focus shifted from development to exchange. Earlier accounts about communities inhabiting coastal areas were seen to offer examples of imported customs. Buchner, for example, had remarked in 1886 on the application of leeches on the West African coastal areas as a practice possibly acquired from the Europeans.[51] Ethnographers had reported that Suaheli youth quickly adopted Arab, Indian and European habits.[52] In 1898 Junior Surgeon Schreber reported the application of lion's fat for rheumatism among the Suaheli, Arabs and Indians, and hinted at the importation of this practice.[53] Imported foreign substances would sometimes also be used differently, as in the case of gunpowder that was administered for acceleration of delivery[54] and artificial abortion.[55] However, examples of the adoption and adaptation of practices from other medical traditions were observed not only in coastal communities but also in interior areas. The Wahehe were reported to have learned how to suture wounds from the Arabs, and from the Europeans the practice of quarantining smallpox patients and their relations.[56] Other communities were thought to have acquired the knowledge of variolation (namely immunisation by inoculation with the pus from less severely diseased patients) from neighbouring groups in colonial times. Some Kiziba societies allegedly 'imitated' real variolation by rubbing drugs into the usual superficial incisions of the skin.[57]

Two manuals were available to guide aspiring researchers travelling to Africa: the *Anleitung zu wissenschaftlichen Beobachtungen auf Reisen*, edited by G. Neumeyer,[58] and the Berlin Museum's *Anleitungen für ethnographische Beobachtungen und Sammlungen in Afrika und Ozeanien*.[59] Both of these were well known and widely used by doctors in East Africa.[60] The manual edited by Neumeyer covered various topics that were considered of interest to explorers (like geography and meteorology). The chapter on medicine however, written by a professor of hygiene, August Gärtner (1848–1934), made only three references to native health and medicine. Gärtner held that the natives' eating habits were adapted to their digestive organs, that their 'medicinal and stimulant drugs' were either 'used by civilised nations, too – and in a better and more effective form – or that they were completely inactive', and that their hygienic conditions and related customs deserved further study.[61] The chapter on ethnology, written by the physician and professor of ethnology Adolf Bastian, focused on the relationships between climate, seasonal cycles and 'native' ideas. Bastian does not refer to medicine at all – although he mentions surgical instruments among a list of the many collectable objects.[62]

The second manual focuses exclusively on ethnographic observations and the collection of artefacts. It was edited on behalf of the Royal Museum of Ethnology in Berlin by its director, the physician Professor Felix von Luschan (1854–1924). The paragraph on medicine stipulates that only doctors should investigate 'indigenous therapies'. Other areas of particular interest were highlighted: use of poisons, epidemic and endemic diseases, syphilis, yaws, leprosy, alcoholism, famine, and surgical operations, including skull trepanations. Sample questions for further research were provided, such as 'Are there real doctors, surgeons, birth attendants (male or female), or just sorcerers (*Zauberer*)?'.[63] However, the author also advises lay people to confine themselves to the collection of drugs.

As these two widely read handbooks indicate, the ethnography of the time oscillated between the attempt to contribute to medical sciences (mainly epidemiology and pharmacology) on the one hand and the ethnological pre-occupation with material culture, linguistics and the spectacular on the other. Generally the interests of scholars at home corresponded with those of the people 'in the field'. Hans Krauss, a physician formerly employed by a railway construction company in German East Africa, clearly defined the prevailing double motive for collecting information on indigenous medicine: 'On the one hand, for under-standing a tribe it seems necessary that its medical views are known, too, on the other hand it might be possible to enrich the pharmacopoeia at home by some precious drugs'.[64]

European 'science' and African 'beliefs'

Those who turned their attention to indigenous medicine were faced with a difficult task. As is evident from a number of accounts, reliable information was hard to come by. Informants, often the doctor's servants, were afraid of punishment by healers and neighbours when they were asked to name the drugs in use.[65] Men, and European men in particular, were excluded from childbirth and the rituals surrounding it. The practical difficulties of access contributed to the image of African medicine as something mysterious. However, the reluctance to disclose expert knowledge and to let Europeans observe medical procedures was often due to gender-specific role prescriptions and professional secrecy rather than to mystery – phenomena not altogether unknown from European history and the Hippocratic as well as the emerging biomedical traditions. The secular character and the instrumental use of healing knowledge (rather than its alleged magico-religious nature) were evident in the case of a group of Wahehe healers who were keen to demonstrate their medicinal herbs to the German medical officer in order to get the desired written confirmation that allowed them their practice.[66]

Once information, however reliable, had been gained, the criteria of contemporary Western scientific medicine were applied to assess indigenous practice. Of these, one of the most important was the extent to which diseases, prophylactic measures and treatments were identified and explained in rational terms – 'rationality' being defined by positivist science. With regard to disease causation, Europeans were keen to find out whether rational theories such as those of infection or of contagion were preferred in indigenous explanations. It was found that the Wahehe[67] 'rationally' attributed the transmission of recurrent fever to tics and that the Massai[68] knew that mosquitoes carried malaria. Although it was immediately concluded that this was common knowledge among other Bantu groups too,[69] further research failed to confirm this.[70]

Examples of 'rational' methods of disease prevention were also found. Some indigenous groups used insect repellents,[71] the isolation of yaws patients[72] or lepers,[73] and variolation.[74] 'Rational' therapies included the prescription of rust for anaemia,[75] splints for bone fractures,[76] and embryotomy for obstructed labour.[77] Sometimes the rationality of a method was contrasted with its allegedly irrational native rationale. The distinction between rational action and irrational explanation had been made earlier by Buchner. He considered the West African practice of applying wet, slowly drying bark to bone fractures as a primitive, but acceptable and rational measure. However, he strongly rejected the local explanation, which was shared by non-medical Europeans, as scientifically unacceptable: 'Yet the Negroes and their pupils, the Negroid white, see its mysterious healing power not in its purely mechanical effect, but in the juice of the Mukumbi bark that is similar to our gum arabic'.[78]

Another paradigm that was invariably applied in the assessment of indigenous practices by Europeans was the distinction between scientific medicine and belief in the supernatural. Here the effects of African healing procedures were recognised and explained in rational, scientific terms, but indigenous frames of reference were rejected as based on religious belief or mere superstition. The effectiveness of herbs was accounted for in pharmacological terms, and medical rituals were explained with reference to contemporary psychology: 'In the healing of diseases, magic (*Zauberei*) certainly plays a role at least equal to that of effective drugs: for the Negro doctors, too, do not want to dispense with the healing power of suggestion'.[79] Observers thought that 'The real value of this magic consists in the frequent suggestive effect and – in the honorarium that the fetish doctor may claim'.[80]

The paradigm of 'suggestibility' was used frequently to explain the effect of African rituals. It had been introduced into medicine by the French neurologist

Hippolyte M. Bernheim in the 1880s. Bernheim claimed to have discovered the effective principle that had been:

> connected with the worst excesses of ignorance, superstition and fraud, hidden like gold embedded in a thick layer of dead rock. Nothing other than suggestive therapy was behind all the mysterious things of ancient magic, and still is behind the magical arts of primitive peoples.[81]

This theory claimed not only that it could explain therapeutic success, but some illnesses too. Thus in East Africa possession states were seen as 'products of suggestive influence', and the belief in the presence of spirits was explained as a lack of ability to distinguish 'between truth and products of imagination, like with our children and certain hysteric individuals'.[82]

As the development of 'modern' European medicine was characterised by a struggle for the separation of medical practices from religion and superstition, the perceived inextricable link between these areas in African society constituted a conceptual challenge to European doctors. 'Physician, conjurer and sorcerer is one and the same with the Wasuaheli, the coastal tribe of German East Africa.'[83] The conviction that a clear difference could be made between medicine and belief in the supernatural, resulted in seemingly clearly delineated categories of remedies mentioned in ethnographic studies. As Luschan had demanded in his questionnaire, ethnographers in the field tried to clearly distinguish between doctor and sorcerer among the different peoples – and often failed.[84] Nevertheless, the division of indigenous remedies into 'medications' and 'charms' ('*Arznei und Zaubermittel*') was continued. The accounts of what was, to European eyes, acceptable 'medical' treatment appeared carefully separated from those of healing practices, like prayers and incantations.

Africans were considered wanting also in respect of the European doctor's dogma of 'diagnosis must precede treatment'. The perceived lack of interest in the identification of diseases on the part of African doctors was frequently commented on unfavourably: 'The right diagnosis is less important to him than the right drug. [...] Thus the disease is never ascertained, but the cause and the remedy only'.[85] European doctors found it unproblematic to 'correctly' identify the disease and to correlate indigenous terms with European disease entities.

Ethnographers who lacked a background in medicine were expected to emphasise in their accounts that they may have wrongly identified a disease – medicine was after all considered to be a science that demanded special training.[86] In a similar vein, medical doctors felt they were better qualified than professional philologists to translate medical terms. Doctors Peiper and Krauss, for example, were keen to point out that some of the translations given by the philologist Velten in his ethnographic work and in his standard Swahili grammar and dictionary[87] were wrong: for the medical expert *ukoma* and *mti* were not cancer and scrofulous ulcers, but leprosy and tertiary syphilis or a swelling of joint and bone.[88] European medical doctors assumed the authority to decide on the accuracy and validity of medical terms – in relation to indigenous healers as much as in relation to non-medical Europeans.

In his account of 'the Suaheli doctor' Peiper used the disease classification system then common in European medicine which ordered according to medical specialities, like infectious diseases, diseases of the nervous system, venereal diseases, etc.[89] This procedure exposed certain problems, in that indigenous classifications could not always be accommodated under a discrete disease category. The Suaheli doctor would refer to the various symptoms of what would in the German system be a single 'disease' as different entities.[90] The diagnostic category of rachitis did not exist in the African system; instead the rachitic symptoms of 'deformed legs', 'deformed arms' and of children's walking disability were identified as different entities, namely as '*matege*', '*vigosho*' and '*kiwete*' respectively.[91] The problem of the incommensurability of different classificatory systems was seen as indicative of the imprecision and ignorance inherent in Suaheli medicine. A similar argument was advanced in the case of apparent 'homonyms' (identical names for different 'diseases') which were seen to indicate a lack of differentiation on the part of the indigenous practitioner.[92] African medicine appears to have been characterised mainly by what were seen as deficiencies when it was compared with European medicine.

Physician, quack or noble savage?

'When somebody wants to have a doctor's advice he goes to his house and tells him that he suffers from such or such disease. The doctor's first question is how will he be recompensed for his services?'[93] This is not the description of European private practice before the introduction of sick funds and health insurance but a German doctor's account of African medicine. The only authoritative German monograph on 'primitive medicine' that was published before 1900 had a section on 'Doctor's honorarium'.[94] German medical men closely observed how much their African colleagues were paid and whether they were paid prior to treatment. They also noticed that African doctors pursued other, often strenuous, work alongside their medical practice, and that patients consulted different healers.[95] For most European doctors, however, the indigenous healer's main objective was personal profit, to such an extent that it distracted from medicine's real purpose: 'Speculation on the patient's purse seems to be the main point for the medicine man when giving the *daua*,[96] the success of the treatment does not matter much to him'.[97]

It could be argued that the question of remuneration was bound to arouse the special interest of medical experts whose professional organisation back home feared that the economic situation of doctors in Germany could create a 'medical proletariat'. There, the right to the exclusivity of professional expertise and the guaranteed income of biomedically trained doctors was continually contested by a range of health care providers: naturopaths, homoeopaths, balneologists and other groups considered as 'quacks'. What is more, throughout the German imperial period, the scope for financial gain by civil doctors in the colonies received adverse attention,[98] while the assumed selflessness and the sacrifices doctors in government service made became a dominant theme later.[99]

Another contentious issue focused on the question of whether African healers ought to be regarded as medical practitioners, especially in the light of earlier ethnographic accounts which had denied the existence of a 'special class of doctors' in Africa.[100] The standard of training and the social standing of African medical practitioners were further points of discussion. Some German doctors saw indigenous healers as the East African counterpart to doctors in Europe and even called some if not all '*Ärzte*' (physicians).[101] Missionaries, military people and ethnologists in contrast generally preferred less medical terms, such as 'sorcerer' and 'magician'.[102]

The fact that, in contrast to non-medical people, German doctors referred to some indigenous healers in these ways is surprising, especially in view of the air of superiority assumed by them when judging 'primitive medicine'. We can only speculate about the reasons for this. The ambition of doctors trained in scientific medicine to distinguish 'magical' from 'empirical' healing might have been a factor here. By acknowledging some healers as 'proper' doctors and their treatment procedures, even if not 'correctly' understood by them, as medical practice, other healers and their rituals could be excluded from serious medical consideration and banished into the realms of religion and fraud. German views of African healers could therefore oscillate between seeing them as different or deficient types of doctors.

Besides the denigration of indigenous medicine, and its scientific study, a third approach to native African health behaviour can be observed occasionally: a late version of the myth of the noble savage. Typically, the famous East African example of this exceptional glorifying view does not stem from a doctor, but from a medical lay person: the navy officer Hans Paasche (1881–1920), one of the prominent exponents of life reform, temperance, anti-vaccinationism and vegetarianism in Germany.[103] He put his satirical remarks on European health risks, especially smoking, alcohol abuse and urban life, into the mouth of Lukanga Mukara, a fictional explorer sent by his African king to report on the conditions in Germany.[104] This highly successful book had been inspired by Paasche's experiences of his military service during the Maji Maji rising in German East Africa and his later honeymoon trip to its north-western corner, the kingdom of Rwanda.[105] Paasche's work reaffirmed German perceptions of African health-related practices as an equivalent to 'naturopathy'.[106] The general assumption was that their 'natural' way of life made the '*Naturvölker*' ('people of nature') experts in natural remedies.[107] After all, like naturopaths back home in Germany, African healers, too, made use of herbs, heat and water. Bathing in mineral-rich water as a treatment of skin diseases and rheumatism was frequently compared to the flourishing German tradition of health spas and hydro- and balneo-therapy,[108] and figured prominently in East African sanitary and ethnographic accounts.[109] Yet, like naturopathy and other 'heterodox' practices at home, African natural healing was looked upon by some with contempt and suspicion and by others with acceptance and interest.

Those favourably inclined towards naturopathy and critical of vaccination campaigns at home, were keen to make their views felt in the colonies, too.[110] These interest groups were, however, largely unsuccessful. It could be argued that the meteorological and intellectual climates in the colonies made it problematic for doctors to turn their backs on modern scientific medicine.[111] The reported successes of vaccination campaigns and the developments in the newly emerging medical discipline of tropical medicine and hygiene led many colonial doctors to ignore naturopathy – quite unlike some of their colleagues in Germany who found naturopathy helpful in the treatment of various diseases.[112]

Conclusion

Attempts to dominate or replace African healing practices have not necessarily and always characterised the attitudes of Europeans. Yet they became a common feature not only of German colonial imperialism. However, despite the comparatively short duration of German administration in Africa and the fact that no uniform and singular approach towards African medicine prevailed, a shift in perceptions and responses to indigenous healing can be discerned. Earlier, mainly derogatory, views of healers as 'treacherous' and 'noxious' were followed by linguistic and epidemiological studies of particular tribes, the search for new drugs, and, occasionally, a glorification of the 'natural' African way of life.[113]

Three major issues were at the centre of discussions about indigenous medicine: the potential value of indigenous African pharmacopoeia for European medicine; the distinction between 'rational' and 'irrational' ideas and remedies; and the affinities between African medicine and folk medicine, naturopathy and 'quackery' in Germany. These issues mirror in various ways contemporary ambitions and developments within Germany itself. 'Modern scientific medicine' in Northern Europe and America sought to differentiate the effects of substances from beliefs in effects (i.e. the pharmacological from the psychological, the medically beneficent from the noxious) and emerged as the dominant strand of medical discourse from attempts to separate the scientific from the irrational, medicine from religion and politics, professional expertise from lay attitudes – in short: 'orthodox' from 'heterodox' medicine. These polarities also characterise the initially mentioned current images of 'traditional medicine' in East Africa, a medicine that emerged only in colonial times and owes its existence as a clearly bounded category to Western discourse and pre-occupations.[114]

The encounter between the science-based, rational and universalist world view of emergent Western biomedicine and the complexity of the pre-colonial field of healing in Africa has been analysed here in relation to the German protectorate in East Africa. This encounter resulted in the application of the label 'traditional African medicine' for a highly heterogeneous collection of old and new concepts and practices. Being less stringently standardised and explored, this field remains potentially exploitable and promising as well as deficient and dangerous as far as biomedical experts and authorities, and pharmaceutical companies are concerned. For the East African population, as for the medical anthropologist, it offers an enormous variety of health care resources. For the medical historian it serves as an indication that contrary to the persistent unifying ambitions and intentions of Western biomedicine, medical traditions, even if 'invented', are inherently plural.

Acknowledgement

Part of the research on which this contribution is based was financed by a grant from the Volkswagen Stiftung for a project on 'Medical Pluralism in East Africa'. We want to thank the other participants of the conference, the editor and the anonymous reviewers for their helpful comments on earlier versions of the paper.

Notes

1 Prof. Eustace Muhondwa, Institute of Public Health, Muhimbili College of Health Services, University of Dar es Salaam, at the international 'Academic Seminar on the History of Health Care in Tanzania' at Mwalimu Nyerere Conference Hall, Ocean Road Hospital, Dar es Salaam, 3rd May 2001, in his paper on 'Traditional Medicine in the Health System in Tanzania: Past, Present and Future', to be published in the proceedings of the conference by GTZ (German Agency for Technical Cooperation), District Health Support Project, Tanzania.

2 See, for example, D. Nyamwaya, *African Indigenous Medicine. An Anthropological Perspective for Policy Makers and Primary Health Care Managers*, Nairobi, AMREF, 1992.

3 Cf. E. Pies, *Willem Piso (1611–1678), Begründer der kolonialen Medizin und Leibarzt des Grafen Johann Moritz von Nassau-Siegen in Brasilien*, Düsseldorf, Interma-orb Verlagsgruppe, 1981, 88; D. Arnold, 'Introduction: disease, medicine and empire', in D. Arnold (ed.), *Imperial Medicine and Indigenous Societies*, Manchester, New York, Manchester University Press, 1988, 11; P. Boomgaard, 'Dutch medicine in Asia, 1600–1900', in D. Arnold (ed.), *Warm Climates and Western Medicine: The Emergence of Tropical Medicine, 1500–1900*, Amsterdam, Atlanta, Rodopi, 1996, 48–51; D. Arnold, *Colonizing the Body. State Medicine and Epidemic Disease in Nineteenth-Century India*, Berkeley, California University Press, 1993, 11.

4 L. Brandl, *Ärzte und Medizin in Afrika*, Pfaffenhofen/Ilm, Afrika-Verlag, 1966, 94.

5 R. Foskett (ed.), *The Zambesi Doctors: David Livingstone's Letters to John Kirk 1858–1872*, Edinburgh, Edinburgh University Press, 1964, 43.

6 U. Bitterli, *Die Entdeckung des schwarzen Afrikaners. Versuch einer Geistesgeschichte der europäisch-afrikanischen Beziehungen an der Guineaküste im 17. und 18. Jahrhundert*, Zürich, Atlantis-Verlag, 1970, 202–3, found that a lonely traveller like Mungo Park was more able to understand and respect Africans than members of large expeditions who were not so much dependant on the native population.

7 Nevertheless some Europeans continued to consult African healers. B. Struck, 'Afrikanische Aerzte', *Münchener Medizinische Wochenschrift*, 53 (1906): 1723.

8 B. Massin, 'From Virchow to Fischer. Physical anthropology and "modern race theories" in Wilhelmine Germany', G.W. Stocking Jr. (ed.), *Volksgeist as Method and Ethic. Essays on Boasian Ethnography and the German Anthropological Tradition*, Madison and London, The University of Wisconsin Press, 1996, 95–7.

9 U. Bitterli, *Die 'Wilden' und die 'Zivilisierten'. Grundzüge einer Geistes- und Kulturgeschichte der europäisch-überseeischen Begegnung*, München, Beck, (1976), 2nd edn 1991; U. Sadji, *Der Negermythos am Ende des 18. Jahrhunderts in Deutschland. Eine Analyse der Rezeption von Reiseliteratur über Schwarzafrika*, Frankfurt/M. and Bern, Lang, 1979; M. Harbsmeier, 'Towards a prehistory of ethnography. Early modern German travel writing as traditions of knowledge', in H.F. Vermeulen and A. Alvarez Roldán (eds), *Fieldwork and Footnotes. Studies in the History of European Anthropology*, London, New York, Routledge, 1995.

10 A.B. Sadji, *Das Bild des Negro-Afrikaners in der Deutschen Kolonialliteratur (1884–1945). Ein Beitrag zur literarischen Imagologie Schwarzafrikas*, Berlin, Reimer, 1985.

11 Closer observation as enabled by established colonial rule changed many judgements on the savage. For the changing perceptions of 'the' Africans by British doctors in East Africa during imperial colonialism see M. Vaughan, *Curing their Ills. Colonial Power and African Illness*, Cambridge, Polity Press, 1991, 29–53.

12 An illustrative example is the question of the Africans' conversion to Christianity. Whereas famous 18th-century authors like Peter Kolbe and Rousseau doubted the enduring success of conversion and saw African animism as real religion, mission theorists in late 19th century believed that this 'superstition' could be completely displaced by Christianity. A. B. Sadji, *Das Bild des Negro-Afrikaners in der Deutschen Kolonialliteratur (1884–1945). Ein Beitrag zur literarischen Imagologie Schwarzafrikas*, Berlin, Reimer, 1985, 89.

13 For very short, quite differing and necessarily oversimplifying accounts of German colonial attitudes towards African medicine in German East Africa see E. K. Feierman, 'Alternative medical services in rural Tanzania: A physician's view', *Social Science and Medicine*, 15 B (1981): 400; A. Beck, *Medicine, Tradition and Development in Kenya and Tanzania 1920–1970*, Waltham/MA, Crossroad Press, 1981, 61–2, 69–70; A. Redmayne, 'Note on health services and the indigenous population under the German administration', in E.E. Sabben-Clare, D.J. Bradley and K. Kirkwood (eds), *Health in Tropical Africa During the Colonial Period*, Oxford, Clarendon, 1980, 115–17; M. Turshen, *The Political Ecology of Disease in Tanzania*, New Brunswick/NJ, Rutgers University Press, 1984, 145–9; J. Iliffe, *East African Doctors. A History of the Modern Profession*, Cambridge, Cambridge University Press, 1998, 29.

14 W.U. Eckart, *Medizin und Kolonialimperialismus: Deutschland 1884–1945*, Paderborn, Schöningh, 1997, 190–1.

15 The term 'healer' will generally be used for referring to those Africans with a special expertise in questions of health and illness – practitioners without formal 'biomedical' training. There is a discussion about the appropriate expression in medical anthropology which reveals the deficiencies of all terms in question. 'Practitioner of Traditional Medicine' (TPM), as proposed by WHO committees, would presuppose the dichotomy to be analysed here. Local terms like *'waganga', 'walacha'* or *'abalossi'* would not allow the generalizations by observers that have to be studied here.

16 M. Buchner, 'Die Medicin der Neger', *Münchener Medicinische Wochenschrift* 33, (1886): 625–6.

17 W. Steuber, 'Als Schutztruppenarzt in Deutsch-Ostafrika', *Münchener Medizinische Wochenschrift*, 82 (1935): 778–82. He published this article as a retired Senior General Surgeon, referring to his early colonial service, and included it, complemented only by a section on 'European shooting' *(Europäerschießen)*, as chapter '6. Medical Cultivation' *(Ärztliche Kulturarbeit)* of his autobiography W. Steuber, *Arzt und Soldat in drei Erdteilen*, Berlin, Vorhut-Verlag Otto Schlegel, 1940, 63–76.

18 Steuber, *Arzt und Soldat*, 58, 74.

19 Unknowingly, Steuber did exactly what the CMS-Missionary Thomas O'Neill had written in his diary 11 August 1876: 'We are obliged to follow the example of the quacks at home: look grave, examine tongue or pulse, and give anything we have at hand – brandy, castor oil, pyretic saline, or baking soda' (quoted after J. Bückendorf, *"Schwarz-weiß-rot über Ostafrika!"* Münster, Lit-Verlag, 1997, 275).

20 *Mganga*, plural *Waganga*: the Swahili and – in different forms (e.g. Kinyarwanda/Kirundi: *umuganga*; Congo and West Africa: *nganga*) – also more general Bantu term for (some) medical practitioners. Cf. J.M. Janzen, 'Towards a historical perspective on African medicine and health', in J. Sterly (ed.), *Ethnomedizin und Medizingeschichte. Symposion vom 2. bis zum 4. Mai 1980 in Hamburg*, Berlin, Verlag Mensch und Leben, 1983, 123.

21 Steuber, *Arzt und Soldat*, 83.

22 For short accounts on indigenous healing by German medical explorers before 1885 see B. Siegert, *Deutsche Ärzte als Forschungsreisende im 19. Jahrhundert bis zum Eintritt des zweiten Kaiserreichs in den Kreis der Kolonialmächte*, Münster, Dr. med. dent. thesis, 1990.

23 Circular letters 13 October 1895 and 12 May 1896, reprinted in *Arbeiten aus dem Kaiserlichen Gesundheitsamte*, 14 (1898): 647–8.

24 *'Shauri'* is the term taken from the Arabic for the traditional meetings intended to come to a decision in a more or less formal way.

25 Correspondence Brieger – Colonial Office, 1903–7, Bundesarchiv R 1001/5987, 112; 127–8; 156; 5988, 79–81; 258–65.
26 Kaiserliches Gesundheitsamt (Imperial Health Office), Bericht zu Negermedizin aus Deutsch-Ostafrika, 15 September 1911, Bundesarchiv R 1001/5790, 106–9.
27 E.g. Friedrich Fülleborn got special leave for his general exploration of the south of the colony, described in his *Das deutsche Njassa-Ruwuma-Gebiet, Land und Leute, nebst Bemerkungen über die Schire-Länder*, Berlin, Reimer, 1906; Otto Dempwolff for his ethnography published as *Die Sandawe. Linguistisches und ethnographisches Material aus Deutsch-Ostafrika*, Hamburg, Friederichsen, 1916; in contrast, Peiper had to use a vaccination campaign for his meticulous study on infant mortality and nutrition, cf. O. Peiper, 'Über Säuglingssterblichkeit und Säuglingsernährung im Bezirke Kilwa (Deutsch-Ostafrika)', *Archiv für Schiffs- und Tropenhygiene*, 1910, 8, 233.
28 The *Kolonialabteilung des Auswärtigen Amtes* (Colonial Department of the Foreign Office) became the *Reichskolonialamt* (Imperial Colonial Office).
29 Cf. W. Baumgart, 'German Imperialism in Historical Perspective', in A.J. Knoll and L.H. Gann (eds), *Germans in the Tropics. Essays on German Colonial History*, New York, Westport/CT, London, Greenwood, 1987, 151.
30 Cf. M. Gothsch, *Die deutsche Völkerkunde und ihr Verhältnis zum Kolonialismus*, Baden-Baden, Nomos, 1983, 243–4.
31 Cf. the interview with Lucien Hubert, Député des Ardennes, in the German Embassy in Paris , 5 January 1910. Copy of the Foreign Office, Bundesarchiv R 1001/6131, 38.
32 Lucien Hubert, 'Exposé des motifs', typescript, Bundesarchiv R 1001/6131, 46:

> 'Raisons d'humanité, raisons d'utilité, raisons scientifiques […] Le moment est venu d'entreprendre une étude systematique et générale de leurs moeurs, de leurs coutumes, de leurs besoins: et pour cela il faut une entente internationale.'

33 Gothsch, *Die deutsche Völkerkunde*, 244–5; W. Smith, 'Anthropology and German Colonialism', in A.J. Knoll and L.H. Gann (eds), *Germans in the Tropics. Essays on German Colonial History*, New York, Westport/CT, London, Greenwood, 1987, 47.
34 E.g. the first German chair for ethnology, then called *Völkerpsychologie* (ethnopsychology), was given to the former ship's doctor Adolf Bastian (1826–1905), and the first anthropological society, the *Berliner Gesellschaft für Anthropologie, Ethnologie und Urgeschichte*, had been founded by him and the physician Rudolf Virchow (1821–1902).
35 Many ethnographic contributions were based on collections only – without the author's visit to the peoples concerned, e.g. F. v. Luschan, 'Beiträge zur Ethnographie des abflusslosen Gebiets in Deutsch-Ost-Afrika', in C.W. Werther (ed.), *Die mittleren Hochländer des nördlichen Deutsch-Ost-Afrika. Wissenschaftliche Ergebnisse der Irangi-Expedition 1896–97*, Berlin, Paetel, 1898.
36 K. Weule, *Wissenschaftliche Ergebnisse meiner ethnographischen Forschungsreise in den Südosten Deutsch-Ostafrikas*, Berlin, Mittler, 1908; E. Kotz, *Im Banne der Furcht. Sitten und Gebräuche der Wapare in Ostafrika*, Hamburg, Advent-Verlag, 1922.
37 Noticeable exceptions written by non-medical authors are an ethnographic monography about the Massai by a captain of the troops in German East Africa (M. v. Merker, *Die Massai. Ethnographische Monographie eines ostafrikanischen Semitenvolkes*, Berlin, Reimer, 1904, 174–91 on medicine, 245 on diseases, 340–9 on medicinal plants); a travel report by the botanist, explorer and later Vice-Governor of German East Africa Franz Stuhlmann (*Mit Emin Pascha ins Herz von Afrika*, Berlin, Reimer, 1894, on disease with the Wanyamwési pp. 84–6; the A-lûr 492–529; the Latúka 774–803); and the collection on the Swahili customs by philologist Carl Velten (*Sitten und Gebräuche der Suaheli*, Göttingen, Vandenhoeck and Ruprecht, 1903, on pregnancy and delivery 3–29; on medicine and diseases 242–57).
38 According to the use of terms in German, here 'ethnography' denotes the collection and representation of data on foreign peoples and 'ethnology' their comparative analysis. The English terms 'cultural anthropology' and 'social anthropology' are today often synonymous with the German 'Ethnologie', but this specific meaning developed only after World War I.
39 E.g. J. Jensen (ed.), *Die Konde. Ethnographische Aufzeichnungen (1891–1916) des Missionssuperintendenten Theodor Meyer von den Nyakusa (Tanzania)*, Hamburg, Klaus Renner, 1989.

40 Cf. Smith, 'Anthropology', 47–8.

41 R. Koch, 'Anthropologische Beobachtungen gelegentlich einer Expedition an den Viktoria-Njanza', *Zeitschrift für Ethnologie* 40 (1908): 449–68.

42 'Full' ethnographic monographs by medical doctors are A. Widenmann, *Die Kilimandscharo-Bevölkerung. Anthropologisches und Geographisches aus dem Dschaggalande*, Gotha, Justus Perthes, 1899, and H. Claus, *Die Wagogo. Skizze eines ostafrikanischen Bantustammes*, Leipzig and Berlin, Teubner, 1911. The other doctors' writings focused on medicine, linguistics, folklore, or travel. E.g. O. Dempwolff, 'Beiträge zur Volksbeschreibung der Hehe', Baessler Archiv 1913, IV, 3, 87–163, is an ethnography only excluding the fields already covered by others, i.e. medicine as well as history, cult, law, war and hunting; others, like H. Claus, 'Die Wangómwia', *Zeitschrift für Ethnologie*, 42 (1910): 489–94, included physical anthropology.

43 E.g. with experience in East Africa in 1911 the physicians Dempwolff, Fülleborn and Steuber, the missionary Cleve, the military officers Ramsay and Paasche; cf. *Zeitschrift für Ethnologie*, 43, (1911): 2–22.

44 For their 'biomedical' publications see the bibliographies in G. Olpp, *Hervorragende Tropenärzte in Wort und Bild*, München, Verlag der Ärztlichen Rundschau Otto Gmelin, 1932, 137–8 (Fülleborn) and in W.U. Eckart, *Medizin und Kolonialimperialismus: Deutschland 1884–1945*, Paderborn, Schöningh, 1997, 588.

45 Dempwolff became a specialist in Bantu and Austronesian languages and was appointed professor of linguistics in 1931. For a short biography cf. H. Jungraithmayr and W. J. G. Möhling (eds), *Lexikon der Afrikanistik. Afrikanische Sprachen und ihre Erforschung*. Berlin, Reimer, 1983, 71–2.

46 E.g. Staff Surgeon Dr. Seyffert used his Health report on the station Arusha, 1912–13, for a broad description of dresses and ornaments with the *Wameru* and *Waarusha*. Bundesarchiv R 1001/5750, 171–8.

47 Cf. K.E. Müller, 'Geschichte der Ethnologie', in H. Fischer (ed.), *Ethnologie. Einführung und Überblick*, Berlin, Reimer, 4th edn, 1998, 31–4.

48 K. Sprengel, *Versuch einer pragmatischen Geschichte der Arzneikunde*, vol. 1, Halle, Gebauer, 1st edn, 1792, 19–25.

49 M. Bartels, *Die Medicin bei den Naturvölkern. Ethnologische Beiträge zur Urgeschichte der Medicin*, Leipzig, Grieben, 1893, 4.

50 M. Bartels, 'Das medizinische Können der Naturvölker', in M. Neuberger and J.L. Pagel (eds), found. by Th. Puschmann, *Handbuch der Geschichte der Medizin*, vol. 1, Jena, Fischer, 1902, 10–19.

51 Cf. 'Die Medizin', 625.

52 Cf. Velten, *Sitten*, 3. African names are generally written as in the German sources and do not follow modern Swahili orthography which is added occasionally. Bantu peoples can be named with or without the plural prefix 'Wa-'.

53 Cf. 'Ueber Medizinen', 664–5.

54 Cf. Hösemann, 'Ueber Negermedizin im Bezirk Udjiji', *Arbeiten aus dem Kaiserlichen Gesundheitsamte*, 1898, 14, 651; Krauss, 'Der Suaheli-Arzt', 2045. Yet there is the opinion that gun powder was not completely foreign to the Africans: (according to Weck, 'Die Einstellung der abendländischen Medizin zur Heilkunde der afrikanischen Eingeborenen', 23) Lafitte, La pharmakopée indigène en Afrique occidentale Française', in *Les grandes épédemies Tropicales*, Paris, 1938, believed, 'that it was known in Africa in ancient times how to produce gun powder.'

55 Schreber, 'Ueber Medizinen', 664.

56 W. Weck, 'Der Wahehe-Arzt und seine Wissenschaft', *Deutsches Kolonialblatt*, 1908, 1048–51 (engl. tansl. by A. Redmayne, 'Hehe medicine', in *Tanzania Notes and Records*, 70, (1969): 29–40).

57 M. Zupitza, 'Die Heilmethoden der Wasiba. Sultanate: Kisiba, Bugabu, Kyamtwara, Kyanya, Ihangiro', *Arbeiten aus dem Kaiserlichen Gesundheitsamte*, 14 (1898): 653.

58 2 vols, Berlin, Oppenheim, 2nd edn, 1888; Hannover, Jänecke, 3rd edn, 1906.

59 Berlin, Gebr. Unger, 3rd edn, 1904; a later revised version became a special volume of the *Anleitung zu wissenschaftlichen Beobachtungen* under the title *Anleitung zu wissenschaftlichen Beobachtungen auf dem Gebiet der Anthropologie, Ethnologie und Urgeschichte*, Leipzig, Jänecke 1914.

60 Dempwolff, *Sandawe*, 71, refers to F. v. Luschan, *Anleitungen für ethnographische Beobachtungen und Sammlungen in Afrika und Ozeanien*, hg. v. Königlichen Museum für Völkerkunde Berlin, Berlin,

Gebr. Unger, third edition 1904, was the first, separate booklet; later, revised versions are: F. v. Luschan, *Anleitung zu wissenschaftlichen Beobachtungen auf dem Gebiet der Anthropologie, Ethnologie und Urgeschichte*, Leipzig, Jänecke, 1914, which is a reprint (in a single, special volume) of the contribution with identical page numbers: F. v. Luschan, 'Anthropologie, Ethnographie und Urgeschichte'; Steuber, *Arzt und Soldat*, 62, mentions G. v. Neumeyer, *Anleitung zu wissenschaftlichen Beobachtungen auf Reisen* vol. 2, Hannover, Jänecke, 3rd edn 1906, 1–123.

61 A. Gärtner, 'Heilkunde', in Neumeyer, *Anleitung zu wissenschaftlichen Beobachtungen auf Reisen*, vol. 2, 2nd edn, 1888, 38, 45–6, 78.

62 A. Bastian, 'Allgemeine Begriffe der Ethnologie', in Neumeyer, *Anleitung zu wissenschaftlichen Beobachtungen auf Reisen*, vol. 2, 2nd edn, 1888, 236–51, 255.

63 Luschan, *Anleitung*, 113–4.

64 Krauss, 'Arzneien', 2044.

65 H. Krauss, 'Geburt und Tod bei den Wasuaheli', *Münchener Medizinische Wochenschrift*, 54 (1907): 2488; O. Peiper, 'Schwangerschaft, Geburt und Wochenbett bei den Suaheli von Kilwa', *Archiv für Schiffs- und Tropenhygiene*, 14 (1910): 461; Peiper, 'Der Suaheli-Arzt', 563–4.

66 Weck, 'Einstellung', 21.

67 Weck, 'Wahehe-Arzt', 1049. B. Möllers, *Robert Koch. Persönlichkeit und Lebenswerk 1843–1910*, Hannover, Schmorl und von Seefeld, 1950, 689.

68 Merker, *Massai*, 174–91.

69 B. Möllers, (cf. note 68), a disciple and biographer of Robert Koch, committed such a generalisation typical for readers of ethnographic accounts when he supposed this knowledge to be common among the indigenous peoples.

70 Weck, 'Wahehe-Arzt', 1049.

71 Cf. Ibid. 1049.

72 [n.n.] *Medizinal-Berichte über die Deutschen Schutzgebiete [...] für das Jahr 1905/06*, hg. von der Kolonialabteilung des Auswärtigen Amts, Berlin, 1907, 83.

73 Schreber, 'Ueber Medizinen', 667.

74 Ibid., 664. Schreber sees the different incidence of people with small pox scars in different areas as a proof of the traditional method's efficacy. Steuber, *Arzt und Soldat*, 84, doubts the success of this measure.

75 Krauss 'Suaheli-Arzt', 518; Weck, 'Wahehe-Arzt', 1050.

76 Schreber, 'Ueber Medizinen', 665; Weck, 'Wahehe-Arzt', 1050.

77 Dempwolff, *Sandawe*, 147.

78 Buchner, 'Medicin', 625.

79 Fülleborn, *Njassa-Ruwuma-Gebiet*, 219.

80 B. Struck, 'Zahntherapeutisches von den Eingeborenen Afrikas', *Münchener Medizinische Wochenschrift*, 53 (1906): 1921.

81 H. Bernheim, *Neue Studien über Hypnotismus, Suggestion und Psychotherapy*, translat. by S. Freud, Leipzig, Wien, Deuticke, 1892, 15.

82 Vix, 'Beitrag zur Ethnologie des Zwischenseengebiets von Deutsch-Ostafrika', *Zeitschrift für Ethnologie*, 43 (1911): 511.

83 Krauss, 'Arzneien ', 2044.

84 E.g. Fülleborn, *Njassa-Ruwuma-Gebiet*, 218, 313.

85 Weck, 'Wahehe-Arzt', 1049.

86 E.g. the missionary Meyer, cf. J. Jensen (ed.), *Die Konde*, 112.

87 For Veltens life and work cf. Jungraithmayr and Möhling (eds), *Lexikon*, 257.

88 Cf. Peiper, 'Suaheli-Arzt', 564, 569; Krauss, 'Der Suaheli-Arzt' (1908): 518.

89 Cf. Peiper, 'Suaheli-Arzt', 564–73.

90 Peiper, 'Suaheli-Arzt', 564, 569; Krauss, 'Der Suaheli-Arzt' (1908): 518.

91 Peiper, 'Suaheli-Arzt', 571.

92 Weck, 'Wahehe-Arzt', 1051, mentions the 'false' use of the same term, *Litawangu*, for pneumonia and pulmonary plague.

93 Peiper, 'Suaheli-Arzt', 562.

94 Bartels, *Medicin*, 56–9.

95 Peiper, 'Suaheli-Arzt', 563.

96 *'Daua'*, modern spelling *'dawa'*, is the Kiswahili term taken from the Arabic for all kinds of remedy not distinguishing between medical and other existential problems, the spheres of nature and of religion.

97 O. Gärtner, 'Ueber Negermedizin', *Arbeiten aus dem Kaiserlichen Gesundheitsamte*, 14 (1898): 648–51.

98 Cf. Anonymus, 'Privatärzte in Deutsch-Ostafrika', *Münchener Medizinische Wochenschrift*, 54 (1907): 1312.

99 P. Manteufel, 'Der kolonialärztliche Beruf', *Die Medizinische Welt*, 41 (1934): 1430; A. Hauer, 'Allgemeine Tätigkeit des Arztes in afrikanischen Kolonien', *Deutsche Medizinische Wochenschrift*, 65 (1939): 1032.

100 Buchner, 'Die Medicin', p. 626.

101 Fülleborn, *Njassa-Ruwuma-Gebiet*, 309–12; Peiper, 'Suaheli-Arzt', 561; Krauss, 'Suaheli-Arzt', 517; Weck, 'Wahehe-Arzt', 1048–9.

102 Cf. missionary Br. Becker, 'Etwas über die Zauberer der Wasuahili', *Nachrichten aus der ostafrikanischen Mission*, 7 (1893): 2–5, where mganga is translated by 'Zauberer' only; cf. in C. W. Werther (ed.), *Die mittleren Hochländer des nördlichen Deutsch-Ost-Afrika. Wissenschaftliche Ergebnisse der Irangi-Expedition 1896–97*, Berlin, Paetel, 1898, the two ethnographic contributions by Lieutenant C.W. Werther, 'Die Irangi-Expedition. Reisebeschreibung unter besonderer Berücksichtigung der kulturellen Verhältnisse der berührten Gebiete', 44–5: *'Zauberdoktor'* and *'Medizinmann'*; and anthropologist Luschan, 'Beiträge zur Ethnographie des abflusslosen Gebiets in Deutsch-Ost-Afrika', 356: *'Zauberpriester'*. *'Zauberdoktor'* also in the influential work of the philologist Carl Velten, *Sitten*, 3; *'Zauberer'* is used by Captain Merker, *Rechtsverhältnisse und Sitten der Wadschagga*, 1902, 19, 30, 34.

103 A. Nothnagle, 'Hans Paasche – ein lebensreformerischer Visionär', *Zeitschrift für Geschichtswissenschaft* 45 (1997): 773–92.

104 H. Paasche, *Die Forschungsreise des Afrikaners Lukanga Mukara ins Innerste Deutschlands*, Hamburg-Bergedorf, 1921.

105 H. Paasche, *"Ändert Euren Sinn!" Schriften eines Revolutionärs*, Bremen, Donat, 1992, 155–63; W. Lange, *Hans Paasches Forschungsreise ins innerste Deutschland. Eine Biographie*, Donat, 1995, 33–57, 71–111.

106 'Naturopathy' translates the German 'Naturheilkunde' which developed during the first decades of the nineteenth century as a (romantic) counter-movement to the emerging 'orthodox' medicine that was based on the exact sciences and perceived as mechanistic and disrespecting nature; cf. C. Regin, *Selbsthilfe und Gesundheitspolitik. Die Naturheilbewegung im Kaiserreich (1889–1914)*, Stuttgart, Franz Steiner, 1995, 23–32.

107 L. Külz, *Tropenarzt im afrikanischen Busch*, Berlin, Süsserott, 1907, 91. Külz was more inclined to naturopathy than his colleagues and in 1927 became the editor of an unsuccessful journal on balneotherapy, the *Illustrierte medizinische Bäder-Zeitung der 'Biologischen Heilkunst'*.

108 B. Struck and C. Potozky, 'Die Hydrotherapie der Afrikaner', *Deutsche Medizinische Wochenschrift*, 30 (1908): 1315–17; Buchner, 'Medicin', 626, had judged the local 'hydrotherapeutic treatment' for rheumatism without 'drying or wrapping in warm plaids' as 'generally noxious'.

109 Cf. the answers to the relevant question posed by chief medical officer Becker to his district medical officers in *Arbeiten aus dem Kaiserlichen Gesundheitsamte*, 14 (1898): 646; Fülleborn, *Das deutsche Njassa-Ruwuma-Gebiet*, 281, 447.

110 Cf. the undated Letter to the Colonial Office, ca. 1905, R 1001/5639, 57.

111 Dr. Wilhelm Arning, military doctor in German East Africa (1892–96 and 1914–17) and a leading colonial politician, argued forcefully against naturopathy in the Reichstag (the German parliament) in 1910; cf. C. Regin, *Selbsthilfe und Gesundheitspolitik. Die Naturheilbewegung im Kaiserreich (1889–1914)*, Stuttgart, Franz Steiner, 1995, 426–7.

112 Page 44 informs about the foundation of the *Verband deutscher Ärztevereine für physikalisch-diätetische Therapie (Naturheillehre)*/Association of the German Medical Societies for Physical-Dietetic Therapy (Naturopathy) in 1904, and in the index of persons (pp. 483–6), about the names of many doctors practising naturopathy *(Naturärzte)*.

113 A further study of (not only) German attitudes to East African medicine that had to be omitted here could demonstrate a similar shift from attempts to suppress to those to combine, as explored by Patricia Laing in Chapter 9 of this volume in regard to 'Western medical constructions of Maori healing'.

114 For the development of African 'traditional' medical systems and their increasing similarity to biomedicine see S. Feierman, 'Change in African therapeutic systems', *Social Science and Medicine*, 13 (1979): 278. See also Reis in this volume (Chapter 6). Concerning the anthropologist's task to avoid creating this 'invented' domain, see R. Pool, 'On the creation and dissolution of ethnomedical systems in the medical ethnography of Africa', *Africa*, 64 (1994): 1–20.

6 Medical pluralism and the bounding of traditional healing in Swaziland

Ria Reis

As elsewhere in Southern Africa, people in Swaziland have access to biomedicine as well as to traditional healers and healing churches. Illness narratives, the stories by which people give meaning to their experience with sickness,[1] demonstrate the complex patterns of health seeking that spring from this medical pluralism, especially when it comes to conditions that neither doctors nor healers can cure. In my research on medical pluralism and epilepsy in Swaziland most people with epilepsy were found to resort to many different treatment options in the course of their life with the disorder.[2] Apparent eclecticism of patients is mirrored by increasing numbers of Swazi healers creatively combining ideas and practices from different medical traditions.[3] Moreover, for more than three decades both the Swazi government and the national association of traditional healers have advocated co-operation between doctors and healers.[4]

In this chapter I will argue that the image of a hybridisation of traditional and modern medical ideas and practices, in the sense of two previously clearly bounded unities being crossed whilst the boundaries are still discernible in the new creation, corresponds neither to actual developments in the medical domain nor to the aspirations and strategies of the actors involved.

Paul Unschuld maintains that the legitimacy of a conceptual system of medicine derives from the correspondence of its ideas concerning the emergence, nature and appropriate treatment of illness with the socio-political ideas concerning the emergence, nature and appropriate management of social crisis by a social group or an entire society.[5] He argues that such a system loses its vitality and creativity when its particular context of social ideology and social structure vanish. In line with this I will argue that the remarkable resilience and vitality of traditional concepts and practices concerning illness and healing in Swaziland depend upon the successful resistance of Swazi society against the destruction of its socio-political ideal of a nation originating from, united by, and fertile and prosperous through, the preservation of 'Swazi tradition', more specifically its institution of sacred kingship. In fact, medical ideas and practices, including those of biomedicine, are evaluated for their compatibility to 'Swazi tradition'. In the context of medical pluralism in Swaziland, 'integration' should be understood, not as the incorporation of traditional healers in the national health services, but the other way around: as traditional medicine incorporating biomedicine.[6]

In the following analysis I will look, first, at the therapy choices of people with epilepsy, second, at the practice of a traditional healer, and, third, at the public debate on the legitimacy of traditional healing. This will show the changing and permeable character of traditional medicine. It will also highlight the differences in the public's perception of the legitimacy of biomedicine and of different traditional approaches to health and illness.

The patients

During medical anthropological fieldwork in Swaziland (1987–1988) 164 people with epilepsy or their carers were interviewed about their experiences with seizures and their therapy choices.[7] More than half of them were contacted on their visit to a health care facility. The others were identified, often at their homes, during a prevalence study in a rural community. All were diagnosed before or during the research by a psychiatrist or psychiatric nurse as suffering from epilepsy. Almost all had seizures characterised by convulsions and sudden loss of consciousness. Swazi healers consider such seizures a specific disease called *sifosekuwa* (*sifo* = disease; *kuwa* = to fall). Biomedicine also classifies such seizures as specific, albeit as only one specific seizure type among many others through which epilepsy, the tendency to have seizures, may make itself known.

The interpretations of first seizures clearly related to specific individual circumstances. A pregnancy, a car accident, a heavy drinking spree or family conflicts during or shortly before the first seizure would be seen as direct or indirect causes, and therapy choices would be made accordingly. Heredity would be considered only if other members of the family were known to suffer from seizures. A person with epilepsy would not usually rely upon home medication but seek professional help shortly after the first seizure, either at a clinic (49 per cent) or with a healer (51 per cent). First choices clearly correlated with the suspected cause: of those who suspected traditional causes, such as sorcery or accidental contact with traditional medicines, 73 per cent went to a healer (and 27 per cent to the clinic). Of those that suspected other causes 37 per cent went to a healer (and 63 per cent to the clinic). In the course of their life with epilepsy 75 per cent of patients would consult both doctors and healers. Treatment with modern anti-epileptic medication would begin within a year after the first seizure (60 per cent), but would be interrupted for longer periods or stopped altogether after one or two months (64 per cent). In the prevalence study a biomedical treatment gap of 80 per cent was found, that is: of every ten people with active epilepsy, eight did not use modern medication at the time.[8] However, unless seizures were diagnosed as signs of immanent healership,[9] traditional therapies were also followed only for limited periods, and discontinued if they did not lead to success within a reasonable period of time. Therefore, people did not receive treatment of any kind for the better part of their lives with epilepsy.

Most people related changes in their perceptions over the years. Emphasis usually shifted from interpretations in terms of animal spirits sent by evil medicine or accidental contact with fumes of traditional medicines, to the idea of epilepsy being a contagious or hereditary disease. On the other hand, five people who had interpreted their first seizure as 'just an illness' after years of suffering came to believe that they had been bewitched. The notion of 'demons' as cause of epilepsy also gained in popularity over time: only two patients had suspected demons after the first seizure, whereas at the interview 16 per cent attributed their seizures to demonic powers.

Such shifts in interpretations may be considered illustrative of the 'subjunctivity of illness narratives', a terminology by which Byron Good describes the open-endedness of the narratives of his informants with seizures in Turkey.[10] Their stories characteristically presented multiple perspectives and divergent interpretations, thus opening up to a variety of possible future solutions and stimulating the listener to comment and think along. Likewise, my informants in Swaziland often proved as curious about my opinions about epilepsy as I was about theirs.[11] But unlike the narratives described by Good, there often was a desperate tinge to the narratives of people with epilepsy in Swaziland.

For one thing it was clear that patterns of dependency could seriously restrain one's freedom to choose. Children with epilepsy, cognitively impaired people and young mothers have little say in therapy choice. In fact only 15 per cent of my informants had decided where to seek help by themselves. In interpretations of epilepsy no gender differences were found, but therapy choices did vary according to the decision-maker's position in the household. Whenever adult men or paternal grandmothers were central to the decision-making the patient would be sent to a traditional healer rather than to the clinic, whereas if women and maternal grand-mothers took the decision, one could expect the reverse.

The dominance of men in decision-making corresponds with traditional relations within the extended family. Swazi girls by definition are marginal in their patrilineal group, which they will leave at marriage. Incorporation in the patrilineal group of their husband is gradual and in fact only final when the woman dies and from then on will belong to the ancestors of her husband's patrilineage.[12] The strongest position of a woman is when as a widow she will be co-heading the household as the mother of a married son and will have authority over daughters-in-law and grandchildren.[13] Until she is grandmother of her son's children, her position in the homestead is relatively marginal. Elsewhere I dwell more extensively upon the question why structural marginality would lead to a preference for Western health care, or, conversely, why a dominant position in the household would lead to a preference for traditional healers.[14] Here I will only mention that female-headed households are usually poorer than male-headed households, as women have less access to finances.

Traditional treatments for epilepsy are more costly than the free anti-epileptic medication provided by the clinic, and are therefore not easily available to single women. Also, young mothers are more successfully reached by Western health care, the reproductive role of women being the stepping stone of public health programmes. Through such programmes women develop relations based on trust with local clinic staff. The wish to preserve these relations may prevent them from visiting healers, the more so since some nurses openly discredit those who make use of traditional healing. It can also be argued, however, that a more stable embeddiment of adult men and their mothers in the household coincides with a stronger commitment to the traditional structures embodied by the chief and his council, still the most powerful organisation at the local level in Swaziland.[15] This may restrict the freedom of adult men and their mothers to choose, because higher standards of loyalty to the traditional powers apply to them. As will become clear, supporting traditional healing may testify to such loyalty.

Whereas patterns of dependency restrain people's freedom to choose, the apparent open-endedness of illness narratives is also determined by a culture-specific perception of illness. Although explanations of seizures were found to differ widely, they all rested upon the idea that something foreign to the body has entered it, by touching, eating or inhaling. This notion is embedded within a dominant perception of what it means to be a human being. People are constantly thought to interact with other living entities (animals, plants, humans). They also interact with ancestors. If there is a hint of a duality here, it is lived undivided in the body. It certainly does not concern the dichotomy of body and soul that dominates the basic assumptions of biomedical science.[16] Neither does it concern the medical anthropological dichotomy of 'naturalistic' and 'personalistic' aetiologies.[17] Healers treat their patients by making them inhale the fumes of heated medicines. Accidental contact with such fumes may cause illness. This could be considered a naturalistic explanation, whereas 'evil medicine', i.e. sorcery, could be classified as personalistic. However, both explanations depend upon the notion that something harmful has entered the body through its weak spots. But this substantiality cannot be reduced to the physical reality from the perspective of Western science. The fumes of traditional medication are not visible or tangible through Western scientific methods, though they are substantially there, as they hover around healers after a therapy or can be smelled by them in diagnostic rituals in the bodies of their patients.[18]

The same applies to the spirits of animals harassing people with epilepsy. Such *tilwane* (wild animals) are not beings with a will of their own: they are animal substances manipulated through sorcery. Or, one could say they are manipulated animal powers. The undivided integration of matter and power in Swazi notions of the origin and nature of illness forms a core problem in efforts to translate Swazi concepts into Western categories of thought. However, the embodiment of power in matter also offers an important key to the understanding of these concepts. What traditional healers diagnose are traces: traces of medicines left in the atmosphere after treatment, traces of harmful matter therapeutically removed from a patient and buried on the crossroads; traces of evil medicine hidden in food, buried under one's threshold, or ritually sent as animal spirits; substantial powers of wild animals left in their tracks or strange matter blown by the winds from afar.[19] The notion of 'traces' bridges the duality of power and matter. A trace is an impression of something or some person, but it also denotes a very small quantity of a substance.

Since epilepsy is conceived of in these terms, any treatment should aim at removing such traces of illness. Consequently, it is not considered appropriate by Swazi people with epilepsy to suppress the tendency to seizures by administering daily medication for many years, or even life-long, as doctors do on the basis of their perspective on epilepsy as a chronic disorder. This explains part of the treatment gap for epilepsy.[20] Lay people evaluate modern treatment as more effective, but the more successful the modern medication, the sooner will the patient stop the treatment. Once the person finds himself without epileptic seizures, he will conclude that he is cured and discontinue the treatment. The return of the seizures is merely taken to prove that the chosen treatment approach was inadequate.

In contrast, traditional therapies aim to remove the cause of the seizures. The perceptions of healers basically correspond to those of their patients. Healers purify the body of the patient by administering enemas, inducing vomiting or sneezing, and by ritually expelling evil spirits. However, the correspondence between patients' and healers' understanding of illness and healing does not necessarily lead to treatment success. On the contrary, patients reported little or no effect of purification techniques and rituals. But the failure of traditional treatment was ascribed to the perceived inadequacies of a specific healer. The belief that *sifosekuwa* can be cured was not doubted. Traditional healers explained that to speak of an incurable disease would be a contradiction in terms. People who have sustained burns due to a seizure or who became cognitively or motorically impaired are no longer thought to be ill; they are damaged. As long as the seizures have not led to irreversible physical or cognitive damage, both patients and healers hope and search for the removal of the falling disease.

In the final instance, the diverse patterns of therapy choices and the open-endedness of the illness narratives of Swazi people with epilepsy derive from the perceived failure of both doctors and healers to answer a fundamental need of people with epilepsy. This need – that the illness may be removed – is culturally shaped by the perception of man as a vulnerable entity in a dangerous world.

The healers

Traditional healers are trained to counter the dangerous or immoral forces causing illness and misfortune. From early ethnographic descriptions, a dichotomy emerges distinguishing the female *sangoma* (diviner) and the male *nyanga yemitsi* or *lugedla* (specialist in medicines, herbalist).[21] People would consult a diviner for diagnosis and subsequently visit a specialist in medicines for appropriate treatment. A survey of traditional healers in the early 1980s[22] indeed revealed healer practice to correlate with gender in Swaziland. Half of the registered healers mainly practised herbalism, 90 per cent of them being male, in contrast to the only 10 per cent male among the healers mainly practising divination. In the late 1980s, in contrast, Gort reported that Swazi healer types could no longer be distinguished by name, sex, or medical practice.[23] The term *inyanga* then referred to a herbalist or a traditional healer in general, and healers in turn called themselves *sangoma* or *inyanga*, usually practising combinations of herbalism, divination and biomedicine, with some even using alternative techniques derived from Asian or Western contexts.[24] As many women as men were found to practise healing.[25] Gort interpreted this as evidence of the disappearance of the previously found 'classic' diviner and herbalist dichotomy.

A decade of change in the medical practice of one of my key informants, a young female diviner, may serve as an example. In 1988 Make Mkhombe, as I will call her, stood out as a prototype of the 'classic diviner'. As the brilliant daughter-in-law of the matron of a well-known healers' college,[26] she was recognised in the community as an authority in divinatory and exorcistic techniques and as a specialist in the treatment of a women's disease that caused infertility and was thought to be due to witchcraft. Although her ancestor hut displayed a small collection of containers with traditional medicines, Make Mkhombe explicitly distanced her healership from herbalism. As an adolescent she had wanted to become a nurse, and she favoured co-operation with biomedicine, but she condemned the use of modern medicines by traditional healers.

Nonetheless, six years later, in 1994, Make Mkhombe's stock of medicines had expanded enormously. Having joined the church of her mother, she now considered herself a Christian. The ancestors would still occasionally visit her to give their diagnoses, but she now focused almost entirely on acquiring new medical techniques, and enthusiastically told of meetings organised by the national healers' association. She had even co-organised a workshop on improved preservation and dosage of herbal medicines. She proudly showed recent photographs of her performances during healing rituals, as well as many pictures of white people who had visited and consulted her. She had plans to build a combined clinic, where she hoped to co-operate with a modern physician.

Three years later, in 1997, the ancestor shrine had all but disappeared from her ancestor hut. It now featured an enormous office desk, topped by telephone and fax. Although she had not been able to realise her plan for the clinic, her activities had brought her to an international conference overseas as a representative of African traditional healers. She showed pictures of herself in traditional gear making a show of bone-throwing, a typical divinatory method, at the conference. She confided, however, that in reality her ancestors had agreed not to 'disturb' her anymore, unless she transgressed their moral rules, for instance by misusing her healing power. In the meantime she had acquired new divinatory techniques from a Western alternative healer, which she now considered her main professional asset.

The position of biomedicine, as seen from a traditional healer's perspective is clearly expressed in the floor plan of the co-operative clinic that Make Mkhombe had originally planned.[27] Her explanation of how patients would be referred reflects the traditional belief that some diseases are the domain of doctors and others are preferably treated by healers.[28] It also shows that healers acknowledge that therapy choices are ultimately made by the patients themselves.

> ... it will be decided by the patient, because they will be informed that there are two sectors in that clinic, the modern and the traditional. So if signs and symptoms of the patient show that it needs a doctor I will refer to the doctor

and the doctor will refer or call me to check the patient if he is not clear about the affliction of that particular person, and I will do the same. … A person who has *tilwane* [lit. animal spirits] , is he who will know that he is supposed to be seen by a traditional healer as he was knowing that the affliction is caused by magic powers.[29]

This account coincides with the description of Green and Makhubu of medical pluralism in the sense of two medical systems being available, each with its own advantages and limitations.[30] This view is supported also by some Swazi health officials who advocate the co-operation between healers and Western-trained doctors. However, terms like 'alternative sectors of health care' and 'intersectoral co-operation' hide that one medical tradition may overarch the other, or that such 'sectors' may be entities difficult to compare from the perspective of the actors involved.

The floor plan of the clinic also reveals an implicit notion of a hierarchical relationship between the two co-operating partners.[31] First, some facilities such as the reception and waiting room, administration and pharmacy, kitchen and store rooms as well as the patients' wards, are shared. Importantly, the consultation rooms are separated. From the waiting room the first door opens to the doctor's consultation room. This mirrors the widespread opinion of Swazi healers that Western health care is most efficient in the fight against acute symptoms, and should, in such cases, be the first port of call.

Between the two consultation rooms lie the storage room for modern and traditional medication and their shared toilets. Surprisingly, the doctor's treatment room also lies on this corridor, in such a way that the healer has to cross this room on her way to store room or bathroom. The treatment domain of the doctor is treaded by both. In contrast, the traditional treatment rooms are solely accessible from the healer's consultation room. One of these rooms is also the only round structure in the entire clinic, resembling the traditional style houses still preferred by many Swazi.

On the eve of the new millennium, in 1999, Make Mkhombe finally drew on traditional, biomedical as well as Western alternative methods. Because of her emphasis on a variety of medical techniques she was now considered a specialist in medicines in the area: people labelled her an *inyanga* rather than a *sangoma*. However, she still felt keen on pointing out that she carried her ancestors. One way of proving this point was by showing prospective patients a copy of an English book published on her life as a diviner. The book displays many pictures of her in traditional attire, performing the rituals identified with divinership.[32]

These changes in the practice of a particular healer seem to reflect the developments described by Gort. The distinction between herbalism and divination became blurred; techniques from very different cultural backgrounds were combined. However, the question arises why Make Mkhombe still found it necessary to project a public image of an ancestor-inspired *sangoma*. To answer this question we have to look at how the elements of various different origins are integrated within her practice.

Technical and divine knowledge

Although the classic herbalist and diviner may not exist as clearly delimited types in reality, as 'ideal types' they represent two different, culturally sanctioned healing powers: herbalism and divination. Herbalism addresses the substantial aspect of people's interactions with their environment. It relates to botanical, animal and human substances, and to the (ritual) methods to make them work. Such knowledge may be acquired from other specialists in medicines and derives from the ancestors only in the sense that this is the case for power in general.[33] Herbalistic knowledge can be acquired by any aspirant to the healing profession.

Divinatory healing power, in contrast, cannot be acquired of one's own volition; the ancestors decide whom they will give it to. They force their descendants to accept this gift by sending them a serious illness that is cured only if they consent to undergo the necessary apprenticeship. This will lead them into an irreversible transformation, making them part of an institution, a sisterhood of healers, all selected by their respective ancestors to embody their presence in society.[34] Ancestral healing power addresses the social-moral aspects of people's interactions with their environment. It enables healers to 'sense' (see, feel, smell) the problems in human relationships and in the moral order that underlie so much illness and misfortune. No herbalist or Western-trained doctor, however well qualified, is likely to have access to divinatory knowledge. Traditional healers and Western physicians have in common that they can acquire medical knowledge and skills through learning and training. This shared technical rather than spiritually linked background enables biomedicine to be considered as yet another 'technical' source of learning that could usefully be drawn on. Indeed, some judge biomedicine to be superior to the technical knowledge of traditional herbalism.

However, Swazi traditional healing has always been dynamic and open to innovations.[35] The introduction of biomedicine is a case in point. At the end of the nineteenth century tales circulated in Southern Africa about the powerful weapons of the Whites, as well as about their knowledge of strong medicines.[36] Since medicines were conceived of as matter 'manipulated' with a view to influencing a person's fortune, medical specialists were always treated with respect as well as with fear and suspicion. The Swazi Dlamini, for example, like other leading families in the region, had always taken care to integrate, safeguard and control the medical knowledge of the groups which they incorporated into their kingdom.[37] So, when word of the powerful medicine of the 'Wjites' reached the Dlamini King in the 1890s, an invitation was sent out. In 1893 a Scottish missionary doctor answered the King's call. His fame rapidly spread: three months after his arrival he was consulted by the queen-mother,[38] and the advance of biomedicine in Swaziland is said to have begun.

Although most healers recognise the specific expertise of biomedicine in relation to acute illness and symptom relief, biomedicine and traditional healing are not considered health care sectors of equal value existing side by side. In particular, those healers who are inspired by ancestors have access to a dimension accessible neither by specialists in traditional medicines nor by modern physicians.[39] The healing power relating to this socio-moral dimension is principally superior even to the supreme technical knowledge of biomedicine. Only healers empowered by the ancestors can counter the immoral forces of evildoing. For healing power derived from merely acquired, learned, knowledge such as herbalism or biomedicine, does not offer legitimacy in the moral domain. On the contrary, such mere technical knowledge can potentially be used for evil purposes. Significantly, the siSwati term for traditional medication, *umutsi* (siZulu: *muti*) denotes both wholesome and evil medicines. Because of their specialist knowledge herbalists are therefore specifically vulnerable to accusations of sorcery.

An extreme example of misusing technical knowledge is ritual murder, whereby a selected victim, often a child, is killed and parts of the body are removed to be used in traditional medicine – it is thought that mutilation takes place before the killing. From the findings of mutilated bodies there appears to be a preference for certain body parts: sexual organs, right arm, tongue, eyes. Ritual murder is an old phenomenon in southern Africa; it has been reported on in early colonial manuscripts, though its context has changed. Colonial reports spoke of 'doctoring the fields': human parts were supposedly used to ensure the fertility of the soil. Since the beginning of the twentieth century ritual murders are associated with competition over scarce power positions and commercial interests. Waves of ritual murders have taken place in neighbouring countries, for instance in Lesotho in the beginning of the century when the colonial government drastically reduced the number of chiefs in Lesotho,[40] or more recently in the early 1980s among the South-African Venda over newly available power positions due to political reforms. In Swaziland the Mpolonjeni murders are a well-known example. In 1988 three subsequent chiefs of the ruling Dvuba family died under suspicious circumstances. When the third body was found with characteristic mutilations the population of that chiefdom asked the king to take over the administration.[41] Usually, however, ritual murders in Swaziland take place as isolated cases. Those found guilty often prove to be wealthy or powerful people who wished to improve their position, but also healers that contributed their knowledge in choosing the victim, the killing method and the parts that had to be removed.

In an important article Ngubane maintains that ritual murder is the ultimate expression of an accepted conceptual principle in Swazi culture, namely that by sacrificing, fortune may be gained, human sacrifice forming the apex of a hierarchy of sacrifices.[42] Certain circumstances simply ask for the sacrifice of a human being, and in the final instance the involvement of healers in ritual murders stems from their professional role. I agree with her conclusion, but would add that this is the case even if the murder aims merely at the acquisition of 'human material' for medicines. The substantial powers of such material are not thought to be essentially different from that of any other material; it is only of a higher order. There is some evidence that 'human material' – not only from ritual murders, but also from graves and graveyards – is being traded and that this trade does not recognise national boundaries.[43]

As far as I know, no ritual murders are ascribed to biomedically trained doctors. However, as some modern medical practices such as blood transfusion and organ transplants involve the manipulation and interference with the human body, biomedicine can be perceived as not considering the use of 'human material' as inherently evil. This argument is at times used in defence of traditional healing practices. The reaction of Make Mkhombe when a doctor offered her painkillers to treat her headache is illustrative of suspicions raised also in regard to biomedical prescriptions: 'They are very white. They haven't been made of human bones, have they?'

As argued before, divinistic powers are considered as gifts of the ancestors. Healers exercising such powers are representatives and keepers of the moral order.[44] They would lose their healing power if they got involved in immoral practices, such as sorcery or ritual murder. This means that healers are vulnerable to accusations of immoral practices the more they focus on merely 'technical' knowledge. I believe this is why Make Mkhombe needs to convince her clients that her ancestors are still with her, even though she almost exclusively practises herbal, Western alternative and some basic biomedical techniques. As I have argued elsewhere,[45] for those who consult healers, a history of ancestor illness testifies to their true calling and legitimacy, since it proves their involuntariness and clears them of selfish motives.

Although parts of biomedicine can be embraced by healers as new medical knowledge to be learned and appropriated, it cannot replace the superior healing power inspired by the ancestors and the moral legitimacy that is seen to go along with it. The domain of divine ancestral authority is inaccessible to and not adequately 'catered for' by biomedicine. In the Swazi context the practice of biomedicine by itself or in combination with herbalism does not necessarily guarantee moral legitimacy.

The public's view of tradition

Swaziland's legal system is essentially dualistic, recognising two parallel systems functioning side by side – European-style courts functioning under Roman-Dutch law and chiefs' courts functioning under Swazi common law. Roman-Dutch law applies to all inhabitants, but white people cannot be brought to trial at a chief's court. Moreover, serious crimes leading to criminal persecution, can only be dealt with by European-style courts. Under common law, publicly recognised *tangoma* [pl. *sangoma*] are still credited with the moral authority necessary to counter social evil. Their diagnostic and curative practices are considered legitimate and necessary by most traditional leaders. In November 1985, for instance, a strike of lightning killed two children at a primary school and injured some 15 other children. Since witches are able to manipulate lightning, the chiefs in the area decided to ask the king to consent to a seance, during which several *tangoma* would 'sniff out' evildoers among all people possibly involved.[46] On another occasion a *sangoma* (who had successfully treated a woman for her infertility, she successfully conceived children but refused to pay for the healer's work claiming that the children were the result of her private prayers), was set in the right by the chief. He ordered the woman to pay her healer since 'they had made a fair agreement'.[47] Many other court cases too testify to the fact that the aetiology of witchcraft still forms part of a fundamental perception of reality.

Under Roman-Dutch law, however, medicine relying on 'higher powers' and explanations of illness in terms of witchcraft are liable for punishment. It claims that the supernatural forces of traditional healers and witches are fictive – literally the legal statutes speak of 'pretended power of divination or other pretended supernatural power'. In practice the anti-witchcraft law is not actively enforced. In fact it is clearly contradicted by the late King Sobhuza's Order in Council in 1954, mandating the registration of healers and providing a standardised fee schedule.[48]

But even in European courts, attitudes to witchcraft are ambivalent. The belief in such powers can be taken as mitigating circumstances. In 1986, for instance, a tragic case was brought to High Court. A young man had murdered his grandmother, because his family and a traditional healer had convinced him that she had bewitched him, so that he suffered from epilepsy, getting injured during a seizure. In consideration of the boy's honest belief he was sentenced to five years in jail rather than being executed.[49] The legal position of Swazi healers is very different from that of Maori healers described by Patricia Laing.[50] While the wording of the Swazi anti-witchcraft act resembles the Maori *Tohunga* Suppression Act in its description of traditional medicine as superstition, Swazi healers benefited greatly from support by Swazi traditional leaders who kept most of their political and legal power during the merely six decades of British indirect rule. At present the contradictions originating from the dualistic legal system are still unresolved, to the chagrin of both proponents and adversaries to traditional healing.

During my stay in Swaziland (1985–1988), the status of traditional healing was given daily attention in the media. The images of traditional healing created in these public debates clearly channel public emotions. Murders originating in the belief in witchcraft or for ritual purposes, deaths at the hands of healers experimenting with modern medication, and tales of nightly visits to healers by people of high status, easily played upon such emotions. For instance, at the verdict of the boy with epilepsy, the judge strongly accused traditional healers of stimulating false belief and primitive practices out of greed, and called for the arrest and trial of 'witchdoctors' and diviners:

> People believing in this practice were mostly witch-finders and diviners and it is surprising enough why such people are not brought before the courts for prosecution as they are the ones behind this quick-spreading bad disease. ... They spread these primitive, unhealthy and unpleasant beliefs to innocent people and in turn people go about hating their neighbours and sometimes go to an extent of murdering the alleged bewitchers.[51]

People who believe in witchcraft typically argue that the hostile stance towards healers is a relic from the colonial period that should be discarded by now. The organisation of traditional healers regularly calls for a change in the colonial anti-witchcraft law. Listen to the angry reaction of the editor of *The Times of Swaziland* when in a letter to the editor, a Mr. S. had called the traditional healers 'devil's children':

> The obviously poor opinion that Mr. S. holds of the country and its people is insulting. … In this country we abide by a clearly defined legal system, among which, witchcraft is a moral and criminal offence. Surely, in the twentieth century, Mr. S. does not believe that we should be re-colonized, so that we can be civilized. In this country we have accepted that herbs do not have to come from any glorified address in Europe to be effective as medical cure…. Mr. S. and all those who hold similar beliefs, please GET OUT with your demons and leave us in peace.[52]

It is significant that the editor speaks of the liability of witchcraft instead of that of witchcraft accusations. He considers witchcraft a reality and traditional healing the inalienable heritage of the Swazi people. The moral value of traditional interpretations of illness and therapies is claimed against ethnocentrism and colonialism.

The emotional appeal of this argument depends upon the invocation of an image of Swaziland as a bounded unity. Some pronounced characteristics indeed seem to confirm this image. The country is one of only three remaining kingdoms in Africa, the dynasty of its present king dating back to the beginning of the sixteenth century. Nation and polity are not the same, however. Not all people living in Swaziland belong to the Swazi nation. It is the loyalty to the king which makes a person a Swazi and which gives him access to rights over land, still the basis of existence in Swaziland.[53]

The institution of sacred kingship forms the prime representation of the Swazi nation as a bounded entity. The Swazi king is not only the representative of the nation – a sort of high priest – in a certain sense the king is the nation. The wellbeing of the king, especially his fertility, is directly connected with the wellbeing of the nation and the fertility of the soil and the people.[54] One could also say that the king embodies Swazi identity: he is the only person who is allowed to change traditions or even destroy them.[55] The defence of traditional healing in terms of these representations of 'Swazi-ness' is therefore of special importance. The argument runs like this: If one is against traditional healing, one is against the nation, and one betrays the Swazi people, the king and one's identity as a Swazi. The existence of ancestors and their moral power cannot be denied, since this would mean the denial of the power of the royal ancestors, and therefore of the sacred kingship and the legitimacy of social-political structures.

The power of this complex set of ideas was made acutely clear in 1987, when the originally British pastor of the Rhema church in Swaziland became the first foreigner to be kept prisoner for sixty days without trial under an emergency law that was installed to control political opponents and plotters against the king. In the four years of his stay in Swaziland Phil Dacre had regularly sent letters to the editor about the dangers of the belief in witchcraft and traditional healers.[56] In 1987 he published an article in his church magazine with the title 'Incwala;

witchcraft, sex orgies and traditions?', in which he described the secret rituals of the Swazi nation as un-Christian and against morality, and stated that the rituals enforced the belief in witchcraft. After months of imprisonment he explained during a trial that he had received a vision of God in which he had seen part of the ritual and examples of traditional medicines. He only had wished to warn the nation against un-Christian practices. The judge, however, as well as public figures and commoners perceived his actions as an attack on the integrity of the Swazi nation: a political act.[57]

The defence of the legitimacy of traditional healing in terms of 'Swazi-ness' can be understood as part of a process of 'cultural closure', 'a search for fixed orientation points and action frames, as well as determined efforts to affirm old and construct new boundaries'.[58] However, another process may be involved, too. Whereas healers see themselves as guardians against witchcraft and sorcery, they are in turn portrayed by their opponents as the very agents of these immoral powers. The Swazi Traditional Healers' Association has therefore adopted a formal policy to counter such accusations. To become a member of the organisation – and thus avoid the risk of inviting accusations of quackery or immoral activities – healers have to specialise. 'Being general' figures in negative opposition to this, as it is associated with the use of technical knowledge for non-medical purposes, such as commercial or political aims. It is to these non-medical domains, where competition reigns and one may prosper, that evil medicine and ritual murders allude to. To prevent accusations of immoral activity, some healers therefore choose to present their practice as being located squarely within the boundaries of 'the medical' as it is perceived by biomedicine.[59] For, according to people who believe in witchcraft, misfortune and illness share the same origin. To distance themselves from practices that may threaten their moral position, healers claim definitions of illness and health that are very different from these traditional perceptions. In that sense traditional healing indeed becomes an 'invented tradition'.[60] Paradoxically, healers have come to claim the very domain as part of their traditional heritage against which they at times struggle to defend their professional position.

Conclusion

Social scientists and health professionals pleading the cause of African healers commonly understand 'integration of traditional and modern healing' as the incorporation of traditional healers into the national health system, for instance at the level of primary health care, thereby extending and/or enriching that system.[61] This case study has highlighted the reverse. Swazi healing easily incorporates biomedicine into the traditional idiom of illness and healing, and, as it is based upon learned knowledge, gives it a place like herbalism next to but also morally inferior to divination. Elsewhere in this voulme Laing maintains that the notion of biomedicine and Maori healing as competing entities within a medically plural system is based upon the construction of Maori healing as merely spiritual and biomedicine as merely material, thereby doing no justice to the complexities involved. Likewise, Swazi advocates of co-operation between Western doctors and healers often suggest a division of labour, allocating technical medical care to the first and spiritual or psycho-social care to the latter. However, from the perspective of healers and their patients, the contrast is not between biomedicine and traditional healing. Divinatory healing power is thought to be superior to and to overarch both herbalism and biomedicine. Therefore, Swazi medical pluralism cannot be understood as two medical systems being available side by side, each with its own advantages and limitations, from which patients may freely choose and practitioners may construct hybrid practices.[62] On the basis of age, gender, cognitive capacities and their position in the household, people with epilepsy are bounded to biomedicine and traditional healing in varying but compelling ways.

Strategies to co-operate with healers by combining the best of two medical systems, are based upon the assumption that healers, doctors and health planners would be free to dissect different medical traditions, using elements in chosen combinations. By focusing upon changes in the practice of a diviner, I have argued that the appropriation of biomedical and other foreign practices by traditional healers – in other words: the localisation of biomedicine in Swaziland – takes place within the context of hierarchically ordered healing powers. Biomedicine cannot replace the superior healing power inspired by the ancestors, necessary to counter the evil lurking in difficult human relationships. Neither can herbalists escape the ambivalence inherent in their healing techniques. In the context of witchcraft beliefs healing aims at curing illness as well as enhancing (material) well-being and prosperity, the domains where the prime motivator for sorcery, jealousy, reigns. Healers are eager and free to learn new medical techniques. However, they have to answer the moral implications involved in such choices. Some do this by claiming ancestral power whilst practising as herbalists. Others claim to focus upon illness from the biomedical perspective, whilst defending the unique character and legitimacy of traditional healing in terms of 'Swazi-ness', a concept connecting the belief in witchcraft and in the efficacy of ancestral healing with the legitimacy of the king.

Notes

1 '… stories of sickness … not as "clinical histories" but as moral tales of remorse and regret, as social dilemmas, as cultural ironies, as the imperative stuff of myth and tragedy'. A. Kleinman, *The Illness Narratives. Suffering, Healing, and the Human Condition*, New York, Basic Books, 1988, p. 14. See also A. Kleinman, *Writing at the Margin; Discourse between Anthropology and Medicine*, Berkeley, Los Angeles/London, University of California Press, 1995.

2 R. Reis, *Sporen van Ziekte. Medische Pluraliteit en epilepsie in Swaziland (Traces of Illness; Medical Plurality and Epilepsy in Swaziland)*, Amsterdam, Het Spinhuis, 1996.

3 E. Gort, 'Changing traditional medicine in rural Swaziland. The effects of the global system', *Social Science and Medicine*, 29, 9 (1989): 1099–104.

Coining Swazi approaches to illness 'medical traditions' honours their historical depth and geographical distribution. See R. Reis, 'The wounded healer as ideology: The work of Ngoma in Swaziland', in R. Van Dijk, R. Reis and M. Spierenburg (eds), *The Quest for Fruition through Ngoma. The Politicial Aspects of Healing in Southern Africa*, London/Athens, James Currey/Ohio Press, 2000. J.M. Janzen, *Ngoma. Discourses of Healing in Central and Southern Africa*, Berkeley, Los Angeles/Oxford, University of California Press, 1992. To speak of biomedicine as a medical tradition draws attention to its historicity and cultural character. E.N. Anderson Jr., 'Health care and culture'. *Reviews in Anthropology*, 8, 1 (1981): 45–58.

M. Last, 'Professionalization of indigenous healers', in Th.M. Johnson and C.F. Sargent (eds), *Medical Anthropology. Contemporary Theory and Method*, New York, Praeger, 1990, p. 351.

4   L.P. Makhubu, *Towards the Integration of Traditional and Modern Medicine*, Unpublished Paper for Swadev workshop, 1–10 May, 1978. E.C. Green and L. Makhubu, 'Traditional healers in Swaziland: Towards improved cooperation between the traditional and modern health sectors', *Social Science and Medicine*, 18, 12, (1984): 1071–9. See also E. Gort, *Changing Traditional Medicine in Rural Swaziland. A World Systems Analysis*, Unpublished Master's thesis, Columbia, Columbia University, 1987.

5   P.U. Unschuld, 'Epistemological issues and changing legitimation: Traditional Chinese medicine in the twentieth century', in C. Leslie and A. Young (eds), *Paths to Asian Medical Knowledge*, Berkeley, Los Angeles/Oxford, University of California Press, 1992, pp. 44–61.

6   Parts of this chapter are revised and condensed versions of paragraphs in my doctoral thesis on medical plurality and epilepsy in Swaziland. Reis, *Sporen van Ziekte*, 1996. An earlier version of this chapter was presented at the Society for the Social History of Medicine Conference in Southampton, 15–16 September 1998, 'Plural medicine – orthodox and heterodox medicine in western and colonial countries during the 19th and 20th centuries'. I thank the participants at the Conference for their inspiring debate. I am specifically grateful to Waltraud Ernst, Maarten Bode, Danielle Willems, and the anonymous reviewers for their invaluable and constructive criticism.

7   The first part of the research took place during a three year residence in Swaziland (August 1985–November 1988). In 1994 the research area was revisited to discuss current developments in health care with key informants and to investigate the viability of some of the central findings. In 1997 the fieldwork area and a small income-generating project that was initiated by a group of people with epilepsy on the basis of the research, were revisited. Of the interviewed people with epilepsy, 48 per cent were male and 52 per cent were female. Approximately 40 per cent were children below 16 years of age, and approximately 15 per cent of the people interviewed had cognitive impairments. In these interviews parents or other family members participated as well. Almost all informants suffered from generalised tonic-clonic seizures.

8   These figures are estimates. S.D. Shorvon and P.J. Farmer, 'Epilepsy in developing countries', *Epilepsia*, 29, Suppl. 1 (1988): S50 define 'treatment gap' as the percentage of patients in a defined population on any one day, with active epilepsy, not receiving anticonvulsant medication. The prevalence study in Swaziland, however, took place in a three-month period. A person was defined as having active epilepsy, if he or she had had two (non-febrile) seizures confirming to the phenomenology of epileptic seizures, the last one no longer than three years before. Almost all registered patients had generalised seizures. Since in any population partial seizures account for a considerable percentage of patients, one may expect the treatment gap for epilepsy to be even higher than the 80 per cent calculated from the research data. Non-compliance may also be higher than the estimated 64 per cent. A check of the patients records of the local clinic six years after the prevalence study revealed the 'disappearance' of 80 per cent of the registered patients.

9   Only 4 per cent of the visits to a traditional healer led to a diagnosis of ancestor calling.

10   B.J. Good, *Medicine, Rationality, and Experience. An Anthropological Perspective*, Cambridge, Cambridge University Press, 1994. Kleinman, *Writing at the Margin*, p.150.

11   Since visits to a traditional healer or faith healer were not always spontaneously mentioned, I would sometimes explicitly ask for it. Some people reacted by asking if I could recommend them a good healer.

12   R. Astuti, '"Cattle Beget Children" – but women must bear them. Fertility, sterility and belonging among women in Swaziland', in H.J. Tieleman (ed.), *Scenes of Change: Visions on Developments in Swaziland*, Leiden, African Studies Centre, 1988, p. 200.

13   M. Russell, 'Are households universal?', *Development and Change*, 24, (1993): 765.

14   R. Reis, 'Socio-structural factors and the treatment gap for epilepsy in Swaziland', Unpublished paper presented at the international workshop on the Treatment Gap in Epilepsy organised by

the International League Against Epilepsy Commission for the developing World, Marrakesh, 1–2 May 1999.

15 P. Fine, 'Traditional leadership and development in rural Swaziland', Unpublished report of the International Voluntary Service Field Office, Mbabane, 1983.

16 D.R. Gordon, 'Tenacious assumptions in western medicine', in Lock, M. and D.R. Gordon (eds), *Biomedicine Examined*, Dordrecht, Kluwer Academic Publishers, 1988, pp. 19–56.

17 Foster, G.M. and B.G. Anderson, *Medical Anthropology*, New York, Alfred A. Knopf, 1978.

18 R. Reis, 'Een neus voor goed en kwaad' (A nose for good and evil), *Medische Antropologie*, 6, 1 (1994c): 51–65. Reis, 'Socio-structural factors and the treatment gap for epilepsy in Swaziland', unpublished paper presented at the international workshop on the Treatment Gap in Epilepsy organised by the International League Against Epilepsy Commission for the developing World, Marrakesh, 1–2 May 1999.

19 H. Ngubane, *Body and Mind in Zulu Medicine. An Ethnography of Health and Disease in Nyuswa-Zulu Thought and Practice*, London, Academic Press, 1997.

20 The other part being the fact that people may wait a long time before they visit a clinic. About 40 per cent of the people with epilepsy identified during the prevalence study had not visited a clinic for more than a year after their first seizure. For more details see R. Reis, 'Anthropological Aspects', *Tropical and Geographical Medicine*, 46(3), (1994a): S37–9, and R. Reis, 'Evil in the body, disorder of the brain: Interpretations of epilepsy and the treatment gap in Swaziland', Tropical and Geographical medicine, 46(3), (1994b): S40–3.

21 See H. Kuper, *An African Aristocracy*, London, Oxford University Press, 1961. B.A. Marwick, *The Swazi*, London, Frank Cass and Co., 1966; Gort, *Changing Traditional Medicine*, p. 93; Green and Makhubu, 'Traditional healers', p. 1072; Ngubane, *Body and Mind*, pp. 106, 190 (for the Zulu); R.W.S. Cheetham and R.J. Cheetham, 'Concepts of mental illness amongst the rural Xhosa people in South Africa', *Australian and New Zealand Journal of Psychiatry*, 10, 39 (1976): 40 (for the Xosa); G.L. Chavunduka, 'Traditional healers and the Shona patient', *Zambeziana*, vol. III., Gwelo, Mambo Press, 1978, p. 20 (for the Shona).

'*Sangoma*' is a generic term for a healer claiming a certain type of power and authority based on claims to a specific association and communication with the spirit world. See Van Dijk, Reis and Spierenburg (eds), *The Quest for Fruition*, p. 7. In contact with clients, i.e. when the *sangoma* takes the healing role, this power is expressed and performed in divination. Some divination techniques may be practised by healers who have not gone through the training specific for *tangoma* (pl. *sangoma*), and therefore technically are not *tangoma*. However, if asked these healers will claim a link with the ancestral world.

In mediamistic healing, that is, healing appealing to extra-human agencies, divination is a collective term for different techniques by which *tangoma* may divine (may see visions, dream, smell evil, hear the whispering of ancestors sitting on their shoulders, speak with ancestral tongues, etc.). See, for instance, A.I. Berglund, *Zulu Thought-Patterns and Symbolism*, London, C. Hurst and Company, 1976; J.M. Janzen, *Ngoma. Discourses of Healing in Central and Southern Africa*, Berkeley, Los Angeles/Oxford, University of California Press; 1992. W.M.J. Van Binsbergen, 'Four-table divination as trans-regional medical technology in southern Africa', *Journal of Religion in Africa*, 25, 2 (1995): 114–40; R. Devisch, 'Perspectives on divination in contemporary sub-Saharan Africa', in W. Van Binsbergen and M. Schoffeleers (eds), *Theoretical Explorations in African Religion*, London, KPI, 1985, pp. 50–83.

Some *tangoma* may predominantly use one technique and then be associated with that technique. Bone throwing is one technique among many. Hence confusions frequently arise, as when Janzen, *Ngoma*, p. 38, maintains that '*takoza*' is the technically correct term for *tangoma* that practise the *femba* (a specific divination ritual), whereas *thokoza* (in siSwati *(ku)tfokota* means being happy) is the addressing term by which the specific type of spirit that 'does' the *femba* is welcomed. See Reis, 'The wounded healer as ideology', p. 74.

In my view the distinction between diviners and *tangoma* appears fluid and changeable mainly because the terms address different things. The term 'diviner' addresses the techniques by which healers who communicate with the spirit world in a specific way do their 'healing work'. The term *sangoma* (from the proto-Bantu construction **-goma*) addresses the specific type of power that makes divination (and other 'work' based upon the communication with ancestors) possible. See A.E. Meeussen, *Bantu Lexical Reconstructions*, Tervuren, Musee Royale de l'Afrique Centrale, 1980, L9; Van Dijk, Reis and Spierenburg (eds), *The Quest for Fruition*, p. 6; Reis, 'The wounded healer as ideology', p. 62. See also: Berglund, *Zulu Thought-Patterns and Symbolism* (specifically chapter 5, 'Diviners-servant of the shades').

22   Green and Makhubu, 'Traditional healers'.

23   Gort, 'Changing traditional medicine in rural Swaziland. The effects of the global system'; *Social Science and Medicine*, 29, 9 (1989): 1099–104.

24   As K. Gardner, *Global Migrants, Local Lives. Travel and Transformation in Rural Bangladesh*, Oxford, Clarendon Press, 1995, observes, other 'cores' than only Western biomedicine may be discerned, thus complicating the understanding of globalisation as a process involving streams from core to margin (p. 273).

25   Gort, 'Changing traditional medicine', pp. 1101–2.

26   See H. Ngubane, 'Aspects of clinical practice and traditional organization of indigenous healers in South Africa', *Social Science and Medicine*, 15B (1981): 361–5, for a description of the regional importance of the training colleges of diviners in southern Africa.

27   This floor plan was drawn by an architect on her instructions and sent to me by mail. Discussions ensued by correspondence.

28   Green and Makhubu, 'Traditional healers', p. 1073.

29   Make Mkhombe, personal correspondence.

30   Green and Makhubu, 'Traditional healers', pp. 1073, 1077; E.C. Green, 'Can collaborative programs between biomedical and African indigenous health practitioners succeed?', *Social Science and Medicine*, 27, 11 (1988): 1125–30.

31   Although I do not engage in a full symbolic analysis here, Cunningham's remark that order in building expresses ideas about unity and difference, was taken as inspiration. See C.E. Cunningham, 'Order in the Atoni house', in R. Needham (ed.), *Right and Left. Essays on Dual Symbolic Classification*, Chicago/London, The University of Chicago Press, 1973, p. 204.

32   Personal communication of Danielle Willems, a Dutch graduate student who in 1999 spent several months in Swaziland for fieldwork purposes.

33   A. Fogelquist, *The Red-Dressed Zionists. Symbols of Power in a Swazi Independent Church*, Uppsala, Uppsala Research Reports in Cultural Anthropology, 1986, p. 48.

34   Janzen, *Ngoma*; Van Dijk, Reis and Spierenburg (eds), *The Quest for Fruition through Ngoma. The Political Aspects of Healing in Southern Africa*, London/Athens, James Currey/Ohio Press, 2000.

35   C. Leslie and A. Young (eds), *Paths to Asian Medical Knowledge*, Berkeley, Los Angeles/Oxford, University of California Press, 1992, p. 6.

36   F.J. Perkins, 'A history of christian missions in Swaziland to 1910', Unpublished Doctoral Thesis, Johannesburg, University of Witwatersrand, 1974, p. 47.

37   Kuper, *An African Aristocracy*, pp. 169–79; H. Kuper, *Sobhuza II. Ngwenyama and King of Swaziland. The Story of an Hereditary Ruler and His Country*, London, Gerald Duckworth and Co., 1978, p. 62. Marwick, *The Swazi*, p. 218.

38   Perkins, 'History of christian missions', pp. 303–4.

39   E.C. Green, 'Traditional healers, mothers, and childhood diarrhoeal diseases in Swaziland: The interface of anthropology and health education', *Social Science and Medicine*, 20, 3 (1985): 277–85.

40   Kuper, *Sobhuza, p.* 176.

41   'Chief found mutilated', *Times*, 19-09-88; 'Take Over!', *The Times* 26-09-88.

42   H. Ngubane, 'The predicament of the sinister healer: Some observations on "ritual murder" and the professional role of the inyanga', in M. Last and G.L. Chavunduka (eds), *The Professionalisation of African Medicine*, Manchester, Manchester University Press, 1986, p. 197.

43   'Woman sold her daughter! How?', *Observer*, 17-05-88; 'Murdered child's arm in South Africa', *Observer*, 19-05-88; 'The return of the ritual murderers', *The Times*, 29-06-88. Or see for more recent cases: *Observer*, 08-08-97, and in South Africa: *The Mercury*, 15-07-97. R. Reis, 'Menselijk materiaal als medicijn: over rituele moord in Swaziland' (Human material as medicine; on ritual murder in Swaziland), *Medische Antropologie*, 9, 2 (1997): 362–76.

44 Green and Makhubu, 'Traditional healers', p. 1073.

45 Reis, 'The wounded healer', (2000): 61–75.

46 *The Swazi Observer*, 30-11-85 [n.p.].

47 *The Times of Swaziland*, 05-06-84 [n.p.].

48 Gort, *Changing Traditional Medicine*, pp. 73–4, 88, n.32.

49 *The Times of Swaziland*, 10-09-86 [n.p.].

50 Laing, chapter 9 in this collection.

51 See 'Arrest these witches!', *Times of Swaziland*, 10-09-86; 'I wanted death but home will do', *The Times of Swaziland*, 08-10-87.

52 *The Times of Swaziland*, 20-05-87.

53 Foreigners may become Swazi by being granted Swazi citizenship by the king. This happened to king Sobhuza's official biographer, the anthropologist Hilda Kuper. See M. Russell, 'Jilda Kuper 1911–92', *Africa*, 64, 1 (1994): 145–9; K.O. Adinkrah, '"We shall take our case to the king". Legitimacy and tradition in the administration of law in Swaziland', *The Comparative and International Law Journal of Southern Africa*, 14, 1 (1991): 234.

54 See J.M. Schoffeleers (ed.), *Guardians of the Land: Essays on Central African Territorial Cults*, Gwelo, Mambo Press for the University of Salisbury, 1979; R.P. Stevens, *Lesotho, Botswana, and Swaziland. The former High Commission Territories in Southern Africa*, London, Pall Mall Press, 1967, p. 192; W.M.J. Van Binsbergen, *Religious Change in Zambia: Exploratory Studies*, London/Boston, Kegan Paul International, 1981, p. 123.

55 J.S.M. Matsebula, *A History of Swaziland* (third edition), Cape Town, Longman Penguin Southern Africa, 1988, p. 19.

56 For instance: 'Witchcraft or herbalism?', *The Times*, 18-7-85; 'Stop this muti fervour!', *Observer*, 9-2-85.

57 For instance, the famous Swazi historian Matsebula, who served as crown witness, judged Dacre's action as '… wrong, scandalous and above all crushing to the dignity of indigenous and self-respecting Swazis'. 'Sedition trial commences. "It's scandalous"', *Observer*, 24–09–87.

58 B. Meyer and P. Geschiere (eds), *Globalization and Identity. Dialectics of Flow and Closure*, Oxford, Blackwell, 1999, p. 2; B. Anderson, *Imagined Communities. Reflections on the Origin and Spread of Nationalism*, London, Verso Editions, 1983; S. Harrison, 'Cultural boundaries', *Anthropology Today*, 15, 5 (1999): 13.

59 R. Pool, 'Afrikaanse medische systemen: vragen bij een antropologisch construct', *Medische Antropologie*, 4, 1 (1992): 47–55.

60 E. Hobsbawn and T. Ranger (eds), *The Invention of Tradition*, Cambridge, Cambridge University Press, 1983, pp. 4–9.

61 *The Promotion and Development of Traditional Medicine. Report of a WHO Meeting*, Geneva, World Health Organisation, 1978; Green, 'Collaborative programs', p. 1128; P. Ventevogel, *Whiteman's Things. Training and Detraining Healers in Ghana*, Amsterdam, Het Spinhuis, 1996, pp. 45–50.

62 Of all patients, 14 per cent consulted a *sangoma* first, 15 per cent a herbalist, 12 per cent a non-specified traditional healer, and 10 per cent a faith healer.

7 Nurses as culture brokers in twentieth-century South Africa

Anne Digby and Helen Sweet

Conventional accounts of the history of health care in South Africa have focused on biomedicine, its development and dissemination.[1] It is only the extent of contemporary health problems, first with sexually transmitted diseases, and currently with the AIDS pandemic, that is resulting in a fuller account being taken of the cultural beliefs and practices of the African population. A longer-term historical view of medicine in southern Africa provides a fascinating view of the subtle shifts in the relationship between Western and traditional medicine, in which the latter achieved only fluctuating visibility through colonial eyes. In contrast to the colonists, however, missionaries were always particularly sensitive to the presence of a pluralistic medicine in southern Africa, although they tended to see indigenous medicine as mere superstition, with 'witch doctors' practising magic and sorcery. It was in the rural hospitals administered by missionaries that many African nurses were trained. The work of these nurses was at the intersection of two healthcare worlds, and this chapter explores the different ways in which they may have acted as culture brokers between the 'modern' Western medical model of their training and the African 'traditional' medicine of many of their patients.

The first subject for investigation is the work of the nurse in the mission hospital in relation to her perceived role in brokering social change by furthering the substitution of indigenous medicine by Western culture (including both medicine and Christianity). Second, her work in the district clinic of the mission is examined to clarify whether in these more remote locations, where greater professional independence was possible, the nurse developed a rather different informal role in facilitating interaction between different forms of medicine[2]. Finally, the African nurse's more recent role within the community is discussed in relation to her work in helping the patient understand, gain access to, and negotiate different health-care options. Emphasis is placed on the extent to which the nurse respected the patient's culture, without seeking to change the patient's health care choices, and the degree to which she effectively acted as an advocate in trying to empower the patient to become an informed consumer of health care options.[3]

Mission hospitals

The mission hospital was a significant location in which to analyse the ways in which nurses may have acted as culture brokers in working to further the displacement of indigenous by Western medicine. During the nineteenth century there was an appreciation in European missionary societies of the value of medical missionaries, especially in areas where mission penetration was otherwise extremely difficult (as in China or India), or where disease made their activity problematic (as, for example, in West Africa).[4] South Africa, in contrast, was a relatively accessible and healthy place so that although there were isolated examples of professionally trained missionaries, many who practised medicine in the early missions were amateurs. However, from the early twentieth century the value of a more specialist mission was universally recognised, so that by 1944 there were over 40 medical missionaries in South Africa together with more than 50 mission hospitals,[5] and by 1975, 117 mission hospitals had been built. These provided the main source of Western health care in rural areas with a preponderantly black population.[6]

Early medical activity by missionaries and their wives was usually a short-term, humanitarian response to the request by Africans for European medicine. A missionary in the London Missionary Society (LMS) wrote that 'My heaviest secular duties as a missionary are medical … they [the patients] frequently occupy me in seasons of severe sickness from morning 'till night'.[7] But medical activity soon encompassed an evangelistic strategy prompted by the sluggish progress of Christian conversion. 'Civilisation is making its way slowly – with exceeding slowness – among them, and by far the larger proportion are still heathen', wrote James Stewart of Lovedale.[8] It was at Lovedale that the Free Church of Scotland founded Victoria Hospital, one of the earliest mission hospitals in South Africa. Here Dr. MacVicar pioneered the training of African nurses. MacVicar described the mission hospital as an 'instrument of love', and as the most 'essential Christian thing in the practical life of the people', so that it should be recognised as a powerful missionary agency'.[9] The Methodist Church also highlighted the distinctive roles of missionary doctor and nurse when it reminded mid-twentieth-century recruits that 'It is not only the bodies that receive attention in our hospitals and clinics, but the souls as well. … incident after incident testifies that the cure of souls is just as steady and just as permanent as the cure of disease'.[10]

For earlier missionaries this 'cure of souls' involved displacement of traditional belief systems through Christian conversion. The former were seen as involving witchcraft, sorcery or magic and thus as misguided, uncivilised, barbaric or evil. Dr. McCord of the American Zulu mission, had (with Dr. MacVicar) pioneered the training of black nurses. He spoke of his hopes in training young African men as nursing auxiliaries and anticipated that it 'would ultimately put the witchdoctor out of business'.[11] Similarly Dr. Gale, of the Free Church of Scotland, wrote in 1936:

> Equally important is it that the doctor should have the active cooperation of his nursing staff. In my own hospital I have had the loyal help of Native nurses from the beginning. The approach to Native patients is, of course, easier for

them, both by reason of their knowledge of the vernacular and because of their more ready recognition of Native ideas furtively expressed. It is essential that the nurses should have had a full training, in order that they may be unshaken in their knowledge of and belief in scientific medicine. Incomplete training has obvious dangers ... Their help is needed, not only in the treatment of disease itself, but also in the task of liberating the Native masses from the ignorance and superstition which shackle them alike in sickness and in health.[12]

The missionary view that Christian conversion should replace indigenous culture was later criticised in the official *Report of the Native Churches Commission* in 1925. 'The attitude of antagonism to native customs, especially on the part of older missionaries, has taken often an unwise direction. ... Civilisation and Christianity are not convertible terms'.[13] In Britain an appreciation of the need for greater cultural relativism had become apparent. For example, the Church of Scotland's advice to newly recruited missionary nurses and doctors in 1945 was that 'while keeping their own standards high [they] should not be unduly discouraged if they find different standards abroad. The difference in culture, customs and outlook which leads to different standards must be kept in mind, and local traditions and taboos must be taken into account'.[14] Thus substitution or displacement as an objective was being succeeded very gradually by awareness in some quarters that more complex relationships were involved. Yet the desirability of cultural displacement was still common in white South African society, and was encapsulated in a headline of *The Star* in Johannesburg in 1943, 'More native nurses needed to stop witchcraft'.[15]

There were 800 black nurses in South Africa in 1948, a figure which grew rapidly to 75,000 by 1989.[16] Mission hospitals performed an important role in the training of nurses. Mission culture viewed the patient in the hospital as a spiritual as much as a medical opportunity. Saving bodies and souls for Christ in this context was intended to displace traditional healing systems personified by the so-called 'witchdoctor'. 'In medical work we do our bit, and leave the priest and catechist to come and gather up the fruit', commented a mission hospital matron in 1933.[17] The bishop of her diocesan area of Kimberley and Kuruman was convinced that 'A very vital part of the work is the training of African girls'.[18] This view was not confined to the missions and churches. Charlotte Searle, the doyenne of nursing historians in South Africa commented in 1961 that 'Scientific medicine had ... to conquer witchcraft and nursing [was] its standard bearer'.[19]

In contrast to urban hospitals under provincial administration, mission hospitals have been largely neglected in the historiography of South African health care. Similarly the hospital rather than the district has been the focus for an analysis of the nurse's work. We suggest that the African nurse played a pivotal role as a culture broker between two different cultural systems of health care. However, our observations are tentative ones because the available sources of information to assess the success of failure of this process are the reports of mission hospitals which provide a mainly one-sided colonial discourse. Only oblique information on the African nurse's own attitudes and self-evaluation is available, and there are large spaces where one would like a much fuller record of the patient's response.

The Jane Furse Hospital

This hospital had been started by the Society for the Propagation of the Gospel (SPG) in 1922. It stood in a remote part of the eastern Transvaal, serving an African population of about 80,000 within the 'Native Reserve of Sekukuniland'. Peter Delius's work shows how this area, once the centre of a proud Pedi Kingdom, had by this time been deplorably reduced by political conquest and segregationist governmental intervention, as well as by disease, drought and dearth. Where once the Berlin Missionary Society had had an unchallenged mission presence, other denominations – Roman Catholic, Dutch Reformed, and Wesleyan – now co-existed, whilst the SPG gave an additional Anglican dimension to mission activity.[20] The stressed nature of life on an increasingly over-populated reserve provided a fertile ground for sustaining belief in magic and witchcraft.[21]

The stance of white staff at the hospital towards the local inhabitants' practice of indigenous medicine was largely negative. Their views were common among many missionaries of the nineteenth and early twentieth centuries in tending to conflate the healing work of traditional practitioners with the destructive work of 'sorcerers'. They also viewed cultural beliefs – such as the conviction that the ancestors had power to influence the incidence of disease – as indicative of magic or superstition. A statement by South Africa's prime minister was quoted approvingly in the earliest days of the Jane Furse Hospital. 'General Smuts has lately told us that the Medical Missionaries "can do most". We can fight the spirit of magic and witchcraft most effectively through the doctor and the nurse'.[22] Thirty years later the medical superintendent indicated the continuity of mission policy in that there was still a 'determined attack on ignorance, superstition and disease of body and soul'.[23]

Ida Cordon, the first hospital matron, saw traditional medicine as a powerful competitor to missionary medicine, precisely because each was holistic in character, and embraced both physical and spiritual components: 'Bewitchment is our greatest enemy, and the greatest obstacle to overcome in our work'.[24] Cordon worked closely with the wife of the African priest who, in the early days of the hospital, acted as the outpatients' untrained nurse and interpreter, going 'round to each [patient] in turn, filling in their particulars on the Outpatient Case Sheets. Very often in reply to her question: "O bolaoa keng?" ("What is the matter?") she receives the information, "Ke loue" ("I have been bewitched")'.[25]

At its inception the hospital was operating in an area where white faces were a rarity, and the 'white man's medicine' unknown to most. Gradually six outreach clinics were established to introduce the population to Western medicine. The low fee compared favourably with the payment to local healers and this, together with the efficacy of Western medicine, led to ever-increasing numbers of patients.[26] Clinics acted as necessary feeders to the hospital which, for some time, was regarded apprehensively as culturally alien and personally disorientating. In this context the hospital's account of an early outpatient is instructive. She was

> from a distant kraal, new to European ways, whose baby screams at the sight of a white face. She, herself, discusses everything with a friend and demands

of nurse for the twentieth time how and when the medicines are to be used. Tentatively she takes out the cork, smells it, licks it, finally samples the contents of the bottle, then swaps for a friend's bottle and they compare notes.[27]

As the work of the clinics became better known people were prepared to travel for two days on foot to reach the central hospital.[28] The staff of the Jane Furse Hospital found, as did colonial practitioners elsewhere, that surgical operations for inpatients were especially well thought of by the local population. Matron Cordon wrote that 'An operation makes a fair show and does much for our fame'.[29] One such case was an old lady who had a 'huge open sore on her thigh which she had had for a very long time' and who was discharged cured. 'The people of the neighbouring village would not believe that she had been healed, so they all walked over *en masse* to see the old lady, to make quite sure that what they had heard was true!'[30]

In 1929 a permanent clinic with a resident African nurse was set up and another two were planned in order to bring Western medicine to a widely scattered population. In the clinic the district nurse was not only to treat, but to teach health care and hygiene.[31] The hospital was heavily reliant on African nurses whom it recruited and trained. The first two female probationers were recruited in 1922, and by 1947 there were 22 of them. Probationers were able to train as registered nurses in 1939, and one of their number, Nurse Makwena, was promoted to sister in 1944. In addition, African orderlies were employed in the hospital from 1944. The hospital had become more and more convinced of the importance of having African nurses, in order to communicate effectively with patients.[32] Yet its policy of outreach was frustrated by a shortage of trained African nurses who would run the district clinics on a day-to-day basis.[33]

Another important rationale in recruiting African nurses was the need for someone who might help in the translation of patients' symptoms into the terms of Western medicine so that medical staff could treat them appropriately. Dr Ethel Smith, the assistant medical officer, wrote:

> a young native man came complaining that a lizard was growing inside him. On enquiry, we discovered that he had swallowed, or thought he had swallowed, a little lizard four months previously, since when he had felt it growing bigger and bigger ... Every morning when he got up, and latterly for a good part of the day as well, the lizard was reported to 'want to come up,' which made him cough; but so far his efforts to assist it had been unsuccessful. As it grew it pressed upwards on his lungs, and made breathing rather difficult. ... A physical examination was made, and the troublesome 'lizard' was found to be a steady growth of the Tubercle Bacillus in both lungs.[34]

Although the nurse was the principal point of contact between Western and indigenous medicine, the healer and the hospital doctor might also show interest in a rival form of healing. The missionary doctor was very occasionally prepared to apply the psychological approaches of the African healer for 'psychosomatic' cases. Dr. Smith wrote that in several cases:

The trouble was 'swallowed flies'. So convinced was the patient of this origin of his ailment, that unless I could somehow fall into line with his superstition I was certain he would continue to imagine the presence of the flies – and therefore of his disease. Obviously strategy was indicated! An emetic was given, and at the psychological moment (when the patient was too occupied to be very observant) two or three dead flies were introduced into the basin. The patient saw them and went home happy – and cured![35]

A healer might be prepared to try out the efficacy of certain sorts of Western medicine. The hospital boasted that 'From time to time, too, she [the nurse] enters the name of a native witch-doctor upon the list of patients'.[36] The institution also highlighted the failures of traditional medicine. 'The cases we dread most are the maternity patients who have been dosed with SeSotho medicine. It is from a certain root and produces symptoms so alarming that even the old women are frightened and send an urgent message to the hospital for help'.[37] But while the hospital reported problems arising from indigenous medicine, there is no parallel account of dissatisfied patients who, in the absence of satisfactory rationales provided by the doctor for their illness, left the hospital or clinic in favour of indigenous healers.

St Michael's Mission

The first matron of the Jane Furse Hospital, Ida Cordon, was later the principal agent in the development of another SPG hospital in South Africa – St Michael's Mission Hospital. Equally remote, it was situated at Batlharos, thirteen miles from Kuruman, in the Bechuanaland Protectorate, now in the Northern Cape. The area had become more isolated as the main strategic route from the Cape to Central Africa, which had formerly run through Kuruman, shifted eastwards towards the mining districts of Kimberley and Johannesburg. A new racial as well as natural landscape had also emerged because the limited supplies of natural water were increasingly appropriated by white inhabitants.[38] The dry land no longer supported the local African population, so that a hospital report commented on the increasing poverty and malnutrition of the people.[39] The hospital drew patients from a 60 mile radius (an area the size of Belgium), serving a much more thinly populated region than the Jane Furse Hospital. Its hinterland had a population of only 28,000 Africans, less than half of its sister institution.[40] The size of its hinterland meant that clinics and a district dispensary were even more essential than they had been at Jane Furse, so that a central significance was accorded to the district nurse and her work as culture broker. Shortly after the hospital began, a second centre of work was also opened in the form of a dispensary at Motito, nearly 25 miles from Batlharos.

District nursing was a demanding job. As a mission report explained to its largely white readership:

African diseases are sometimes different from English ones. This is well known but unfortunately not all are to be found in textbooks. Such common conditions as 'stopping of the heart', 'general body pains', 'waist pains', and 'pain running all down the right side into the toes' are nowhere described.[41]

However, since the last mentioned symptoms are typical of what would in every Western medical textbook be referred to as sciatica, it is likely that linguistic problems were complicating transcultural diagnosis. Indeed, nurses recruited from England found the work of transcultural assimilation particularly daunting. Nurse Bisset, for example, wrote from the Motito Dispensary that:

> One's powers of diagnosis and treatment are often taxed severely by the description given of symptoms, for instance there was a woman whose 'stomach was full of water and that water was boiling' [and] 'the man who said he was bewitched and had therefore had a headache for three years' but was found by us to be only needing glasses, and another woman who said her soul smelt, not to mention the extraordinary parts of the body to which abdominal pains can travel!'[42]

Given the problems faced by European nurses, African colleagues were increasingly given the responsibility of running the dispensary. Treatment of outpatients at the dispensary was complemented by health education and preventive work in homes and schools.[43] After a decade of such work it was reported that local people were 'showing greater confidence in their [the staff of the dispensary] ministrations'.[44]

Although hospital reports indicate that those with a white skin appeared obtuse about ethnic and linguistic differences amongst Africans, and thus learned very slowly, if at all, being a black 'African' nurse was in itself not a sufficient qualification for the role of culture broker at the dispensary. The first district nurse at St Michael's, Nurse Minah Molefe, had trained in the Transvaal at the Jane Furse Hospital, where a BaPedi culture within a wider BaSotho society prevailed. Described at first as the matron's 'right hand' at St Michael's Mission Hospital, she also participated in district work. But after a year she indicated that she was about to leave because she did not like the country. Possibly, she initially found the culture alien or the BaTswana unwelcoming or suspicious, although she was still working in the area several years later.[45]

Her successor of a decade later was a Xhosa-speaking nurse, who had trained at Lovedale Hospital in the eastern Cape. Nurse Frances Tuta was reported to have quickly learned the local language of 'Sechuana'. The Bishop of Kimberley and Kuruman approved of her work, which he interpreted as being that of 'an African girl ministering to Africans'.[46] In reality Nurse Tuta found that her different cultural background militated against her acceptance. She admitted that 'Health visiting has not been done successfully owing first to [my] inability to speak the language well, and secondly to the people fearing that these visits only aim at interfering with their customs. Only five homes have been visited with success and twelve visits paid in all'.[47] If she had spoken SeTswana more confidently, her powers of negotiation and mediation would probably have been more successful, but attempting to promote a new set of beliefs and practices with blunt linguistic tools compromised her work as broker between the medicines of indigenous and Western cultures. Predictably, she left the following year.[48]

The case of Nurse Tuta is interesting also because it exposes, and makes visible, the system of power relations within the reserves. Without the backing of the local chief, African district nurses would have been unable to work in the community. Nurse Tuta's initial lack of success resulted in the chief permitting her to do her work within his kraal, thus explicitly placing his power behind Western medicine and displaying approval of her work.[49] Other nurses would also have operated within this patriarchal tribal system and therefore would have needed the backing of the traditional leader for the successful operation of their clinic.

It was not until the appointment of Nurse Kagelelo Andrease in 1955 that a nurse was found who worked on the district for a much longer period. Her circumstances were different in that she married a local man, had a family, became successfully integrated into the local community, and secured the approval of traditional leaders for her work. Nurse Andrease ran the outpatients department at the hospital, as well as taking eight district clinics. The matron described her as 'a very valuable District Nurse as she is conversant with all the people of the district'.[50] Nurse Andrease was privileged over her predecessors not only because local people knew her, and would therefore trust her as she introduced them to the unfamiliar concepts and practices of Western medicine, but also because she was familiar with the belief systems that her patients brought to these encounters. According to Dr Merriweather, a later missionary doctor working in Bechuanaland (later Botswana), those working with the BaTswana needed to understand that traditional belief about disease had no conception of germs or infection. Any attempt to translate SeTswana diseases, for example, into a Western typology was fraught with difficulties for both traditional and Western healers. For example, there was no agreement (even amongst traditional healers themselves), on whether a well-known SeTswana disease, *thibamo*, equated with TB, or whether tuberculosis was but one manifestation of a larger disease cluster which arose from the breaking of taboos. SeTswana culture attributed disease either to the breaking of taboos which displeased the ancestors, or to bewitchment.[51]

Culture and medicine

The nurse as the agent of displacement had been predicated on the assumption that because of her training she would find the superiority of Western medicine over indigenous medicine compelling, and that in the institutional context of a mission hospital she would gradually distance herself from her own traditional culture. The supervision of the African nurse by a European matron and European sisters was intended to reinforce this process of assimilation. The work of the nurse in St Michael's Mission not only involved translation between medical systems with different conceptualisations of disease, but also involved religion. Western medicine and Christianity were inseparable in this context. Contestation between medical systems was therefore subsumed within a more cosmic struggle between God and the devil personified by the witch doctor. The dominant belief under

Matron Cordon's regime at St Michael's Hospital was that 'ignorance, superstition and witchcraft ... play no small part in disease and death'.[52] It was clear that attempts to colonise the African body had to do more than surgically replace holistic indigenous healing by Western scientific medicine. At the mission it was assumed that those who used Western medicine would become Christian, and concomitantly that the heathens who converted to Christianity would forgo traditional medicine. The constituents in this equation were well understood by the BaTswana. An 89-year-old Motswana woman, Esther Seipei Moholong, remembered Matron Cordon as the pioneer who had had formidable determination in 'making people realise the benefit of Western medication' at a time when 'about 90 per cent of our people were still superstitious and suspicious of Western methods of healing and curing diseases'.[53] Disease brought the heathen to the dispensary where they came into contact with the Christian mission in all its aspects.[54]

The integration of medicine with religion might be personal as well as professional as, for example, when Jane, the district nurse, married the native priest to the mission, the Reverend J. Setlhabi.[55] 'In the dispensary and hospital we have many opportunities of talking of spiritual things and of fighting superstition and the power of the witch-doctor', wrote Matron Cordon.[56] Elsewhere she talked about outpatient work with her first nurse, Minah Molefe, and the native priest, and in doing so borrowed some of the vocabulary and conceptualisations of indigenous culture. She wrote that 'We answer any call, *smell out* any sick that are under witch doctor's spells, and attend all who come for medicine' [emphasis added].[57] In this remarkable passage the nurses and priest substituted for the witch doctor as 'smeller out' of the cause of affliction. The Motito dispensary was in the front line of the battle since, according to mission reports, it was here that initiation schools 'with all their attendant evils' 'tested and strengthened' the resolve of Christians. In this cultural confrontation it was not only Western medicine that was in the Motito armoury, but also, as a white sister remarked, the 'unseen force of prayer which is such a tremendous help in our fight against the mighty force of superstition and witchcraft against us'.[58]

In working at the intersection of two contrasting worlds, the African district nurse seldom possessed either the professional self-confidence or the technical tools to be the effective conversion agent her superiors desired. Paradoxically, the relative success of different district nurses attached to the St Michael's Mission suggests that, rather than achievement resulting from *distancing* themselves from their cultural background, the African district nurse might operate more effectively if she was seen (as was Nurse Andrease) to be *both in and of the local community*, and to be operating with the sanction of traditional authority. A simple model of the nurse as the agent of substitution propounded by the missionary societies thus does not adequately explain her actual role.

If a displacement thesis is insufficient to explain the role of the nurse, how well does it fit the patient? Even *within* traditional medicine a pluralistic choice of remedy and practitioner was found, so that a simple exchange *between* Western and indigenous medicine is likely to be too narrow. Patients in southern Africa frequently consulted several indigenous practitioners and highly esteemed healers whose therapeutic armoury contained resources obtained from distant places.[59] Thus, Africans were ready to be eclectic consumers of varied forms of medicine and it was unlikely that they would invest all their hopes of relief or cure in a single kind of practice.

The experience of both mission hospitals suggests that a slow process of cultural osmosis was occurring in which there was a very gradual and selective take-up of particular aspects of Western medicine. BaSotho and BaTswana people admired Western surgery and some Western medicaments, and their adoption of these aspects of biomedicine showed that they recognised their superior efficacy in specific situations. However, their delayed recourse to other hospital or dispensary treatments, notably in cases of tuberculosis, indicated that their first port of call was frequently indigenous healing and, more specifically, herbal medicines.[60] In addition, even if Western medicine provided efficient remedies, it did not usually attempt to address the wider cultural meaning of illness. Traditional medicine addressed the 'why me?' of the sufferer, attributed meaning and significance to the illness, as well as an interpretative rationale for it, within a longer and wider framework embracing individual, family, wider social group and ancestors.

Medical pluralism was not given adequate recognition in the simple displacement model represented historically by the mission hospital and its nurses. The model did not acknowledge the resilience of traditional beliefs amongst patients and nurses, nor appreciate the force of attractive alternative choices offered to patients by different medical systems. A better fit between hypothesis and reality was the model of the community nurse as the patient's advocate in relation to a recognised set of medical options. This was sufficiently well grounded to last into the later democratic, post-colonial situation.

The community nurse

The next part of this chapter discusses the nurse acting as a culture broker in the community, as an advocate and mediator in the empowerment of the patient within a multicultural society. Whilst the theory of transcultural nursing provides a fruitful approach, oral histories of several nurses and doctors will be drawn on to present valuable supportive evidence.

The theory, study and practice of 'transcultural nursing' has become formalised since the mid-1950s with courses being developed at undergraduate and graduate level, specifically to provide 'culturally competent, responsible and safe nursing care'.[61] Much has been written about nurse advocacy, and to avoid becoming unnecessarily pre-occupied with nursing and anthropological theoretical constructs, the model put forward by Jezewski has been adopted. This defines culture broadly as: 'a system of *learned* and *shared* standards for perceiving, interpreting, and behaving in interactions with others and with the environment'.[62] Within each culture, she suggests, health care has its own, separate or sub-cultural set of beliefs, customs, values, symbols and language. The culture broker has to bridge these two cultures in order to empower the 'lay' recipient of that care.

Although Jezewski was writing about the American healthcare system, there is a particular relevance to the South African nursing experience in the paradox that as a culture broker the nurse's ability to identify with the patient has often arisen as a result of their own 'relative powerlessness and marginality in a physician-dominated medical system'. A (political) recognition of the right of the individual to choose his or her form of health care is now recognised as fundamental to the freedom of the individual in post-apartheid South Africa. Patients need to be empowered in order to make that informed choice, rather than being forced to accept only the 'Western' biomedical system – and its associated, culturally limited explanations for the aetiology of disease. Equally, in the aim for equity of healthcare provision, it is argued that the patient should not be limited to traditional medicine because demographic or economic constraints deny them access to the biomedical system. Understanding of, and respect for, the patient's culture, is therefore clearly of paramount importance in enabling the nurse to perform the role of advocate.

Historically, the nurse has often found herself in-between patient and biomedical doctor as 'translator' – not only compensating for the linguistic differences but also taking into account cultural divisions. Laurel Copp refers to this form of advocacy as providing a 'communication bridge' between the health team on the one hand and the patient and the patient's family on the other.[63] This is illustrated in an interview with Shirley Mashione-Talbot, the daughter of a Lovedale-trained nurse who worked in Gauteng during the 1950s and 1960s. First she described the diplomacy used in overcoming the language and cultural barrier:

SMT: for example, [the doctor] would say to my mother, 'And how old is he?' [...] But they had a way of actually knowing when they were born, because they'll say, 'During the time ... five years before ... you know, the big harvest', [or some significant life-event such as] drought, or a disease which killed a lot of cattle [...] because most of it was related to cattle and property, and events like that. [...]

Interviewer: [Helen Sweet] And did she have to translate these dates for the doctor?

SMT: Yes. Yeah. Yes, because they would say, 'Ten years before the big drought', or 'After the big drought', or 'the wars', because the wars was another landmark, a very big landmark. And there were some historical things that happened in South Africa, you know, which they would point to, this side or that side, or the same time, or whatever. So she was able to do that [on the patient's behalf].[64]

Nevertheless, the nurse did not see herself as the doctor's handmaiden or as a practitioner working solely within Western medicine, but had a pluralistic understanding of the advantages and disadvantages of traditional medicine. Evelyn Barbee's research in Botswana describes the resulting tensions as placing the nurse in a 'pivotal' position in which she finds herself 'ensnared in a dialectic between medical and traditional beliefs'.[65] This is illustrated by the work of Mavis Makhetha who was one of first non-white nurses trained at Pretoria General Hospital. In the 1950s she became a district nurse in Kronstad with the King Edward VII Order of Nurses, where she found herself occasionally working with a healer as her colleague. She remembered that:

> There were also occasions when we got a call to find the family witchdoctor or *sangoma* bedecked in all her trimmings, palpating the patient. That is where tact came to our rescue. You had to really convince her that our method of delivering was best. You kept her at hand to coax a fretful 'primip' and of course to hand you whatever you needed. They responded very well to the partnership idea, though you did all the work your way. But woe betide you if you came up with a high-handed approach! We always ended up being great friends.[66]

Another illustration was given in an interview with the daughter of the Lovedale-trained nurse (quoted above), where it is evident that she was aware of the advantages and disadvantages of different kinds of medicine, including traditional medicine. This is demonstrated in an example she gave, in which her mother dealt with the unsatisfactory outcome of parents consulting traditional healers about a child:

SMT: he had stomach pains, and they took him to the traditional healers. And do you know what it was? Appendicitis, and it burst, and he died. And my mother just said, 'Please, let's do it the other way. I won't stop you, you know'. And she explained what it was, that it could have been dealt with, and all that, but [she would say] 'It's happened. Let's make sure it doesn't happen again', and things. But, yes, sometimes she would have serious difficulty where, you know, things haven't worked with traditional healers. And sometimes she would advise them to go and get herbs from them, you know, if there was someone who was good.

HS: Oh, would she?

SMT: Oh yes. Yes. If she knew that a herb would do better, she would advise them. Yes, yes.

HS: What about the doctors who were visiting, did they have any relationship with the healers?

SMT: No, no, no, no.[67]

In a more general study of health care in South Africa it has been suggested that 'Persons who object to traditional medicine are especially those who encounter the failures of traditional healers and have to rectify them', and that 'the attitudes of doctors, nurses, pharmacists and paramedical personnel in respect of cooperation are scarce'.[68] However, this would appear to ignore the difference articulated on a number of occasions (both by nurses and doctors) between the nurse 'on duty', particularly in the hospital's biomedical environment, and the nurse 'off duty', in a different cultural environment. A Western doctor who worked in a Transkei mission hospital describes this disparity:

I can remember having some nurses … . I don't know, I had some kind of social evening. And once you got them talking, they would sort of talk about how their cousin was cured of this or that, with a traditional healer. Now, if you talked to them in any kind of formal situation, they would have nothing to do with traditional healers, because traditional healers were not, you know, they were not scientific.[69]

We have termed the view expressed here as 'latent pluralism' since it signifies a pluralistic attitude but one that was, and still is, hidden or publicly denied in response to social tensions between the individual as a trained member of a respected health profession and the individual's background, culture and belief system. The number of African nurses who either believe in, or actively consult, traditional medicine as a result of these tensions, is unknown but the figure may be as high as 90 percent.[70] This may be likened to the considerable numbers who are able to reconcile traditional customs and beliefs with their Christian faith. The hidden or latent aspect of this, in the case of the nurses, may be due to inculcated awareness from their training of some inconsistency in using both systems, yet, where these are reconciled, the potential for the integration or coexistence of traditional and biomedicine must be greatly increased.[71]

We found another form of 'empowerment advocacy' that is of a more political nature – informing the patient and upholding the patient's ethical and legal rights.[72] Attempting to redress material deprivation within an unjust society, in a community situation where social marginalisation is being felt most strongly, is probably a still greater responsibility and has led to the image of the community nurse in more than one African township as 'district nurse, community worker and social worker'.[73] One of these township nurses started a crèche, carried out daily school visits to dispense vitamin supplements and initiated feeding schemes. These activities were ostensibly aimed at school-children, but they had the additional advantages of providing cooking and nutritional education for the women, teaching them to grow and use a variety of fresh vegetables and to use offal to make stock. The nurse used her professional position to ask help from neighbouring (white) farmers for lambs' fleeces for the children to sit on at school, and for donations of used toys and money. She founded a women's football team to raise money for blankets for the elderly, and designed, and organised the making of, crutches for the large number of polio victims in the community. Added to this, her daughter explained, 'they would bring prisoners sometimes that were hurt, to be bandaged and everything, and, you know, she'd be talking in a language, advising them what to do when they get to court and all that, while she's bandaging them'.[74]

Four young doctors of the Alexandra Health Centre in another large Johannes-burg township were well aware of the nurses' community role during the 1950s:

relations between doctor and nurse have also improved greatly, as closer cooperation and understanding become possible … Our nurses are of the people, speak the languages, and have much to teach us about the community

... In this community which is unfamiliar with scientific medicine, domiciliary practice has much to offer that the hospital does not give ... nurses can do much to combat ignorance and prevent disease.[75]

At the time (in 1955) there was a population of approximately 80,000, with 16,500 domiciliary visits annually, of which 13,500 were by district nurses. Almost 40 years later in Khayelitsha, Cape Town, a community nurse highlighted a similar situation: 'I think my most important role is being a facilitator and trainer'. She also referred to the low doctor–patient ratio and to a majority of doctors not being able to speak local African languages, and noted that the relationship between traditional medicine and Western medicine had only recently begun 'to be discussed by medical staff, as are cultural issues of language and culture in general'.[76] As during earlier decades, the main problems were poverty and associated multiple health problems, particularly malnutrition.

Conclusion

We have argued that the African nurse, although rarely receiving attention in studies of medical pluralism, played a significant and evolving role as culture broker in integrating different forms of medicine and health care provision in South Africa. The training of the African nurse in missions was predicated on the assumption that those who worked there would help broker the displacement of indigenous medicine because of their total commitment to Western biomedicine. This supposition probably equated to a substantial extent with the reality of work with inpatients within the hospital ward, since here the culture of Western medicine, when reinforced by close supervision by a doctor, sister or matron, would have been very powerful. In the more remote outpatient dispensary or clinic, however, the circumstances were different. Here the nurse had a greater degree of professional independence and was operating within a cultural context where the claims of Western medicine confronted entrenched traditional values, customs and practices. It seems likely that in these circumstances the district nurse acted informally as a mediator or culture broker in advising the patients on their optimum choices between indigenous and Western medicine. For a more recent period more evidence is available to substantiate the role of the African nurse as culture broker in the community. The nurse empowered the patient by acknowledging, discussing and providing access to chosen options for care and treatment within both Western and traditional medicine.

The chapter therefore suggests that, because of her dual allegiance, the African nurse operated strategically to benefit her patients within a significant borderland between traditional and Western medicine. She was able to do this most effectively when she had the sanction of traditional power structures and was well known to local people. In such circumstances she could act successfully in an enabling way on behalf of her community as cultural mediator and patient advocate. The philosophy which informed these actions is encapsulated by the Xhosa saying: 'Ubuntu ungamntu ngabanye abantu' ('People are people through other people').[77]

Acknowledgement

The financial assistance of the Wellcome Trust for this research is gratefully acknowledged. We have also benefited from helpful comments by delegates to the RCN History of Nursing Society's 'Millennium History of Nursing' Conference at Edinburgh, the Society for the Social History of Medicine Annual Conference 'Medicine, Magic, Religion' at Southampton, and the 'International Healthcare Conference 2000' held by the University of South Africa in Pretoria, and also by members of the Medical History Seminar at the University of Cape Town Medical School.

Notes

1   See, for example, the two standard works on nineteenth century-medical history, E.H. Burrows, *A History of Medicine in South Africa up to the end of the Nineteenth Century*, Cape Town, A.A. Balkema, 1968, and P.W. Laidler, and M. Gelfand, *South Africa: Its Medical History 1652–1898: A Medical and Social Study*, Cape Town, C. Struik, 1971.

2   Whilst nurses at this time were predominantly female outside the locale of the mining hospitals, and medical aides were the nearest male equivalent, by the end of this period there were a small but growing number of male nurses trained by mission and state hospitals.

3   M.A. Jezewski, 'Culture brokering as a model for advocacy', *Nursing and Health* 14, 2 (1993): 78–85.

4   R.J. Johnston (ed.), 1888, *Report of the Centenary Conference of the Protestant Missions of the World*, London, Exeter Hall.

5   D.G.B.A. Gerdener, *Recent Developments in the South African Mission Field*, Cape Town/ Pretoria, N.G. Kerk-Uitgevers, 1958, p.236.

6   M. Gelfand, *Christian Doctor and Nurse: The History of Medical Missions in South Africa from 1799–1976*, Sandton, R.S.A., Mariannhill Mission Press, 1984, pp. 344–7.

7   School of Oriental and African Studies (SOAS), London, WCM, box 30, folder 3 jacket B, 11 May 1857, T. Durant Philip to Rev. Dr. Tidman, Secretary of the London Missionary Society.

8   National Library of Scotland, accession 7548, D 80, Report on the State of the African Mission of the Free Church, 1863.

9   Typescript summary of the General Missionary Conferences of South Africa, Rhodes University, Cory Library, 1904–32, p. 19. This statement was given to the conference in 1904.

10   Methodist Church of South Africa. *Is it Nothing to You?* Pietermaritzburg, Methodist Church of South Africa Missionary Department, 1946.

11   General Missionary Conferences of South Africa, 1904–32, pp. 88–9.

12   G.W. Gale, 'The rural hospital as an agent in native health education.' *South African Medical Journal*, 10, 8 (1936): 541–3.

13   South African Government. *Report of Native Churches Commission*, Government Printers, 1925.

14   National Library of Scotland, accession 7548, c 82, Church of Scotland Foreign Mission Committee, 1949–53, 4 October 1945, 'Notes for missionary doctors and nurses'.

15   Quoted in S. Marks, *Divided Sisterhood: Race, Class and Gender in the South African Nursing Profession*, Basingstoke, St Martin's Press, 1994, p. 82.

16   S. Marks, 'The legacy of the history of nursing for post-apartheid South Africa', in A.M. Rafferty, J. Robinson, and R. Elkan (eds), *Nursing History and the Politics of Welfare*, London and New York, Routledge, 1997, pp. 32–3; and C. Searle, *Towards Excellence: The Centenary of State Registration for Nurses and Midwives in South Africa, 1891–1991*, Durban, Butterworths, 1991, p. 269.

17   U.S.P.G. Medical Missions Records, Rhodes House (1907-7), M340, St Michael's Mission Hospital *Report*, 1933–4.

18   U.S.P.G. Medical Missions Records, Rhodes House (1907-7), M509, correspondence of the Bishop of Kimberley and Kuruman, letter to Dr. Houlton, 23 August 1945.

19   C. Searle, 'Professional advancement of the African nurse', *South African Nursing Journal*, February (1961): 28.

20   P. Delius, *The Land Belongs to Us. The Pedi Polity, the Boers and the British in the Nineteenth-century Transvaal*, Johannesburg, 1983, pp. 108, 122–3; P. Delius, *A Lion Among Cattle: Reconstruction and Resistance in the Northern Transvaal*, Oxford, 1996, pp. 25–33, 89.

21   Delius, *A Lion Among Cattle*, pp. 121, 201, 203; South African Government. *Report of the Commission of Inquiry into Witchcraft Violence and Ritual Murders in the Northern Province of the Republic of South Africa*, 1995.

22   U.S.P.G. Medical Missions Records, Rhodes House (1907-7), M338, Jane Furse Hospital, *Report*, 1923 (hereafter JFH *Report*).

23   JFH *Report*, 1950.

24   JFH *Report*, 1929.

25   JFH *Report*, 1924.

26   JFH *Reports*, 1938 and 1941.

27   JFH *Report*, 1940.

28   JFH *Report*, 1941.

29   JFH *Report*, 1930.

30   JFH *Report*, 1938.

31   JFH *Report*, 1940.

32   JFH *Report*, 1942.

33   JFH *Report*, 1946.

34   JFH *Report*, 1924.

35   JFH *Report*, 1924.

36   JFH *Report*, 1924.

37   JFH *Report*, 1940.

38   N. Jacobs, 'The flowing eye: Water management in the Upper Kuruman Valley, South Africa', *Journal of African History*, 37 (1996): 227–60.

39   U.S.P.G. Medical Missions Records, Rhodes House (1907-7), M338–M340, St Michael's Mission Hospital *Reports*, (hereafter SMMH *Report*) 1933–4.

40   SMMH *Report*, 1945–6.

41   SMMH *Report*, 1965–6.

42   SMMH *Report*, 1945–6.

43   SMMH *Report*, 1941–2.

44   SMMH *Report*, 1945–6.

45   SMMH *Reports*, 1935, 1936–7, 1939–40.

46   SMMH *Reports*, 1948–9, 1950.

47   SMMH *Report*, 1950.

48   SMMH *Report*, 1952.

49   SMMH *Report*, 1953.

50   SMMH *Reports*, 1955, 1967.

51   A.M. Merriweather C.B.E. (1992) *Medical Phrasebook and Dictionary: English and Setswana*, Gabarone, Pula Press.

52   SMMH *Report*, 1933–4.

53   Moffat Mission, Kuruman, Service of thanksgiving to celebrate the 75th Anniversary of the SMMH.

54   SMMH *Report*, 1933–4.

55   SMMH *Report*, 1938–9.

56   SMMH *Report*, 1940–1.

57   SMMH *Report*, 1939–40.

58   SMMH *Reports*, 1944–5, 1941–2.

59   C. Van Onselen, *The Seed is Mine. The Life of Kas Maine, a South African Share Cropper*, Oxford, Currey, 1996, pp. 73, 127, 207, 454, 483, 515; A.C.S.M. Musingeh, *A History of Disease and Medicine in Botswana 1820–1945*, Unpublished Cambridge PhD thesis, 1984, pp. 67, 69, 74.

60   See also Reis' chapter in this collection (Chapter 6).

61 M.M. Leininger, *Transcultural Nursing Leadership with Progress in Theory, Education and Practice*, Unpublished paper, ICN Centennial Conference, London, June 1999.

62 Jezewski, 'Culture brokering', pp. 78–85

63 L.A. Copp, 'The nurse as advocate for vulnerable persons', *Journal of Advanced Nursing*, 11 (1986): 255–63.

64 Oral testimony: Shirley Mashione-Talbot, Liverpool, 1999.

65 E.L. Barbee, 'Tensions in the brokerage role: Nurses in Botswana', *Western Journal of Nursing Research*, 9 (1987): 253.

66 South African Nursing Association, *South African Nurses of Distinction*, vol. 1, 1986–92, p.75.

67 Oral testimony: Shirley Mashione-Talbot, Liverpool, 1999.

68 H.C.J. Van Rensburg, E. Pretorius, and A. Fourie, *Health Care in South Africa. Structure and dynamics*, Pretoria, Academica, 1992, p. 335.

69 Oral testimony: Dr Anne Savage, London, 1999.

70 This approximation was suggested by several oral history interviewees, at least one of whom was a practising nurse.

71 M.H. Logan, and E.E. Hunt, *Health and the Human Condition: Perspectives on Medical Anthropology*, North Scituate, Mass., Duxbury Press, 1978, p. xvii, suggests that the role of culture broker in promoting reciprocal understanding and respect, may be played by medical anthropologists who are similarly aware of cultural differences.

72 N. Turner, '"Better Service" takes over from district surgeons', *The Sunday Independent Reconstruct Supplement*, 12 December 1999, p. 3, refers to the restructuring in Gauteng of the service previously provided by district surgeons, and now includes separation of forensic and medico-legal services with 300 nurses and doctors receiving special training.

73 Oral testimonies: Xoliswa Ndingaye, 1999, Shirley Mashione-Talbot, 1999.

74 Oral testimony: Shirley Mashione-Talbot, 1999.

75 M. Susser *et al.*, 'Medical Care in a South African Township', *Lancet*, 1 (1955): 912–5.

76 K. de Selincourt, 'A measure of South Africa's health care', *Nursing Times*, 88, 33 (1992): 39–40.

77 A. Sparks, *The Mind of South Africa*, London, Heinemann, 1990.

8   *Kexue* and *guanxixue*

Plurality, tradition and modernity in contemporary Chinese medicine

Volker Scheid

China embraced modernity as a consequence of military weakness and defeat at the hands of Japan and the Western colonial powers. Ever since, technicism and the valorisation of scientific knowledge have been constant guides on China's tortuous path through the twentieth century. Medicine was one of the domains at which modernising efforts were directed quite early. This led to confrontations between proponents of Chinese and Western medicine,[1] culminating in 1929 in an ultimately unsuccessful attempt to abolish Chinese medicine. The strategy on which Chinese medicine's defence in these struggles was based involved a fundamental acceptance of the discourse of modernity. Following the establishment of the People's Republic in 1949 modernisation was further accelerated resulting in Chinese medicine's gradual integration into a state orchestrated plural healthcare system.[2]

Following several failed attempts to create a new medicine out of the synthesis of Chinese and Western medicine,[3] contemporary Chinese physicians emphasise inheritance (*jicheng*) and development (*fazhan, fayang*) as being of equal importance for the modernisation of their tradition. Beyond such general statements no consensus exists, however, about the precise manner of combining the old and the new or about transforming one into the other. Thus, after almost a century of modernisation, modern and traditional forms of Chinese medicine still exist side by side, interpenetrating each other in complex ways. Medical lineages and the personal transmission of knowledge continue to be important even as Chinese medicine is reshaped to fit the evolving requirements of a modern education system. Diagnostic and therapeutic practices increasingly integrate biomedical knowledge and technology but remain fundamentally informed by classical texts. Innovation is inspired by the transfer of information from biomedicine and other Western healing practices and by the changing dictates of political economy, but also by unresolved questions in the literary canon dating back all the way to the Han dynasty.[4]

This raises important scholarly questions. If contemporary Chinese medicine is different from its traditional predecessor, where runs the boundary between the two? Are contemporary transformations of Chinese medicine categorically different from those of previous periods? If Chinese medicine is no longer traditional, what does this imply for the claims of biomedicine to be the only truly modern medicine? If several distinct forms of modern medicine (modern Chinese medicine and modern biomedicine in China, or modern Chinese medicine in China and modern Chinese medicine in the US or the UK) can exist side by side, what implications does this have for our perceptions of modernity?

These questions arise wherever Western biomedical and non-Western or non-biomedical Western medical practices meet each other. Whether in nineteenth-century Africa or Bradford, twentieth-century India or China, or on the internet today, struggles for legitimacy in the medical domain are united by the fact that they are mediated through discourses of tradition and modernity.[5] In this chapter I want to employ the problematic nature of these discourses as a starting-point for a self-reflective analysis of plurality in contemporary Chinese medicine and beyond. 'Self-reflective' in this context denotes my conviction that such an effort can no longer take concepts such as culture, practice, system, tradition and modernity as neutral concepts that allow us, as social scientists, to map out social space and describe historical processes.[6] A medical 'system', for instance, even where it is explicitly constructed as a methodological device for the operationalisation of empirical research, makes claims about the nature of the world that mix up common sense belief, Enlightenment notions of science and observed behaviour.[7] The notion of 'tradition' evokes automatic oppositions to modernity, even though much of what we would tend to label as modern, such as biomedicine, turns out to be very traditional by the terms of these very definitions.[8] And the idea of culture, finally, can be shown to become important in Western scholarly discourse precisely at that historical moment during which 'Atlantic nations began to establish their domination over much of the rest of the world' and to embark on a 'process of self-definition through contrast with characteristics imputed to colonized others'.[9]

Thus, while I shall employ Western perspectives on modernity to examine contemporary transformations of Chinese medicine, it is an equally important objective of my chapter to interrogate the construction of these perspectives by confronting them with the ethnographic realities of Chinese medicine in contemporary China.

Three perspectives on modernity in Chinese medicine

Three broad and very different strategies for analysing the modernisation of Chinese medicine are available. The most conventional of these defines the modern by means of shared universal attributes. Standardisation and regularisation of knowledge and practice, professionalisation, a belief in progress and the ability to improve the human condition by means of science and technology, emphasis on the global and universal coupled with a disregard for the local and specific, and the emergence of bureaucracies in the service of nation states are typical items on such a list.[10]

On the plus side, this perspective allows us to tie transformations in Chinese medicine to similar changes in other social domains and, by implication, to global theories of historical and social development. It fails, however, to account for the actual complexities and contradictions of specific historical transformations. Nationalism and dialectical materialism, for instance, have contributed as much to the shaping of contemporary Chinese medicine as the discourse of modernity. Consequently, the modernisation of Chinese medicine in China has proceeded along a very different path to that in the West.[11] That scholars cannot agree on the point at which the transition between traditional and modern Chinese medicine might have occurred further underlines the fact that the entire distinction is far from self-evident.[12]

Analysing modernity as an essentially local phenomenon has therefore become an alternative strategy increasingly adopted by scholars seeking to account for such plurality. These authors still use the notion of modernity to link inquiries across disciplines, historical periods and geographical areas. Understanding the dynamics of its actual unfolding, however, is considered possible only in relation to concrete contexts of practice.[13]

From this perspective, the modernisation of Chinese medicine in Nationalist China, for instance, can be interpreted as having emerged through the historically specific dialectic between scientism and nationalism that shaped not only Chinese medicine but also Chinese perceptions of science.[14] Modernisation of Chinese medicine in post-Mao China can, alternatively, be analysed as being structured by a different set of contradictions. These include the imperatives of social development prescribed in Deng Xiaoping's theory of 'four modernisations', the forced movement of Chinese medicine into hospitals as an important aspect of state-controlled healthcare, and Chinese medicine's status as a national treasure decreed by Mao Zedong. This conjunction of forces demands the utilisation of science and technology as primary tools for the development of Chinese medicine without permitting a questioning of the tradition as a whole.[15]

This perspective permits us to tease out of a particular constellation of events those forces that are specific and unique to it without surrendering the benefits that accrue from a comparative point of view. It also enables the identification of modernity and its constitutive practices as locally configured and therefore as implicitly plural. Finally, such analyses explicitly challenge conventional narratives of modernisation. They show that modernity does not simply displace what went before, but that new and old practices interpenetrate each other in complex and complicated ways.

A final obstacle, however, impedes the way to a non-Orientalist analysis of Chinese medicine that would free itself from the colonial burden of representing the Asian other in such a way as to enhance the identity and superiority of the West: the continued reliance of local history and ethnography on fundamental categories of thought (such as tradition/modernity, science/ethnoscience, nature/culture, fact/fetish) constructed within the discourse of modernity itself. Arranging phenomena that are not intrinsically modern into a conceptual grid dictated by the concerns of modern (or postmodern) authors is never achieved without some degree of what the Indian social scientist Ashis Nandy has termed 'epistemic violence'.[16] The consequences of such violence no longer reveal themselves in the obvious distortions of imperialist Orientalism, but more subtly in the tenacious persistence of a teleology that limits understanding and constrains adaptability.

Two examples relevant to the ethnography of contemporary Chinese medicine suffice to demonstrate these effects. Inquiries into local processes of modernisation are most often organised within the framework of a world system's perspective. Contemporary ethnographies and postcolonial writings thus focus on the encounter of local groups and persons with the forces of globalisation and the macro-processes associated with capitalist political economy in its many forms. Relationships between tradition and modernity are therefore interpreted as being marked by distinctive qualitative differences that construct modern regimes of power/knowledge as naturally hegemonic. As a consequence, relationships between the modern and traditional are most often viewed through a framework of resistance and accommodation, where tactical resistance or subversive deferral constitute resources by which non-modern forms of life can undermine – but never actually overcome – the hegemony of the modern.[17] Consequently, academic investigations of Chinese medicine in the West often focus on the loss of traditional skills and concepts and view its future with considerable apprehension.[18]

Second, even where modernity is conceived as locally emergent, its opposition to traditional forms of practice invariably impinges on judgements regarding the desirability of local transformations. Medical practice, where such transformations have direct implications for all those involved, provides a pertinent example. In contemporary China, where scientism is state sponsored, most of the physicians and patients I talked to viewed the modernisation of Chinese medicine as desirable. In the West, on the other hand, where the popularity of Chinese medicine is supported by a romantically inspired critique of modernity, its associations with tradition are emphasised by many of its practitioners. This, in turn, makes it very difficult for advocates of modernisation to view Chinese medicine as anything else than a return to outdated modes of thought and practice. The result, in China as in the West, is a foreclosing of multiple other options of engagement with Chinese medicine. Such options may be less easily recruited to oppositions between tradition and modernity but may enable less prejudicial judgements regarding the benefits of different medical traditions in the increasingly plural healthcare systems arising everywhere as a result of twenty-first-century globalisation.

If the (often unreflected) narrative of resistance and accommodation that produces such one-sided accounts is surrendered to a more pluralistic perspective – a perspective that gives up the tradition/modernity dichotomy – a reconfigured space of cultural production can be established. In this space Western medicine and modernisation lose their status as singular points of reference. Instead, dynamics of local identity formation, microeconomics, interpersonal relations and clinical experience become equally important factors driving the transformations of contemporary medicine.[19]

I thus turn to a third perspective that has evolved in the field of science and technology studies and resolves the dilemma of modernity by denying it any special qualitative characteristics. Its proponents show, first, that the existence of qualitative differences between tradition and modernity cannot be sustained on an evidential basis and, second, that knowledge and society, nature and culture co-construct each other within practices that are always locally emergent. Models such as Donna Haraway's 'cyborg', Bruno Latour's 'actor-network', or Andrew Pickering's 'mangle of practice' thus succeed in tying nature and culture, tradition and modernity into heterogeneous and unpredictable constellations without *a priori* privileging one above the other.[20]

I wish to argue that by dissolving in this manner the essence of previous conceptions of modernity, the ethnography of Chinese medicine is empowered in three ways at once. First, the theoretical models made available by this research tradition provide medical anthropologists with conceptual tools that explain how and why the modern and traditional, kept apart in thought, align without difficulty in practice. Second, they provide inspiration and resources for an emergent multi-perspectival ethnography that decentres the resistance and accommodation framework organising much contemporary work. Third, by disabling the reductionist pressures implicit in all teleology, plurality is established as a natural condition of social practice rather than a surface phenomenon in constant need of elucidation.[21]

Yet, in as much as writers such as Latour, Callon and Pickering conceive of the practices that construct alignments of nature-culture in terms of abstract models that are then tested in concrete contexts, research in this tradition is liable to problems affecting all global theory. Differences between Western and Chinese medicine, for instance, or between Chinese medicine practised in different places, by different people in different times clearly involve more than differences in the size of their networks, or in the agents that these networks connect. Accounting for the actual complexity and contradiction of local practice thus requires, at the very least, to embed such models in the thick description of local ethnography. This is what I propose to do now by means of a short case study.[22]

A day in the life of Professor Rong

The person at the centre of my study is Professor Rong with whom I enjoyed the privilege of studying from September to December 1994 while carrying out field-work for a doctoral dissertation in medical anthropology. At the time I had already practised Chinese medicine in Britain for over a decade. This allowed me to enrol as an advanced student (*jinxiusheng*) at the Beijing University of Chinese Medicine and Pharmacology (*Beijing zhongyiyao daxue*) and study with venerated senior physicians (*laozhongyi*) at different teaching hospitals. I also built up an extensive network of private contacts, a process considerably enabled by my status as a foreign practitioner of Chinese medicine with some experience. This helped me to stand out from my fellow Chinese students as well as from Westerners studying in Beijing, most of whom were beginners. It was through these private networks that I became a student of Professor Rong, even if officially this relationship was part of my university-based training.

Professor Rong is a leading physician, author and educator, whose multiple involvement in the practice, transmission and modernisation of Chinese medicine over four decades suggested him to me as the ideal focal point for an investigation of networks in Chinese medicine. The following is an account of a typical day in the working life of Professor Rong, his students and disciples.

At about 7.50 a.m. Professor Rong (who was 73 years old in 1994) and his son and disciple Dr Rong Jr are picked up at their home by the professor's three PhD students. The students escort their teacher to his surgery where he is already expected by ten or more patients and Dr Lu. Dr Lu, a grey haired woman in her early fifties and a professor herself, is the second disciple of Professor Rong. As Professor Rong and his entourage approach the clinic, the students, who usually file behind their teacher, quickly move to the front. One opens the door for the professor and helps him take off his coat, while the other two busy themselves with arranging the consulting room. As soon as Professor Rong has seated himself he begins his consultations. By lunchtime he will have attended to between 60 and 70 patients.

Each consultation proceeds according to the same pattern. Professor Rong examines pulse and tongue, asks a few questions and then writes out a one or two line assessment and diagnosis followed by a prescription into the case history booklet which serves as a treatment record. The booklet is passed to the student seated opposite who copies the prescription on a prescription pad. The student keeps one copy for himself and passes another to the patient who has already vacated the chair for the next person in line. The two other students also copy Professor Rong's prescriptions and notes. If the necessity arises, they deal with patient queries and problems, ensuring that as few intrusions as possible are made into Professor Rong's precious consulting time.

The role of Professor Rong's two disciples in assisting their teacher is different. One sees a small number of patients in an adjacent windowless cubicle. Usually, these are new patients whose assessment interview would make more demands on Professor Rong's time. Following the consultation with the disciple, each patient takes this prescription to the next room where, following a short inspection of pulse and tongue, Professor Rong makes a few alterations to the prescription. He crosses out some of the drugs and replaces them with others in a gesture that has both educational and symbolic significance.[23] The student may have made a mistake, but patients coming to Professor Rong for treatment would not be happy if they only received the benefit of his disciples' knowledge.

The second disciple, meanwhile, copies Professor Rong's notes and prescriptions for filing in Professor Rong's archive. If Professor Rong is out of town attending a conference or giving a lecture, his disciples treat his patients. His students do not attend on these days. The son also assists his father during surgeries held at their home in the evenings and on Sundays, where Professor Rong treats many high-standing cadre and business leaders.

In the afternoon, Professor Rong usually attends a meeting of one of the many committees of which he is a leading member. His disciples may organise the archive of their teacher's case records and assist him with the writing and preparing of manuscripts. Students, instead, are busy with their own doctoral dissertations. The topic of each is research into formulas designed by Professor Rong. Such research involves tracing the historical lineage of the formula, biochemical analyses and animal experiments, documenting individual case histories, conducting clinical experiments and running clinical trials.

Discipleship: the endurance of tradition

Contemporary Chinese distinguish clearly between the students (*xuesheng*) and disciples (*tudi*) of a given teacher. Prior to the establishment of schools and colleges on a nation-wide basis in the late 1950s, discipleship was the main avenue for the transmission of medical craft.[24] Social relations between master and disciple are modelled on the filiation between father and son, one of the five cardinal relationships (*wu lun*) of Confucian ideology.[25] These relationships embody a hierarchical relation of non-equals. The father/master, as the senior element in the relationship, was accorded authority and a wide range of prerogatives over the son/disciple circumscribed by rules of correct conduct (*li*). Such rules were considered essential to the performance of filial duties and the harmony of the relationship.[26]

The hierarchical structuring of discipleship and the mutual obligations this entails is clearly visible in the relationship between Professor Rong and his disciples. Disciples walk behind the professor. They must assist his work at any time he requires. They subordinate personal ambition to their teacher's accumulation of status by contributing to a book, which will be published under his name. All disciples with whom I spoke also emphasised that their teacher was very strict and that they feared him because of that. Yet, such strictness was simultaneously also considered to be an expression of care and concern.

There is no uniform way by which one becomes a disciple. Before the establishment of Chinese medicine colleges in the 1950s apprenticeship would often start at an early age either within one's own family or by moving into the household of the teacher. Discipleship then involved the memorisation of canonical works and the participation in peripheral activities such as compounding medicines and boiling herbal decoctions. Today apprenticeship rarely begins before university training has been completed.[27]

Disciples are admitted by their teacher based on various factors ranging from kinship ties and perceived merit to political pressure. The state, which never managed to totally eliminate discipleship, co-opted them instead into the state education system. In the late 1970s the Ministry of Health (MoH) and its local sections began to confer the title of *ming laozhongyi* (famous senior physician of Chinese medicine) to a small number of selected practitioners.[28] *Ming laozhongyi* are entitled to teach disciples thereby raising their own status above that of other physicians. For the apprentice an official certificate marks successful completion of discipleship. This establishes her as *tudi* of Dr X and confers onto her some of the *mingqi*, or fame, of her teacher.

Professor Rong has no other disciples besides his son and Dr Lu. Other famous professors in Beijing admit short-term disciples under the system outlined above. Gradients of apprenticeship as well as their common denominators and their links to patterns of tradition become discernible in comparing these different discipleships. The hierarchical ordering of all discipleship is reflected in ritualised behaviour (*li*) which still demands of disciples to kow-tow on formal occasions at one end of a continuum and to pour tea for their teacher during consultations at the other. *Li* demands of teachers to be stern and strict on the outside and caring on the inside.

The relation between Professor Rong's son and his father is an extension of a pre-existing father/son relationship and shares in its mutual obligations and symbolic connotations. Dr Rong Jr carries on a long-established family line apparently going back nine generations. He lives in the same household as his father and communicates with him in a Southern dialect that remains unintelligible to either Dr Lu or his students. He helps his father with all consultations including those reserved for rich and influential patients carried out at their home.

The relation between Professor Rong and his second disciple, Dr Lu, is an extension of a bureaucratic relationship between superior/inferior. By way of this apprenticeship Professor Rong has successfully inserted his family medical lineage into the modern bureaucratic organisation of the state education system. As professor of formulas, the same department of which Professor Rong himself is Emeritus Professor, Dr Lu is now the second link in a new chain of transmission. This chain has assimilated state education into lineage descent, but has also had to accommodate itself to these new contexts. Whereas for nine generations Professor Rong's line has been transmitted through the male line according to traditional ideologies of patrilineal descent, the realities of modern socialist education have opened a space within that tradition in which women take up important and visible positions.

In contradistinction, the relationship between temporary disciples and their teacher is from the outset temporally limited even if its effects endure. In that sense, it has the character of a strategic alliance rather than of a structural bond. A student can thus be the disciple of a famous physician without being part of his line in a narrow sense. Vice versa, a teacher may publicly claim a student as his disciple by providing a preface for one of her books, but there is no pressure on either to maintain a publicly visible relationship of enduring obligations. Temporally limited discipleships also permit students to study with different teachers in succession, a practice well documented in the history of Chinese medicine.

The above examples show how master/disciple relationships of different grades of proximity, of various degrees of longevity and of different functional character are established on the basis of various socially effective relations: cognatic blood ties, bureaucratic hierarchies and social network. These grades of proximity express themselves, too, in how disciples learn from their teacher, and how they themselves become masters. For Dr Chao, a short-term disciple of another famous physician, learning consisted largely in access to her teacher's way of diagnosing and prescribing by being permitted to attend consultations. In the course of these consultations, there was no formal instruction and Dr Chao had to rely on her background knowledge to interpret her teacher's prescriptions. On rare occasions where teaching became verbal, it was structured to test whether she had succeeded in retracing her master's steps. If her answer demonstrated that this was not the case, she was guided to a text that might help her overcome her interpretative difficulties. As a disciple Dr Chao was expected 'to have [her master's] train of thought, exactly his train and no other. As a disciple of Professor Xu' she told me, 'it was impossible for me to study different methods. If I wanted to do so, I had to do it secretly. Still now, I had better not let other people know.'[29]

Professor Rong's disciples also rely on interpretative understanding but have many opportunities to have their interpretations corrected in practice and to engage with their master in explicit discourse. Vice versa, the pressures and expectations brought to bear on them increase with this proximity. Not only are they required to think like their teacher, even in middle age he corrects their prescriptions and thereby controls their practice as physicians.[30]

Studentship: the influence of the modern state

Agency and social relations within the education system developed by the Chinese state since the 1950s differ in many respects from discipleship. Whereas the latter expresses traditional forms of social organisation, morality, and implicit or even secret knowledge, state education (henceforth referred to as studentship) self-consciously declares itself as modern, universal and scientific. However, there are also points of crossover that attest to the historical contingencies that have shaped studentship out of and against discipleship.[31]

Professor Rong forms relations with students in two contexts. First, in a direct and immediate manner as lecturer, teacher and supervisor. Second, in an indirect, mediated manner as the author of textbooks and the member of committees that determine what and how students learn. Such knowledge, too, is continually tested, though not in the context of clinical practice but in the form of uniform nationwide written exams. Such tests employ a mixed format of multiple choice and short answer questions as well as the filling in of blanks in given sentences with standard phrases. In the emphasis on testing memorised knowledge a clear link is thereby established with official examinations in imperial China but also with learning in the context of discipleship.[32] Simultaneously, such examinations are as much a cause as an expression of the standardisation of traditional medical knowledge that accompanied its modernisation. Nationwide exams only become meaningful if individual results are comparable. For that the education system must produce roughly equivalent local contexts of learning or, at least, transmit in these contexts a common core of testable knowledge.

There are several important preconditions for the success of such an undertaking. First, political control of education must be sufficiently centralised to arrange and supervise a smoothing process whereby previously diverse contexts of learning are progressively homogenised. Second, teaching materials and curricula must transform personalised practices that accord a high value to implicit knowledge into shared, explicit and highly formalised knowledge.[33]

Professor Rong's contribution to such efforts began in the early 1950s. Following training in Western medicine at his local hospital he joined the teaching staff at the Chinese Medicine Improvement School (*zhongyi jinxiu xuexiao*) in Nanjing, the capital of his native Jiangsu province.[34] Due to a conjunction of historical and social factors, the courses established at this college later became a model for the founding of the first Chinese medicine colleges. Throughout the last four centuries, Jiangsu has been an important centre of Chinese medicine where many of its most innovative and influential physicians lived, practised and published. As importantly, Lu Bingkui, the person in charge of organising these courses in Nanjing, later became director of the Chinese Medicine Bureau at the MoH. In this role Lu moved a staff of young doctors – including Professor Rong – from Jiangsu to Beijing where they soon played an important role in establishing Chinese medicine as an academic discipline.[35]

The influence of Jiangsu physicians is reflected nowhere more so than in the first major textbook of Chinese medicine produced under direct supervision of the MoH. This text, entitled *Outline of Chinese Medicine (Zhongyixue gailun)*, was compiled mainly by the Nanjing Chinese Medicine College in 1957/58.[36] Professor Rong was a member of the editorial committee that drafted the initial manuscript. The presentation of the entire field of Chinese medicine within a single text has since been superseded by a series of more specialised textbooks. Professor Rong's own career development mirrored this process of specialisation. He became professor of formulas *(fangjixue)* at Beijing College of Chinese Medicine. He has contributed to all editions of the standard textbook on which state examinations in the subject are based and is currently a member of the committee that supervises the publication of common teaching materials for tertiary level Chinese medical education.

While in his own practice Professor Rong draws on the formulas discussed in his textbooks, the manner in which he selects, modifies and combines them cannot be read off from the texts that introduces them to undergraduate students. This is because in practice physicians hardly ever use standard formulas. More usually, they adjust formulas to the presentation of a patient by adding and subtracting *(jiajian)* various drugs. Chinese medicine formulas in this sense do not have prescriptive character. Rather, they function as models from which the virtuosity of a physician – a virtuosity which becomes nowhere more visibly manifest than in the act of composing a prescription – is developed.[37]

When I asked a PhD student how she would define the difference between students and apprentices, she gave the following reply.

> [Students and disciples] receive different treatment. [My professor] wants to hand down his ideas and experiences to his disciples, whereas students only need to study in school. He will instruct them in doing papers so they graduate and may become professors themselves.

Discipleship here is related to clinical practice while studentship constitutes the passage into an institutional career. This career, however, centres on medical practice and involves clinical as much as theoretical teaching. Hence, while certain categorical distinctions seem to exist between studentship and discipleship – embodied in the specialisation of modern state education and the separation of theory and practice – they are also related to each other by way of historical contingency.

Such contingency is embodied literally in Professors Rong and Xu, who are masters to disciples and teachers to students. It surfaces in the stereotypical attributes expected of any good teacher in contemporary Chinese medical schools. A demeanour reflecting authority coupled with an obligation to care for students beyond merely imparting to them knowledge remain close to the characteristics of a traditional teacher.[38] We already noted how Professor Rong succeeded in inserting his line into the university infrastructure and how the state managed to influence access to and certification of certain types of discipleship. Further crossovers occur where students manage to construct particularistic ties to individual teachers.

Due to the sheer number of students educated in university courses and the relatively short periods of time they are taught by the same teacher the forging of particularistic teacher/student ties during undergraduate training remains an exception.[39] Nevertheless, it does take place. While I was studying at the gynaecology department at another Chinese medicine hospital in Beijing, one of the consultants was frequently accompanied by one of his final year undergraduates. In his spare time, this student followed the consultant in the same manner described above for the disciples of Professors Rong: copying prescriptions, attending to patients and, in the evening, typing and editing his teacher's manuscripts.

Opportunities for developing particularistic ties present themselves increasingly with the duration of one's education. Postgraduate students often select a course because they wish to study with a specific supervisor. Students benefit directly and indirectly from having a famous physician such as Professor Rong as their supervisor. Given the social organisation of Chinese society and the influence of those placed in positions of power a supervisor may be able to actively help with employment, promotions, research opportunities, housing, introductions, references and even holidays. Having studied with a *ming laozhongyi* also, of course, adds to a student's face. A reciprocal pressure on physicians to show their standing by becoming a supervisor is the reverse side of this coin. Unlike most other countries China certifies individuals, more usually than departments or programmes, to accept graduate students. The supervision of doctoral degrees, in particular, is reserved for eminent physicians. That one is a 'doctoral supervisor' (*boshi daoshi*) is therefore prominently displayed on the visiting cards of all those entitled to claim such status, just as their students proudly present themselves as 'doctoral candidates' (*boshisheng*).

Once a particularistic teacher/student relationship has been established, it takes on some of the characteristics of master–disciple relationships. Physicians, who had completed postgraduate studies, invariably mentioned to me how deeply their practice had been influenced by the style of their supervisor. Contexts and modalities of learning also frequently resemble those described for master–disciple relationships, as we saw with Professor Rong's doctoral students: the copying of prescriptions during clinical practice and the referral of students to source texts rather than the explicit resolution of questions. Even secret prescriptions (*mifang*), simultaneously functional emblems of knowledge and power and material representations of the bond between generations of practice, may be passed on by teachers to students.

A very different case was that of a doctor in his mid-thirties, who occupied positions of seniority in the state education sector far above of those of comparable age and experience. Heir to one of the most respected acupuncture lines in north China, I met him instructing foreign students in the secret traditions of his line. He told me that in his opinion the very notion of secret knowledge was an anachronism at the end of the twentieth century. A less charitable explanation would be that trading in his line's secret knowledge had become a profitable business, which permitted extensive travel abroad.

This latter example alerts us that besides learning relationships facilitated by kinship(-like) ties and/or bureaucratic educational structures more spontaneous exchange relations are possible. These are mediated by factors extending from emotional bonds to financial transactions and have assumed a new social importance in post-Maoist China.

Guanxixue: *learning and the art of social networking*

The role of particularistic exchange relations, known locally as *guanxi*, in Chinese social life is so striking that an ability to form 'pluralistic' identifications with others on the basis of shared attributes has been identified a fundamental aspect of Chinese social behaviour. More recent ethnographies demonstrate, however, that *guanxi* relationships are neither unique and invariant features of an enduring Chinese culture, nor are they local reflections of universal relationships of an instrumental nature. Rather, they constitute interpersonal bonds that conjoin emotional, moral and instrumental concerns into a constantly re-emergent conception of what constitutes self in relationship to others. *Guanxi* thus represents the use of inherited cultural tools in the pursuit of contemporary ends, a process in which both *guanxi* and the users of *guanxi* are continually redefined. His fame as a physician and his insertion into a wide range of different networks make of Professor Rong an ideal exemplar from which the role of *guanxixue* (the art of establishing *guanxi*) in contemporary Chinese medicine may be read off.[40]

The first observation we can make is that being in the right place at the right time – without which it is, of course, impossible to insert oneself into any network – seems to have been of crucial importance. As the son of a nationally renowned paediatrician who had died early, Professor Rong occupied an ideal position from where the traditional and the modern in the emergent Chinese medicine of the new China could be tied together. Professor Rong was also fortunate enough to belong to a local place-based network that became an important force in the shaping of Chinese medicine both nationally and locally in Beijing. His move from rural Jiangsu to the capital Beijing, finally, positioned Professor Rong closer to new centres of power with which useful *guanxi* ties could be established. Vice versa, with each new appointment Professor Rong occupied increasingly important 'gatekeeper' positions that made it desirable for others to nurture his acquaintance.

Establishing *guanxi* with a person of Professor Rong's standing is a crucial career move for PhD students. I gathered much anecdotal evidence that Professor Rong was popular because he helped his students in a manner that a good teacher is expected to do, such as obtaining employment after graduation. Professor Rong counts among his patients politicians, business people and other members of the elite. My informants were in no doubt about the considerable influence exerted on the development of Chinese medicine via such personal networks. 'You have to learn that in China policies change as people change', was a lesson my friends and teachers never tired of impressing on me.

An important example for the direct influence exerted on the development of Chinese medicine by individuals via *guanxi* networks is the compilation of national textbooks. As stated previously, MoH committees made up of physicians and educators decide upon the content of these books. According to my informants the leading members of such committees exert an extraordinary amount of influence which allows personal preferences to enter official discourse. Less powerful networks, however, also subvert such hegemony. When I studied warm pathogen diseases (*wenbing*) in Beijing, for instance, my teacher took great care to emphasise that his way of teaching the subject differed from that of official textbooks. He supplied us with photocopies of his own articles and a book written by a local professor. This text organises the subject in a substantially different way from the set textbooks edited by physicians from the south. Depending on the identity of their teachers, students of *wenbing* at Beijing now learn enough of the dominant southern interpretation to pass their exams but acquire this knowledge mediated through local interpretations.[41]

These examples highlight *guanxi* networks that depend for their functioning on the reproduction of official hierarchies. Professor Rong occupies a central node in many such networks precisely because of his official positions. Other networks insinuate themselves across or even against the hierarchical structures of state and family. PhD students, for instance, exchange amongst themselves the prescriptions of their supervisors providing themselves with access to otherwise closely guarded knowledge. Yet, these prescriptions did not thereby pass into general circulation but remained restricted to specific *guanxi* networks.

There exist many other such lateral exchange networks. They cut across social domains, personal identities, time and space. They connect by means of digital technology, financial transaction, ethics and emotionality and blur clinical, economic, and political domains. Working within particular hospital departments I noticed repeatedly how physicians defined themselves against members of other departments or other hospitals. Different departments had secret prescriptions that were known to their own physicians but not to outsiders. Physicians who have studied under the same supervisor sometimes connect to each other like disciples of the same master and introduce their own students into such networks.

Physicians also establish *guanxi* connections with various groups of lay persons (and vice versa). The boundaries between medicine, art, philosophy and other academic disciplines thus become highly permeable. Intellectuals and scholars can possess considerable medical knowledge and some of the doctors with whom I studied were accomplished painters and calligraphers. The merging of clinical and the socio-economic domains, on the other hand, become obvious in the course of daily surgeries. Patients use *guanxi* to be introduced to a specific physician, or construct it spontaneously by playing on some joint identification. A common surname or home province is sufficient to put into play an emotional attachment that obliges a doctor to be just that little bit more attentive. Doctors, equally, are never shy to seize an opportunity for widening their own *guanxi* networks. As one of my teachers – a physician of the highest sophistication and moral integrity – advised me, being a physician in Beijing was desirable simply because it opened doors that in the country one did not even know existed.

It should be clear from these few examples that *guanxi* networks do not merely arise from the rational calculation of individuals but that they draw on an ethics of relationship which implicate specific inflections of emotionality, selfhood and morality. *Guanxixue* thus embodies patterns of agency that are developed and utilised by social actors in the stabilisation of specific syntheses, yet that reciprocally also define these actors. *Guanxi* networks have increased in size and importance since the 1980s and have formed alternative subjectivities to those enabled by traditional kinship and modern socialist bureaucratic types of social organisation. The re-emergence of the individual as social actor as well as a reaffirmed admissibility of traditional patterns of social behaviour have facilitated this renewed importance of *guanxixue*. Other factors, however, have worked against a sliding back of social behaviour/organisation towards pre-revolutionary patterns. The bureaucratic organisation of the socialist state has remained in place, the cultural hegemony of modernisation and scientification have been further amplified and individual agency is very much defined nowadays as a pursuit of economical goals.[42]

These changes are easily documented in the domain of Chinese medicine. There is considerable evidence, for instance, for the renewed importance attached to individual actors. Textbooks, even individual chapters of textbooks, are again traceable as the work of individual authors who write in distinctive styles and put forward controversial opinions. The last decade has witnessed the re-entry into Chinese medicine of traditional philosophy and a self-conscious 'return to the sources' which is unashamedly concerned with reworking the own tradition rather than learning from the West. Modernisation and the integration of Chinese medicine and Western medicine still remain national political goals, however, whose importance is emphasised by the economical and political benefits (real or imagined) seen to accrue from the internationalisation of Chinese medicine. Yet, while the state still controls education, it no longer can rely on the willingness of the practitioners it trains to care for the masses out of purely humanistic motivations, be they of a socialist or traditionalist inflection. Increasingly what counts for doctors is personal fame, which can be translated into personal wealth. And if the former cannot be had the latter will have to do on its own. Many young doctors are now leaving the profession for better paid positions in private industry, one of the most common options being employment by pharmaceutical companies.

Professor Rong, like other physicians, has made the appropriate transitions. We already encountered him as a successful entrepreneur in his surgery. The doctoral dissertations of his students double as pharmacological studies that will, in the future, be used to support the marketing of his patented prescriptions. In his capacity as chairman of government committees he is negotiating with the Food and Drug

Each has its own strengths

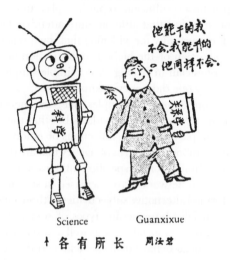

Science   Guanxixue

↑ 各 有 所 长   周汝昌

Figure 8.1 Cartoon from *China Youth Daily* (Zhongguo qingnian bao), 20 December 1984

Administration (FDA) about US licences for traditional pharmaceutical products. Several of his students are now living and working abroad where they use his name to promote their own, yet also facilitate their teacher's transition into an international renowned master physician.

In an environment where tradition again counts for something though only if it is suitably modernised, where the state still provides the basic structures of education and medical practice but individual status is newly important, where opportunities for jobs, housing and promotion are always scarcer than the number of applicants, *guanxixue* emerges as a product of specific historical contradictions. Contemporary physicians of Chinese medicine have become what they are by passing through a state-controlled education system based on a vision of medicine as a social product. In practice they increasingly need to assert their own individuality or remain shackled to a system that cannot deliver for them their aspirations. No wonder they should attempt to construct, in medical as well as social terms, their own lines of connection.

Networks and agency

In the introduction to her ethnography of *guanxixue* in contemporary China, Mayfair Yang reprints a cartoon from a Chinese newspaper, which opposes *kexue* (science) and *guanxixue* as two modes of making progress in life (see Figure 8.1).

In my encounters with Chinese medicine I have often been reminded of this cartoon because it condenses into a single image part of the dynamic that characterises contemporary Chinese medicine as much as contemporary Chinese society. Chinese medicine emphasises tradition yet is distinctly modern. It claims to be a forward looking unitary science but also defines itself through multiple genealogies of experience. It thinks of itself as distinctly Chinese (where Chinese-ness naturally evokes networks of descent) and as a universal medical system. These currents appear to be contradictory yet they also provide stability to an ongoing transformation that connects actors, institutions, technologies and signifiers into complex relations systems.

My case study shows how within a small consulting room in the north of Beijing multiple relations converge on and radiate out from a single centre. This centre is Professor Rong. From a different perspective, however, Professor Rong merely constitutes an intersection of networks through which different kinds of things (information, emotions, favours, money) travel and are exchanged. The manner in which Professor Rong and the networks to which he is connected construct each other in an ongoing process of transformation challenges conventional analyses of medical pluralism and the problematic disjunction between tradition and modernity to which they are related.

Professor Rong is the representative of a distinctive medical tradition, a professor within a modern educational institution, and an individual Chinese person. He actively configures what it means to be a scholar-physician, a teacher of Chinese medicine and an individual in contemporary China. Yet, the institutions, moral norms and social contexts in which he finds himself equally configure him. Discipleship, studentship and *guanxixue* thus do not represent stable 'forms of life', 'styles of reasoning', 'institutions', 'cultures' or 'practices' that might somehow be read off Professor Rong as an exemplary subject. More useful, in my opinion, is to think of Professor Rong in terms of multiple and contradictory 'subject position-alities' that simultaneously relate him to different institutions, moral norms, medical doctrines and practices.[43]

These institutions, norms, doctrines and practices all have different historical origins. They are condensations of diverse and not necessarily congruent processes of historical transformation that link each to different networks of peoples and things in both the past and the present. Professor Rong's rewriting of traditional formularies is a seamless continuation of similar work carried out for at least a thousand years. He is instrumental in shaping a national curriculum that has a history of less than fifty years. And he discusses the marketing of Chinese medical formulas with the FDA as a result of the very recent globalisation of Chinese medicine.

Elements of traditional practice are transformed by being connected to modern ones imported from the West. Modern institutions, however, are equally reshaped by tradition in a process that signifies more than just resistance. Professor Rong introduces conventional moral codes into the supervision of his doctoral students, while they draw on modern Chinese notions of *guanxixue* to get a job at the end of their studies. Professor Rong uses the biomedical research of his students as a tool to promote his traditional formulas in a late twentieth-century commercial context, while his students use forms of association made possible by the modern institution in which they study to circulate his personal prescriptions. Professor Rong has managed to insert his medical line into the university system, but socialist education has made possible transmission through a female disciple from outside his family.

Such a network model (loosely based on Bruno Latour) catches well some aspects of these ongoing transformations because it does not impose onto our analysis *a priori* definitions of practice or historical periods, tradition or modernity. Networks can extend across analytical domains relating to each other bodies (organic, inorganic, technological, social, institutional, political), selves (social, psychological), and signifiers (concepts, texts, signs). Individual nodes within a given network can connect to other networks without these networks forming a necessary totality. Hence it is possible – and not at all odd – that contemporary physicians formulate prescriptions by drawing on Chinese medical literature from the Han and bio-medical knowledge from the *New England Journal of Medicine*, that networks of descent stretch from Qing Southern China, to a Beijing *laozhongyi* and on to his disciple in the United Kingdom, and that they simultaneously circulate knowledge, status, money and favours. A network model also explains why some nodes accrue more power than others through positioning themselves in such a way that certain flows must pass through them.

The network metaphor, however, also suggests a stability that is never actually there. Anthropological studies of *guanxixue*, for instance, demonstrate that the a-temporal quality of the network metaphor with its implicit focus on structure fails to capture the dynamism of local agency that can only be captured as process. It is such agency that uses networks to channel through them other flows than originally intended. Studentship can thus be transformed into particularistic personal ties for the exchange of money and favours or moved in the direction of ritually ordered discipleship. It is through such agency, too, that networks are created and modified, broken down and destroyed. State education, for instance, has seriously undermined the importance of discipleship. Yet the very rarity of such relationships has also therefore made them into something special.

One way to perceive of agency in structural terms is to depict agents as foci from whom radiate out effects that disperse as they move progressively outward. Professor Rong's relationship with his graduate students and disciples support such a model. In each case relations are developed and affirmed through similar ritualised performances, while intensity diminishes with increasing social distance. However, Professor Rong's status as master and teacher is not entirely determined by the structural order into which a specific relationship is embedded. It also reflects his actual achievements within these relations. Such achievements are continually threatened in the context of practice. Whether as a physician or as a teacher, Professor Rong is continually on stage. He must demonstrate anew in each consultation that he is a *ming laozhongyi* and to each PhD student that he is a powerful person whose patronage is worth fostering.[44]

The origins of plurality

In Chinese thought relational networks (*guanxiwang*) are established and maintained through the art of *guanxixue*. Yet, the art of *guanxixue* is made possible only by the existence of networks that can be constantly rewoven in the pursuit of specific goals. New elements can always be inserted into such networks while older strands are thrown out – and later perhaps rediscovered. Continuity and constant transformation thus go hand in hand. It is in the ensuing tension and codetermination between agency and structure that plurality is grounded. Walter Benjamin has captured within one beautiful and haunting image, the image of the *origin*, the ontological primacy of plurality within the coming-into-being of any conjunction of subjectivity and network:

> Origin [Ursprung] although a thoroughly historical category, nonetheless has nothing to do with beginnings [...] The term origin does not mean the process of becoming of that which has emerged, but much more, that which emerges out of the process of becoming and disappearing. The origin stands in the flow of becoming as a whirlpool [...]; its rhythm is apparent only to a double insight.[45]

Our ability to grasp this impermanence bestows an important advantage on a pluralist perspective in the analysis of medical practice. Anthropologists have repeatedly drawn our attention to the short-term value of narrow conceptions of science and modernity implicated in dismantling the richness of traditional knowledge.[46] Another facet of the same short-termism is the homogenisation of traditional knowledge itself. The political mechanisms contributing to such homogenisation are manifold and cannot be discussed here. They are accelerated, however, by romanticised perceptions of traditional healing systems prevalent not only amongst anthropologists but also among advocates of so-called alternative medicines.[47] Such romanticising – and the homogenising comparisons between biomedicine and tradition with which it is associated – impedes our capacity to render visible the fragmentation of all medical practices and to challenge the regimes that benefit from hiding their synthetic nature. Above all, it makes it more difficult to discern the diverse and not always predictable alignments between different medical practices – alignments that – as many contributions to this volume show – exist not only in contemporary China and that will become ever more obvious and important in the rapidly transforming landscapes of medicine in the West.

Notes

1 Throughout this chapter I use the term 'Chinese medicine' to refer to the medicine of the scholarly élite in Imperial China and the contemporary transformations of this medicine as taught and practised mainly within the state controlled healthcare system. Although the choice of term is misleading in several ways (it does not encompass all Chinese medical practice; Chinese medicine is increasingly practised by non-Chinese outside of China), it equates to the term *zhongyi*, which is used within contemporary China to designate this practice. J. Farquhar, *Knowing Practice: The Clinical Encounter in Chinese Medicine, Studies in the Ethnographic Imagination.* Boulder: Westview Press, 1994, has provided the best analysis of the constitution and use of this medicine in contemporary clinical practice to date (but see also the references cited in fn. 2). I follow S.D. White, 'Deciphering "integrated Chinese and Western medicine" in the rural Lijiang basin: state policy and local practice(s) in socialist China', *Social Science and Medicine* 49 (1999): 1333–47, in using 'Western medicine' (the literal translation of the Chinese term *xiyi*) to refer to the practice of biomedicine as it has developed in China throughout the last century or so, including its

distinctive practice in the PRC. See G. Henderson and M.S. Cohen, *The Chinese Hospital: A Socialist Work Unit*. New Haven, CT: Yale University Press, 1984, and C. Maldener, 'Grundzüge des chinesischen Gesundheitswesens (I und II)', *ChinaMed*, 5 & 6 (1995): 17–23, for some discussion of this.

2   Various aspects of the modernisation of Chinese medicine throughout the last century are discussed by H. Ågren, 'Patterns of tradition and modernization in contemporary Chinese medicine', in A. Kleinman, P. Kunstadter, E. Alexander and J. Gale (eds), *Medicine in Chinese Cultures: Comparative Studies in Chinese and Other Cultures*, Washington: US Dept. of Health Education and Welfare Public Health Service, 1974, pp. 37–59; B. Andrews, 'The making of modern Chinese medicine, 1895–1937', PhD thesis, Cambridge, 1996; R. Croizier, *Traditional Medicine in Modern China*, Cambridge, MA: Harvard University Press, 1968; T. Deng, (ed.), *Zhongyi jindai shi (A History of Chinese Medicine in the Modern Era)*. Guangzhou: Guangdong gaodeng jiaoyu chubanshe, 1999; E. Hsu, *The Transmission of Chinese Medicine*, Cambridge: Cambridge University Press, 1999; H. Jia, 'Chinese medicine in post-Mao China: standardization and the context of modern science', PhD thesis, Department of Anthropology, University of North Carolina, 1997; S. Lei, 'When Chinese medicine encountered the state: 1910–1949', PhD thesis, Department for the Conceptual Foundations of Science, University of Chicago, 1998; T. Ots, *Medizin und Heilung in China* (2. Auflage), Berlin: Dietrich Reimer Verlag, 1990; N. Sivin, *Traditional Medicine in Contemporary China*, Ann Arbor: Centre for Chinese Studies, The University of Michigan, 1987; P. Unschuld, 'Epistemological issues and changing legitimation: traditional Chinese medicine in the twentieth century', in C. Leslie and A. Young (eds), *Paths to Asian Medical Knowledge*, Berkeley: University of California Press, 1992, pp. 44–63; X. Xu, '"National essence" versus "science": Chinese native physicians' fight for legitimacy 1912–32', *Modern Asian Studies* 31, 4 (1997): 847–78; and H. Zhao, *Jindai zhong xi yi lunzheng shi (History of the Polemics between Chinese and Western Medicine in Modern Times)*. Hefei: Anhui kexue jishu chubanshe, 1989.

3   One can discern at least three such attempts. The first was carried out by individual Chinese physicians from the turn of the century to about 1950. The second encompassed efforts by the Chinese state during the 1950s to unite Chinese and Western medicine. The third is the attempt to construct an integrated Chinese and Western medicine initiated during the Cultural Revolution and now institutionalised as a distinct branch of (Chinese) medicine called 'integrated Chinese and Western medicine' (*zhongxiyi jiehe*). In as much as these attempts are ongoing my statement simplifies a much more complex situation.

4   I use the terms 'modern' and 'traditional' in relation to Chinese medicine with some hesitation. They are suggestive of a discontinuity that is difficult to sustain. Although many elements of Chinese medicine have been transformed in the course of the last 100 years, even more remain the same. Traditional also implies that prior to the encounter with modernity Chinese medicine was static and unchanging. This is not the case as Sivin, *Traditional Medicine in Contemporary China* and P. Unschuld, *Medicine in China: A History of Ideas*. Berkeley: University of California Press, 1985, demonstrate. I discuss this issue at length in V. Scheid, *Contemporary Chinese Medicin Synthesis and Plurality*, Durham, NC: Duke University Press, in press.

5   See Bradley (Chapter 2), Bruchhausen and Roelke (Chapter 5), Hardey (Chapter 12), Liebeskind (Chapter 4) and Reis (Chapter 6) in this volume.

6   The critique which informs this statement is too complex and multi-faceted to review here in detail. B.J. Good *Medicine, Rationality, and Experience: An Anthropological Perspective, Lewis Henry Morgan Lecture Series*, Cambridge: Cambridge University Press, 1994, and S. Franklin, 'Science as culture, cultures of science', *Annual Review of Anthropology* 24 (1995): 163–84 provide summaries and reviews for the realms of medicine and science respectively.

7   See Reed in this volume (Chapter 10).

8   Take Giddens' definition of tradition used by Reis, this volume, that defines it as a kind of enduring truth that is protected by certain guardians who have unique access to this truth even if on the outside the forms of tradition change considerably over time. That, to me, seems a very good description of modern biomedicine and science in general.

9   J.D. Farquhar and J.L. Hevia, 'Culture and postwar American historiography of China', *Positions* 1, 2 (1993): 486–525.

10 There are innumerable ways to define modernity and my list is by no means meant to be complete. M. Weber, *Economy and Society*, Berkeley and Los Angeles: University of California Press, 1968, provides the most commonly cited reference pointing to such factors as rationalisation, mechanisation, bureaucratisation, secularisation and the disenchantment of social and religious life. More recent influential attempts to define the uniqueness of modernity include M. Berman, *All That Is Solid Melts into Air: The Experience of Modernity*, New York: Penguin, 1982; M. Foucault, *Discipline and Punish: The Birth of the Prison*, Harmondsworth: Penguin, 1979; A. Giddens, *The Consequences of Modernity*, Cambridge: Polity Press, 1991 and *Modernity and Self Identity*, Cambridge: Polity Press, 1990; and J. Habermas, *The Philosophical Discourse of Modernity*, Oxford: Polity Press, 1987.

11 A pertinent example is the work of Georges Soulié de Morant, *Chinese Acupuncture*. Brookline, MA: Paradigm, 1994, a key figure in reviving interest in acupuncture in the West during the first half of the twentieth century. Although not Chinese, Soulié de Morant succeeded in many ways to construct what the Chinese themselves have found difficult to accomplish – a coherent medical system that integrates Chinese medicine and biomedicine. Contemporary transformations of Chinese medicine in the West are analysed by H.A. Baer *et al.*, 'The drive for professionalization in acupuncture: a preliminary view from the San Franscisco Bay Area', *Social Science and Medicine*, 46, 4–5 (1998): 533–7, and L. Barnes, 'The psychologizing of Chinese healing practices in the United States', *Culture, Medicine and Psychiatry* 22 (1998): 413–43.

12 Lei, 'When Chinese Medicine Encountered the State', for instance, constitutes the rejection of the proposed ban on Chinese medicine in 1929 as an epistemological event that marked the transition to modern Chinese medicine. He thus sees continuities between the transformations of Chinese medicine before and after 1949, while socialist reform after 1949 appears to mark a distinct transition for other writers such as Andrews, *The Making of Modern Chinese Medicine*, Hsu, *The Transmission of Chinese Medicine* and Sivin, *Traditional Medicine in Contemporary China*. Naturally, the two perspectives do not exclude each other, though they demonstrate that perceptions of continuity and change are as much a consequence of perspective as of perceived facts.

13 The different modernity offered by non-capitalist and non-Western societies has been the stimulus in criticising homogenising perceptions of modernity as derived from the Enlightenment and the Industrial Revolution in the West. Examples of such critiques with special relevance to the Chinese case are A. Ong, 'Anthropology, China and modernities', in H.L. Moore (ed.), *The Future of Anthropological Knowledge*, London: Routledge, 1995, pp. 60–92, and 'Chinese modernities: narratives of nation and of capitalism', in A. Ong and D. Nonini (eds) *Underground Empires: The Cultural Politics of Modern Chinese Transnationalism*, pp. 171–202, London: Routledge, 1997; L. Rofel, 'Rethinking modernity: space and factory discipline in China', *Cultural Anthropology* 1, 1 (1992): 93–114 and *Other Modernities: Gendered Yearnings in China After Socialism*, Berkeley: University of California Press, 1999; and M. Yang, 'The modernity of power in the Chinese socialist order', *Cultural Anthropology*, 3 (1988): 408–27.

14 See S. Hua *Scientism and Humanism: Two Cultures in Post-Mao China*. Albany, NY: Suny Press, 1995; W. Hui, 'The fate of "Mr Science" in China: the concept of science and its application in modern Chinese thought', in T.E. Barlow (ed.), *Formations of Colonial Modernity in East Asia*, Durham, NC: Duke University Press, 1997, pp. 21–81; and D. Kwok, *Scientism in Chinese Thought 1900–1950*. New Haven and London: Yale University Press, 1965, for the development of scientism in China. X. Xu, *'National Essence' Versus 'Science'*, discusses the role of nationalism in the transformation of Chinese medicine. It is interesting to note that authors who subscribe to a distinctive difference between modern and traditional Chinese medicine such as Andrews' *The Making of Modern Chinese Medicine* are very much aware of the interplay between modernisation and nationalism but suggest to discuss these separately from each other.

15 Various aspects of the modernisation of Chinese medicine in post-Mao China are discussed by G. Henderson, 'Issues in the modernization of medicine in China', in D.F. Simon and M. Goldman (eds), *Science and Technology in Post-Mao China*, Cambridge, MA: The Council of East Asian Studies/ Harvard University, 1989, pp. 199–221; Hsu, *The Transmission of Chinese Medicine*; J. Farquhar, 'Market magic: getting rich and getting personal in medicine after Mao', *American Ethnologist*, 23, 2 (1996): 239–57 and 'Technologies of everyday life: the economy of impotence

in reform China', *Cultural Anthropology*, 14, 2 (1999): 155–79; Jia, 'Chinese Medicine in Post-Mao China'; and S.D. White 'Deciphering "integrated Chinese and Western medicine"'.

16   A. Nandy (ed.), *Science, Hegemony and Violence: A Requiem for Modernity*, Dehli: Oxford University Press, 1988.

17   A. Ong, *Spirits of Resistance and Capitalist Discipline: Factory Women in Malaysia*, Albany: Suny Press, 1987, provides an exemplary ethnography relating to China.

18   M. Porkert, 'Die chinesische Medizin verkürzt und verbilligt', *Chinesische Medizin* 13, 3 (1998): 80–5; N. Sivin, 'Reflections on the Situation in the People's Republic of China, 1987', *American Journal of Acupuncture* 18, 4 (1990): 341–3, and P. Unschuld, 'Epistemological issues and changing legitimation', are prominent examples. Many Western practitioners of Chinese medicine, too, perceive a loss of tradition in contemporary China that needs to be recovered in the West as L. Barnes, 'The psychologizing of Chinese healing practices in the United States' demonstrates. The resonance between these academic and professional positions points to shared but unacknowledged background assumptions regarding the relation of tradition and modernity in their production.

19   J. Farquhar, 'Multiplicity, point of view, and responsibility in traditional Chinese healing', in A. Zito and T. Barlow (eds), *Body, Subject and Power in China*, pp. 78–99; Scheid, *Synthesis and Plurality in Contemporary Chinese Medicine*, and White 'Deciphering "integrated Chinese and Western medicine"' provide ethnographic evidence of the importance of such factors.

20   D. Haraway, 'A Cyborg manifesto: science, technology and socialist feminism in the late twentieth century', in *Simians, Cyborgs, and Women: The Reinvention of Nature*, London: Free Association Books, 1991, pp. 149–81 and 'Situated knowledges: the science question in feminism and the priviledge of partial perspective', *Feminist Studies*, 14 (1988): 515–99; B. Latour, *Science in Action*, Cambridge, MA: Harvard University Press, 1987 and *The Pasteurization of France*. Cambridge, MA: Harvard University Press, 1988; B. Latour and S. Woolgar, *Laboratory Life: The Construction of Scientific Knowledge* (2nd edn) Princeton, NJ: Princeton University Press, 1986; and A. Pickering, *The Mangle of Practice: Time, Agency, and Science*, Chicago: University of Chicago Press, 1995, and 'Explanation, agency, and metaphysics: a reply to Owen Flanagan', in B. Herrnstein-Smith and A. Plonitsky (eds), *Mathematics, Science, and Postclassical Theory*, Durham, NC: Duke University Press, 1997, pp. 90–4. S. Franklin's, 'Science as culture, cultures of science' provides a useful overview of the impact of science studies on anthropology. See B. Latour, 'Postmodern? No simply amodern. Steps toward an anthropology of science', *Studies in the History and Philosophy of Science*, 21, 1 (1990): 145–71; *We Have Never Been Modern* (translated by Catherine Porter), Cambridge, MA: Harvard University Press, 1993, and 'A few steps towards an anthropology of the iconoclastic gesture', *Science in Context*, 10, 1 (1997): 63–83, for a consistent and explicit effort at dismantling the boundaries between tradition and modernity.

21   For an in-depth discussion of the theoretical issues raised here see G. Marcus, 'Ethnography in/ of the world: the emergence of multi-sited ethnography', *Annual Review of Anthropology*, 24 (1995): 95–117.

22   Such decontextualisation is, in fact, a criticism that has been made of both Latour and Pickering, e.g. D.J. Hess, 'If you're thinking of living in STS: A guide for the perplexed', in G.L. Downey and J. Dumit (eds), *Cyborgs and Citadels: Anthropological Interventions in Emerging Sciences and Technologies*, Santa Fe, NM: School of American Research Press, 1997, pp. 143–64. Haraway's work is less open to such critique precisely because it emphasises local situatedness. Hence, her cyborg model has perhaps been particularly influential among anthropologists, e.g. G. Downey and J. Dumit, *Cyborgs and Citadels: Anthropological Interventions in Emerging Sciences and Technologies*, Santa Fe: School of American Research Press, 1997.

23   The students told me that this was what patients would expect.

24   The Imperial Medical Academy (*Tai yi yuan*) was the major exception to this general rule until the end of the Qing dynasty. Modern schools of Chinese medicine influenced by Western models of education began to appear from the late nineteenth century onward. While these schools used classroom teaching for the transmission of doctrine, they still relied on master disciple relationships in the transmission of clinical skills. T. Deng, *Zhongyi jindai shi*, pp. 108–213 and personal information from interviews with Chinese physicians.

25 N. Sivin, 'Text and experience in classical Chinese medicine', in D. Bates (ed.), *Knowledge and the Scholarly Medical Traditions*, Cambridge: Cambridge University Press, 1995, pp. 177–20, shows how discipleship developed in pre-Han China derived from or superimposed on filiations between father and son. That this is indeed the case was demonstrated to me during my fieldwork. All disciples I interviewed likened discipleship to family-like relationships.

26 These relationships are enumerated for the first time in their standard sequence by Mencius who also joins them with their appropriate emotive tenor. Although formulated within the context of family kinship, their content applied equally to relations outside the family. Eastman, E. Lloyd, *Family, Fields, and Ancestors: Constancy and Change in China's Social and Economic History, 1550–1949*, Oxford: Oxford University Press, 1988, p. 35.

27 The biographies contained in Zhou Fengwu, Zhang Qiwen and Cong Lin (eds), *Ming laozhongyi zhi lu (Paths of Renowned Senior Chinese Physicians)*, 3 vols. Jinan: Shandong kexue jishu chubanshe, 1981–5, contain many descriptions of traditional apprenticeship.

28 In 1978 MoH statistics account for 85 *laozhongyi* in Beijing of whom 28 were *ming laozhongyi* Zhonghua renmin gongheguo weishengbu zhongyisi. *Zhongyi gongzuo wenjian huibian (Collection of Documents Relating to the Work of the Ministry of Public Health on Chinese Medicine)*. Beijing, 1985, p. 294.

29 Not all masters are as stern and many will, in fact, encourage their disciples to study with other physicians. Where a teacher does not encourage such learning, students circumvent this problem by studying with different teachers subsequently.

30 It must also be mentioned that patients come to be treated by Professor Rong, not by his disciples. Making a few changes in their prescription thus functions also as a gesture in Professor Rong's relationship with his patients demonstrating his concern for their well-being.

31 As discussed in the introduction, modernity in China in general and education in particular have been shaped by particularly Chinese transformations. In the course of this chapter it is not possible to discuss these in detail. I thus use general terms such as state where it would be more precise to refer to socialist state, Maoist state, etc.

32 Medical examinations in the Song dynasty, for instance, were equally stereotyped. See G. Lu and J. Needham, *Science and Civilization in China*, (rev. by N. Sivin), Vol. 6 part 6, Cambridge, Cambridge University Press, 2000, pp. 95–113. For the kind of examinations typical of Chinese Medicine state education see Quanguo gaodeng jiaoyu zixue kaoshi shizhi daowiyuanhui. *Zhongyi zhuanye kaoshi jihua (Chinese Medicine Professional Examination [Study] Program)*. Shanghai: Shanghai zhongyixxue yuan chubanshe, 1986.

33 This process has been examined in detail by Hsu, *The Transmission of Chinese Medicine.*

34 These schools operated between 1950 and 1956 and functioned as centres for the further training of licensed practitioners of Chinese medicine. Kim Taylor, 'Paving the way for TCM textbooks: the Chinese medical improvement schools'. Paper presented at the The Ninth International Conference on the History of Science in East Asia, The East Asian Institute, National University of Singapore, 23–27 August 1999, has argued that their main function therefore was the control of these practitioners by the state.

35 A biography of Lü Bingkui outlining the developments described here can be found in the Introduction to 'Lü Bingkui cong yi 60 nian wenji' weiyuanhui, ed. *Lü Bingkui cong yi 60 nian wenji (Festschrift for Lü Bingkui's 60th Anniversary as Physician)*, Beijing: Huajia chubanshe, 1993.

36 The history of the compilation of the 'Outline' is described in the introduction to the third edition by J. Meng and Z. Zhou (eds), *Zhongyixue gailun: xiuding ben (Outline of Chinese Medicine: Revised Edition)*, Beijing: Renmin weisheng chubanshe, 1994.

37 See J. Farquhar, 'Time and text: approaching Chinese medical practice through analysis of a published case', in C. Leslie and A. Young (eds), *Paths to Asian Medical Knowledge*, Berkeley: University of California Press, 1992, pp. 62–71 and *Knowing Practice*, for detailed ethnographic descriptions and analyses of such prescribing.

38 See M. Schoenhals, *The Paradox of Power in a People's Republic of China Middle School*, Armonk, NY: M.E. Sharpe, 1993, for a discussion of how studying in China is concerned with helping students to embody socially sanctioned models of virtue.

39   In Beijing I observed student groups ranging from one to twelve during clinical training. Students would rarely follow the same physician for longer than two to three months.

40   Ethnographies of *guanxi* in contemporary China are provided by A. Kipnis, *Producing Guanxi: Sentiment, Self, and Subculture in a North China Village*. Durham, NC: Duke University Press, 1997; Y. Yan, *The Flow of Gifts. Reciprocity and Social Networks in a Chinese Village*. Stanford: Stanford University Press, 1996 and M. Yang, *Gifts, Favours, and Banquets: The Art of Social Relationships in China*, Ithaka, NY: Cornell University Press, 1994.

41   Compare the presentation of the topic in S. Zhao, D. Hu and J. Liu, *Wenbing zongheng (Warm Diseases in Detail)*, Beijing: Renmin weisheng chubanshe, 1982; with S. Meng (ed.), *Wenbingxue (Warm Diseases)*. Shanghai: Shanghai kexue jishu chubanshe, 1985.

42   My observations fit that of Kipnis, Yan and Yang, which detail an increasing disassociation between *guanxi* and *renqing* (feelings social in nature and requiring empathy with others) that previously rooted *guanxixue* to an ethics of moral obligations, emotional attachment and empathy. Since the 1980s *guanxi* is becoming more and more detached from *renqing* and thus devalued in moral terms. It is what one has to do to get things done but does not necessarily entail anymore the feelings of *renqing* previously associated with such relations. Still, the deep emotional attachment between Professor Rong and his students clearly demonstrates that *guanxi* and *renqing* still sustain each other in the domain of contemporary Chinese medicine.

43   On the definition of subjectivity and subject positionality as an object of study see J. Henriques, *Changing the Subject: Psychology, Social Regulation and Subjectivity*, London: Methuen, 1984. J. Farquhar and J. Hevia, 'Culture and postwar American historiography of China', *Positions* 1, 2 (1993): 486–525, as well as A. Zito and T. Barlow, 'Introduction: body, subject, and power in China', in *Body, Subject and Power in China*, pp. 1–22, discuss the issue from the perspective of Chinese studies.

44   Such observations are confirmed by Schoenhals, *The Paradox of Power in a People's Republic of China Middle School*, a detailed study of education in the PRC. Based on participant observations in a Chinese secondary school (*zhongxue*) Schoenhals argues that a paradox of power exists in cultures of face and shame such as the Chinese. This cedes to inferiors a certain power over superiors in spite of the hierarchical character of the system. Superiors have more face but are constantly on stage and must live up to the standards expected of them. This, according to Schoenhals, gives each class session the character of a performance.

45   W. Benjamin, *Gesammelte Schriften, vol V: Das Passagenwerk* (ed. Rolf Tiedeman), Vol. 5. Frankfurt/Main: Suhrkamp, 1982. Quoted in Susan Buck-Morss, *The Dialectics of Seeing: Walter Benjamin and the Arcades Project*. Cambridge, MA: MIT Press, 1991, p. 8. Interestingly, Latour in 'Postmodern? No simply amodern' also looks to 'origins' as a source of plurality but derives his notion from the work of the French philosopher Serres.

46   L. Nader, 'Anthropological inquiry into boundaries, power, and knowledge', in L. Nader (ed.), *Naked Science: Anthropological Inquiry into Boundaries, Power, and Knowledge*, New York and London: Routledge, 1996, p. 11.

47   A. Kleinman, *Writing at the Margin: Discourse Between Anthropology and Medicine*, Berkeley: University of Berkeley Press, 1995, p. 35; M. Valussi, 'What does "alternative medicine" really mean?', *European Journal of Herbal Medicine* 3, 1 (1997): 38–44.

9 Spirituality, belief and knowledge

Reflections on constructions of Maori healing

Patricia Laing[1]

When ethnographers study indigenous healing it is becoming more common for them to work as apprentices to indigenous healers just as many medical anthropologists train in Western medicine. This was the case for me when I studied with Samoan healers in the late 1970s and early 1980s.[2] The knowledge and practices I learnt in Western Samoa were the basis on which I was accepted as a student of Maori healing in the mid 1980s. However, the starting point for this discussion of spirituality, belief and knowledge in constructions of Maori healing is my own experience of breast cancer.[3] My studies of Maori healing informed how I developed explanations for my illness, the central place I assigned to spiritual dimensions in my healing, and how I used a plurality of therapies in remaking my world. My intention is to provide a case-study based on my expertise in medical anthropology and my own experience of how medical pluralism works in Aotearoa New Zealand where indigenous healing practices, alternative therapies and Western medicine intersect.

A popular characterisation that directly influenced the management of my breast cancer is that Maori are a spiritual people and Europeans are a material people and therefore not spiritual.[4] This distinction has its historical origins in a mid-nineteenth-century account of Maori healing by Shortland, suggesting that because illness causation was attributed to spirits Maori had no physical treatments.[5] While contesting accounts were published at the time[6] Shortland's ideas became a rationalisation for *tohunga* treating Maori people experiencing spiritual distress while Western doctors treat ailing Maori bodies. Furthermore, Europeans were not seen as recognising the spiritual dimension in explanations of illness and healing.[7]

The contrast between Western medical knowledge and indigenous healing belief asserts the rationality and dominance of one variant of scientific medicine. Yet, as Cant and Sharma (1999) suggest, the way Western medicine identifies the boundaries between its knowledge and that of alternative modalities varies from country to country, leading to many versions of what constitutes Western medical knowledge.[8] Despite this variability Western medicine asserts not only its dominance in relationship to alternative therapies but also to indigenous knowledges.

Byron Good writes about how illness is present in a 'lived body' and at times of illness the body is a 'disordered agent of experience'. Although women with breast cancer often have no initial awareness of being ill I went to the Western doctor because I experienced dull chronic pain. Good offers an approach 'focused on the body's creative source of experience',[9] which I found a useful starting point. The narratives I constructed to explain my breast cancer and plan my healing included spirituality as a source of knowledge. I drew on Maori healing, alternative therapies and several versions of Western medicine.

The inclusion of spirituality in my healing narrative led me to reflect on how spirituality is integrated into illness explanations and healing stories. Good says:

> The scientific world is only one of several worlds or 'subuniverses' in which we live, worlds which include those of religious experience, of dreams and fantasies, of music and art, and of the 'common-sense' reality which is paramount in much of our lives. These are not simply forms of individual experience, but diverse worlds, with distinctive objects, symbolic forms, social practices, and modes of experience.[10]

Although I agree with the point being made, I am uneasy about placing dreams alongside fantasies when in my world-in-the-making dreams and spirit guides are a part of 'common-sense' reality. The spirituality to which I refer does not coincide with religious experience when it is equated with faith and church-going. Rather, informed by the *mana wahine* construction, feminist spirituality and Anthroposophical medicine, it is constituted out of the celebration of the seasons and lunar cycles, daily rhythms of lived experience, and caring for the land because its products sustain us.[11] (Mason Durie, a Maori psychiatrist and Professor of Maori Studies has identified as *mana wahine* the period from 1931–75. He uses the term – which can be loosely translated as 'women's authority' – to refer to Maori participation in health when Maori women took the lead.)

The first part of this chapter outlines how Maori and European scholars, particularly anthropologists and ethnologists, constructed Maori healing as *belief* not only because that was the conventional anthropological approach but also with a political purpose. Since spirituality or *wairuatanga* is central to Maori healing a discussion of the spiritual dimension or *te taha wairua* could traverse the entire history of the relationship between Maori healing and Western medicine in Aotearoa New Zealand.[12] The shifts and changes in Western medical constructions of Maori healing included using the law in an attempt to suppress *tohunga*, Maori healers, as quacks and witches,[13] and 'marrying' Western medicine and Maori women's *mana wahine* construction of healing and health.[14]

The second part of this chapter explores the importance of illness explanations and healing stories for remaking a life-world. Such narratives may extend beyond a body that experiences spirituality, dreams and common sense reality as discrete worlds. When composing them a person may contemplate and draw on the interactions between multiple worlds to arrive at a new and different sort of integration. This contemplative need to interact with multiple worlds can offer a partial explanation for the way people use multiple healing modalities that represent contrasting and contradictory ideas.[15]

Maori healing knowledge as belief

Byron Good's review of the concept of 'belief' in anthropological texts suggests that science juxtaposed 'belief' and 'knowledge' on the basis of what was, or was not, seen as factual.[16] The history of what was identified as knowledge or belief in the colonial construction of Maori healing practices has as much to do with movements of political power as it has to do with factual or counterfactual assertions. The hand of politics can be identified in the 'scientific' construction of *tohunga* as quacks and witches. In 1940 Ngata and Sutherland, with the intention to protect, re-positioned Maori healing as 'belief'. Once Maori healing was no longer seen as being in competition with Western medicine the scenario changed from one of suppressing medical pluralism to one concerning the boundaries between religion and medicine in healing labour. Recently, Mason Durie criticised anthropologists for constructing Maori healing as belief because this denies it contemporary medical relevance. Similarly, a Maori health researcher, Sam Rolleston, recommends 'That an effort be made towards removing the negative attitudes towards *tohungaism*[17] amongst health professionals'.[18] When I composed explanations for my breast cancer I learnt how the judgements of what constitutes belief and knowledge flow into how healing labour is distributed, and how these distributions constrain our ability to remake our worlds.

The suppression of *tohunga*

Towards the end of the nineteenth century there was intense competition among aspiring Maori leaders with visions of what the future would hold for Maori. *Tohunga's* prophecies synthesised Maori cosmology and Western religious ideas as a basis for model settlements. Among the most famous were Te Whiti o Rongomai and Tohu at Parihaka,[19] Rua Kenana at Maungapohatu,[20] and Te Puea at Ngarawahia.[21] Other *tohunga* moved about and gathered followings that stretched the resources of the places where they stayed.[22] Young, Western-educated Maori, such as Maui Pomare, Peter Buck and Apirana Ngata also envisaged the future. Pomare and Buck were trained in Western medicine and saw its establishment as dependent upon the suppression of *tohunga*. In 1900 the Maori Councils were given the task of licensing *tohunga*, regulating their relationships with medically qualified practitioners, and preventing them from establishing settlements.[23] But Councils were fearful of the retribution *tohunga* might unleash on members and therefore did not prosecute.[24] Pomare convinced the government that special legislation was needed and the *Tohunga* Suppression Act (*TSA*) was passed in 1907. The *TSA* was directed at Maori knowledge of spiritual origin, referred to in the legislation as 'superstition' and 'belief'.

In the treatment and cure of Maori three offences were created under the *TSA*:

1 'practising on their superstition or credulity';[25]
2 'possessing or pretending to possess supernatural powers';[26]

3 'foretelling future events', with the intention to 'induce the Maori to neglect their proper occupations and gather into meetings where their substance is consumed and their minds unsettled'.[27]

The suppression of *tohunga* continued to be debated after the passing of legislation. Raymond Firth undertook anthropological research in the late 1920s that described how important a *tohunga* was in most aspects of community life. 'He was continually requisitioned to officiate at the crises of life, such as birth, marriage and death, on occasions of baptism, war, illness, loss of property by theft, attempts to gain someone's affections or to lay a curse on an enemy'.[28] Firth concluded:

> [Because of] the essential role of magic in primitive industry ... it should not be wantonly or ignorantly broken down or be made the subject of repressive legislation. The practice of magic or 'sorcery' should be a craft, if not honoured by the white man, as it is by the native, at least wisely tolerated. Few Europeans realise how greatly the industry and welfare of the native are contingent upon the unimpaired retention of his whole magical system.[29]

While opposing the suppression of *tohunga* Firth still described 'economic magic' – the rituals for safety, success and sustainability in economic endeavours – as 'born in irrational belief' and 'cradled in illusory power',[30] that 'tended to buttress by its supernatural sanction a number of regulations of rational utility'.[31]

Reframing Maori healing

Despite the campaign and legislation to suppress Maori healing, knowledge from spiritual origins has continued to inform Maori decision-making in personal, economic and political settings.[32] Apirana Ngata, a long time member of parliament and Minister of Maori Affairs, was opposed to the suppression of *tohunga* because their activities had much wider relevance than being merely in competition with Western medicine.

Ngata and Sutherland's view, in contrast, was that in times of crisis Maori 'throw up either great fighting chiefs, or fanatics ... to fire the people to demonstrate actively and physically their continued opposition to the *pakeha*[33] and their determination to drive him into the sea whence he came'.[34] They identified fighting chiefs and fanatics with *tohunga* and described them as priestly leaders involved in religious cults. This had two consequences. Firstly, they minimised Maori opposition to European settlers by characterising it as cult activity and mere ritual and belief:

> One of the most prominent features of the Ringatu church was what may be termed faith healing. Today it is probably the feature which attracts to the church considerable numbers of the Maori people, including reputedly devout members of other communions. The featuring of cure, or attempted cure of illness by means other than the administering or application of physical

remedies has in the case of the Maoris come down the generations. Culturally it may be associate with the practice of *makutu* or witchcraft and communication with *atua* or supernatural beings through the medium of the priestly class known as *tohunga*. It is probable that the beliefs and superstitions that centre in what is now known as Maori 'tohungaism' survive from that period in pre-*pakeha* days when the Maori world was peopled with gods and personified spiritual forces whose names identified them with the various departments of everyday life. There is no doubt that the healing by the laying on of hands referred to in the scriptures gave signal confirmation to Maori beliefs in these matters. This feature in the framework of the Ringatu religion and of other sects that have arisen among the Maori people thus has the support both of native antecedents and of biblical practices. It has the dual tradition solidly behind it hence its strength.[35]

Secondly, Ngata and Sutherland indicated a setting wherein the healing activities of *tohunga* could flourish out of direct competition with Western medicine:

> Where the *pakeha* (or Maori for that matter) doctor and nurse fail, the patient or his relative will declare that the affliction must be *mate Maori*, a disease peculiar to the Maori and curable only by resort to Maori means, and the doctor who has declared the case hopeless resigns the patient to their charge. There have been some isolated cases of spectacular recovery and, just as the single swallow does often make the summer, so 'tohungaism' and faith-healing associated with Maori religious cults goes on.[36]

In a similar vein, the anthropologists Ernest and Pearl Beaglehole constructed a three-fold typology of Maori sickness in 1947:

1 illness and accident with a physical causation which could be treated using herbal remedies or Western medicine;
2 illness with no apparent physical causation considered to be *mate Maori* which only *tohunga* could treat;
3 black magic that was said to be dying out.

The first two types the Beagleholes saw as 'folk medicine' or 'pseudo-science of sickness causation' which 'competes with *pakeha* scientific medicine for success in the cure of sickness'.[37] However, from the point of view of Western medicine, Maori had not had a pharmacopoeia before contact.[38] Healers who used herbal remedies, massage and steam baths were not seen to commit an offence under the TSA as long as they did not pretend that they had supernatural powers. *Tohunga* who treated the second type of illness using 'a combination of religious prayer, séance-possession, and magic'[39] were vulnerable to being prosecuted under the Act. These were the *tohunga* whom Ngata and Sutherland identified as faith healers. According to Ernest and Pearl Beaglehole some Maori were confused by this identification: 'Even those who appear to be sceptical of tohunga treatment are not sceptical because the treatment involves a belief in Maori spirits and ghost. Rather are they doubters because the *tohunga* mixes Roman Catholic or Church of England prayers with mediumistic seances and magical treatment'.[40]

The Ratana movement exemplifies the scenario where the relationship between religion and Western medicine is the major issue when seeking to understand the distribution of healing labour. Ratana (1873–1939) was a faith healer who mixed Christian theology and Maori magic. '[H]e persuaded thousands to sign a covenant of belief in the Trinity and to reject the belief in *tohunga*'.[41] Ratana believed paganism caused Maori illness.[42] Although he was anti-*tohunga*, he exhibited all the characteristics the *TSA* was designed to prohibit. He established a settlement known as Ratana Pa, claimed God as the source of his healing and had a vision for the future of Maori.[43]

Te Puea, a famous chieftainess fearful of being charged as a *tohunga*, was particularly concerned about the influence Ratana's approach would have on Maori cosmology.[44] The *mana wahine* construction of Maori healing and health originated in her approach.[45] Her synthesis of Maori and Western knowledge for healing drew on a 'cosmology that was essentially that of pre-European Maori'.[46] Rather than accept the division of labour Ngata and Sutherland articulated, a version of which Ratana practised, Te Puea is said to have kept the spiritual aspect of healing alive among her people and hidden from her medical advisers.[47] She focused on ameliorating Western medical opposition at the quotidian level organising opportunities for the complementary use of Western medicine and Maori healing, and participating in public health and health education projects.[48]

Consistent with Good's analysis, anthropologists considered Maori healing as beliefs that were '[q]uite reasonable, even if mistaken'.[49] For Ngata, constructing Maori healing as belief gave it a future. Following Ngata and Sutherland's 1940 reinterpretation of *tohunga* activities, Johannes Anderson gathered what information he could about *tohunga* 'to increase the sympathetic interest in the beliefs and philosophies of the Polynesians, an interest that has for some time been active'.[50] He wondered if 'there is not something beyond our ken – whether this old race had not preserved a knowledge of forces that we have yet to acquire'.[51] He wrote that the spiritual and magical activities of *tohunga* were comprised of 'relics of a very ancient system of knowledge' and of 'absurdities' which future investigation might find 'some foundation for in fact'.[52] With similar intentions Ernest and Pearl Beaglehole headed a chapter 'Being Religious – Being Sick; the Tangi' and noted that '[w]hatever sophisticated distinctions the pakeha may make between being religious on the one hand and consulting a doctor for sickness on the other hand, the Maori is much less sure of these distinctions'.[53]

In the late 1960s Joan Metge distinguished between Western medical assessments of standards of Maori health and sickness due to mystical causes that faith healers treat.[54] Metge suggests that the *TSA* was repealed in 1963 because 'it distinguished unnecessarily between Maori and Pakeha faith healers'.[55] Ngata and Sutherland's 'reinterpretation' had articulated what *tohunga* and their followers were doing, and had ensured continuing access to Maori healing in the face of Western medical opposition.

Despite the repeal of the TSA health professionals and anthropologists still recognised faith healers as the appropriate practitioners to treat the spiritual dimensions of Maori illness, and Western doctors as the appropriate practitioners to treat physical illness. This distinction entered into the imagination of Maori and other New Zealanders to such an extent that it became a defining feature of the relationship between Maori and European. Ruth Brown, in her paper 'Maori Spirituality as a Pakeha Construct', takes Keri Hulme's Booker Prize winning novel *the bone people* (1983) as a starting point for asking what '*pakeha*' are doing when they attribute spirituality to Maori and not to themselves.[56] Brown teases out some of the confusion and silences created by this attribution given the evidence that in the Maori world 'spirituality and entrepreneurial activity are not necessarily exclusive'.[57] She concludes that if we seek a peaceful relationship between Maori and '*pakeha*' then open debate needs to replace the silences around the 'myths about spirituality and national identity'.[58]

Mason Durie maintains that Maori are more spiritual than '*pakeha*'. On the other hand he criticises medical anthropologists for reinterpreting Maori concepts of illness into 'mental and psychic realms, scarcely relevant to the vast majority of human illnesses and hardly applicable to contemporary times'.[59] Good's analysis of the characterisation of indigenous healing as belief in contrast to Western medical knowledge suggests that the medical anthropologists whom Durie criticises were using a conceptual framework conventional in their discipline. Good acknowledges with reference to indigenous healing practices 'that the emergence of "belief" as a central analytical category in anthropology was a fateful development'.[60] In Aotearoa New Zealand this 'fateful development' contributed to the preservation of Maori healing at the same time as it bound Maori and Europeans into an unhealthy relationship. Prior to Durie's criticism attempts to understand the relationship between Western medicine and Maori healing were located at the intersection between religion and medicine rather than in a consideration of medical pluralism. To enhance the prospects of healing at individual, community and societal levels open debate is needed concerning the strengths and weaknesses of locating Western medicine's relationship with Maori healing at the intersection of religion and medicine rather than as competitive healing systems.

Illness explanations and healing stories for remaking a life-world

The attribution of spirituality to Maori and materiality to Europeans resulted from a mid-nineteenth century Western medical assertion concerning the spiritual causation of Maori illness and consequent lack of a pharmacopoeia. These attributions were debated among some medical men and criticised by some Maori, anthropologists, and *pakeha* women working with Maori. They were consolidated in the process that established Western medical dominance in Aotearoa New Zealand involving the suppression of *tohunga*, a process that paralleled the establishment of Western medicine in many colonies.[61] A response among some Western and traditionally trained Maori was to accept Ngata and Sutherland's reinterpretation of *tohunga* as faith healers in order to retain access to their healing practices. Anthropologists could support this Maori response because it too was consistent with the common anthropological distinction between knowledge and belief. The significance of these historical distinctions rests in how they flow into illness explanations and healing stories constructed today.

When my diagnosis of breast cancer became known in 1995 Maori people explained my illness in spiritual terms while Europeans mostly explained it in physical ones. I will explore the voids in both Maori and European people's resources for explaining illness and narrating stories of healing created as a result of the way spirituality and materiality are attributed. This pattern of attribution denies the agency of the ill person and his or her family in the healing process, which my studies of Maori healing and my own experience suggest is crucial for healing.

Everyday activities and seasonal celebrations are becoming fashionable as the focus of both men's and women's spirituality. John Bluck in *Long White and Cloudy: In Search of Kiwi Spirituality* and John Hunt in *We Spirited People: A personal, enriching and uniquely New Zealand guide in Celtic Spirituality* explore the possibility of extending the boundaries of spirituality beyond church walls into 'the landscape, history and community of this time and place'.[62] While men such as Bluck and Hunt search for their spirituality in landscape and community, my companions to date have been predominantly women. Goddess spirituality emerged in Aotearoa New Zealand at about the same time as it gained a foothold in other parts of the world.[63] From the late 1960s Goddess spirituality found expression in both Maori and European women's traditions.[64] The Maori women's tradition includes Te Puea, the women in the Women's Health League and the Maori Women's Welfare League. As well as locating their spirituality in everyday activities focused on ancestors they use Christian or one of the syncretic religions based on Maori and Christian traditions such as Ringatu,[65] or Ratana[66] for rituals of remembrance and celebration. While Maori men and women have an unbroken tradition of spiritual kinship it is only recently that I have seen European men and women beginning to share a spiritual journey that honours both God and Goddess in public.

This spirituality offers knowledge I needed to remake my world and heal from breast cancer. The genre to which narratives describing these worlds-in-the-making belong offers alternatives to the inclusions and exclusions represented in the notions of Maori spirituality and European materiality. This genre suggests the existence of complex patterns of relationships involving spirituality, religion, medicine and magic. A debate that locates Western medicine's relationship with Maori healing at the intersection of religion and medicine or sees them as competing entities within a medically plural system may not do justice to this complexity.

Illness explanations, resource voids and denials of agency

Maori explained my illness in terms of breaking *tapu*. *Tapu* and *noa* are concepts central to Maori healing 'noa denoting safety, tapu protection'.[67] They are a complementary pair signifying sacred and profane, 'set apart under ritual restriction' and 'allowing relaxation and freedom of action'.[68] *Tapu* and *noa* are used to shape people's understandings of their bodies – 'the human body (especially the head and the genital area) were regarded as tapu and thus to be protected from inappropriate touching'.[69] They also regulated relationships within families, extended kin groups, tribes, and between tribal groups. They prescribed people's activities in the environment and the management of food, water and other resources including knowledge. 'Tapu', according to Tait, 'means far more to the Maori than just prohibitions ('Don't touch this', 'Don't go there'). Tapu is the spiritual essence of all things'.[70] It flourishes 'through tika (justice), pono (integrity, or faithfulness to tika) and aroha (love). By continually striving to act with tika, pono and aroha in day-to-day life, tapu flourishes and mana [spiritual power] radiates outward like the ripples of a stone dropped into a pond'.[71]

The manifestation and regulation of the shifting and changing relationships between *tapu* and *noa* was the expert prerogative of *tohunga* and the reason why Firth cautioned that *tohunga* should be 'if not honoured by the white man ... at least wisely tolerated'.[72] The importance of *tohunga* in managing *tapu* and *noa* motivated Ngata and Sutherland (1940) to protect them so that *tapu* could continue to flow in the land, forests and fisheries, and in people. While *tapu* and *noa* as a regulatory system may not be as influential in people's lives as it once was,[73] the idea that *tapu* is the spiritual essence of all things is still widely recognised, particularly at times of illness.

A public health nurse, working in the Gisborne District Health Office in 1983, described a potentially deadly medical intervention:

> An elderly Maori woman had a detached retina. She was seen by a specialist who suggested she have a graft, not being told that she had a bit of somebody else's outfit in her eye. And things were going to be fine and she actually had what they thought was vision in the eye, she'd seen light and things. Until, several days later, one of the nurses, in some way – inadvertently – let slip that she had a piece of somebody else's eye: 'Wasn't it marvellous what medicine could do these days'. And from there on that woman nearly went off her head. She rejected the graft, physically as well as emotionally. She was almost moribund. She was terribly ill, and getting shocking head pains and wanting to die. With the permission from the hospital the family brought her up to a woman healer.
>
> The healer massaged her and used oil and vinegar and all sorts of things and then said at the end of the session, 'You must take this woman back down, and this must be removed. If you don't she will die. You had no right to put it there in the first place, and it should never have been there'. So back to hospital the family went. [The graft was removed and the woman recovered.] ... The doctors were amazed because the emotional rejection also became a physical rejection. A thing that had been healing beautifully, and they were delighted with suddenly just didn't take. It just all went wrong.[74]

The retina from an unknown person was regarded as *noa,* an implanted foreign-body desecrating the sacredness of the woman. This story illustrates how important the congruence of illness explanations and treatment can be for healing to occur. It also suggests that patients and families using a plural medical system must be fully informed about what is involved in treatment.

In another research project I interviewed Maori people who had been admitted to Wellington Hospital in 1985. One woman, explaining why she did not want to be interviewed, and why I should think very carefully about what I was doing, told a story illustrating how illness is a punishment for transgressing a *tapu.*[75] When her father died he had been teaching her and her elder brother about *whakapapa* or genealogy, and Maori history. He said that if he died without finishing the task then they 'must give up' because they did not know how to protect themselves from the energies and strengths that were woven into the *whakapapa* or genealogies, *waiata* or songs, and *tikanga* or traditional ways. An error could mean death. Her brother did not heed his father's words and after a short time became ill. He sought the healing of his father's brother who said he would become a cripple if he did not act in accordance with his father's and his ancestors' wishes. The young man changed his ways, was healed successfully and has remained well.

For Maori people illness is a time when a person is in close contact with forces from the spiritual realm and thoughts of the principles of *tapu* surface again. Some of the Maori patients of my 1985 study did not observe all the rules of *tapu* and *noa,* but to 'protect' themselves they prayed with their families, ensured that family members were available to bathe and feed them, and wore *kaitiaki* or protective carvings around their necks. Several families told stories of upsetting the medical and nursing staff by their presence in hospital wards for these purposes.

When I became ill with breast cancer several Maori suggested, with concern rather than criticism, that I, or a member of my family, may have become too involved in Maori preparations for claims to the Waitangi Tribunal.[76] Different groups of Maori people over the years had asked me to share my skills so that they could undertake research for themselves. My involvement had included discussing possible ways to manage sacred knowledge. Another member of my family could have unwittingly behaved in a way that upset the balance and harmony that is at the centre of Maori concepts of *tapu* and *noa.* Any member of a family can become ill when one of them breaks a *tapu.*[77]

The Maori explanations for my illness were a powerful reminder of the obligations I had undertaken when I was invited to study Maori healing. Several old people had shared aspects of their knowledge with the understanding that I would use it for the purposes of challenging negative attitudes to *tohunga* and Maori healing. At the time when I became sick I was about to give up on this project because I found it so difficult. In health discourse, talk about spirituality was very much a Maori prerogative and until recently they were mostly silent about it.[78] Once Maori began talking openly about spiritual healing and reclaimed the body or *tinana* and the physical dimension of healing or *te taha tinana,* Europeans began tentatively to speak about spirituality in health forums.[79] An important explanation for my illness was my loss of courage to express myself on the subject of the relationship between

Maori healing and Western medicine. This upset my relationship with the old people, many of whom were now ancestral spirits, thus causing a breach of *tapu*.

Many New Zealanders of European descent do not have contact with Maori people who offer them spiritual explanations of their illnesses. Most seek explanations only in what Byron Good describes as the 'folk beliefs' of Western medicine.[80] In restricting themselves to physical explanations they miss out on a world of images and stories that could assist their healing. Doctors support them in the decision to restrict themselves to Western medicine. The doctor's response to my calm when I received the positive results from the biopsy taken from my breast was to describe how difficult most women found the process of coming to terms with their diagnosis. For him the options after a mastectomy were radio-therapy, chemotherapy or perhaps removing the ovaries.[81] He discounted all the alternative therapies that are offered to treat cancer emphasising the excessive cost of them. The surgeon knew nothing of my interests in the anthropology of indig-enous healing in the Pacific, and the relationship between indigenous healing and Western medicine. The idea that spirituality might have an essential part to play in healing was outside his medical considerations. For him my illness was physical and he could cut it out of my body.

Exhausted and sick, one part of me wanted to give over my care to the surgeon. I was impressed by the strength of my socialisation into the Western medical patient's view that the doctor was the expert and that if any healing were possible Western medicine would effect it. Another part of me raged at this passivity. How could I take this passive course which would deny twenty years of research that had taught me the importance of spirituality to healing? How could I forget the Maori lessons that control over one's healing was a part of the treatment,[82] that giving up one's agency hastened death? Knowledge of the medical pluralism of the *mana wahine* approach strengthened my resolve to become the agent of my own healing.

Spirituality, materiality and healing stories

When I became ill I was so used to hearing about the materialist Europeans that I had come to doubt my own spiritual experiences. This doubt influenced my commitment to the elders who had taught me something of Maori healing. The illness acted as a spur to straighten out my ideas. To do this I joined a women's ritual group, sought counselling, Western medical care, and alternative therapy that honoured human existence as the mediation of the spiritual and material dimensions.

In women's ritual groups, learning to use the resources from the unseen world 'for the good of all, past, present and future, seen and unseen' is an essential part of 'Goddess spirituality'. This includes self-healing through the use of storytelling, daily and season rituals and celebrations. Like other women who have been drawn to the rituals of the Goddess I constructed my spirituality by drawing on notions from diverse traditions. These include Maori, Samoan, Anthroposophical,[83] Chinese,[84] Tibetan,[85] and others.[86] Juliet Batten's *Celebrating the Southern Seasons: Rituals for Aotearoa* provides information from Aotearoa and Pagan and Christian Europe as a basis for creating seasonal rituals.[87] These offer among other things a framework for each participant to develop a personal programme of healing work and creativity. For instance Spring is a time 'to contemplate what quality, action or new attitude [we] wish to plant in our lives'.[88] In Summer we acknowledge and honour our own and others' achievements.[89] In Autumn we 'contemplate our own inner harvest to see how it contains the seed of whatever new crop is to come in spring'.[90] And winter is a time to withdraw within and reflect on what we are gestating.[91] A focus on seasonal, lunar and daily cycles opens up a multiplicity of images and understandings from the cultures of the world that can contribute to our healing stories.

Batten also indicates a vision for Maori/'*pakeha*' relations that has the potential to liberate us from the Maori/spirituality – European/materiality bind. She suggests that the meaning of women's spirituality in New Zealand may 'be about daring to belong and daring to connect with the spirit of this land'.[92] The women who create healing rituals with Juliet Batten are a part of a movement among women that is a worldwide phenomenon among mostly middle class, well-educated women. Susan Greenwood in her paper 'Feminist Witchcraft: A Transformatory Politics' (1989) is critical of the possibility that 'feminist witchcraft', as she calls it, can offer a basis from which to effect political change to benefit women and their families. Yet the *mana wahine* approach is infused with a spirituality that pervades their everyday activities and succeeds in doing this exactly. At the very least, the women's spirituality movement provides access to a network of alternative therapists and indigenous healers that honour the integrity of what it means to be human. Furthermore, Maori and European women who participate in this movement keep open the possibility of transforming the silences around our spirituality and national identities, and provide models inclusive of spirituality, religion, medicine and magic.

Batten suggests that the greed of some people for the land has left 'a legacy of oppression and exploitation that can easily overshadow the genuine attempts of many to sustain practices based on integrity and respect'.[93] She thinks that wounds and dislocations can begin to be healed if we bring 'the Green Man to meet Tane, God of the forest, the Great Mother to Papatuanuku, the seven goddesses of the Pleiades to the "little eyes" of Matariki, the Celtic goddess Brigid to Mahuika, and Hecate to Hine-nui-te-po'.[94] A dance performance consistent with this approach, produced by Keri Kaa, won national and international acclaim. I saw it the day after having chemotherapy and it warmed the freezing cold that this treatment produced in my physical body. The effect of this meeting of the gods and goddesses is to change the vantage-point from which we write our healing stories. From this planetary point of view we can contemplate the future of the earth and her people and compose individual illness and healing narratives in this context. The old stories and legends signal the way forward and transform Firth's 'irrational beliefs cradled in illusory power' and Anderson's 'absurdities' and 'relics' into a different kind of knowledge that they may have intuited. This knowledge concerns how human beings mediate spiritual and physical existence.[95]

The Western medical processes I used had to be made consistent with this new world-in-the-making, and therefore I sought practitioners who explained breast cancer as an illness in both spiritual and physical terms. Susan Love, an American breast surgeon, acknowledges that 'The psychosocial and mind/body connections … affect how long a woman with breast cancer will live'.[96] It is on the basis of the scientific research that supports these connections that Love is open to her patients using complementary and alternative therapies. Christiane Northrup, an American obstetrician/gynaecologist, is informed by feminist approaches to scientific knowledge and Western medicine. She goes further than Love towards practising 'holistic medicine'. She draws on Chinese, Ayurvedic and other conceptions of human beings in order to understand how to integrate emotional and psychosocial aspects for the purposes of healing. They are also the source of her understanding of how energy works in a person contributing to illness and healing.[97] Northrup drew on Chinese and Ayurvedic understandings to develop a Western medical approach to healing herself and then her patients. She concludes that '[r]egardless of whether we believe in angels, God, Jesus Christ, the human spirit, the Blessed Virgin, the Great Spirit or the Goddess Gaia, being in tune with our spiritual resources is a vital healing force. Committing ourselves to remember our spiritual selves and receive guidance for our lives is a part of creating health'.[98] Her work models a healing process within which the ill person and/or his or her friends and family can synthesise knowledge from multiple sources to narrate a story of healing.

Peter Heusser in his paper 'A basis for the understanding of anthroposophical medicine and cancer therapy' indicates how Rudolf Steiner's approach integrates spirituality within Western medicine. Steiner's view was that:

> The modern natural science which is oriented entirely towards the inorganic world can be used as the foundation for technological work but not for the healing of diseases. For the essence of an illness is to be found at the place where the spiritual and corporeal elements are connected. If one says that natural science is the only possible science, and that it cannot arrive at the spirit because of its boundaries then one also has to say that any real medicine is impossible. In order to acquire spiritual knowledge one has to have the inner courage to add active cognitional forces to the passive ones. Contemporary natural science has lost this courage, because it always looks for sense perceptible supports whenever valid knowledge should be developed. It cannot be a science which gives medicine any support. This is why a medical method is being developed here [in Anthroposophical medicine] which is based on an insight into spiritual existence.[99]

There is one anthroposophical medical practice in Wellington. I sought an assessment of my cancer status from the doctor, Rene de Monchy, which showed that the diagnosis of breast cancer was, at least at first sight, unexpected. Intensive counselling, informed by anthroposophical ideas among others revealed that one explanation for my breast cancer was that the essence of my illness was to be found at the place where the spiritual and corporeal elements are connected.

My reflections on the construction of Maori healing suggest that our attention needs to be redirected. Instead of focusing on questions about the relationship between medicine and religion, and the relationship between healing modalities within a system of medical pluralism, we need to consider first and foremost what resources a sick person needs to heal. The *mana wahine* approach in Maori healing, the women doctors using a 'holistic approach', and Anthroposophical medicine offer models of medical pluralism in which patients can be agents of their own healing. This agency is an essential part of integrating knowledge from various healing modalities. It enables illness explanations and healing stories to be narrated in which spirituality and materiality can be reconnected. This also raises questions about the implications of historical constructions of Maori healing, not only for divisions of healing labour but also the consequences of reconnecting the spiritual and physical dimensions of ourselves for our sense of community, the organisation of our society, and our national identities.

Acknowledgements

My thanks to the Maori people with whom I worked in the Department of Health in the 1980s, particularly Dr Pat Ngata, Lorna Dyall, and the late Dr John McLeod. The late Professor Eru Pomare, Dean of Wellington Clinical School, University of Otago was a friend and colleague whose conversations have informed my thinking. My thanks to the Ngati Porou people of Tokomaru Bay who welcomed me and challenged my thinking on healing and health from 1983 onwards. Tainui people at Waahi Pa and Inez Kingi showed me how marae-based health centres organised traditional healing, alternative therapies and Western medicine to improve Maori health for which I am most grateful. This paper is based on research funded by the Medical Research Council of New Zealand and the Health Research Council of New Zealand.

Notes

1 I have published previously as Patricia Kinloch.
2 See P. Kinloch, *Talking Health But Doing Sickness*, Wellington, Victoria University Wellington Press, 1985.
3 In April 2002 it will be seven years since I received a medical diagnosis of breast cancer.
4 R. Brown, 'Maori spirituality as Pakeha construct', *Meanjin*, 48, 2 (1989): 252–8; H. Tait, 'The unseen world', *New Zealand Geographic*, 5 (1990): pp. 87–91; M. Durie, *Whaiora Maori Health Development*, Auckland, Oxford University Press, 1988 (2nd edn); J. Bluck, *Long White and Cloudy: In Search of Kiwi Spirituality*, Christchurch, Hazard Press, 1998; J. Hunt, *We Spirited People: A Personal Enriching and Uniquely New Zealand Guide to Celtic Spirituality*, Christchurch, The Caxton Press, 1998.
5 See E. Shortland, *Transactions and Superstitions of the New Zealander*, London, Longman Green, 1856 (2nd edn).
6 See, for instance, A.S. Thomson, *The Story of New Zealand: Past and Present – Savage and Civilised*, London, John Murray 1859.
7 Durie, *Whaiora*, pp. 77.

8 For a discussion of how the boundaries are set in Aotearoa New Zealand see K. Dew, *Borderland Practices: Validating and Regulating Alternative Therapies in New Zealand*, PhD Thesis, Wellington, Victoria University Wellington, 1998.

9 B. Good, *Medicine, Rationality and Experience: An Anthropological Perspective*, Cambridge University Press, 1994, p. 118.

10 Ibid.

11 P. Heusser, 'A basis for the understanding of anthroposophical medicine and cancer therapy', *Journal of Anthroposophical Medicine*, 8, 2 (1991): 5–38; J. Batten, *Celebrating the Southern Seasons: Rituals in Aotearoa*, Birkenhead, Tandem Press, 1995; Bluck, *Long White and Cloudy*, 1998; Hunt, *We Spirited People*, 1998, P. Laing, 'Blood and bone: feminist reflections of Maori health', in M. Jolly and V. Lukere (eds), *Engendering Health in the Pacific*, Honolulu, Hawai'i University Press, forthcoming.

12 See M. Nicolson, 'Medicine and racial politics: changing images of the New Zealand Maori in the nineteenth century', in D. Arnold (ed.), *Imperial Medicine and Indigenous Societies*, Manchester: Manchester University Press, 1988, for some of the nineteenth-century changes.

13 M. Voyce, 'Maori healers in New Zealand: The *Tohunga* Suppression Act', *Oceania*, 60 (1989): 99–123; M. Durie, *Whaiora: Maori Health Development*, Auckland, Oxford University Press, 1998 (2nd edn).

14 P. Laing, 'Blood and bone: Feminist reflections on constructions of Maori health', in M. Jolly and V. Lukere (eds), *Engendering Health in the Pacific*, Honolulu, Hawai'i University Press, forthcoming.

15 See S. Cant and U. Sharma, *A New Medical Pluralism? Alternative Medicine Doctors, Patients and the State*, London, UCL Press Ltd, 1999.

16 See B. Good, *Medicine, Rationality and Experience: An Anthropological Perspective*, Cambridge University Press, 1994, p. 20.

17 Maori is recognised as an official language in New Zealand. Most books published in New Zealand on Maori topics no longer italicise Maori words. I italicise here because of a wider international audience.

18 S. Rolleston, *He Kohikohinga: A Maori Health Knowledge Base: A Report on a Research Project for the Department of Health*, Wellington, Department of Health, 1988, p. 23.

19 D. Scott, *Ask that Mountain: The Story of Parihaka*, Auckland, Heinemann, 1975.

20 J. Binney *et al.*, *Mihaia: The Prophet Rua Kenana and his Community of Maungapohatu*, Wellington, Oxford University Press, 1990; P. Webster, *Rua and the Maori Millenium*, Wellington, Victoria University Press, 1979.

21 M. King, *Te Puea: A Biography*, Auckland, Hodder and Stoughton, 1977.

22 Voyce, 'Maori healers in New Zealand: The Tohunga Suppression Act' *Oceania*, 60 (1989): 99–123; R. Lange, *May the People Live: A History of Maori Health Development 1900–1920*, Auckland, Auckland University Press, 1999.

23 Voyce, 'Maori healers in New Zealand', p. 106; Lange, *May the People Live*, pp. 144–5.

24 Voyce, 'Maori healers in New Zealand', p. 107.

25 *Tohunga* Suppression Act, 1907, S2, 1.

26 Ibid.

27 *Tohunga* Suppression Act, 1907, S2, 1 and Preamble.

28 R. Firth, *Economics of the New Zealand Maori*, Wellington, Government Printer, 1959, p. 300.

29 Ibid., pp. 278–9.

30 Ibid., p. 275

31 Ibid., p. 276.

32 P. Ngata and I. Sutherland, 'Religious influence', in I. Sutherland (ed.), *The Maori People Today: A General Survey*, Wellington, New Zealand Institute of International Affairs and the New Zealand Council for Educational Research, 1940, pp. 336–73; Firth, *Economics of the New Zealand Maori*; Durie, *Whaiora*.

33 *Pakeha* is a Maori name used to refer to non-Maori of European descent. Despite its common usage many Europeans dislike it because they understand it to have derogatory connotations. In this chapter I have used it in quotes when discussing the ideas of authors who have used it. I

168   *Patricia Laing*

think that different peoples within Aotearoa New Zealand need to think about what they call
themselves. This will make the terms Maori and European problematic too. I draw the reader's
attention to this, but I do not have the space to elaborate on it in this paper.

34 Ngata and Sutherland, 'Religious influence', p. 350.
35 Ibid., p. 360.
36 Ibid., pp. 360–1.
37 E. and P. Beaglehole, *Some Modern Maoris*, Wellington, New Zealand Council for Educational
Research, 1946, pp. 219–20.
38 E. Shortland, *Transactions and Superstitions of the New Zealander*, London, Longman Gress, 1856
(2nd edn); W. H. Goldie, 'Maori medical lore: notes on the causes of the disease and treatment
of the sick among the Maori people of New Zealand, as believed and practised in former times,
together with some account of various ancient rites connected with the same', *Transactions of the
New Zealand Institute*, 37 (1904): 1–120; E. Best, 'Maori medical lore', *Journal of the Polynesian
Society*, 13 (1904): 213–37.
39 E. and P. Beaglehole, *Some Modern Maoris*, p. 219.
40 Ibid., pp. 228–9.
41 Voyce, 'Maori healers in New Zealand', p. 115; Ngata and Sutherland, ' Religious influence'; E.
Schwimmer, 'The aspirations of contemporary Maori', in E. Schwimmer (ed.), *Maori People in
the Nineteen-sixties: A Symposium*, Auckland, Blackwood and Janet Paul Ltd, 1968; King, *Te Puea*.
42 Voyce, 'Maori healers in New Zealand', p. 114.
43 Scott, *Ask that Mountain*; Schwimmer, 'The aspirations of contemporary Maori'.
44 King, *Te Puea*.
45. Laing, 'Blood and bone'.
46 King, *Te Puea*, p. 161; Durie, *Whaiora*, p. 46.
47 King, *Te Puea*.
48 Laing, 'Blood and bone'.
49 B. Good, *Medicine, Rationality and Experience: An Anthropological Perspective*, Cambridge University
Press, 1994, p. 18.
50 J. Anderson, *The Maori Tohunga and his Spirit World*, New Plymouth, Thomas Avery and Son Ltd.,
1948, pp. viii–ix.
51 Ibid., p. 29.
52 Ibid., p. 41.
53 E. and P. Beaglehole, *Some Modern Maoris*, p. 203.
54 J. Metge, *The Maori of New Zealand*, London, Routledge and Kegan Paul, 1967, p. 83.
55 Ibid., pp. 83–4.
56 Brown, 'Maori spirituality as Pakeha construct', p. 252.
57 Ibid., p. 254.
58 Ibid., pp. 257–8.
59 Durie, *Whaiora*, p. 67.
60 B. Good, *Medicine, Rationality and Experience: An Anthropological Perspective*, Cambridge University
Press, 1994, p. 7.
61 See D. Arnold (ed.), *Imperial Medicine and Indigenous Societies*, 1988; B. Good, *Medicine, Rationality
and Experience: An Anthropological Perspective*, Cambridge University Press, 1994.
62 Bluck, *Long White and Cloudy*, p.108.
63 K. Rountree, *Re-membering the Witch and the Goddess: Feminist Ritual-making in New Zealand*, PhD
thesis, Hamilton, Waikato University, pp. 197–8.
64 See C. Kearney, *Faces of the Goddess: New Zealand Women Talk about their Spirituality*, Birkenhead:
Tandem Press, 1997; Batten, *Celebrating the Southern Seasons*.
65 J. Binney, *Redemption Songs: A Life of Te Tooti Arikirangi Te Turuki*, Auckland, Auckland University
Press with Bridget Williams Books, 1997.
66 Ngata and Sutherland, 'Religious influence'; E. and P. Beaglehole, *Some Modern Maoris*;
Schwimmer, 'The aspirations of contemporary Maori'.
67 Durie, *Whaiora*, p. 9.

68 J. Metge, *New Growth From Old: The Whanau in the Modern World*, Wellington, Victoria University Press, 1995, p. 85.

69 Ibid.

70 Tait, 'The unseen World', p. 88.

71 Ibid., p. 90.

72 Firth, *Economics of the New Zealand Maori*, p. 279.

73 Metge, *New Growth From Old*, p. 85.

74 Author's interview transcript, research project on the relationship between Maori Healing Processes and Western Medicine, 1983.

75 Many instances exist of Maori people becoming ill and dying as a result of transgressing a *tapu*. See, for example, E. and P. Beaglehole, *Some Modern Maoris*; Anderson, *The Maori Tohunga and his Spirit World*.

76 For a discussion of the issues for anthropologists involved in assisting Maori with claims to the Waitangi Tribunal, see J. Metge, 'Kia Tupato! Anthropologists at work', *Oceania*, 69, 1 (1998): 47–60. These claims are intended to compensate Maori for breaches of the Treaty of Waitangi (1840).

77 See Tait, 'The Unseen World', p. 91.

78 Durie, *Whaiora*, p. 77.

79 Ibid.

80 Good, *Medicine, Rationality and Experience: An Anthropological Perspective*, pp. 37–47.

81 For all care options, see S. Love, *Dr Susan Love's Breast Book*, Reading and Massachusetts, Perseus Books, 1995.

82 P. Laing and P. Ngata, 'Maori health practices research and development project: final report', *Medical Research Council Research Review (1986)*, 1987, pp. 123–5; Durie, *Whaiora*.

83 R. Steiner, *Occult Science – An Outline*, London, Rudolf Steiner Press, 1909 (translated 1962–3 by G. and M. Adams, reprinted 1969); R. Steiner, *Man and the World of Stars: The Spiritual Communion of Mankind*, New York, Anthroposophical Press Inc., 1922 (translated by D. Osmond); R. Steiner, *The Four Seasons and the Archangels: Experience of the Course of the Year in the Four Cosmic Imaginations*, London, Rudolf Steiner Press, 1923.

84 H. Beinfield and E. Korngold, *Between Heaven and Earth: A Guide to Chinese Medicine*, New York, Ballantine, 1991.

85 S. Rinpoche, *The Tibetan Book of Living and Dying*, London, Rider, 1992.

86 B. Brennan, *Light Emerging: The Journey of Personal Healing*, New York, Bantam Books, 1993; Starhawk, M. Macka Nightmare, and the Reclaiming Collective, *The Pagan Book of Living and Dying: Practical Rituals, Prayers, Blessings and Meditations on Crossing Over*, New York, Harper Collins Publishers, 1997; W.I. Thompson, *The Time Falling Bodies Take to Light: Mythology, Sexuality and the Origins of Culture*, New York, St Martin's Press, 1984.

87 While the women's spirituality movement is often linked to both neo-pagan and New Age movements, and the movement does draw ideas from both of these, it leans much more towards neo-paganism than New Age. For a discussion of the similarities and differences between these movements see M. York, *The Emerging Network: A Sociology of the New Age and Neo-pagan Movement*, London, Rowman and Littlefield, 1995.

88 Batten, *Celebrating the Southern Seasons*, p. 87.

89 Ibid., p. 121.

90 bid., p. 152.

91 Ibid., p. 56.

92 Ibid., p. 20.

93 Ibid.

94 Ibid, p. 21.

95 See, for instance, C.P. Estes, *Women Who Run with the Wolves: Myths and Stories of the Wild Woman Archetype*, New York, Ballantine, 1992.

96 S. Love, *Dr Susan Love's Breast Book*, p. xx.

97 See C. Northrup, *Women's Bodies Women's Wisdom: The Complete Guide to Women's Health and Well-being*, London, Piatkus, 1995; and also Brennan, *Light Emerging*, 1993; Beinfield and Korngold, *Between Heaven and Earth*, 1991.
98 Northrup, *Women's Bodies Women's Wisdom*, p. 489.
99 Cited in Heusser, 'A basis for the understanding of anthroposophical medicine and cancer therapy', pp. 3–4.

10 Local–global spaces of health

British South Asian mothers and medical pluralism

Kate Reed

This chapter aims to explore the influence of globalisation on the health beliefs[1] and behaviours of British south Asian[2] mothers in Leicester, UK. This includes an exploration of the significance of geographical location, space and the way in which the erosion of national boundaries affects the women's health beliefs and behaviours. The research for this chapter is based on a larger project, which involved in-depth interviews with thirty south Asian women living in diverse parts of Leicester. It takes a gendered and generationally specific approach. It focuses on women who have either been born in or who have lived in Britain from the age of five or younger. Previous research[3] has demonstrated the important role of mothers in mediating family health; the project explores this role by drawing on respondents who are all themselves mothers. The project adopts a theoretical framework that highlights global syncrecy on the one hand, and the importance of context on the other.

The concept of syncrecy is used to look at the way in which Western and non-Western cultures are mixed both locally and globally in a reciprocal context. The concepts of syncrecy and syncretism have been used in research on health, ethnicity and identity to denote crossovers and tensions between categories of difference.[4] The benefit of using these concepts here lies in their resistance to completely collapsing categories of difference. Whilst recognising crossovers, syncrecy and syncretism also allow the potential for tensions between different categories.[5] The research explores the tension for British Asian women between west and non-west. This exploration of syncrecy is juxtaposed with an exploration of the importance of context (social, economic and spatial) on the beliefs and behaviours of women within the study.

The chapter's aims are threefold: first, it explores respondents' use of health discourses within Britain. This relates within the study to women's location in Leicester, focusing on their use of south Asian medicines. Their employment of such products will be explored in the context of their position as 'British Asian', as women socialised within the west who are also part of a wider globally dispersed ethnic group. This section will also look at their use of other non-Western health systems, particularly in the context of increases in alternative medicine in general. Second, the chapter explores the way in which women take and bring back a plurality of health goods to and from India. This transcultural flow of health goods highlights the significance of the south Asian diasporic network, enabling women to use of a variety of health discourses in a multiplicity of locations. In its deconstruction of borders and boundaries it forms part of the wider process of globalisation and emphasises the tension of the local–global dynamic.[6]

Finally, the chapter explores respondents' use of health products and health services within India, both Western and non-Western. Again, this emphasises the impact of globalisation and respondents' connections through diasporic networks. Globalisation has made visits to the homeland or 'imagined' homeland[7] easier and has opened access to health products and services through south Asian diaspora members in other locations. Before turning to explorations of these research findings, existing literature will be explored.

Locating health: plural medicine and previous research

Existing studies on the health beliefs and behaviours of minorities have tended to find mixed results regarding the use of Western and non-Western medical discourses. Donovan found that the use of South Asian medicines was confined in the UK almost exclusively to people of Afro-Caribbean descent, not Asian.[8] Others have found the converse to be true.[9] Eade paints a more complex picture.[10] Drawing on data from his study on the health beliefs and behaviours of Bangladeshi Muslims in Tower Hamlets, London, he argues that minorities within the west draw on a plurality of discourses including both non-Western and Western. Eade locates this use of different discourses as part of the dynamic and contested process of cultural construction as conditions are adapted to the conditions of urban life within the west. This approach is useful in the context of this research exploring the beliefs and behaviours of 'British Asian' women who are raised and socialised within differing cultures which may at times conflict.

The picture becomes more complex still when we consider the question of whether Western and non-Western medical systems can be seen as completely distinct. Brady *et al.* argue that Western and non-Western medical systems should not be looked at separately.[11] They argue that both merge together and are not in fact polar opposites. Leslie suggests that medical systems are in themselves syncretic incorporating into their centres a mix and match of different systems which makes them far from coherent and bounded.[12] I would argue that one cannot look at systems in simple isolation from one another, since systems often share a common feature. However, I would argue that to see systems themselves as syncretic or blurred, as only ever a mix and match of difference, denies that systems have characteristics that are specific only to them. A denial of difference between systems also fails to take into account the long history of unequal relations between biomedicine and non-Western systems. In an earlier chapter in this volume, Bradley highlights the tendency to emphasise the 'otherness' of heterodox medicine. Indeed in the eyes of the state, biomedicine is still viewed as superior to any alternatives, which have to strive for official recognition.[13] It is more fruitful for the operationalisation of empirical research to recognise that while there may be crossovers between medical systems, they remain on the whole distinct. However, as will be explored within this chapter, lay people themselves may use these systems syncretically, mixing and matching them and creating something new in the process.

In situating systems as separate there is also the issue of 'naming' them. Ideas about what constitutes alternative, indigenous, non-Western, unorthodox, or non-conventional medicine remains a contested domain. All the terms suffer from the same problems. All set Western medicine up as 'normal' and anything else as abnormal or fringe. In light of this, I chose the term non-Western medicine. I argue that in these circumstances it is not the term itself which is important but the way in which it is used. Because the term non-Western is in some respects as problematic as any of the other terms, I use it with caution.

The term 'non-Western' can also have negative connotations when focusing on minority use of non-Western discourse. Bowes and Domokos are strongly critical of research that has focused on south Asian use of non-Western practices, describing them as derogatory and patronising.[14] It is necessary to be sensitive in an engagement with non-Western discourse. However, it is important to recognise the role of plural medicine and medical subcultures present in all cultures and to explore the use of non-Western discourses. For instance within this chapter women's use of plural medicines in differing contexts is not necessarily a negative experience and can be seen in many ways as enabling, offering women alternatives to Western medicine in Britain.

Before moving on to explore the findings of the study, it is necessary to provide information on the methods used in order to give some background to the research. The project is based on thirty in-depth interviews with British South Asian women from Leicester. The respondents of the study adhere to various religions, they come from a range of social classes and their ages range from early twenties to early forties. The women all have at least one child under the age of ten. Respondents were drawn from playgroups and women's centres. Initially an informal pilot discussion group was conducted in order to refine the method for the main body of interviewing. This involved women from a community playgroup, all of whom had small children. The main interviewing process was staggered over a seven-month period. I analysed the data by developing initial theories, which were then explored in the field. Having collected the data, themes were identified through the continual process of transcription. Themes were categorised and then related back to the initial theories. On writing up the interviews have remained confidential and names have been changed.

Research findings: localising the global, Leicester in a national context

Migration from the Indian subcontinent to Leicester during the 1960s came at the height of Leicester's industrial boom.[15] Today, while Leicester's Asian population includes Ugandan, Kenyan, Tanzanian, Punjabi, Pakistani, Bangladeshi, and those from the rest of the subcontinent, the population is heavily weighted towards East

African Asians and Gujarati people, both Muslim and Hindu. According to census data 23.7 per cent of the population of the district of Leicester are of Asian origin. This is compared with 71.5 per cent white, 2.4 per cent black, and 2.4 per cent ethnic other.[16] Many women within the study had moved from other parts of the country to Leicester to marry.[17] These women came mostly from Blackburn, Birmingham and London. The women from Blackburn were all Muslim, those from Birmingham were Sikh and those from London were Sikh, Muslim and Hindu. The majority of women who had been born in Leicester were Hindu. There were some women within the study who had migrated to Britain from either East Africa, India or Pakistan, with one respondent from Trinidad. Women from countries other than Britain had quite frequently moved through several places in Britain before marrying and settling in Leicester.

Jeffers *et al.* argue that Leicester is a city where boundary crossing interactions between various minority and white populations are significant.[18] It is also argued to have a close-knit traditional Asian community as compared to other areas such as Blackburn and London, which have smaller and more scattered populations.[19] Because of the significant amount of people moving to Leicester to marry, these regional differences become mixed. Women within the study talked about how this was quite often reflected in beliefs and behaviours. Several respondents felt that people who were originally from Leicester often had 'traditionally' Indian ideas about health and health care and were more likely to use Indian health products.

In terms of Asian medical services, Leicester has one Ayurvedic clinic. There are also a number of Hakims who practise the Muslim medical system, Unani. While being aware that Vaidas and Hakims' (Hindu and Moslem healers') clinics existed in Leicester, views on the availability and use of the services and satisfaction with them were mixed. Hakims were widely talked about and many women knew of clinics and practitioners. Most were quite cynical about them though and saw Hakims as unsatisfactory, and too expensive. Many women in the study were worried about coming into contact with someone who was not properly qualified. This applied to both Ayurvedic clinics and Hakims. As Sita remarked:

Sita: Yes, now that holds me back, what if I come into contact with someone who isn't fully qualified? People practise and they say they are qualified but I don't know, somehow I'm reluctant to use it.

This line of argument is supported by Karseras and Hopkins who suggest that while healers in the subcontinent must be qualified this is not so in Britain.[20] Anyone can call themselves a Vaida or a Hakim, with the obvious danger that patients suffering from a serious but potentially treatable condition could be consulting an untrained person with little experience. Respondents were less likely to hold these types of views about Western medical practitioners in Leicester.

Because of Leicester's cultural diversity, women within the study felt it was a really good place to be able to get Asian health products as opposed to other areas of the country they had either visited or lived in. Access to and use of Asian products in some ways appeared to be actually far more important than use of

Asian medical services. Within the research women were much more likely to use Asian products than they were to visit official Asian medical healers. In talking about the availability of products in Leicester, Samina, a Muslim woman originally from Blackburn, argued:

Samina:　In Leicester I've seen it [laughs], you can get everything in Leicester, where I come from, in Blackburn, we always get them sent down from India. Tiger balm, don't forget the Tiger Balm!

This was a quite commonly held view, particularly when women within the study talked about balms for general health. Respondents related this issue of significant availability of health products in Leicester to the multi-cultural nature of the city. They appeared very proud of their knowledge of these products and even of Asian health care within Leicester. I would argue this gives us our first example of what Clifford calls 'diaspora discourse'[21] which blends together notions of both host and homeland, connecting members of the south Asian diaspora in a number of locations and aiding access to a plurality of products and services. Health goods flow between members of the south Asian diaspora in different locations, from Leicester through other national and international contexts.

Many respondents talked about the use of other health products or health care which were neither Western nor south Asian. Women within the study also went to visit alternative practitioners such as those practising acupuncture; this was mostly for general illness, such as hay-fever, and bodily aches and pains. Women went to other cities in order to get certain treatments or visit particular healers. Respondents found out about alternative practitioners and clinics in other contexts through friends' recommendations. They often sought out healers in other places when they had exhausted health care resources within Leicester. Indian health care services and, more importantly, health care products are reasonably widely available in Leicester. Other types such as Traditional Chinese medicine, though available, are less easy to find in Leicester, perhaps due to a lack of Chinese population.

Respondents' use of a broad range of non-Western products reflects an overall growth within Britain in the use of alternative health care. It fits in with general arguments about dissatisfaction with approaches in Western healthcare. As Worsley argues, many people in Britain, after consulting their GP, feel dissatisfied and turn to experiment with non-Western medicine.[22] Women in the study were on the whole keen to try alternative practices, although none expressed a desire to use only alternative practices. As Gurinder explained, women also linked increased use of alternative health care with more general shifts in the National Health Service and Western society in general:

Gurinder: I think it is age but it is also with the way society is. I mean it [Western medicine] is not always the answer and the doctors don't always diagnose you the right way. I think it is the way the NHS [National Health Service in Britain] is going.

It is important to recognise power dynamics within this global spread of non-Western discourses. It must also be located within the argument of the wider issue of the power of global marketing and health.[23] The global marketing of cultural products through the media is important. This indicates a celebration of ethnic difference in a very post-modern sense, making difference not only acceptable but also fashionable.

Respondents also identified their position as 'British Asian', as giving them access to a range of cultural resources not readily available to other populations. This relates to their membership within a wider diasporic network. As 'British Asian', women in the study occupy a unique position. They have access to both Western and non-Western health discourses through Western socialisation and as part of an ethnic minority group that is geographically dispersed. Because of the ability of diasporas to connect multiple communities, women are able to access a whole range of products and services within Leicester.

Ultimately the respondents' location in Leicester and their related connections with members of the British Asian diaspora in other locations affected their beliefs and use of different types of health discourses. Within the next section I will look at how the use of these products is extended from along local and national lines to global contexts, focusing on the transcultural flow of goods and capital.

From here to India (and back): the transcultural flow of health products

Much of the literature on globalisation looks at how separate places become effectively a single community through the continuous circulation of people, money, goods and information.[24] This culturally homogenising type of argument has been heavily criticised. As Grewal argues, such reference to transcultural flows of goods should be seen instead as scattered hegemonies which are the effects of mobile capital as well as the multiple subjectivities that have replaced the unitary European subject.[25] As other authors have pointed out, the movement of any forms of capital in a global era should not be seen as one way. Relating to health, Worsley argues that today so great is the flow of people and ideas across the globe, cultural exchanges overcome political barriers.[26] He argues that though Western remedies may diffuse particularly rapidly, the traffic is not all one way. Within the context of diaspora, globalisation with its deconstruction of borders and boundaries makes it possible for products and people to traverse diasporic networks particularly efficiently.

This was reflected in respondents' accounts when they talked about how they bought both Western and Asian health products, and brought them back to the UK and also taking certain things out to other countries. This occurred when respondents were on holiday or visiting family. Such exchanges mostly took place between Britain and India. I argue that rather than seeing this as part of the argument for cultural renaissance or homogenisation, it relates rather to the push and pull of both local and global forces, which form part of the process of globalisation as national boundaries are opened. Women went to India to buy non-Western *and* Western health products, which were then circulated within the local context. At the same time the reciprocity of the local/global process was emphasised through taking goods over to India and dispersing them within family networks there. As Sita explained:

Sita: I take multi-vitamin tablets, my family in India really like us to take them if anybody's going over.

Women took health products from the UK over to family in India and various other places because family saw them as better than the products available there. These were mostly things like vitamin tablets and pain killers. Respondents also talked about certain products they went to India to buy.

In discussions on cultural pluralism, India is often cited as a premier example.[27] It has many variations in language, religion and social status and other cultural traits. Such pluralism is also reflected within health care in India, as Ayurveda, Sidha and Unani are available alongside biomedicine.[28] Women drew on such plural health systems in India. Respondents' need to draw on these resources in India depended on their location in the UK and for women in Leicester, as already demonstrated, they could access most South Asian balms in Leicester. Women went over to buy non-Western goods already available in Leicester, mostly because it was cheaper to get them from India, where no tax has to be paid. Some Asian balms could only be obtained in India. Some non-Western health products (such as skin products) were also available only in India. As Gurinder, a Sikh woman, argued:

Gurinder: My dad has psoriasis and he's had medicine from India for that. There's this special tablet that I think is specifically for people with eczema and psoriasis. It worked on him; it is like a little herbal remedy you get from India.

Other goods that women went to India to buy specifically were herbal tablets for diabetes. Some women also went to India for specific Western health products, because certain things are available there and not in Britain. Ramila, a Hindu woman talked about going to India for diet pills:

Ramila: Next time I go (to India) I want to get a diet pill that makes you lose weight, that you can't get here. You can get that there. You know – amphetamine, what you used to be able to get here, but are banned now.

Respondents' position as British Asian affected their access to a plurality of health resources. This was most notable in two different ways: British Asian women appeared to have greater access to Asian medical products and services because they were part of an ethnic group with greater access to products and services through the South Asian diasporic network, as argued previously. It was also the case that the women's status as part of a mobile group with a significantly globally dispersed network heightened access to both Western and non-Western products in other contexts. These types of cultural exchanges on a global level have been demonstrated in other research on diasporic communities, not however relating to exchanges in health products. Parker argues in his research on British Chinese people that their connections to places of origin are made through material exchanges.[29] Cultural commodities from Hong Kong are exported within days to distribution companies in France, North America and London.

Some women felt quite cautious about either sending things over to India or bringing them from India back to Britain. This is because they were cautious over the content of products bought in India. This can also be related to respondents' caution about breaking the law regarding non-payment of tax duties and importation of banned goods. In this sense sometimes respondents' would talk about buying and bringing things back only when someone else had already tried it. Within the study, women also talked about the flow of labour and the way in which people received work qualifications in different countries. When talking about biomedical doctors in India, many women talked about how they got their medical training in the UK or America. This often impacted on whether or not women trusted doctors in India.

Using plural health care services in India

Many respondents were open to using Western health care in India, or had used health care there generally if they needed to when visiting. It was also common for respondents to use health facilities in India for specific treatments. Some women even had a family doctor in India, in case they needed to use one when they visit family. Respondents often explained this use of health care in India by reference to its cheapness. However, it also appeared that women used it because of marked differences in care between Britain and India and in some respects treatment seemed better in India. This reflects Worsley's argument that despite the inter-nationalism of Western medicine, marked cultural differences, subscribed to by patients and doctors alike, persist in each country.[30] Women talked about how you could go private in India and pay a lot less but get good treatments. Gurinder related this to being viewed there as being 'from abroad':

Gurinder: To them 100 or 200 rupees, it is like private, so, and getting your best treatment just for a little bit more, so I would prefer to. You know that little extra care, particularly if you're from abroad; they do treat you a lot better in India.

Women went to India for various treatments because they felt that they performed them better there.

Many women talked about how they used health care in India when they felt they were not being treated properly in the UK. Shahnaz talked about how her sister in-law's husband died of cancer. He had been mis-diagnosed in the UK, so went to India and was treated more promptly, albeit too late to save his life.

Shahnaz: He wasn't actually seen until the September of 1996, they said there wasn't anything wrong with him. In December he was getting worse. He changed GPs and the new GP realised it was bad and finally got things rolling. The state of his health deteriorated so much that he eventually went to India. With the first doctor, the first examination he had, they diagnosed him as having cancer.

Shahnaz felt that if her relative had finished his treatment in India he might have survived. Such dissatisfaction with Western health care was located in the women's accounts around more general arguments about poor standards within the National Health Service. Women on the whole complained about waiting lists, inability to get appointments and poor or wrong diagnosis. While many authors have talked about the poor treatment of minorities and migrants within the health service, relating this to the practice of racism,[31] women were reluctant to talk about inadequacies as a result of racist practices.[32] This may or may not be related to the problematic nature of interviewing across race. Respondents were keener to attribute unhappiness with the health services to a general deterioration in health care.

In this sense using health care both generally and for specific reasons and in emergencies in India can be seen as a pragmatic alternative for British Asian women to health care in the UK. India can be interpreted as a site open only to Indians or diasporic Indians because of connections. It is not open in the same way to white British people. Rather than seeing this move to health care in India as a quest for authenticity, we must analytically reframe such quests amid a widening field of available positions of pragmatism.[33] As Shahnaz demonstrates, India opens up possibilities for women and their health, which are not as accessible for white Britons and other populations:

Shahnaz: You shouldn't need to go to India to get treated. We (Asians) have got some place to go to but what about white people who are born here they haven't got another country to go to, you know.

However, respondents often argued that although they would use biomedicine within India and were glad they had that option if needed, they nevertheless preferred to use health care in the UK if they had the choice.

There was a significant split here between women visiting India as if it were part of a 'homeland' and those who felt like they were 'foreigners' there. This tied in with respondents' identity in general and whether they saw themselves as British Asian women, as Indian women, Muslim women etc.[34] The split was mostly keenly felt between those who had roots, or family origins in East Africa or the Caribbean, and those families who were more directly from India. The latter on the whole were far more comfortable with visiting India and using health care there. This did not automatically stop those from other countries using health care in India and in fact they were more likely to do so than use health care in their own countries of origin.

Mostly when women talked about using health care in India it was to use Western health care. One woman had used a Hakim while in India and some women went to practitioners who used herbal remedies and religious and spiritual healers. Sita argued that whether you used non-Western health care in India depended on what kinds of family contacts you had within a wider diasporic context, whether for instance you had Ayurvedic practitioners in your family.

Sita: What sort of background they have, like I was saying, my grandfather was very much into Ayurveda but still once he passed away we would rather stick to a normal [Western] doctor over there. In India your GP is like your family member, it's literally like, you know, it's called a family doctor.

Women seemed to use a variety of health products and systems in India just as they did in the UK. This usage has a global dimension in that it transcends local specificity. As Kishwar, a Muslim woman, argued as she talked about using health care for fertility problems in many diverse contexts:

Kishwar: Due to having problems having children, the doctor diagnosed that there was a problem with him [her husband]. So we had to go to various herbalists from India, people's recommendations and things, and we've also used private health care such as BUPA and even, like, to Harley Street in London.

Many women within the study were also very wary of using health care (just as they were with health products) in India, either Western or non-Western. They were fearful as they felt doctors and other medical professionals might not be properly qualified there. As Gurinder commented:

Gurinder: If I was there, I wouldn't go personally, because you are dubious in India because doctors aren't, you know, qualified. You know here because they've got their medical certificates and stuff, but in India I don't know, doctors scare me a bit because you hear stories. That patients go to the doctors and they're not very literate. They go to the doctors and they get told they have to have this major surgery, they end up with a kidney missing and obviously the doctors have sold it on as transplants without the knowledge of the patients you see.

This was quite a commonly held view among respondents which exemplifies women's apparently paradoxical view of health care products and services in India as both enabling and constraining. In contrast to the story of one of Shahnaz's family members, as outlined earlier, most women quite often felt that health care was better in the UK, with better-qualified staff and better facilities.

Many respondents, however, related this mistrust to particular geographical areas of India, and said their use of health care there depended on what area they were in. As is the case with health care in many geographical contexts, Meade, Horin and Gesler suggest that there is a spatial and social imbalance in the quantity and quality of available health care.[35] Regional differences in health care system mixes and health outcomes create huge inequalities in health care delivery systems and this was reflected in the women's accounts.

Conclusion

The chapter draws on original research into the health beliefs and behaviours of British Asian mothers in Leicester. It has aimed to contribute an understanding to the significance of geographical location, space and globalisation on these women's use of plural medicine. The findings of the study demonstrate how space, context and diasporic networks significantly influence the women's beliefs about and use of different health discourses. Women's position as 'British Asian' also plays a key role. As 'British Asian', women are socialised within Britain and within a wider diasporic network. This gives women equal access to both Western and non-Western discourses.

Within the study women also actively seek other non-Asian, non-Western discourses which can be related to more general shifts towards use of alternative medicine. Globalisation also opens up boundaries enabling women to move goods transculturally and utilise health care and products in India. This demonstrates women's syncretic use of health discourses and the influence of the decentralised Asian diaspora in all its diversity. Women draw on these diasporic networks in order to create spaces of health, which give them an alternative to Western health products and care in Britain. These spaces enable women to use a plurality of discourses in a number of diverse locations.

In a broader sense the findings highlight the difficulties of conceptualising and distinguishing between and within Western and non-Western medical discourses. They demonstrate the usefulness of distinguishing between the two but also suggest that we must recognise the dangers of seeing them as completely separate. It is important to remember that these findings are based on a regionally specific study and are therefore limited in terms of their relevance to general claims about pluralism. However, I feel they do highlight a more general need for a globally dynamic approach to pluralism, one which emphasises the argument that pluralism is built upon multiple transnational networks, networks which can be regionally situated but transcend national boundaries. This is something worth exploring within new research, focusing on different diasporas in other national and international contexts.

Notes

1 Within the conceptual framework of the study a distinction between health beliefs and health behaviours was recognised along the lines of McAllister and Farquhar's distinction: beliefs as feelings about lifestyles and health, and behaviours as health related activity. However the distinction was not seen as fixed and the aim was to see whether respondents themselves made the distinction. Within the findings no clear-cut distinction was made. McAllister, G. and Farquhar, M., 'Health beliefs: a cultural division?', *Journal of Advanced Nursing*, 17 (1992): 1447–54.

2 Census data uses the term 'Asian' to refer to those migrants originating from Asia. At this level the data doesn't distinguish by region. The more regionally focused definition 'south Asian' refers to those from India, Pakistan and Bangladesh, see Ballard, R. (ed.), *Desh Pardesh: The South Asian Presence in Britain*, Hurst and Company, London, 1994. *See* Marett, V., *Immigrants Settling in the City*, Leicester University Press, Leicester, 1989, for a breakdown of Leicester's Asian population by regional grouping. The term 'British south Asian' or 'British Asian' is used in this context to refer to those with south Asian parentage who have been born and/or raised within Britain.

3 Blaxter, M. and Paterson, E., *Mothers and Daughters: A Three Generational Study of Health Attitudes and Behaviours*, Heinemann Education Books, London, 1982. Graham, H., *Hardship and Health in Women's Lives*, Harvester Wheatsheaf, London, New York, 1993.

4 Fitzpatrick, R. (1984) 'Lay concepts of health and illness' in Fitzpatrick R., Hinton, J., Newman, S., Scambler, G. and Thompson, J. (eds), *The Experience of Illness*, London, Tavistock. Parker, D., *Through Different Eyes: The Cultural Identities of Young Chinese People in Britain*, Aldershot, Avebury.

5 Reed, K. (2000), 'Dealing with difference: researching health beliefs and behaviours of British Asian mothers', in *Sociological Research Online*, Vol. 4 No. 4, <http://www.socresonline.org.uk/4/4/reed.html>

6 The term discourse is used here in the Foucauldian sense. For Foucault discourses are 'large groups of statements', rule governed language terrains defined by what Foucault refers to as 'strategic possibilities'. For Foucault, at any given moment in a particular context, there will be a particular discourse of medicine: a set of rules and conventions, systems of mediation and transposition which govern the way health, illness and treatment are discussed, when and by whom. For a more general overview of the term see Hawthorn, J., *A Glossary of Contemporary Literary Theory* (3rd edn), Arnold, London, 1998.

7 'Imagined homeland' here is a play on Anderson's ideas of imagined communities. Anderson talks of a nation as an imagined political community. He sees it as imagined because the members of even small nations will never know of their fellow members, meet them, hear them. However, according to Anderson, in the minds of each lives the image of communion. Drawing on Anderson, imagined community within the research is then used to denote in a spatial context the women's relationships to India or Africa. They may never have lived in these places (or have any intention of doing so), or visit them that frequently, know many people there. However, in the minds of many of the respondents these places still maintain the quality of mythical homelands.

8 Donovan, J., *We Don't Buy Sickness It Just Comes: Health, Illness and Healthcare in the Lives of Black People in London*, Gower, Aldershot, 1986.

9 Armstrong, D. and Pierce, M., 'Afro-Caribbean lay beliefs about diabetes: an exploratory study', in Kelleher, D. and Hillier, S. (eds), *Researching Cultural Differences in Health*, Routledge, London, 1996.

10 Eade, J. 'The power of the experts: the plurality of beliefs and practices concerning health and illness among Bangladeshis in Tower Hamlets, London', in Marks, L. and Worboys, M. (eds), *Migrants, Minorities and Health: Historical and Contemporary Studies*, Routledge, London, 1997.

11 Brady, M., Kunitz, S. and Nash, D., 'Australian aborigines' conceptualisations and the World Health Organisation', in Marks, L. and Worboys, M. (eds), *Migrants, Minorities and Health: Historical and Contemporary Studies*, Routledge, London, 1997.

12 Leslie, C., 'Interpretations of illness: syncretism in modern Ayurveda', in Leslie, C. and Young, A. (eds), *Paths to Asian Medical Knowledge*, University of California Press, Berkeley and Los Angeles, 1992.

13 Cant, S. and Sharma, U., *A New Medical Pluralism? Alternative Medicine, Doctors, Patients and the State*, UCL Press, London, 1999.

14 Bowes, A. and Domokos T.M., 'South Asian women and health services: a study in Glasgow', *New Community* 19, 4 (1993): 611–26.

15 Marett, V., *Immigrants Settling in the City*, Leicester University Press, 1989.

16 Leicester County Council. *Census: Electoral Wards Profiles (City)*, Leicester County Council, Leicestershire, 1991.

17 In the study 16 women were British born, originating from a range of areas including Blackburn, Birmingham, Leicester and London. 14 of the women interviewed were born outside of the UK. These women came from East Africa, India, Pakistan, and Trinidad. 7 women in the study were Muslim, 15 were Hindu, 7 were Sikh and 1 was Catholic.

18 Jeffers, S., Hoggett, P. and Harrison, L., 'Race, ethnicity and community in three localities', *New Community*, 22, 1 (1996): 111–26.

19 Ibid.

20 Karseras, P and Hopkins, E., *British Asians: Health in the Community*, Chichester, Hampshire, 1987.

21 Clifford, J., *Routes: Travel and Translation in the Late Twentieth Century*, Harvard University Press, Cambridge, MA, 1997.

22 Worsley, P., *Knowledges: What Different Peoples Make of the World*, Profile Books, London, 1997.

23 Morley, D. and Robins, K., *Spaces of Identity: Global Media, Electronic Landscapes and Cultural Boundaries*, Routledge, London, 1995.

24 Clifford, J., *Routes: Travel and Translation in the Late Twentieth Century*, Harvard University Press, Cambridge, MA, 1997.

25 Grewal, I. and Kaplan, C., *Scattered Hegemonies: Postmodernity and Transnational Feminist Practice*, University of Minnesota Press, Minneapolis, 1994.

26 Worsley, *Knowledges*.

27 Meade, M., Horin, J. and Gesler, W., *Medical Geography*, Guildford Press, London, New York, 1988.

28 Ibid.

29 Parker, 'Through Different Eyes'.

30 Worsley, *Knowledges*.

31 Ahmad, W.I.U. (ed.), *Race and Health in Contemporary Britain*, Open University Press, Buckingham, 1993.

32 Authors such as Rhodes have highlighted the difficulties of researching across race. He asks whether it is possible to elicit sensitive information relating to race when interviewing in a differing racial context? Within the context of this research it was sometimes difficult to tell whether women felt they had not been subject to racist practices within the health service, or whether they were saying they had not because I was white and they felt that they could not speak to me about it. Rhodes, P.J., 'Race of interviewer affects: a brief comment', *Sociology*, 28, 2 (1994): 547–58.

33 Bausinger, H., *Folk Culture in a World of Technology*, Indiana University Press, Bloomington, 1990. Narayan, K. 'Songs lodged in some hearts: displacements of women's knowledge in Kangra', in Lavie, S. and Swedenburg, T. (eds), *Displacements, Diaspora and Geographies of Identity*, Duke University Press, Durham, NC, 1996.

34 Women drew on medical discourses that related directly to their own religion, Hindu women drawing on Ayurveda and Muslim women on Unani. However, women drew also on folk remedies that were syncretic in origin.

35 Meade, M., Horin, J. and Gesler, W., *Medical Geography*, Guildford Press, London, New York, 1988.

11 Indian indigenous pharmaceuticals

Tradition, modernity and nature

Maarten Bode

That India is now a big city culture and certainly in my generation and much more so in subsequent generations, that India includes large amounts of what you may call adulterated material. ... For me this notion of hybridity, of melange, of things being mixed together, has been essential.

(Salman Rushdie in *India Today*, 14 July 1997)

In the last decades of the nineteenth century Indian entrepreneurs started the industrial production of Ayurvedic and Unani (Greco-Islamic) medicines. At the end of the twentieth century the turnover of this industry was much larger than government funding of Ayurvedic and Unani education, treatment and research.[1] However, in contrast to government policy towards Indian medicine this industry has not received much attention from scholars interested in the study of contemporary Indian medical traditions.[2]

Around 8,000 licensed pharmacies produce a wide range of Ayurvedic and Unani medicines.[3] It is common for Unani firms to produce Ayurvedic medicines such as 'Supari Pak' and 'Chyawanprash'. Among these companies, many are small and have a largely local clientele. I will focus on three of the biggest companies which sell their products all over India and, increasingly, abroad. The Ayurvedic companies Dabur and Zandu hold around one third of the market in Ayurvedic products while Hamdard produces around 70 per cent of the Unani pharmaceuticals in India. The total sale of Ayurvedic products in 1997, including Ayurvedic soaps and cosmetics, was estimated to be between Rs. 1,500 *crores* (US$ 375 million) and Rs. 2,300 *crores* (US$ 575 million) while Hamdard claimed in the same year an annual sale of Rs. 110 *crores* (US$ 27.5 million).[4] Though Hamdard boasts as many as 1,200 pharmaceutical products and the therapeutic indexes of Dabur and Zandu mention at least 300 products, a handful of these are responsible for the large sales figures. For example, three products (a tooth powder, a hair oil and a vitality booster) comprise around 40 per cent of the sales of Dabur while 'Rooh Afza', a *sarbat* (sweet syrup, sweet medicine)[5] for which many health benefits are claimed, does the same for Hamdard.

The marketing of Indian indigenous pharmaceuticals has substantially determined the way the Indian public looks upon its medical traditions.[6] Indian medicines are not only the fresh drugs prescribed by a professional 'naturalist'[7] or the home remedies prepared in Indian kitchens, but increasingly high tech products associated with factories and laboratories. Their ambiguity challenges dichotomies which have been too easily taken for granted such as 'Western/indigenous' and 'traditional/modern'.[8] Nowadays the term 'modern' can also be applied to Indian health traditions such as Ayurveda and Unani *tibb*.[9] Though Ayurvedic and Unani preparations have their roots in classical sciences these substances are increasingly produced, researched and marketed along modern lines. Companies use modern production and research technology and advertisements appear on television and in glossy, English-language magazines. Large producers like Dabur, Zandu and Hamdard also offer financial incentives to 'encourage' retailers and chemists to raise the sales of their products. At the same time a significant number of recipes come from classical texts and traditional medical concepts are used in the marketing of Indian medicines. Indeed, Indian health products are modern and traditional at the same time. Although, logically speaking, 'traditional' and 'modern' exclude each other, in practice these qualities go together.[10]

Especially large companies like Dabur, Zandu and Hamdard have been instrumental in the reworking of traditional medicines into modern health products. In this chapter I will analyse the way over-the-counter Ayurvedic and Unani pharmaceuticals are projected by the industry. How do these large companies 'manage the paradox of being natural and traditional, while remaining contemporary', as one of Dabur's directors put it.[11] Analysis of promotional material as well as interviews with managers will provide us with insight into the dialectic relationship between tradition and modernity, which marks Indian health traditions and Indian society today. Besides, to sell their products Dabur, Zandu and Hamdard tap into popular Indian notions of health and disease. For example, advertisements target the moral dimensions that are part and parcel of discourses about health and illness in the Indian context.

The commodification of Indian indigenous medicines

In June 1998 *India Today*, a prominent Indian weekly with 15.9 million readers, contained an advertising special on Ayurvedic medicines. It included five pages with advertisements and small articles about three companies. Allen Laboratories promoted its capsules for fighting dandruff, hair loss and premature greying by toning up the stomach and liver. Baidyanath, a large north Indian company established in 1918, selected five products out of its range of five hundred: two *rasayanas* (tonics, vitalisers), a medicinal tooth powder, a digestive, and a medicine for the treatment of dysmenorrhoea. Dabur restricted itself to a food supplement and 'Pudin Hara', a digestive already mentioned in their therapeutic index of 1930.

Most Ayurvedic and Unani medicines don't find their way to patients and consumers through the prescriptions of traditional healers. I estimate[12] that at the moment 80 to 90 per cent of Ayurvedic and Unani pharmaceuticals are sold directly to consumers by retailers such as chemists, small grocers as well as supermarkets and beauty parlours.[13] This reality differs from the image of the scholarly traditional healer who prescribed medicines after carefully having examined his patients. Self-medication seems to be the rule for most Indian indigenous pharmaceuticals. One of the reasons is the fact that a large majority of the students who finish their education at one of the colleges of Ayurveda or Unani *tibb* start to practise Western medicine. Rather than promoting the cause of traditional medicine by offering teaching facilities and stimulating confidence in Indian medicine the more than 'hundred badly-funded Ayurvedic and Unani colleges' have mainly functioned as 'backdoors', i.e. backdoor entrances, to the practice of Western medicine for those who failed to get access to Western medical training.[14] The larger part of the training in these 'traditional colleges' is usually in Western medicine and allied modern sciences. Following graduation students will make use mainly of Western disease categories and medical prescriptions. Therefore, the practice of institutionally trained Ayurvedic and Unani physicians often does not differ from that of biomedically trained physicians.[15] Indeed, the prestige of modern medicine as well as the lack of proper training in traditional medicine has deprived the traditional pharmaceutical industry of physicians for the prescription of their products.[16] Another reason for the dominance of over-the-counter marketing is the large number of medicines for common diseases like cough and body aches, as well as tonics and cosmetics in the product range of most companies. At least from a modern perspective one could argue that for these products a prescription is not needed.

The profusion of advertisements for Unani and Ayurvedic pharmaceuticals complements the increasing consumerism that marks India in the 1990s. Producers of Indian medicines advertise their products widely. Different media are used including television, radio, cinema, billboards, neon signs, print media, beauty contests, sales exhibitions and even 'international' scientific conferences. Advertisements for Indian indigenous pharmaceuticals are also seen in the streets of India's cities. A walk through Delhi proves my point. A police boat carries the name of the largest producer of Unani medicines. An Ayurvedic company uses city buses for drawing the public's attention to its 'brain tonic'. Above Chandni Chowk, the famous bazaar in the old city, towers an advertisement for an Ayurvedic hair oil that cools the brain. Along Delhi's Ring Road an Unani company uses the road demarcations to advertise its Ayurvedic health tonic demonstrating the intertwining of Indian medical traditions. Because of the costs involved these advertisements are usually for the most 'fast-moving' products of the companies. For other products an army of salespeople tries to influence retailers to 'counter-push' their products. The retailers get financial incentives and signboards that carry the name of the shop next to images of some medicines made by the company that offers the signboard. Product brochures carry the statement 'For medical practitioners only'. This indicates the importance companies attach to maintaining a medical image for their products although it does not deter them from selling them straight to patients.

Who are the customers to whom these commercial messages must appeal? In contrast to India's more advanced hard liquor industry, producers of indigenous pharmaceuticals have just started collecting statistical data about their customers.[17]

It was only recently that the Himalaya Drug Company, a large producer of Ayurvedic medicines that is known for its progressive marketing and production, hired a marketing firm to collect socio-economic data about consumers and evaluate their reactions to advertisements for Ayurvedic Concepts, the company's new over-the-counter product line. Even large companies like Dabur and Hamdard remain largely dependent upon piecemeal data collected by their sales staff when they visit retailers. This fact is illustrated by the assistant manager of Dabur Research Foundation who said 'Occasionally we dispense one of our new products to a sample of around four hundred people and ask them their opinion. However, such systematic studies are still exceptional in the Ayurvedic industry'.[18] Though members of the lower middle class and daily wage earners are certainly important customers for Hamdard, Dabur and Zandu, indigenous brand medicines are 'increasingly marketed to the more affluent middle classes'.[19] Newspaper articles, advertisements and industry statements' indicate that people like office workers, executives and affluent farmers are an important new consumer market for indigenous medicines. This trend is also reflected in the price of some of these products, as a statement of the assistant advertising manager of Hamdard illustrates: 'only more affluent people can afford to buy our brain tonic Rogham Badan Shirin on a regular basis'.[20] The recent release of a CD-ROM entitled 'Ayurveda Authentica' by Dabur also demonstrates that middle-class consumers are an important target for these companies' marketing efforts. In their campaigns companies capitalise on anxieties among the better-off about side-effects caused by Western medicines and offer 'gentle' remedies for chronic ailments such as hypertension and diabetes, health problems that affect the richer strata of Indian society.

'Chyawanprash', a general health tonic produced and marketed by Dabur, Zandu and Hamdard, is the best known Ayurvedic tonic. It is named after a sage who was its first user. The sage obtained the tonic from the Asvins, the physicians of the gods,[21] after losing his eye-sight and vigour due to an overcurious and sexually demanding princess. Though many Ayurvedic and Unani companies sell this product, Dabur is the largest producer of 'Chyawanprash'.[22] Due to heavy advertising on television and in the print media the product has had a great impact upon the popular image of traditional medicine in India. In India Dabur's Chyawanprash is often seen as the symbol of commodification of Indian medicine, as a statement by a manager of Dabur testifies: 'after Dabur turned 'Chyawanprash' into a commodified family tonic the number of buyers rose to 25 million. The product familiarised the Indian middle class with Ayurveda as a codified tradition'.[23] In an advertisement in *India Today*, Dabur emphasises the health benefits of the product by stating:

> Modern Science has ample evidence today to prove that the unique immuno-modulatory action of Dabur Chyawanprash restores the balance of antibodies. … It has powerful anti-oxidants which neutralise the harmful effects of modern living. Protecting you from illness. Making you stronger. From within. … Based on the 3000-year old Ayurvedic recipe in Charaka Samhita, fortified with 48 herbs, roots, fresh fruits and minerals. Completely natural, free from side effects.[24]

Both Ayurveda and Unani *tibb* attach great importance to enhancing vigour and disease resistance. Emaciation, the wasting away of body constituents, is viewed as the blue print for disease.[25] This explains the large number of tonics marketed by the indigenous industry. The *sarbat* 'Rooh Afza', India's best selling Unani tonic, is a case in point. The tonic is not mentioned in any of the canons of the Greek-Arabic medical tradition. Instead it was developed in 1907 by Hakim Abdul Majeed, the founder of Hamdard. Though 'Rooh Afza' is not a traditional medicine in the strict sense, according to Hamdard the product combines 'the essence and virtues' of 'traditional syrups'.[26] Nowadays 'Rooh Afza' makes up approximately 40 per cent of Hamdard's profits. Like in the marketing of Dabur 'Chyawanprash' a blend of traditional and modern science is used to legitimise the product:

> The unique preparation with herbs, vital elements and natural vitamins. People's favourite for over 86 years with scientifically proven natural goodness that balances natural body processes, and body fluids. Its unique ingredients cleanse the blood and correct deficiencies that lead to tiredness, loss of appetite, anaemia and giddiness. Besides being extremely beneficial during vomiting, dehydration, and heat exhaustion, Rooh Afza increases the calcium level in blood as well. Strengthens bones and helps nerves and muscles function efficiently.[27]

'Rooh Afza' is clothed with many images and ideas like science, art, Muslim hospitality – the product is widely used by north Indian Muslims for breaking the fast during Ramadan – nature and beauty. We find most of these on the 'Rooh Afza' calendar that Hamdard distributed in 1999. Next to pictures of young women who are said to be 'completely natural', 'completely beautiful', 'completely happy' and 'completely fit', glitter the names of prominent modern research institutes that have done research on the product such as the All Indian Institute of Medical Sciences. According to the calendar the product 'can actually cool body, mind and soul', is 'anabolic' and 'anti-stress' and 'stimulates cardiovascular and central nervous system activity as well as regulates the balance of electrolytes in the body'. The product's '92 year heritage' is also emphasised on this calendar.

Along with their medicines the producers of Indian indigenous pharmaceuticals also market their medical systems. For example, a brochure of Zandu that mentions 33 of the company's best-selling products, states:

> In the service of ailing humanity Zandu's Effective Ayurvedic medicines are based on time-tested prescriptions by India's ancient physician sages of the Aryan era. Effectively revived with intensive research of the ancient blended with modern know-how. … The essence of Zandu's success lies in the firm belief that Ayurveda propounds no mere technique of herbal or mineral cure, but lays down a whole philosophy of human life and living with a view to the preservation and building of a positive health and happiness, development of immunity to disease, longevity and preservation of youth.[28]

Apart from evoking traditional culture and modern science Zandu legitimises its products by stating that they belong to a holistic medical tradition.

Indeed, the spectrum of ideas and images evoked by the industry is wide. However, after comparing many advertisements and brochures, of which only a few examples have been given, two themes emerge. The first theme symbolised by the *rishi* (seer) sitting in a test tube is the embracing of both tradition and modernity. It is not too difficult to detect in the printed material as well as in the conversations with managers and other employees of the industry the importance of both concepts. What kind of images and ideas are used by the industry to express that their products are both traditional and modern? How do they argue the authenticity of their products in a context in which Western medicine has the upper hand in terms of prestige and power? The second theme is the naturalness and wholesomeness that the producers claim for their products. At first sight this looks obvious. Indeed, everywhere producers of herbal and mineral remedies are capitalising on the fear induced by the side effects of 'chemical' pharmaceuticals. However, in the Indian context at least there is more to this. Underneath an instrumental discourse on the dangers of reductionism and the advantages of holism we can detect a moral discourse about human affinities with, at its centre, the construction of 'naturalness' and 'wholesomeness'.

Tradition and modernity

Religious and historical images are used by the industry to anchor Indian pharmaceuticals in traditional culture. For example, the modern plastic container of Dabur 'Chyawanprash' shows a *rishi* sitting in the Himalayas and a 'free, fact-filled booklet' for its promotional claims that 'Chyawanprash' is 'from the oldest living system of health care'.[29] These images appeal to Indian people because everyone is familiar with the *Ramayana*. In this Hindu epic the monkey king Hanuman flies to the Himalayas to collect the herbs to save Laksman, the brother of Lord Rama who is the hero of the epic, from dying. The streets were empty when this epic was shown on television in 1987–8. The Himalayas represent the abode of potent medical herbs while a *rishi* denotes superior knowledge about life. Most certainly these images will be part of the attraction 'Chyawanprash' holds in the eyes of the Indian public.

Zandu associates its products with traditional culture by emphasising its relationship with 'a philanthropic and famous Ayurvedic physician from Jamnagar, a district in Gujarat' who 'was popular by his nickname Zandu'.[30] According to Zandu this physician 'was the Rajvaidya [royal physician] to Raja Jam Vibha, then king of Jamnagar'.[31] Zandu uses a picture of Dhanvantari, the Hindu god of medicine, to link its products to Indian traditional culture. On the back of one of its brochures we see Dhanvantari, 'Zandu's Symbol of Purity and Effectiveness in Medicine', rising out of the ocean with a container holding Amruth, the nectar of immortality. As Zandu tells us, in Hindu mythology Dhanvantari is one of the gifts the gods provided to humanity by churning the ocean. Indeed, Amruth denotes the god given nature of Ayurvedic medicines. The sun and the moon are present in 'The 10 Minute Guide to Ayurveda' that Dabur published around 1995. In Hinduism, the sun and the moon are deities as well as basic semantic opposites. Among many other things they represent heat and coolness that people who have some basic knowledge about Ayurveda will immediately associate with *pitta* (bile) and *kapha* (phlegm), two of the Ayurvedic humours. Gods, *rishis* and the Indian *sastras* (sciences), also play a prominent role in Ayurveda Authentica, a CD-ROM for the promotion of Ayurveda that Dabur released in 1998. The cover of the CD-ROM evokes Indian traditional culture through the phrase 'Discover India's ancient secrets for health and healing'.

The producers of Unani pharmaceuticals also refer to traditional culture. The Koran and the crescent moon decorate the packaging and the promotional materials of the products of the Ajmal Khan Tibbiya (medical) College Dawakhana (pharmacy), a Unani pharmacy that is part of the Unani medical college of Aligarh Muslim University, one of the largest Muslim universities in the world. Though the products of Hamdard do not carry religious symbols, the use of Urdu poetry for the promotion of 'Rooh Afza' links the product to Delhi's pre-independence Muslim culture that suffered greatly in the aftermath of partition. The majority of Delhi's Muslim population left for Pakistan shortly before and after this nation was created in 1947. The absence of religious symbols in the marketing of Hamdard could be due to Hindu sensitivity towards Islam. Instead of Islam Hamdard uses Unani *tibb* to link its products to tradition. The 'centuries old Unani system of medicine' as well as ancient physicians like ibn Sina and Galen feature in the promotional material of the company.[32] Sculptures at the entrance of the head office off Hamdard at Asaf Ali road, just on the border of old and New Delhi, aim at anchoring Hamdard in world medical history. Among the sculptures we find Abdul Majeed, the founder of Hamdard, in the company of the prominent Unani physician and freedom fighter Ajmal Khan and classical medical authorities such as Hippocrates, Galen and ibn Sina. These statues denote Unani *tibb*'s shared ancestry with Arabic and classical Western medicine.

Do all these images of traditional culture mean that Unani and Ayurvedic medicines are things of the past? Certainly not, for example in an advertisement for a 'brain tonic' the Central Drug Research Institute, a modern research centre based in Lucknow, is mentioned alongside the *Rig Veda*, the oldest of the four Vedas holding the greatest authority within Hinduism.[33] In the introduction to its latest therapeutic index Hamdard promises to open 'the doors of research' and enter 'an expansive world of discovery and research'.[34] Images of modern research and production technology are as important for the marketing of Indian indigenous pharmaceuticals as are references to tradition. Pestles and mortars are placed next to computers. A *rishi* is sitting in a test tube (Figure 11.1). Deified planets are combined with pictures of the latest equipment for chemical laboratory analyses. Company brochures contain pictures of modern factory buildings and halls equipped with modern production machinery such as huge metallic containers, electric ovens and packing machines.

Almost all promotional material from the three companies that are the focus of this chapter contain references to modern laboratory and clinical research. For

Figure 11.1 'Sage in a test tube'

Source: © Zandu Pharmaceutical Works Ltd.

instance, Dabur's booklet for 'Chyawanprash', the tonic named after the consummated sage, mentions research on the product by the Banaras Hindu University.[35] Modern medical journals such as the *Journal of the National Integrated Medical Association* and the *Indian Practitioner* are referred to in a brochure for 'Livotrit', Zandu's liver tonic.[36] Hamdard too is keen to offer modern scientific data to 'validate' or 'authenticate' its products. To boost the scientific image of its products Hamdard offers monetary rewards to scientists who do research on its best-selling products. Research monographs have been published on its 'super star product' 'Rooh Afza' as well as on its 'star products' 'Cinkara', a herbal tonic containing 'vitamins, minerals and trace elements', and 'Safi' (pure, just), Hamdard's 'blood purifier for the treatment of skin diseases'. These studies are published as Hamdard National Foundation Monographs. Since the 1970s Hamdard has been developing a new science called 'elementology' that seeks to provide a modern epistemological base for its products. International conferences devoted to elementology have been organised and occasionally Nobel prize winners have been invited to provide international glamour. With the profits of its products Hamdard has built its own university in New Delhi. Jamia Hamdard (Hamdard University) is equipped with laboratories and a hospital for conducting research on Unani and Ayurvedic medicines. Zandu and Dabur also have their own laboratories for researching their products. Indeed, to validate their products the producers of Ayurvedic and Unani medicines use modern research. Is this a new phenomenon caused by accelerated globalisation after the opening up of the Indian economy in the late 1980s and early 1990s? The answer should be negative because as early as the nineteenth century it was propagated that if Ayurveda and Unani wanted to survive these 'native systems should be studied historically and discriminated critically'.[37] Indian medical systems should improve by borrowing from modern medicine, 'the epistemological other'. Consequently dissection and modern pharmacological research became part of these medical traditions. This trend continued after independence with the creation of the Central Council of Research in Indian Medicine by the Indian government in 1970. Also, R.N. Chopra, a modern pharmacologist and the chairman of the first official commission on Indian Systems of Medicine that advised the Indian government in 1947, propagated the use of modern pharmacology because

> there are sure to be others [indigenous medicines] of little therapeutic value that are given merely because they are mentioned in some old manuscripts, and no one has taken the trouble to confirm the truth of these statements. Attempts must be made to separate the good ones from the useless ones and for this a systematic investigation of these drugs must be undertaken.[38]

How could 'certain spurious and superfluous formulations' creep into what has been called by Hamdard 'the vast treasure house of medicines?'. [39] This could be explained by a theory of decline as part of a revival movement that started in Bengal in the nineteenth century. These revivalists think of India's medical traditions as 'ruins that testified to a glorious past' and they propagated 'the revitalisation of tradition through modernity'.[40] Though Hindus and Muslims think of different periods when they speak of a glorious past when Ayurveda and Unani *tibb* flourished, both communities hold foreign rule responsible for their decline. Apart from justifying modern research for sifting the wheat from the chaff, this theory of decline implies the greatness of Indian medicine. 'A system that survived so many onslaughts must have a lot to offer', was the comment of the manager product development of Dabur.[41] This theory of decline as well as the past glory that is an integral part of it is still very much alive in the promotional material of the industry. For example, in the inaugural issue of the English version of its magazine *Ayurved-Vikas* (Blooming Ayurveda), Dabur explains the present subordinated state of Ayurveda by 'invasions' having 'disastrous effects on various aspects of ancient sciences'.[42] In the same article the heyday of Ayurveda is located in the Buddhist period which is projected as the period in Indian history in which 'basic human values' and 'the logical sciences' were prominent. Also, Zandu's symbol Dhanvantari, the Hindu god of medicine, refers to a period when Indian civilisation was at its zenith. A theory of former greatness is also part of the discourse within Unani *tibb*. 'Unani declined, because the British suppressed educated Muslims culturally, educationally and economically', I was told by the superintendent of the Unani wing of the teaching hospital of Jamia Hamdard.[43] Indeed, Unani *tibb* is often linked to the glories of the Indian Mogul empire. By associating their medicines with a glorious past the producers of Indian indigenous pharmaceuticals legitimise their products.

When modern science is the 'arbiter' does this mean that Ayurveda and Unani *tibb* are just adapting to biomedicine? This question has often been answered in the affirmative. For instance, Leslie has argued convincingly that modern Ayurveda, created through the professionalisation of the field in the nineteenth and twentieth century, differs from classical Ayurveda of the first millennium AD, as well as from the 'traditional culture' Ayurveda that marked the second millennium up to the nineteenth century.[44] In his view modern Ayurveda has many things in common with the way biomedicine is taught and practised in India. For instance, modern science dominates Ayurvedic and Unani colleges while the prescription of Western pharmaceuticals and biomedical disease categories are part and parcel of 'indigenous practice'. Likewise, other social scientists like Bala and Banerjee have argued that Indian systems of medicine have become standardised through their interaction with biomedicine and modernity at large.[45] According to Banerjee, Ayurveda has become 'formatted' and 'co-opted' by the 'capitalist enterprise' that she sees as typical of colonial and post-colonial India.

However, at the marketing level adaptation and resistance to biomedicine are paradoxically linked. For example, the slogans 'right effect, no side effect' and 'from deep within' that are used by Dabur represent a critique of Western medicines. Ayurvedic as well as Unani medicines are marketed as natural medicines without harmful side effects. Modern medicines 'have played havoc with the natural power of resistance of the human system', says the marketing brochure on Safi, Hamdard's 'blood purifier'. Modern drugs cause 'unheard of allergies and loss of immunity', because they testify to a 'one-symptom-one drug-one-action-mindset'.[46] With these slogans the industry addresses the fear of side effects of modern medicines. According to the marketing manager of Hamdard, using modern medicines is like 'printing money to fight inflation' because 'Western medicines cure on the one hand and make you sick on the other'.[47] 'Taking Western medicines is like an addiction because it never stops', was the comment of an Ayurvedic physician who runs an outpatient clinic owned by a South Indian manufacturer of Ayurvedic medicines.[48] Next to presenting Indian indigenous medicines as safe alternatives they also claim to be more effective in the long run. While 'Western medicine focuses mainly on the symptoms and not the cause of the illness',[49] Indian indigenous pharmaceuticals are marketed as medicines that fortify the immune system and therefore work 'from deep within'. These medicines have 'the right effect' because by regulating digestion and blood formation they take care of the formation of healthy humours and tissues. Indian medicines 'balance' organs, 'lubricate' tissues and 'clean' canals. Indeed, Indian physiology explains the efficacy of Ayurvedic and Unani medicines. They are said to fortify the innate human power for conserving health and fighting disease.

Natural medicines

Ayurvedic and Unani pharmaceuticals are represented as 'completely natural'. Natural ingredients such as fruits, flowers, vegetables, leaves, roots and minerals decorate labels, advertisements and promotional material for them. The Dabur company has chosen a tree as its company logo and Hamdard's brochures discuss the health benefits of the natural ingredients found in its products. In *Ayurved-Vikas*, Dabur's health magazine, a lot of attention is devoted to the medical proper-ties of 'Indian plant drugs' such as neem, tulsi and amla. A few years ago the firm

Zandu added a leaf to its company logo to emphasise the natural quality of its products. As natural medicines Ayurvedic and Unani pharmaceuticals are presented as green alternatives to 'modern curative agents' that are labelled 'synthetic'.[50] The safety and efficacy of these medicines is guaranteed because their 'ingredients are so well balanced that they cancel out possibly harmful effects on one another while bringing out – even boosting – the curative properties of each'.[51] Next to synergy – the joint action of medical ingredients as well as organ systems – immunity and vitality, which are closely connected within modern Ayurveda and Unani *tibb*, are important markers of contemporary Indian health traditions. To communicate the latter two concepts Hamdard uses the slogan '*hamara angrakshak*' (our bodyguard) in its marketing of 'Chyawanprash'. Both immunity-vitality and synergy are argued on technical grounds. In the case of immunity and vitality, terms such as free radicals, anti-oxidants, *kapha sleshma* (anabolic function) and *ojas* (vital energy)[52] which belong to different knowledge systems, are used simultaneously. But this technical discourse – clothed in biomedical as well as humoral terms – is at the same time, or at a deeper level, a moral discourse about 'wholesomeness' and 'naturalness' in which 'divine intelligence' and the natural order of the universe are important images.

The animated life force is central to the natural philosophy that forms the epistemological base of Indian health traditions.[53] This paradigm offers explicit guidelines for an appropriate way of living marked by 'naturalness', 'appropriateness' and 'wholesomeness'.[54] Indeed, *vaidyas* and *hakims* are naturalists who claim that their cures are based on both the products and the laws of nature. Both are seen as god-given. They are not based upon the mechanism of natural selection of modern science but upon a master plan. Indian health traditions represent the human body as a canopy of the soul and hold its owner responsible for keeping it in good shape. At the same time it is the task of the physician to provide patients with guidelines that seek to bring the body back to its natural state, i.e. health.[55] This places Ayurveda and Unani *tibb* in contrast to biomedicine as a laboratory science which sees illness as a natural object that can be manipulated by positivistic research designs and high-tech medical treatment. To emphasise the philosophical and spiritual status of their medical systems, the producers of Indian pharmaceuticals state that their products embody a 'whole philosophy of life and living'[56] and conquer the evil of disease. For example, in one of its brochures, Zandu phrased it like this:

> The God of Science of Ayurveda, Dhanvantari, with a pitcher containing Amruth (Nectar of Ambrosia), emerging out of the ocean, has a mythical significance to the great event of Samudra Manthan (churning of the Oceans), referred to in the Ved, Puranas and ancient Hindu literature. The emergence of Dhanvantari symbolizes the victory of whatever good and noble over evil.[57]

Zandu tells us that health conquers disease because its sacred medicines contain and activate the life force and therefore restore the body's natural order. In natural philosophies such as Ayurveda and Unani *tibb* disease is seen as preternatural, i.e.

not part of the 'natural order of things'. Treatment tries to restore the balance between the humours which, during illness, have degenerated from pillars that support the body into substances that undermine it. It is revealing that the Ayurvedic word for humour is *dosa*, which literally means 'fault' and 'trouble'.[58] Medicines and dietary and behavioural guidelines aim at balancing somatic components such as humours, tissues and organs. When bodily order has been restored the body's self-healing capacity automatically returns. Hence, it is argued that systems such as Ayurveda and Unani *tibb* do not force the body but rather guide it back to 'its natural pace of disintegration'. Likewise the phrase 'He is the healer' on top of Unani prescriptions indicates that medicines are 'only helpers from the outside' for activating the inner healing force. However as I have noted before, this capacity for self-healing only works well in an ordered body which means that the humoral balance and the life force are closely connected. By restoring the individual balance known as *dehaprakrti* in Ayurveda or *tabiat* in Unani *tibb*, Indian therapeutic agents are said to create the stamina to fight disease. Is this animated life force identical to the biomedical concepts of immunity and disease resistance which are linked to anti-bodies and vitamins? According to the head of the Department of History of Medicine of Hamdard University, the life force transcends these Western concepts because although

> the working of organ systems such as respiration, digestion and evacuation can be explained in physiological terms, these bodily functions are controlled by a conscious agent which cannot be named, measured or located.[59]

Indeed, according to those involved in Indian health traditions, somatic integration eventually depends upon a life force endowed with volition. This is not in contrast with the idea that natural substances such as herbs and minerals can restore health. On the contrary, as we have seen these 'material' substances are effective exactly because they are designed according to a master plan and therefore contain the life force that pervades the universe. This is in line with Indian traditional conceptions of the body in which the spiritual and the material are arranged in a hierarchy.

As we have seen, Indian medical traditions are based on a natural philosophy that provides guidelines for a healthy life that, by definition, is in harmony with the sacred, natural order. Ayurveda and Unani *tibb* provide a moral code that takes care of individual and social hygiene. Healthy bodies make a 'healthy' society and vice versa. Hence corrupted societies and corrupted bodies are dialectically related. Violation of the 'natural' code will lead to illness as illustrated by an Indian story in which the god Soma, the Moon, is punished for breaking a social rule. Because of an excessive passion for one of his wives Soma neglects his other spouses. Consequently the deified planet loses his unctuousness, which is closely related to vital energy, and becomes emaciated. Only by promising to behave properly in the future is the Moon restored to health. Indeed, according to Indian health traditions the body wastes away when the 'natural' rules of life which are engraved in the social code of a 'healthy' society, are violated.[60] Ignoring these rules brings a person into the state of *vikrti* (disorder, impairment of health). Because of a close association between somatic and social order, Ayurveda as well as Unani *tibb* are tailored to provide a vehicle to critique contemporary Indian society and Western therapeutic drugs that nowadays have a prominent place in Indian health care. In regard to medical traditions the marketing manager of Hamdard, stated: 'Indian medicines do not have the side effects of Western drugs, because our natural products embody traditional Indian values which lead to health'.[61] As I have argued in the previous section of this chapter, Indian medicines refer to the glory of the past when India was not a poor developing country but the epitome of civilisation. In contrast, the present is known as the Kali Yuga (the period of darkness), when 'immorality' rules the world. It is a time marked by 'the blurring of categories' and confusion about the right code of conduct. Indeed, a critique of Western medicines easily becomes a critique of modernity and a glorification of Indian traditional culture in which people are said to have followed the 'natural' rules for somatic, mental, spritual and social hygiene.

As a metonym for Westernisation, city life is criticised for providing an environment that denies people the means for a 'natural' life and therefore leads to somatic and mental stress. For example, according to a Zandu publication entitled *Swasth Jivan* (Healthy Life), the environment of contemporary Indian cities undermines the three pillars of health which are: wholesome diet, undisturbed sleep and 'sexual abstinence', i.e. the practice of sexuality according to social rules which usually means marital sexual relations.[62] *Vaidya* Lata, the author of this Hindi work that lists a selection of Zandu's products, states that these three guardians of health conflict with modern life which is marked by 'mental and environmental pollution'.[63] Returning to a 'natural' life-style, of which the consumption of Ayurvedic medicines is just one aspect, is offered as a solution for the ills of modernity. Likewise Dabur claims that 'the answer is now Ayurveda' because its medicines offer the antidote against:

> today's fast and competitive world ... [in which] stress and strain tell upon our health, our diet has become more synthetic and even the modern therapeutic agents are synthetic exposing us to toxins, resulting in various disorders.[64]

Apart from a critique of the synthetic character of Western medicines and the modern, artificial lifestyle to which they are said to belong, Dabur propagates the idea that its Ayurvedic preparations fight the venom created by a modern lifestyle. Indeed, Indian indigenous pharmaceuticals provide a vehicle to criticise Westernisation while also offering a solution for the health hazards caused by 'modern things' such as fast food, alcoholic drinks and excessive ambition. In the same line, Dabur's popular magazine, *Ayurved-Vikas*, blames 'the anger of city life' for 'modern' diseases such as hypertension, diabetes and impotence. In the same article the author strongly suggests that the city makes people prone to disease while its unnatural life deprives people of their inner healing force. Because of its 'unnaturalness' the city is called a 'non-environment' where the inhabitants live a 'machine life' that takes away their vitality and vigour. Within Indian health traditions diminishment of both natural forces is closely connected to disease as a brochure for Hamdard's sexual tonic 'Lahmina' illustrates:

> ... tiresome, demanding life of modern man can lead to general debility, listlessness, high blood pressure and a weak heart. And naturally, this weakness can drastically affect a man's sex life.

In this fragment weakness and sexual impotence as its most powerful image, is once more tied to modernity. Just as in the examples above, Hamdard's tonic embodies a critique of modernity while at the same time its producers promise relief from its ills. In the same line Dabur promises that its 'Chyawanprash' will provide 'the strength to fight and win the daily battle for survival'.[65] Indeed, Indian medicines are offered as antidotes against 'the poison of modernisation'.[66]

Within Indian symbolic contexts the spiritual and the material are not exclusive categories but part of a hierarchy in which matter is potentiated by the metaphysical realm. Nature and its products have both supernatural and physical dimensions, which are not as rigidly separated as they are in the West. When the producers of Indian indigenous pharmaceuticals claim superiority in terms of safety and efficacy they also refer to a metaphysical domain which is as real to them as the modern world containing their factories and laboratories.

Concluding remarks

Large producers of Indian indigenous pharmaceuticals shape Indian medical systems such as Ayurveda and Unani *tibb*. Their use of modern product forms such as capsules, pills and syrups as well as sophisticated production and packaging technology have changed the outlook of Indian bioceuticals. This modern image of Indian health products has been reinforced by marketing schemes, heavy advertising in media such as television and glossy magazines as well as laboratory research. By updating their products the three companies which are the focus of this chapter have changed the archaic image of Ayurveda and Unani *tibb* away from the domain of *vaidyas* and *hakims* dealing in outdated ideas and products.[67] They have made these 'traditional' systems contemporary. Hence for many Indians indigenous medicines are no longer substances prepared and prescribed by traditional healers but modern over-the-counter products used for self-medication.

Increasingly the consumption of Indian medicines has become an urban middle-class phenomenon. Consequently the importance of Indian medicines for diseases such as cholera, elephantiasis and goitre – health hazards that mainly affect the poor – has diminished. Nowadays, the industry projects its products as safe and effective remedies for both chronic and common diseases. The rise of chronic diseases among the Indian middle classes as well as the popularity of preventive health products among these groups has created a favourable epidemiological context for Indian indigenous pharmaceuticals. Because many of these new consumers have a modern education, the producers of Indian pharmaceuticals cannot only refer to traditional medical authorities for the marketing of their products.

Therefore, to legitimise their products the industry 'has added science to culture',[68] which means that they are 'reworked' by laboratory and clinical research. The action mechanisms of Indian medicines are both their researched chemical properties as well as their traditional and divine nature. They derive their power from a sacred and glorified past as well as from modern science. Indeed, like contemporary Indian culture indigenous medicines and the medical traditions to which they belong are hybrid phenomena.

In India it is often said that medical traditions such as Ayurveda and Unani *tibb* incorporate modern medicine in the sense that Ayurveda is the mother of all medical systems and Unani *tibb* has adhered to the truths of Hippocrates and Galen which biomedicine has forgotten.[69] This demonstrates that in the Indian arena traditional and modern medical systems are not considered to be exclusive. Indeed, at least at the rhetorical level the modern is enclosed by the traditional. From another angle it can be argued that Indian medical systems can be pictured as local modernities in the sense that these traditions have been modernised and globalised.[70] However, this does not mean that all medical options available in India boil down to the same thing. Indian medical traditions provide us with ideas and products that differ from biomedical ones. For instance, because Ayurveda and Unani *tibb* are based upon a natural philosophy and include prescriptions for a 'wholesome' life, patients are easily held responsible for their illnesses. Because these modern traditions ascribe illness to a damaged divine life force caused by violating the 'natural' laws of individual and social life, Ayurveda and Unani *tibb* are tailored for a critique on individual and collective lifestyles. Within such an ethical discourse modern life weakens bodies and makes them susceptible to disease. Ayurvedic and Unani pharmaceuticals are marketed as products that can protect and cure the body from the consequences of an 'unwholesome' way of living marked by the consumption of 'synthetic' food and medicines, competition and environmental pollution.

Indian health traditions and biomedicine are both part of contemporary Indian society and are therefore integrated into 'local symbolic contexts', which shape all medical options available in India. Therefore ideas and commodities such as therapeutic drugs are not the exclusive domain of one medical tradition. This is well demonstrated by medical practice in India. For example, Indian biomedical physicians 'have a strong faith in the medical beliefs of their forefathers' which shows itself in prescriptions for Ayurvedic or Unani drugs and the representation of health and disease as a 'moral enterprise'. At the same time, Western drugs and modern medical technology are part and parcel of 'traditional' practice. Indeed the traditional is found in the modern and the modern is in the traditional. Medical pluralism exists within rather than between medical systems. Traditional and modern medical forms are creatively rearranged in the Indian context. This should not surprise us as Indian society at large is marked by the entanglement of the modern and the traditional. After all, the people of the Indian subcontinent have a long history of integrating Indian and Western ideas, practices and commodities.

Acknowledgements

I have benefited from comments by Waltraud Ernst, Bernard Harris, Darshan Shankar, Ria Reis, Dick Plukker, Sjaak van der Geest, Klaas van der Veen, Urmila Thatte, N.B. Brindavanam, Vinay Kamat, and by discussions in the 'PhD club' of the Medical Anthropology Unit, University of Amsterdam.

Notes

1   In 1989–90 the Indian central and state governments spent Rs. 62.54 crores (US$ 15.64 million) on Indian Systems of Medicine, see the Ministry of Health and Family Welfare, *Indian Systems of Medicine and Homeopathy in India 1990*, 1993, p. 297. The turnover of Ayurvedic medicines alone was estimated by the industry to be between Rs. 1,500 crores (US$ 375 million) and Rs. 2,300 crores (US$ 575 million) in 1997. (The conversion to US dollars is based on the exchange rate in 1997 which was forty rupees to one US dollar.) These data are based on written enquiries made by the author. For comparison, the sale of Western medicines was estimated to be between US$ 2,650 million and US$ 3,000 million in 1997. Though the purchasing power of the Indian rupee went down by 50 per cent between January 1991 and January 1998 there remains a large gap between government expenditure on Indian medical traditions and the amount the public spent on indigenous medicines.

2   To my knowledge Charles Leslie was the first scholar who emphasised the importance of research on the indigenous industry for the study of contemporary Indian medical systems. See C. Leslie, 'Indigenous pharmaceuticals, the capitalist world system, and civilisation', *Kroeber Anthropological Society Journal* (1988): 23–31. I benefited greatly from the research materials on the indigenous industry that Charles Leslie handed over to me in 1995.

3   According to the Ministry of Health and Family Welfare on 31 December 1989 there were 7,648 licensed pharmacies producing indigenous pharmaceuticals. *Indian Systems of Medicine and Homeopathy in India 1990*, 1993, pp. 266–7.

4   These data come from two sources: 1) A personal letter from the General Secretary of the Kerala Drug Manufacturers Association of 18 February 1998, and 2) a speech by the manager of the Dabur Research Foundation delivered on 17 February 1998 at the 'International Conference About Medical Plants For Survival', held in Bangalore. The substantial difference in the two figures can be explained by the non-availability of production data of the majority of the 8,000 firms that produce Indian health products. Moreover, there are no official government data on this. The share of Dabur, Zandu and Hamdard in the total sale of Ayurvedic and Unani products is an educated guess based on the following data: 1) According to the assistant manager of the Dabur Research Foundation, the turnover of Dabur in 1997 was approximately Rs. 700 *crores* (US$ 175 million), of which approximately Rs. 500 *crores* (US$ 125 million) came from Ayurvedic products while the remaining amount was earned with the sale of products such as 'bulk drugs and chemicals' and 'food stabilisers'; 2) During an interview held in Delhi on 25 March 1999, the marketing manager of Hamdard told me that in the financial year 1997–8 the turnover of his company approximately amounts to Rs. 110 *crores* (US$ 37.5 million). In a letter dated 16 March 2000, the managing director of Zandu claimed a turnover of Rs. 110.78 *crores* in the financial year 1998–9. Zandu and Hamdard claim a yearly rise of their sales of around ten per cent, volume-wise, while the rise in the sales figures of Dabur is even bigger. For instance, according to data taken in September 2000 from the internet site (*<www.Dabur.com>*), the turnover of Dabur was Rs. 1035.83 *crores* (US$ 258.96 million) in the financial year 1999–2000. This suggests a substantial rise.

5   The translations of Hindi terms in this chapter are taken from R.S. McGreggor, *The Oxford Hindi–English Dictionary*, Oxford, Oxford University Press, 1993. In our times the word 'medicine' has largely become a reserved term for substances on which there exists a large body of modern laboratory and clinical research of which the results are laid down in professional journals.

6   For studies on the meaning of medicines see: S. van der Geest and S. Whyte (eds), *The Context of Medicines in Developing Countries. Studies in Pharmaceutical Anthropology*, Dordrecht, Kluwer Academic Publishers, 1988; S. van der Geest and S. Whyte, 'The charm of medicines: metaphors and metonyms', *Medical Anthropology Quarterly*, 3, 4 (1989): 346–67; and S. van der Geest, S. Whyte and A. Hardon, 'The anthropology of pharmaceuticals. A biographical approach', *Annual Review of Anthropology*, 25 (1996): 153–78.

7   See F. Zimmermann, 'The scholar, the wise man, and universals: three aspects of Ayurvedic medicine', in D. Bates (ed.), *Knowledge and the Scholarly Medical Traditions*, Cambridge, Cambridge University Press, 1995, pp. 297–319.

8   See Chapter 2 by Arnold and Sarkar in this volume.

9   Consult the contribution of Scheid to this volume (Chapter 8).

10 Mark Nichter speaks in this context of 'double think'. M. Nichter, 'Pharmaceuticals, health commodification, and social relations: ramifications for primary health care' in M. Nichter (ed.), *Anthropology and International Health. South Asian Case Studies*, Dordrecht, Kluwer Academic Publishers, 1989, p. 255.

11 G.C. Burman, director, (*<www.Dabur.com>*), September 2000.

12 This estimate is an educated guess based upon written and oral data of the sale of individual products and information about their marketing route. Moreover, in India it is common knowledge that many 'prescription' drugs are sold over the counter, i.e. the chemist does not always ask for a doctor's prescription.

13 There are two exceptions to this rule. First, companies belonging to the Kerala tradition such as the Arya Vaidya Shala and Arya Vaidya Pharmacy market their products via franchises. These franchises, as well as the hospitals of these companies, are run by qualified *vaidyas* holding a degree that is sanctioned by the government. These franchises as well as the company hospitals which resemble the 'Kurorts' of Germany and Austria, are mainly frequented by affluent middle-class people looking for relief from chronic diseases such as arthritis, spondylitis, digestive ailments, depression and sleeplessness. The second exception is the Himalaya Drug Company holding around 7 per cent of the market in Ayurvedic products. The Himalaya Drug Company has around 1200 medical representatives who market their products to physicians who have either a degree in Western medicine (MBBS), Ayurveda (BAMS) or Unani *tibb* (BUMS). The medicines of the Himalaya Drug Company are mainly adjuvants for mitigating the effects of Western medication as well as herbal alternatives for the treatment of common and chronic diseases. However, recently this company started an over-the-counter line called Ayurvedic Concepts. This confirms the increasing importance of the over-the-counter market for the sale of Indian indigenous pharmaceuticals. In this chapter no attention is paid to part-time traditional healers. Many of them prescribe medicines comprised of fresh herbs. See D. Shankar, 'Indigenous health services. The state of the art', in A. Mukhopadhyay (ed.), *State of India's Health*, New Delhi, Voluntary Health Association of India, 1992, p. 157. See also many articles on this topic published in the bimonthly *Amruth* of the Bangalore-based Foundation for the Revitalization of Local Health Traditions (FRLHT).

14 Interview with the director of a large Indian NGO, Bangalore, 5 January 1997. See also C. Leslie, 'Interpretations of illness. Syncretism in modern Ayurveda', in C. Leslie and A. Young (eds), *Paths to Asian Medical Knowledge*, Berkeley, University of California Press, 1992, p. 184.

15 For the practice of such an Ayurvedic physician in a government Out Patient Clinic, see V. Kamat, 'Reconsidering the popularity of primary health centres in India: a case study from rural Maharashtra', *Social Science and Medicine*, 41, 1 (1995): 87–98. For the biomedical Ayurvedic practice of government-trained Ayurvedic physicians in Sri Lanka see N. Waxler-Morrison, 'Plural medicine in Sri Lanka: Do Ayurvedic and western medical practices differ?', *Social Science and Medicine*, 27, 5 (1998): 531–44.

16 For the lack of Ayurvedic education in 'Ayurvedic' colleges, see R. Manohar and D. Shankar, 'Ayurveda today. Ayurveda at the crossroads', in J. v. Alphen and A. Aris (eds), *Oriental Medicine*, London, Serindia Publications, 1995, pp. 102–4.

17 Lecture given by Sanjib Datta Choudurry, PhD, entitled 'Whiskey advertisement in north India', University of Amsterdam, 3 September 1999.

18 This statement has been confirmed during an interview with the marketing manager of Dabur Pharmaceuticals Limited, Delhi, 26 November 1997. However, my consultation in December 2000 of Dabur's internet-site (<*www.Dabur.com*>) shows that the company has professionalised the marketing of its 'fast moving products'. For example, in the case of its newly launched digestive Pudin Hara G the company states that 'pre-launch research' and 'post-marketing surveillance' has been conducted.

19 Interview with the general manager for sales and marketing of Dabur, Delhi, 29 November 1997.

20 Interview with the assistant advertising manager of Hamdard, Delhi, 19 February 1999.

21 See S.C. Banerji, *A Companion to Sanskrit Literature*, Delhi, Motilal Banarsidass, 1971, pp. 29–31.

22 According to the company at the end of 1997 Dabur Chyawanprash had 25 million users and a turnover of Rs. 110 *crores* (US$ 27.5 million).

23 Interview with the assistant manager of Dabur Research Foundation, Delhi, 21 December 1997.

24 *India Today*, 10 May 1999.

25 In the case of Ayurveda, see F. Zimmermann, *The Jungle and the Aroma of Meats. An Ecological Theme in Hindu Medicine*, Berkeley, University of California Press, 1987, p. 177. See also F. Zimmermann, 'The love-lorn consumptive: south Asian ethnography and the psychosomatic paradigm', *Curare*, special issue 7, 91 (1991): 185–95.

26 'The History of Rooh Afza', Hamdard (wakf) Laboratories, 8 pp., no date, probably mid-1980s.

27 'Rooh Afza. Deliciously nutritious recipes. From a family favourite', Hamdard (wakf) Laboratories, 12 pp., no date, probably 1993.

28 A brochure with a *rishi* in a test tube on the cover issued by Zandu Pharmaceutical Works Ltd., no title, no date, probably from the early 1980s.

29 'Think health think Dabur Chyawanprash', Dabur India Limited, 8pp, no date, probably mid-1990s.

30 'A dream come true. Indian expertise, global perspective', Zandu Pharmaceutical Works Ltd., 8 pp., no date, probably 1997.

31 'Zandu, the company that bears the great name', Zandu Pharmaceutical Works Ltd., 4 pp., no date, probably end 1970s or beginning 1980s.

32 'Unani system of medicine. The natural way of healing', Hamdard (wakf) Laboratories, 2 pp., no date, probably mid-1990s. See also Hamdard's brochure for the promoting of its blood purifier 'Safi', titled 'Authoritative research findings on the inter-linkage of blood impurity and diseases of the skin and blood', Hamdard (wakf) Laboratories, 24 pp., no date, probably 1980s.

33 'Brento. Memory booster'. Product information of the Zandu Pharmaceutical Works Ltd., no date, probably from mid-1990s.

34 'Diseases and treatment. Health with Hamdard'. Therapeutic Index, Hamdard (wkf) Laboratories, 56 pp., no date, probably from mid-1990s.

35 'Think health think Dabur Chyawanprash', Dabur India Limited, 8pp, no date, probably mid-1990s.

36 'Alcohol damages but Livotrit protects', Zandu Pharmaceutical Works Ltd., 2 pp., no date, probably mid-1990s.

37 D. Kumar, 'Medical encounters in British India, 1820–1920', *Economic and Political Weekly*, 25 January 1997, p. 168.

38 R.N. Chopra *et al.*, *Indigenous Drugs of India*, Calcutta, Dhur and Sons, 1958 [1933], pp. 5–6.

39 'Diseases and treatment. Health with Hamdard'. Therapeutic Index, Hamdard (wkf) Laboratories, 56 pp., no date, probably from mid-1990s.

40 C. Leslie, 'The ambiguities of medical revivalism in modern India', in C. Leslie (ed.), *Asian Medical Systems*, Berkeley, University of California Press, 1976, p. 362.

41 Interview with the manager product development of Dabur Research Foundation, Ghaziabad, 4 November 1997.

42 *Ayurved-Vikas. A Complete Health Magazine*, Dabur India Publication, 1999 Inaugural Issue, p. 43.

43 Interview with the superintendent if the Unani *tibb* section of the Majeedia hospital, Jamia Hamdard, Delhi, 11 March 1999.

202   *Maarten Bode*

44 C. Leslie, 'The ambiguities of medical revivalism in modern India', in C. Leslie (ed.), *Asian Medical Systems*, Berkeley, University of California Press, 1976, pp. 356–67. See also C. Leslie, 'Pluralism and integration in the Indian and Chinese medical systems', in D. Landy (ed.), *Culture, Disease and Healing. Studies in Medical Anthropology*, New York, McMillan, 1977, pp. 511–18; and C. Leslie, 'Interpretations of illness. Syncretism in modern Ayurveda', in C. Leslie and A. Young (eds), *Paths to Asian Medical Knowledge*, Berkeley, University of California Press, 1992, pp. 177–208.

45 P. Bala, *Imperialism and Medicine in Bengal. A Socio-Historical Perspective*, New Delhi, Sage, 1991; M. Banerjee, *Power, Culture and Medicine: A Study with Special Reference to Ayurvedic Pharmaceuticals in India*, PhD thesis Delhi University, 1995.

46 'Authoritative research findings on the inter-linkage of blood impurity and diseases of the skin and blood', Hamdard (wakf) Laboratories, 24 pp., no date, probably 1980s; 'The 10 minute guide to Ayurveda', Dabur India Limited, no date, probably mid-1990s.

47 Interview with the marketing manager of Hamdard, Delhi, 25 March 1999.

48 Interview with the head physician of the outpatient clinic of the Arya Vaidya Pharmacy, Delhi, 28 October 1997.

49 'Unani system of medicine. The natural way of healing', Hamdard (wakf) Laboratories, 2 pp., no date, probably mid-1990s.

50 'Dabur Ayurvedic specialities', Therapeutic index, Dabur India Limited, 206 pp., 1995.

51 'Think health think Dabur Chyawanprash', Dabur India Limited, 8 pp., no date, probably mid-1990s.

52 According to G. Obeyesekere, 'Science, experimentation, and clinical practice in Ayurveda', in C. Leslie and A. Young (eds), *Paths to Asian Medical Knowledge*, p. 176, *ojas* is the 'vitality that infuses our body'. In a more religious context *ojas* is seen as the seat of *prana* (vital breath) which endows five premordial elements (*mahapancabhuta*) with life. In the English language version of its magazine *Ayurved-Vikas* Dabur defines *oj*, the Hindi equivalent of the Sanskrit *ojas*, as 'the essence of all *dhatus*' (bodily tissues) and 'the essence of our energy'.

53 See for Ayurveda, F. Meyer, 'Introduction', in J. van Alphen and A. Aris (eds), *Oriental Medicine*, London, Serindia Publications, 1995, pp. 11–15, and for Unani *tibb* Chapter 4 of Claudia Liebeskind in this volume.

54 For an exposé about morals in classical and modern medical traditions, consult B.S. Turner, 'Disease and disorder', in his *The Body and Society*, London, etc., Sage Publications, 1996, pp. 197–215. The naturalisation of 'the work of culture' is an important topic of discourse for anthropologists and social historians, and perhaps even more so for those involved in women studies. For example, consult B. Good, 'Semiotics and the study of medical reality', in B. Good, *Medicine, Rationality, and Experience. An Anthropological Perspective*, Cambridge, Cambridge University Press, 1994, p. 114, for the naturalisation of gender differences through the idiom of 'Greco-Islamic' medicine. See also on this topic: B. Good and M. DelVecchio Good, 'The comparative study of Greco-Islamic medicine: the integration of medical knowledge into local symbolic contexts', in C. Leslie and A. Young (eds), *Paths to Asian Medical Knowledge*, Berkeley, University of California Press, 1992, pp. 267–8. For the way the biomedical discourse in the 18th and 19th centuries did 'intermediate' gender differences consult L. Jordanova, *Sexual Visions. Images of Gender in Science and Medicine between the Eighteenth and Twentieth Centuries*, Hertfordshire, Harvester Wheatsheaf, 1989, pp. 1–18.

55 In Ayurveda the term *svasthya* (health), 'being established in oneself', refers to the fact that health is considered to be the normal state of a human being.

56 A brochure featuring a *rishi* in a test tube on the cover issued by Zandu Pharmaceutical Works Ltd., 6 pp., no title, no date, probably from the early 1980s.

57 'A dream come true. Indian expertise, global perspective', Zandu Pharmaceutical Works Ltd., 8 pp., no date, probably 1997.

58 For the Ayurvedic humours, *kapha*, *vata* and *pitta*, which in disease become the body's troubles (*dosa*), see G. Obeyeskere, 'The theory and practice of psychological medicine in the Ayurvedic tradition', *Culture, Medicine and Psychiatry*, 1, 2 (1977): 155–81. Leslie qualifies Ayurveda as a 'moral enterprise', C. Leslie, 'Interpretations of illness. Syncretism in modern Ayurveda', in C.

Leslie and A. Young (eds), *Paths to Asian Medical Knowledge*, Berkeley, University of California Press, 1992, p. 202.

59 Interview Delhi, 5 March 1999. See also 'Unani system of medicine. The natural way of healing', Hamdard (wakf) Laboratories, 2 pp., no date, probably mid-1990s.

60 For the dialectical relationship between corrupt bodies and a corrupt state in the contemporary Indian, see J. Alter, 'Gandhi's Body, Gandhi's Truth: Nonviolence and the Biomoral Imperative of Public Health', *Journal of Asian Studies*, 55, 2 (1996): 301–22.

61 Interview with the marketing manager of Hamdard, Delhi, 19 February 1999.

62 W.S. Lata, *Swasth Jiwan* (Healthy Life), Bombay, Leopard Investments, 1990, p. 2.

63 Interview 17 April 1996.

64 'Dabur Ayurvedic specialities', Therapeutic index, Dabur India Limited, 1995, p. iii.

65 Many more examples can be given. For instance, Zandu's liver tonic 'Livotrit' is marketed as a panacea against modern things such as 'potent drugs', 'increased consumption of alcohol' and viruses that stand for 'environmental pollution'.

66 M. Bode, 'On the consumption of Ayurvedic pharmaceuticals in India. Extracting the poison of modernisation', in A. Gevers (ed.), *Uit de Zevende Faculteit. Vijftig Jaar Politieke en Sociaal-Culturele Wetenschappen aan de Universiteit van Amsterdam* (From the Seventh Faculty: Fifty Years of Political and Social Sciences in Amsterdam), Amsterdam, Het Spinhuis, 1998, pp. 367–78.

67 See also the conclusion of Chapter 3 by Arnold and Sarkar in this volume.

68 Interview with the assistant manager of Dabur Research Foundation, Ghaziabad, 24 March 1999.

69 See Chapter 6 by Ria Reis in this volume in which she draws our attention to the hybridisation of traditional and modern medical ideas and practices in Swaziland.

70 See also Chapter 8 by Volker Scheid in this volume.

12 Health for sale

Quackery, consumerism and the internet

Michael Hardey

In the summer of 1998, a webcast of a woman giving birth attracted an internet audience of nearly one and half million. The following year an electronic auction house received bids of several million dollars for a kidney that was offered for sale on its web site. In October 1999 *The Observer* newspaper in the United Kingdom carried a story about a fashion photographer who published a web page containing photographs of models who were offering to sell their eggs to help make the 'perfect baby'. Before it was approved for consumption in the United Kingdom the prescription drug 'Viagra' was widely available through orders placed on the internet. The medical research database 'Medline' in the United States was used for an average of seven million searches a year in the early 1990s. In 1997 it was made available through the internet to any user and is now involved in over a hundred and eighty million searches a year. About a third of these searches are undertaken by members of the public. In the same year the US Food and Drug Administration (FDA) issued a warning to the public about the 'significant, possibly life-threatening health risks' arising from the use of home abortion kits and female self-sterilisation kits that were advertised on the internet.[1] Statistics about internet use are difficult to compile.[2] However, it has been estimated that over 40.9 million adults in the United States used the internet for health information in the first three months of 2000.[3] In the United Kingdom the home based use of the internet increased over 109 per cent between 1998 and 1999.[4]

The headline-making reports above illustrate some of the more public manifestations of the impact of the internet on the production and consumption of health services, advice and products. The internet is a central part of the new Information and Communication Technologies (ICTs) that include mobile phones and digital television. It has been variously described as a 'consensual hallucination',[5] a 'virtual community',[6] 'cyberspace' and the 'electronic frontier'. This new electronic space is an inherently interactive environment that transcends national boundaries, regulations and cultures. Through a simple graphical interface users can move seamlessly between different forms of health information, practitioners, beliefs and lifestyles. Like any new territory, the internet is rapidly becoming populated by new users who have discovered a resource through which they can publish their experiences, learn about treatments, and lifestyles and make decisions about their health care. The potential social and economic impact of the internet is such that is has been described as the most significant technological advance since the development of the printing press.[7]

Globalisation and health pluralism

The internet has become the generic term used to describe the transmission of digital data between computers according to various protocols and includes the world wide web (WWW), email, usenet newsgroups, chat rooms and other systems of distributing and viewing data. The WWW is based on hypertext which, together with a graphical-based browser, enables users to simply 'point and click' their way across the internet. Estimates of the extent and growth of the internet are diverse, but all point to a massive increase in content and users. In 1993 there were an estimated 623 web sites on the internet.[8] An estimate of the total number of web sites made six years later was over 5.4 million.[9] The number of people with access to these resources is also increasing, with an estimated 11,100 new users per day in the UK.[10] There is a higher rate of domestic computer ownership in the United States but in both cases households with a lower income are less likely to have a domestic connection to the internet.[11] However, workplaces, schools, public libraries and cybercafés also provide public access to computers and information technologies.

As part of globalisation the internet has been associated with the ascendancy of Western medicine. This can be illustrated by examples relating to the practice of medicine and to the spread of medical knowledge. First, email has been used for many years by medical scientists and doctors to support colleagues located in other parts of the globe.[12] It has also become possible for surgery to be conducted through a surgical robot that is at some distance from the principal surgeon. What is described as 'telemedicine' is increasingly being used to deliver Western health care to patients in countries where there are strong indigenous medical traditions. Secondly, biomedical education has taken advantage of the internet to transform local educational services into global resources. These include the National Library of Medicine, which provides students with access to a library of medical images and interactive learning resources. More dramatically, the project provides a complete, anatomically detailed, three-dimensional representation of the male and female human body. Consisting of magnetic resonance images, computed tomograms and cryoscopic sections taken at 1mm intervals, students can 'fly' through the body or study sections in ways impossible in conventional anatomy texts. Western notions of the body and medicine education therefore become local resources for students and others across the globe.

The internet connects people directly to medical and health resources. These include medical libraries and databases, information intended for consumers and published by government organisations such as the National Health Service (NHS) in Britain, individual doctors and practitioners of alternative health care. In addition, through newsgroups and personal web pages people are able to broadcast their experiences of ill health and provide advice to others.[13] This proliferation of information, advice and services on the internet represents a challenge to what has been described as the medical monopoly of expertise and knowledge.[14] It is not therefore surprising that the medical professions have viewed public access to this information with a degree of caution if not hostility. This caution partly reflects the predominance of evidence-based health care that holds that the 'gold standard' for the evaluation of treatments is the randomised controlled trial (RCT). Broadly, it is argued that the public may be exposed to risks by changing their health behaviours in line with information which they may not have understood. Moreover the information may be misleading, incorrect or harm the relationship between doctor and patient. It is also argued that people may consult medical or alternative health practitioners that are not directly involved in their care in order to challenge the competence of their doctors.[15] There are similarities here to the earlier struggle by the medical profession to mark out a territory of expertise and to establish a monopoly of practice by seeking to marginalise competing therapists through a discourse about 'quackery'.[16] One report, while recognising that doctors are increasingly using non-orthodox approaches in patient care, warns that use of internet information that is not produced by medically qualified authors is 'tantamount to information malpractice'.[17]

The attempts by the medical profession to shape users' access to health information on the internet should be seen within the broader context of increasing public scepticism about medicine. In the United Kingdom there have been a number of major scandals involving prestigious medical institutions. At the Bristol Royal Infirmary three doctors have been found guilty of serious professional misconduct after the deaths of twenty-nine babies. Enquires continue into the practice of removing and storing children's organs without their parents' consent. A general practitioner has been convicted of murdering fifteen elderly patients. The General Medical Council, which is responsible for the conduct and registration of doctors, has been criticised for protecting its members rather than the public in the face of long delays in malpractice cases. What has become known as 'mad cow' disease, the dangers of *E. coli* 0157 infection, genetically modified food and many other 'health scares' have captured public attention and highlighted uncertainty and disagreement amongst medical experts.[18] In the face of growing public disquiet the Department of Health has made the provision of information to the public a key policy objective.[19] The internet is regarded as central to this strategy. The potential of providing consumers with information can be seen in the Massachusetts Board of Registration in Medicine internet database of all doctors that includes details of their education, experience and any disciplinary action. However, compared to the United States, there is little information available to the public about individual doctors, the performance of specialist hospitals or the services available in different parts of the United Kingdom.

Many general practitioners refer patients to complementary practitioners and an increasing number of doctors practise some form of complementary medicine.[20] However, the policy discourse about evidence-based practice reflects the medical profession's established response to non-orthodox therapies, and places doctors in the role of guardians of the public interest and safety.[21] This has produced various attempts to develop a standard for the reliability of medical information within the internet. National and international groups, such as Health on the Net Foundation, British Healthcare Internet Association, Internet Healthcare Coalition, and Health Internet Ethics, have all produced criteria against which internet information can be assessed. The global and dynamic nature of the internet as well as the sheer volume of information means that it is impossible to monitor or regulate the flow of material. However, effort has been directed at establishing a 'gold standard' or 'ethical principles' for internet health sites. The idea here is that information providers could display a logo to indicate to consumers that they adhere to a clear set of principles. A different approach had been proposed by the World Health Organisation (WHO) which was attempting to establish a new top-level domain name. Commonly used top-level domain names include 'dot-com' for commercial web sites or 'dot-ac' for academic sites. However, WHO has so far failed in its proposal of a 'dot-health' domain which would only be granted to sites that comply with criteria that ensure the reliability of their health information and advice. The advantage of this approach would be that it would be possible to regulate a particular domain and not involve removing or prohibiting sites from the internet as a whole. Should this proposal be adopted consumers would know that a 'dot-health' site would, for example, not promote or advertise 'unproven' treatments. However, the unregulated diversity of the internet would still be available to consumers.

Researching the internet

As a new and rapidly changing phenomenon, there are few clear methods that have been established to research the internet.[22] This chapter draws on a study of internet users in the United Kingdom and a survey of health-related web pages that have been devised and published on the internet by lay people. The case study of users was based on ten households in the United Kingdom. Collaboration with an internet service provider (ISP) allowed households who used the internet at home to be recruited through an email about the research. All the households described their members as 'healthy' although some contained people who had asthma and eczema. They also had at least one school-aged child and none of the participants had any professional health care qualifications. Over the course of a year two face-to-face interviews were undertaken with the adults in each household. The majority of interviews lasted between one and two hours each and focused on a range of topics related to health and the internet. The interviews were tape recorded and transcribed. Analysis followed a grounded theory approach whereby themes are identified through the 'constant comparative method' that validates the categories against the data they are grounded in.[23]

The internet survey involved an examination of home pages constructed by people that contain accounts of their experiences of ill health. The web pages were identified by using internet search engines, newsgroup correspondence and chat room exchanges. The key words 'my' and 'illness' were initially used to identify web pages. A search was also undertaken using the words 'asthma', and 'multiple sclerosis'. These were chosen as representing conditions that could have an impact on individuals' way of life. In addition, where links were made to other personal pages, these were followed. Thirty-eight newsgroups formed around health and illness topics were monitored to identify any home pages that were posted by participants.

Finally, ten chat rooms about health were monitored for six hours over five evenings to provide further personal pages that participants noted during the course of exchanges. A final total of 132 personal pages were identified through this combination of strategies and about half of these originated in the United States. The web pages were printed and saved onto a computer hard drive. A questionnaire was also sent via email to those authors who published their email address on their web page. Analysis followed the approach adopted in the household case study. It is not claimed that the sample is representative of the entire population of personal web page authors but it is unlikely to be untypical of those concerned with health and illness. In this chapter, I have followed the convention of making the responses to the questionnaire anonymous. The home pages are in the public domain and these have been cited where relevant by providing the URL from which the page was originally accessed. It should be noted that due to the dynamic nature of the internet these home pages may have been removed or subject to wholesale reconstruction since they were accessed for the purposes of this paper.

Dealing with diversity and finding health information

The size and dynamic nature of the internet mean that it can be a confusing and intimidating place. It is rather like a vast collection of books, films and other media that have been dumped in an immense building and are continually added to without any attempt to catalogue the contents. However, a new industry has developed to provide users with a way to organise this apparent chaos. Internet directories, search engines, and portals provide various kinds of maps through which destinations can be identified and journeys undertaken. ISPs and other organisations provide sites or portals that they hope users will use as their initial starting place to the internet. Portals provide structured links to other parts of the internet as well as many resources within the organisation's web resources. The BBC web site is a good example of a portal that contains a large amount of material and annotated links to other parts of the internet. Users can set their web browser to automatically begin any internet session from such a portal site. There are clear commercial possibilities opened up to sites that have the high number of users typical of portal sites. Internet directories typically consist of a list under various headings, such as health, medicine and so forth, that contain annotated links to other sites. With increasing competition between ISPs the quality, extent and ease of use of directories has become important in retaining subscribers.

Richard took part in the household case study and described how he identified information about asthma:

> Sarah [his ten-year old daughter] has asthma. So we were curious to see what there was on the net about it. I started off by going through Yahoo [a

hierarchical directory of links] and found the Asthma Campaign [National Asthma Campaign based in the UK] had a web page. We already had information from them, but we do use this site quite a lot as it has very up to date news and things. Sarah liked their kids' page which I think helps make her feel that she is like lots of other children. ... I was interested in alternative medicine and used a search engine to find sites. Lots of things came up but most were in the States [USA].

Richard's short description shows how users move seamlessly through material that includes medical and alternative medical information from across the globe. Accessing information that originated in other countries can be problematic. For example, reflecting the market-orientated health care system in the United States, many American medical web sites are designed to enable users to type in the names of prescription drugs. This can pose a problem for European users because drugs may be marketed under different names. For example, a drug like benzoyl peroxide that is widely used to treat acne is available in forms that range from a gel to a soap bar, with product names that range from 'Acne-Aid Vanishing Cream' (USA) to 'Xerac BP 5' (Canada). However, although some users included in the study found this frustrating, most had found information about prescription drugs used by members of their household. Jane explained how she discovered information about her prescription drug:

> I was given these antibiotics but they gave me thrush and I couldn't sleep. My GP wasn't terribly helpful, but when we looked up anti-biotics we found a lot about what they could do to you ... you know, side effects that they don't bother explaining to you. Anyway we also found a lot about natural treatments that did not involve drugs as such ... Allergies are probably a lot to do with my problem, so I'm trying this diet we found out about and I'm seeing a homoeopath.

Jane's account illustrates how the diversity of internet health information can shape health behaviours and potentially challenge the treatment provided by medical practitioners. A more deliberate attempt to move beyond the boundaries of biomedicine through the internet is contained in Andrew's account:

> My mother is, well, something of a health fanatic. She had been on at me about chiropractice after I did my back in [minor injury incurred while playing football]. The amount of information about it [back pain] was surprising. I found a lot of interesting things mostly from America [USA] but some from here [UK]. Quite a lot of things were strange about the whole thing but the idea about a pinched nerve and manipulation made a lot of sense. I also knew that it wouldn't do me any harm to give it a go.

Both Jane and Andrew's accounts indicate that the internet is providing users with the knowledge to 'shop around' for therapies and make informed choices about their treatment. The internet therefore encourages people to act as consumers of health rather than patients who only have recourse to medical practitioners.

Apart from search engines and directories, the links provided by individual web sites provide the other major route to health information for users. There is increasing competition between web sites to provide useful links to other sites. A dilemma here for medical sites is the degree to which the publication of a link to another site constitutes a recommendation or the recognition that it fulfils a quality protocol. Indeed it can be argued that medical practitioners involved in the publication of internet information have an ethical responsibility to ensure that all their material is reliable. Rose describes how she has greater faith in information provided by medical centres:

> I feel you can be reasonably confident that the information on the medical sites is reliable. Lots of things [sites] come from America [USA] and you can find out about treatments that may not yet have reached here [UK]. I mean I trust information from medical centres more than I would from some other places but would not just look at those.

Interviewer: Why?

> It depends on what I'm looking for but because it is easy to look at lots of sites I tend to dig around until I think I've had enough.

The accounts above show the ways in which users seek out information and make choices about what they read. The classic sociological formulation of the 'sick role' holds that the patient will seek medical treatment and adhere fully to medical advice.[24] There is supposed to be a relationship of trust between patient and doctor that also implies that the patient is unable to access or understand medical information. This model of the doctor/patient relationship is challenged by the policies that advocate patient choice (albeit within a medical context) and the internet.[25] However, health practitioners continue to act as the route to many medical and social services. This makes it difficult for consumers to make many health decisions independent of medical advice or treatment. Despite such restrictions the extract below taken from the web page of a woman who has asthma shows how the transition from the 'patient role' to the active health consumer envisioned by Giddens is being promoted by the internet.[26]

> I have had asthma ever since I can remember. I have designed this page to help you to cope with living with asthma and to share my experiences and that of other sufferers. I am an IT consultant not a nurse or a doctor. But I am an expert in my own asthma. For me the experience of others has been far more helpful than any amount of medical aids and treatment. I'm not saying you should abandon all medical treatment but you should take charge of your treatment and make sure your GP will treat you in the ways that you want. This Web Site contains an account of my own treatment, that of others who have sent me their stories, email advice and links to other useful sites. You can also find information about how natural remedies may help you.

There is information about acupuncture, hypnotherapy [there follows a long list of approaches with hypertext links to different parts of the site] ... This site is not sponsored by any medical or drug company.[27]

Lay expertise, narratives and support

The extract above represents the growing number of web pages or 'home pages' constructed by individuals who suffer from a chronic illness or other on-going health problem. In design and content such web pages may include personal accounts of illness, diaries, life histories and complex interactive sites which provide on-line advice.[28] The publication of a personal account of illness provides the author with a global audience. The internet is unique in that the most disabled or stigmatised individual has access to the same mode of expression as the able-bodied. In constructing and publishing a narrative, individuals are making sense of illness in an active and constructive process,[29] in contrast to the largely passive response to external circumstances envisaged by the 'sick role'. Furthermore, the boundary between the *patient* or *consumer* of health information and advice and that of the *producer* of health information and advice is becoming blurred.

A common theme in internet narratives is the author's interaction with health professionals as he or she worked through a lengthy period between the onset of symptoms and a formal diagnosis. It is here that the author's desire for a clear aetiology or therapy for the condition often leads them to explore different approaches to health or, on occasion, religious interventions. Some narratives are constructed with the intention of 'converting' visitors to a particular therapy or approach that the author has benefited from. In addition to the publication of web pages, usenet news groups and chat rooms also provide an important source of lay narratives and advice. The former are arranged around specific topics and can be originated and accessed by any user. Like email, users can view previous 'conversations' and contribute to them. In contrast, chat rooms represent a form of instant communication that is again arranged around different topics. Users enter and leave chat rooms and may contribute to the 'conversations' taking place in 'real time'. There are an estimated 29,613 newsgroups and almost every imaginable health-related topic has a dedicated group. In the early part of 2000 it was estimated that approximately 30,000 people posted messages to newsgroups each day and that there were over one million passive readers.[30] Specific groups can be identified by using search engines or usenet resources such as 'Deja News'. Within news groups and chat rooms people exchange experiences and share their knowledge with others. This sharing of stories and advice is particularly important in relation to rare diseases that have few sufferers in any one country. Feelings of isolation or stigma may be overcome by becoming part of what has been described as a 'virtual community of care'.[31]

Given the diversity of news groups it is hard to capture a typical exchange. However, the edited extract below which was taken from a discussion topic from

212 Michael Hardey

'alt.support.asthma' captures a sense of the interactions within news groups (original spelling, punctuation and terminology have been retained).

Topic: Curious about vitamins for asthma...
From: Kate

Hello Everyone!!

    I recently learned that there are some vitamins out there that are excellent for asthma including Magnesium, Vitamin C, Vitamin B6 & B12, and some other various herb remedies as well. Can anyone here tell me if they've used these vitamins and remedies and if you have, how well have they worked for you? Right now, I take Vitamin C, and the B vitamins, and they seem to be doing some sort of good although I'm not really going to know until I'm off of my prescription medication.

    I have also learned about a magnesium/zinc/calcium complex tablet that's good to take for asthma. Does such a tablet exist?? If so, where can I find it?

Topic: Re: Curious about vitamins for asthma...
From: John

The only people making these claims are the frauds who want to get at the contents of your wallet. This is a subject that has been studied in clinical trials and the conclusions are that these are of no value in the treatment of asthma.

    'I have also learned about a magnesium/zinc/calcium complex tablet that's good to take for asthma. Does such a tablet exist?? If so, where can I find it?'

    You can find it at any vitamin store. Of course, it is useless for the treatment of asthma. Have some fun with the people trying to sell the stuff to you. Ask them for citations from medical research journals that validate their claims to current scientific standards. Then when they cannot, remind them that fraudulent claims of health benefits are a felony in the US.

Topic: Re: Curious about vitamins for asthma...
From: Kate

Are you a doctor?

Topic: Re: Curious about vitamins for asthma...
From: John

No. Just somebody who has read (and understood) the source scientific documents on the subject.

    I'm a big believer in alternative medicine wherever it can be effective -- and there are some areas where it is better than conventional medicine -- but it is NOT effective when it comes to asthma. By all means, take vitamins to ensure that you are getting proper nutrition. Vitamin C does have a mild antihistamine effect, which might help somewhat. But don't fool around with asthma — there are no alternative meds out there that really work. Conventional medicine has the right answers for asthma — inhalers and anti-inflammatory meds.

In common with most interactions within newsgroups devoted to health problems the above is an example of an exchange between people who experience a specific problem and want to share their ideas.[32] The exchange shows that users may question the status of members who appear to be offering advice that they anticipate as coming from medical experts. Indeed, it is the advice of people who experience asthma that is valued and some may be inhibited from offering their experiences to an audience that includes health professionals.[33] Scepticism about medical advice is also reflected in the following extract from the case study research:

> The way I look at it, the way you hear about all those doctors who make the wrong diagnosis or otherwise mess up their patients lives, it is important to make up your own mind and listen to people who have experience of asthma.

There is a sense in which those more active in newsgroup advice giving or those who construct their own web pages like 'hystersisters' become, in de Swaan's term, 'proto-professionals'.[34] The newsgroup exchange also illustrates the kind of dialogue that may have an effect on users' health behaviours. This is particularly important when it is remembered that for every person that actively takes part in the exchange, it is estimated that there are as many as twenty passive readers.[35] Like lay advice offered, for example, at a family gathering, there is no reason to suppose that advice offered through a newsgroup will prove to be any more reliable according to clinical criteria. It is therefore not surprising that studies of newsgroup advice have found that much is inappropriate or inaccurate from a clinical perspective.[36] Newsgroups may also be aimed at particular age groups with the intention of providing a space where children and adolescents can exchange experiences about living with chronic illnesses and give voice to emotions and feelings. People with what they regard as stigmatising conditions may seek the anonymity of the internet to develop friendships and support networks. The internet is a space where there is little 'gamble'[37] involved in exposing intimate feelings. Indeed one of the first uses of the usenet system was to support and campaign for people infected with HIV/AIDS. However, such positive aspects of the internet have been questioned and it has been claimed that at least one attempted suicide has resulted from participation in a newsgroup.[38]

Consumption, pluralism and risk

While the content of newsgroups can expose users to risk it is the global nature of the medium, combined with the new opportunities this creates for the consumption and production of health advice and services, that has attracted most attention. The rise of electronic commerce has been described as a 'gold rush' in which 'countless firms will be transformed … including publishing, banking, retailing and deliverers of health care'.[39] The internet provides the means for goods and services to transcend national boundaries and regulations. Advertisements for products that apparently treat obesity, impotence, baldness and virtually any broadly defined health problem are scattered around the internet. In the United Kingdom the direct advertising of prescription drugs to consumers is prohibited. However, direct advertising to consumers has rapidly expanded in the United States and the internet provides a conduit to a global market.[40] Furthermore, pharmaceutical products that are not approved or illegal in one country can be advertised and purchased through the internet. The following advertisement that was distributed to newsgroups and formed an advertising banner on web sites, captures the subversive potential of the internet.

> Viagra by mail-order, and no need to bring a prescription either! Viagra on the web: The easiest and most discreet way to end impotence. Viagra, right over the internet. For as low as $6 per dose. Buy Viagra DIRECT now.

Since this advertisement, Viagra has crossed the boundary from clinical to a recreational drug, known as 'V' and 'poke'.

The tensions between the open nature of the internet, lay users and regulation can be illustrated by drawing an example from the alt.support.psoriasis newsgroup.[41] A product called 'Skin-Cap' was claimed to be a remedy for the unsightly, frequently painful and potentially debilitating skin disease psoriasis. Skin-Cap was advertised on many newsgroups and other health-related sites. The product was widely available in Spain and some other countries but its sale and use was prohibited in the United States and elsewhere. Medical authorities were concerned about a steroid constituent of the product that was thought to have a potentially dangerous interaction with other commonly prescribed psoriasis treatments. However, people who purchased Skin-Cap often found that it dramatically reduced their symptoms. Newsgroups and chat rooms quickly filled with recommendations for the product. These positive accounts were soon followed by warnings from people who had experienced severe side effects. In 1998 the FDA banned the importation of Skin-Cap into the United States. The demand for Skin-Cap engendered through the internet had created a new market for similar products. Within days of the ban on Skin-Cap, a new product manufactured in Spain, called 'BlueCap', was being marketed on the internet.

As the account above suggests the internet, by providing opportunities for the consumption of health products, exposes users to potential risks. However, the following extract from the case study suggests that users are wary of relying on such information:

> I know that using the internet doesn't provide all the answers. But it does give lots of information which we have never been able to see before … as well as contacts with people who have personally experienced asthma. … So, you have to be careful, because you can't just take everything seriously. I find that

I balance up the advice, you know, from the net and doctors. I decide what to take seriously and obviously I wouldn't buy any drugs or anything like that from the net. As I say that would be too risky.

The extract above suggests that access to internet information means that medicinal knowledge is not accepted uncritically. Indeed this can be seen, as Giddens argues, as part of the 're-appropriation' of individuals' critical skills and scepticism that 'relate[s] to all aspects of social life, for example medical treatments, child rearing, or sexual pleasure'.[42] However, this re-appropriation or re-skilling may also have negative aspects in that access to information may engender anxiety and make it difficult for people to make choices about their health.[43] Furthermore, the use of internet information and advice to make demands on health care providers for treatment and services may further disadvantage those who lack the resources or do not desire to use the internet.

Conclusions

Since the emergence of Western biomedicine as a dominant belief system it has generated ever more 'exotic' and inaccessible knowledge.[44] Foucault argued that doctors used this knowledge to re-work the confessional, whereby anxieties are transformed into a therapeutic language so they can be categorised and controlled.[45] Turner has also drawn attention to how doctors use their 'social monopoly of expertise and knowledge'[46] to manage encounters and perpetuate their position of power over patients.[47] This chapter has shown that the internet constitutes a new space in which the categories of, and boundaries between, knowledge and expertise are contested. It is enabling patients to take a leading role in determining their own health and challenge the prevailing relationship found in the consulting room.[48] Advertising, advice, electronic commerce, health promotion and health education material are presented to users through the computer screen. In addition, the beliefs, experiences and advice of others who may share a particular health problem are freely available. Indeed, by providing space for personal stories and experiences the internet is capturing something of the tradition of telling stories and passing on moral tales found in cultures with a predominately oral tradition. As medical authorities have pointed out, such experiences and advice do not accord with the practice of modern evidence-based medicine. However, Beck and Giddens have argued, ideas about 'risk' are central to contemporary Western lifestyles.[49] From the public perspective scientific medical practice is far from risk-free and it may in fact expose the public to risk. The provision of a code of ethics or other standard for health information that might be accessed through a new dot-health domain may help users assess the reliability of material they find on the internet.

Within the space of the internet, there is a diversity of self-help groups, health belief systems, lifestyle guides and products that provide users with resources to construct and reconstruct narratives to maintain or change their self-identity.[50] Reflecting this diversity, non-orthodox therapies have an increasingly important role to play in how people understand health and make decisions about therapies and therapists.[51] Ayurvedic, Unani and other health care systems are all represented in web pages and through contributions to debates within news groups and chat rooms.

As part of a wider process of globalisation the internet is playing an important role providing people with access to a variety of medical approaches in the West. This does not mean that patients are abandoning orthodox medicine – despite the rhetoric in some medical quarters. Rather, life in late-modern societies seems to involve a never-ending cycle of construction and re-construction of the self in which the body and health are central.[52] The internet forms part of this broader pluralisation of lifestyle, based on choice and opportunities. This involves constant self-improvement that draws on information, expertise and relationships both lay and professional, and the recognition that patients can be both consumers and producers of health information and advice.

Notes

1 'FDA Warns Consumers on Dangerous Products Promoted on the Internet', http://www. fda.gov/bbs/topics/answers/ans00803.html
2 M. Cornford, 'Counting the Net', *CMC Journal*, 34 (1999): 5–12. Internet Survey
3 Internet Survey http://www.cyberdialogue/survey/2000.html
4 'Web Growth Summary' http://www.mit.edu:8001/people/mkgray/net/web-growth-summary.html
5 W. Gibson, *Neuromancer*, New York, Ace Books, 1984.
6 H. Rheingold, *The Virtual Community: Homesteading on the Electronic Frontier*, London, Secker and Warburg, 1994.
7 A. Giddens, *Beyond Left and Right*, Cambridge, Polity Press, 1994
8 'Web Growth Summary' http://www.mit.edu:8001/people/mkgray/net/web-growth-summary.html
9 'Totals for Top Servers Across All Domains' http://www.netcraft.com/survey/Reports/199909/graphs.html
10 National Opinion Polls, *Internet User Profile Study*, London, NOP Research Group, 1999.
11 K. Bikson and S. Panis, 'Internet usage', *CMC Journal* 28 (1997): 34–41. R.E. Thomas and C.D. James, 'Informal communication networking among health professionals', *Health Informatics Journal* 8 (1999).
12 R.E. Thomas and C.D. James, 'Informal communication networking among health professionals', *Health Informatics Journal* 8 (1999): 574–81
13 M. Hardey, 'E-health: the internet and the transforming of patients into consumers and producers of health and knowledge', *Information Communication and Society* 5, 2 (2001): 1–26.
14 B.S. Turner, *Medical Power and Social Knowledge*, London, Sage, 1995.
15 A.J. Jadad, 'Promoting partnerships: challenges for the internet age', *British Medical Journal* 319 (1999): 761–4.
16 R. Porter, *Health for Sale: Quackery in England 1650–1850*, Manchester, Manchester University Press, 1998.
17 B. Snow, 'Internet sources of information on alternative medicine', *Database* 21, 4 (1998): 65–73.
18 M. Hardey, *The Social Context of Health*, Buckingham, Open University Press, 1998.
19 Department of Health, *The New NHS: Modern, Dependable*, London, HMSO, Department of Health, 1997.
20 S. Cant and U. Sharma, *A New Medical Pluralism?*, London, UCL Press, 1999.
21 M. Saks, *Professions and the Public Interest. Medical Power, Altruism and Alternative Medicine*, London, Routledge, 1995.

22 M. Hardey, *The Social Context of Health*, Buckingham, Open University Press, 1998.
23 A.L. Strauss and J. Corbin, *Basics of Qualitative Research Grounded Theory Procedures and Techniques*, Newbury Park, Sage, 1990.
24 T. Parsons, *The Social System*, New York, Free Press, 1951.
25 A. Coulter, *Patient Information*, London, Kings Fund, 1999.
26 A. Giddens, *Modernity and Self-Identity*, Cambridge, Polity Press, 1991.
27 Asthma Home, http://hometown.aol.com/asthma.html
28 M. Hardey, 'E-health': the internet and the transforming of patients into consumers and producers of health and knowledge *Information Communication and Society* 5, 2 (2001): 1–26
29 R. Fitzpatrick, 'Lay concepts of illness', in R. Fitzpatrick, J. Hinton, S. Newman, G. Scambler and J. Thompson (eds), *The Experience of Illness*, Tavistock, London, 1984.
30 'Hysterectomy Support', www.hystersisters.com. R. Burrows and S. Nettleton, 'Reflexive modernization and the emergence of wired self-help', in K.A. Renninger and W. Shumar (eds), *Building Virtual Communities: Learning and Change in Cyberspace*, New York, Cambridge University Press, 2000.
31 R. Burrows and S. Nettleton, 'Reflexive modernization and the emergence of wired self-help', in K.A. Renninger and W. Shumar (eds), *Building Virtual Communities: Learning and Change in Cyberspace*, New York, Cambridge University Press, 2000.
32 L. Lamberg, 'Online support group helps patients live with, learn more about the rare skin cancer', *Journal of the American Medical Association* 277 (1997): 1422–3.
33 N. Pleace, R. Burrows, B. Loader, S. Muncer and S. Nettleton, 'On-line with the friends of Bill W: social support and the net', *Sociological Research Online* 5, 2 (200): 134–48.
34 A. de Swaan, *The Management of Normality: Critical Essays in Health and Welfare*, London, Routledge, 1990.
35 M. Smith, 'Invisible crowds in cyberspace: mapping the social structure of the Usenet', in M.A. Smith and P. Kollock (eds), *Communities in Cyberspace*, London, Routledge, 1999.
36 R. Seaboldt and J.A. Kuiper, 'Comparison of information obtained from a Usenet newsgroup and from drug information centers', *American Journal of Health Systems* 54, 15 (1997): 1732–5.
37 A. Giddens, *Modernity and Self-Identity*, Cambridge, Polity Press, 1991.
38 C.H. Cantor and P.J.M. Baume, 'Access to methods of suicide: what impact?', *Australian and New Zealand Journal of Psychiatry* 32, 1 (1998): 8–14.
39 V. Sussman and M. Mannix, 'Gold rush for cyberspace', *US News and World Report* 199, 9 (1995): 72–8.
40 P. Jenkins, *Advertising and the Net*, New York, Basic Books, 1998.
41 'Nesgroup Listing', http://netscan.research.microsoft.com/netscan/
42 A. Giddens, *Modernity and Self-Identity*, Cambridge, Polity Press, 1991, p. 146.
43 G. Williams and J. Popay, 'Lay knowledge and the privileging of experience', in J. Gabe, D. Kelleher and G. Williams (eds), *Challenging Medicine*, London, Routledge, 1994.
44 B. Good, 'How medicine constructs its objects', in B. Good (ed.), *Medicine, Rationality and Experience – an Anthropological Perspective*, Cambridge, Cambridge University Press, 1994.
45 M. Foucault, *The Birth of the Clinic an Archaeology of Medical Perception*, London, Routledge, 1991.
46 Psoriasis Home Page, http://www.psoriasis.org.
47 B.S. Turner, *Medical Power and Social Knowledge*, London, Sage, 1995.
48 L. Weed, 'New connections between medical knowledge and patient care', *British Medical Journal* 315 (1999): 231–5.
49 A. Giddens, *Modernity and Self-Identity*, Cambridge, Polity Press, 1991. U. Beck, 'From industrial society to risk society. Questions of survival, social structure and ecological enlightenment', *Culture and Society* 9, 1 (1992): 97–123.
50 A. Giddens, *Modernity and Self-Identity*, Cambridge, Polity Press, 1991.
51 U. Sharma, *Complementary Medicine Today: Practitioners and Patients*, London, Routledge, 1992.
52 A. Giddens, *Modernity and Self-Identity*, Cambridge, Polity Press, 1991.

13 Limiting pluralism

Medical scientism, quackery, and the internet

Ned Vankevich

American medical doctor, Stephen Barrett, spearheads a popular internet-based campaign to undermine the credibility of what he calls 'quackery'.[1] Many of the therapeutic products, practices and philosophies Barrett groups under the term quackery are often referred to as 'alternative', 'holistic', 'unconventional', 'comple-mentary', 'traditional', 'indigenous', 'non-Western', 'unorthodox', 'folk' and 'mind/body' medicine.[2] According to his web-biography, Barrett is a retired psychiatrist from Allentown, Pennsylvania who has written forty-seven books, including a number of texts on what Barrett considers to be dubious medical therapies and practices.[3] He is also a board member of the *National Council Against Health Fraud*, a scientific adviser to *The American Council on Science and Health*, and a fellow of the *Committee for the Scientific Investigation of Claims of the Paranormal* (CSICOP).[4]

Barrett's *Quackwatch* – a website billed as 'Your Guide to Health Fraud, Quackery, and Intelligent Decisions' – is available on the World Wide Web in English, French, German and Portuguese, with Italian and Japanese versions 'under construction'.[5] According to its mission statement, *Quackwatch* functions as a 'nonprofit corporation whose purpose is to combat health-related frauds, myths, fads, and fallacies'.[6] As further outlined in its mission statement, the main activities of *Quackwatch* include: investigating questionable claims, answering inquiries, distributing reliable publica-tions, reporting illegal marketing, generating consumer-protection laws, improving the quality of health information, and attacking misleading advertising on the internet.[7]

Barrett is a bold, self-described online 'quack-buster' who devotes a large amount of time and energy to promoting the superiority of dominant, science-based medicine over alternative healing therapies.[8] His effort is not misplaced. According to a national survey published in *The New England Journal of Medicine*, visits to alternative medical practitioners have increased over 47 per cent to 629 million between 1990 and 1997, 'thereby exceeding total visits to all US primary care physicians'.[9] Barrett's anti-quackery discourse also includes criticism of prestigious biomedical affiliated institutions including the American Cancer Society, The National Institute of Diabetes and Digestive and Kidney Diseases, and the National Institutes of Health.[10] This chapter explores some of the implications of Barrett's website and the anti-alternative medicine discourse it generates. In doing so, it will situate Barrett's rhetorical campaign within its wider historical, philosophical, and cultural context with an eye toward highlighting some of the potential problems operating within Barrett's polemic.

The site of contention

Dr Barrett's *Quackwatch* is one of the larger websites on the internet promoting a sceptical approach to non-mainstream nutritional products and healing protocols.[11] Barrett divides his homepage into fifteen sections dealing with a variety of issues related to alternative health and healing.[12] Some of Barrett's topic headings deal with 'General Observations' about quackery, 'Consumer Strategies and Education', 'Consumer Protection', 'Research Projects' and 'Legal and Political Action Activities'. A considerable portion of Barrett's critique and rhetorical effort is dedicated to exposing what he calls the hype, misinformation, and over-promotion that many individuals and companies manifest in their zealous desire to capture customers in the alternative health marketplace.[13] Barrett especially targets multi-level marketing (MLM) companies and dedicates a specific website entitled *MLM Watch* to critique them.[14] He concentrates on MLM companies because they most succinctly express the type of excessive and unsubstantiated health claims he deems quackery to promote.[15]

Other major concerns listed on Barrett's *Quackwatch* website include 'questionable products, services and theories', 'questionable advertisements', and 'non-recommended sources of health advice'. On his 'Questionable Products, Services, and Theories' webpage, Barrett lists over fifty procedures that, in his estimation, have little or no diagnostic or therapeutic value. In addition to esoteric items like 'Cytotoxic or Metabolic Intolerance Testing', 'Contact Reflex Analysis', 'Therapeutic Touch', and 'Qigong', Barrett includes more recognisable alternative health practices such as acupuncture, chelation therapy, chiropractic care, homoeopathy, and naturopathy. Under Barrett's 'non-recommended sources of health advice' he criticises books and leading alternative health advocates that he considers are promoting unacceptable forms of medical quackery. His list includes Deepak Chopra's 'Ayurvedic mumbo-jumbo,' Hulda Clark's 'bizarre' cancer cures, and Andrew Weil, whom Barrett deems the chief 'guru' of alternative medicine. Barrett also refers to other well-known personalities in the US alternative therapy market, including medical doctors Robert Atkins, Herbert Benson, Larry Dossey, and Bernie Siegel. It is also important to note that Barrett devotes a good portion of his website to consumer protection and education issues, including topics dealing with his ongoing research projects and the legal action consumers can take to help stop quackery.

At face value, Barrett's goal to protect consumers from the fraudulent, dangerous, and mistaken health information that abounds on the internet, and elsewhere, is laudable, especially given the potential for unconscionable charlatans and the sincerely misguided to take advantage of people's health fears. There is also Barrett's legitimate concern that medical amateurs are doing more harm than good in dispensing unsubstantiated products and information that can lead to a wrong diagnosis or harmful treatment.[16] To support these concerns, Barrett includes an essay entitled 'How quackery harms cancer patients' by William T. Jarvis, Professor of Public Health and Preventive Medicine at the School of Medicine and Public Health at Loma Linda University and President of the National Council Against Health Fraud.[17] Jarvis cites examples of how 'dubious therapies can cause death, serious injury, unnecessary suffering, and disfigurement' and includes a graphic example of a woman who was mistreated with cancer by an unlicensed naturopath who gave her a black herbal salve that burned her nose off.

At the same time, however, Barrett's anti-quackery zeal tempts him to overlook some of the important issues that are taking place in contemporary medical discourse and practice, namely, the phenomenon of medical pluralism, and the understanding that issues of health, illness, and well-being entail a number of complicated psycho-cultural factors that his medical epistemology fails to acknowledge.[18] In order to appreciate the complexity of issues entailed in Barrett's crusade, and to understand why he overlooks significant reasons why patients and consumers embrace alternative and holistic forms of healthcare, it is important to understand the historical context within which Barrett's anti-quackery crusade is located.[19]

Quackery confined

Etymologically, the term 'quack' derives from the Dutch word 'quacksalver,' meaning one who 'quacks (like a duck) or brags about the potency of medicinal products'.[20] The idea of quackery gained cultural currency in Europe during the sixteenth century and, according to Gevitz, originally described the rhetorical and advertising skills of pitchmen who enticed people to buy their medicines.[21] Later, the term quackery came to designate both worthless medicines and therapeutic techniques and the exploitative harm quacks and their products were said to cause.[22]

P.S. Brown notes that as nineteenth-century medicine became professionalised, it urgently needed to 'define its boundaries'.[23] Inglis further reminds us that although the term quack was also applied to charlatans who pretended to have knowledge of medicine they did not possess, many nineteenth-century American allopaths, during their struggle for professional dominance, began to use the term quack for 'all unorthodox practitioners who have not been through a medical school – however well qualified and experienced they may be in their techniques'.[24] The use of the terms quack and quackery thus became a convenient way for nineteenth-century allopathic doctors to bolster their image as the only legitimate form of medical praxis.[25]

James Harvey Young, in his classic works *The Medical Messiahs* (1967) and *The Toadstool Millionaires* (1961), chronicles the rise of quackery and patent medicines (and devices) and the way American legal authorities have sought to suppress unorthodox medicines and therapeutic practices from the nineteenth to the middle part of the twentieth century.[26] Young's *The Medical Messiahs* is especially detailed in its telling of the role the American Medical Association (AMA) and local and national legislation have played in limiting medical diversity.[27] As Young points out, the late nineteenth and early twentieth-century medical 'quack-busters' used

the yardstick of science to expose medical quackery to great effect.[28] They also
helped to enact a number of federal laws aimed at restricting and limiting the
types of 'patent' medicines that could be made and promoted. Previously, American
food and drug laws were primarily 'Jacksonian' or libertarian in spirit. However,
during the 'Progressive Era' (*c.*1900–17) the social climate began to change as
various groups sought to implement governmental and legal control over a number
of cultural practices.[29]

Samuel Hopkins Adam's 'Great American Fraud' series for *Collier's* magazine
epitomizes the type of reform-oriented exposé at work in the popular press during
the early part of the twentieth century.[30] Adam's eloquent and passionate exposure
of unscrupulous and fraudulent promoters of patent medicines served both as a
firebrand and a model for the anti-quackery and anti-nostrum essays, pamphlets
and books the AMA produced during the first few decades of the twentieth century.

During this same period, Morris Fishbein, former head of the AMA, and Arthur
J. Cramp, the former AMA Director of the Propaganda Department and Bureau
of Investigation, were instrumental in formulating American anti-quackery
discourse.[31] Cramp and Fishbein wrote several influential volumes dealing with,
as the subtitle of Cramp's secpnd volume indicates, 'nostrum evil, quackery and
allied matters affecting public health'. Cramp's texts contain a compilation of
articles and essays from the *American Medical Association Journal* designed to expose
a specific person, device or product deemed to be a form of medical fakery or
dangerous nostrum. Such rhetorically successful condemnations of quackery and
patent medicine resulted in the enactment of the first U.S. federal laws restraining
the manufacturing and advertising of 'patent' medicines.[32]

Barrett echoes this tradition when he defines a quack as 'a pretender to medical
skill; a charlatan and one who talks pretentiously without sound knowledge of the
subject discussed'.[33] Although quackery might involve deliberate deception for
Barrett, the 'paramount characteristic' of quackery today is 'promotion' rather
than 'fraud, greed, or misinformation'.[34] Barrett also links the definition of quackery
to those therapeutic products, therapies, and protocols that are not 'compatible
with established scientific concepts'.[35] In spite of the apparent novelty of Barrett's
cyberspace campaign, he is in fact continuing an on-going anti-quackery tradition
that has operated in American medical culture for well over a century.

Before sketching that tradition, it is important to note that I am not implying
that all approaches to health and healing are good and therefore valid. Cramp
and Barrett's exposé of dangerous or fraudulent health products represents an
important social and ethical response to deception and exploitation. However, of
comparable concern is the way some supporters of the dominant medical
establishment have used their authority to thwart and punish those who offer
unconventional healing procedures that some patients have found beneficial.

Quackery and medical scientism

Since the rise of scientific thinking, beginning in the late sixteenth century, dominant
medicine has increasingly sought to ground itself in a scientific understanding of
health and healing.[36] Such an understanding is rooted in an orientation that favours

rational, repeatable, and measurable therapeutic understanding and results. The fundamental theme of Fishbein and Cramp's discourse and of those influenced by them, is that medical charlatans, quacks, and sects, as well as the products and therapies they promote, operate outside the boundaries of acceptable medical science and epistemology, and therefore they need to be constrained.[37] Inherent in this theme is the assumption of the professional and therapeutic superiority of biomedical practice and the institutions, like the AMA and medical research centres that support it. Such assumptions are based upon the premise that empirical-based science is the only touchstone for determining legitimate medical practice and understanding.

For some people, one man and the study he directed on the state of medical educational institutions in North America near the beginning of the twentieth century played a central role in the development of American science-based medical training and practice. Entitled *Medical Education in the United States and Canada*, Abraham Flexner's influential report helped foster the medical conformity that operates in medical schools to this day. Flexner's report is also related to the anti-quackery discourses of Fishbein, Cramp, and Barrett.[38]

Beginning in January of 1909, Flexner began a sweeping evaluation of 155 American and Canadian medical schools and postgraduate institutions, and after ten months of investigation he issued his famous 1910 account.[39] Flexner's document highlighted what he considered to be alarmingly low standards of educational and clinical training taking place in most American and Canadian medical schools.[40] In light of such unfavourable evidence, Flexner sought to bolster the therapeutic practice and credibility of American medical schools by ensuring that a uniform, high level of standards would be met. To help accomplish this goal, Flexner focused on the advances being made in physiology, pharmacology and surgery as well as in the burgeoning fields of pathology, bacteriology, and histology.[41] According to Flexner, 'by the very nature of the case, admission to a really modern medical school must at the very least depend on a competent knowledge of chemistry, biology, and physics. Every departure from this basis is at the expense of medical training itself'.[42]

As John A. Lee observes, it was during the nineteenth century that 'biology began to provide medicine with an empirical basis for a secular, materialist approach to healing'.[43] In keeping with the spirit of such scientific logic, Flexner also promoted a form of medical reductionism whereby health and healing were reduced to sheer chemical and physical components. Examples of Flexner's medical reductionism can be found in his claims that nutrition and waste are 'but chemical problems' and that physiological laws reflect the 'same fundamental sciences upon which the anatomist and the physiologist have already freely drawn – viz., biology, physics, and chemistry'.[44] In essence, Flexner made a strong contribution to what can be referred to as medical scientism or a naturalistic and mechanistic model of health and healing. Such a model is characterised by what Steven Shapin calls explication based on 'ordinary, comprehensible mechanical and material causes'.[45]

The rhetorical power of Flexner's detailed critique of the inadequacy of specific medical educational institutions was so convincing that many of them closed their doors. This was particularly true of medical sects that did not meet his criteria of science-based medicine. Within a few years, most of the 'irregular' medical schools such as those established by homoeopaths, eclectics, and physio-medicalists ceased to operate. Flexner was also unflagging in his critique of what he called 'unconscionable quacks' such as chiropractors and mechano-therapists whose 'tissues of exaggeration, pretence, and misrepresentations' did not even merit 'serious' consideration as a medical sect.[46] In short, Flexner's report helped cement and codify the philosophic and epistemological orientation that enabled the supporters of science-based medicine to articulate a strong case not only against quacks and the patent medicines that abounded at the turn of the nineteenth to the twentieth century, but also against any healing procedure that did not comport with the standards of science-based medicine.[47]

As in the case of Barrett's website, the principle behind Flexner's report to protect the public good by ensuring that medical practice meets specific professional and safety standards was well justified. However, the action of advocates like Flexner and Barrett could also be seen to harbour problematic elements.[48]

Quackery and marginalisation

The anti-quackery discourse of Flexner, Cramp and Fishbein contributes several important elements that operate in Barrett's internet campaign. It helps solidify the epistemological basis of medical scientism that promotes a naturalistic and mechanistic approach to health and healing, and it unleashes a strong drive to induce medical conformity and limit medical diversity by reproving those who do not subscribe to the dominant biomedical model.[49] In addition, it also seems to generate what some consider a hegemonic orientation that is quick to marginalise, judge, and punish medical divergence.[50] A few examples will serve to illustrate this influence.

According to Barrett, alternative medicine has become the 'politically correct term for questionable practices formerly labelled quack and fraudulent' and is

> part of a general societal trend toward rejection of science as a method of determining truths. This movement embraces the postmodernist doctrine that science is not necessarily more valid than pseudoscience. In line with this philosophy, alternative proponents assert that scientific medicine (which they mislabel as allopathic, conventional, or traditional medicine) is but one of a vast array of health-care options. Alternative promoters often gain public sympathy by portraying themselves as a beleaguered minority fighting a self-serving, monolithic 'Establishment'.[51]

There is a lot to unpack in this claim, however, at minimum this assertion and other similar statements made by Barrett indicate that he is aware of the socio-political dimensions, rather than simply the 'scientific' issues at play in the conflict in which he is engaged.[52]

Barrett takes his battle seriously and, like his anti-quackery predecessors, he is quick to employ a variety of tactics to obtain his goals.[53] Like Flexner, Cramp, and Fishbein, Barrett employs denigrating terminology to describe many of the products, therapies, and healing philosophies of which he disapproves. Examples include his calling Ayurvedic medicine 'mumbo-jumbo';[54] his deeming the concern over dental mercury amalgam poisoning a 'scam';[55] his labelling the nutritional supplements that many chiropractors dispense as 'irrationally formulated';[56] and his arguing that the Bates method of vision correction – which Barrett admits did meet with 'considerable success' – has 'attracted large numbers of charlatans, quacks, and gullible followers who then published scores of unscientific books and articles'.[57] Barrett's promotion of medical scientism also leads him, in his 'Questionable Products, Services, and Theories' section, to criticise therapeutic techniques that are considered legitimately 'complementary' by some medical doctors, including acupuncture, chelation therapy, massage therapy, and the use of vitamins and nutritional supplements. To help support his claims, Barrett has a link to Russell Turpin's World Wide Web article 'Characterization of Quack Theories' that exposes many of the pseudo arguments and evidence that proponents of 'quack medicine' and paranormal phenomena often employ.[58]

In addition to such discursive practices, Barrett uses the legal system to accomplish his limiting of medical diversity. According to Morsé Mehrban, a lawyer writing for Barrett's website, 'many people have been defrauding the public for years or even decades without even minimal scrutiny by any government'.[59] To remedy this situation, Mehrban explains how 'any individual activist or consumer-protection group' in California can become a 'private attorney general' who 'carries the full power of the law' to help prosecute 'California-based purveyers [sic] of modern-day snake oils'.[60] In addition, Barrett himself promotes the use of 'lawsuits' as a way for 'individual consumers' to 'strike powerful blows against products marketed with false or misleading claims'.[61]

A number of writers have drawn attention to the way notions of scientism and quackery have been used by advocates of dominant medicine to limit medical plurality by undermining competition and ensuring monopolistic control over how medicine is practised.[62] As Starr notes, dominant medicine has used its gatekeeping power to determine what is legitimate healthcare and to increase its cultural authority and power base.[63] By determining how patients receive medical care, the promoters of dominant medicine have been able to control key sites of medical therapy such as hospitals and the distribution of pharmaceutical drugs. The legitimacy of this practice is often based upon an appeal to the rational superiority of science and the rigorous training medical physicians receive. However, claims about the inherent superiority of medical science and the way its clinical trials, tests and verifications are more valid than alternative health might not be so unequivocal. As Stanley Aronowitz observes, what is at issue is whether our knowledge and practice of science can sufficiently be free of cultural presuppositions to justify the limiting of social freedom.[64]

Aronowitz's insight draws attention to the way some proponents of dominant medicine, like Barrett, sometimes overlook important psycho-cultural, institutional, ideological and economic factors at play in using scientific discourse to bolster claims of epistemic and therapeutic superiority.[65] As Edward Campion reminds us, a number of existential forces are at work when people choose alternative medicine, including fear of medical tests and treatments, the need for emotional comfort and attention, media stories of medical mishaps and mismanagement, a desire for control, etc.[66] In light of this, it is important to explore how Barrett's hegemonic use of the term quackery might unjustifiably collapse the difference between the practice of unscrupulous and exploitative medicinal hucksters and the use of 'unorthodox' and 'fringe' therapies that some people find more beneficial than biomedicine.[67] In doing so, I will focus on several issues that make some of Barrett's anti-quackery discourse problematic.

Medical turmoil

A number of observers, both inside and outside the medical profession, draw attention to troubles facing the field of American biomedicine. In the blunt words of a recent *Journal of the American Medical Association* commentary, the 'fact is the US population does not have anywhere near the best health in the world'.[68] Medical watchdog, Martin L. Gross, draws attention to the amount of medical errors and incompetence besetting contemporary dominant medicine. Drawing upon studies in prominent medical journals such as the *Journal of the American Medical Association* and *The New England Journal of Medicine*, Gross highlights the high number of iatrogenic and nosocomial, or treatment and hospital-induced illnesses, and deaths and maimings caused by the American biomedical establishment each year. Gross is not alone in his assessment.[69] A report to President Clinton published by the Quality Interagency Coordination Task Force, a group organised under the direction of the U.S. federally funded Agency for Healthcare Research and Quality to help improve healthcare, found that 'up to 98,000 Americans die each year as a result of preventable medical errors'.[70] The report considers this issue a 'national problem' of 'epidemic proportion' given that such 'preventable' and 'adverse medical events' add costs in excess of '$29 billion annually' and cause the 'death of tens of thousands' of patients each year.[71] According to statistics compiled by Starfield and others, these numbers are too conservative. In her estimation, over 225,000 people die each year from 'unnecessary surgeries', 'medication errors', 'hospital errors', 'nosocomial infections', and 'non-error, adverse effects of medications'.[72] And these numbers do not include 'adverse effects that are associated with disability or discomfort'.[73]

Gross succinctly outlines many of the institutional and economic causes for this situation including Health Maintenance Organization (HMO) mismanagement, therapeutic zeal that results in unnecessary surgeries and medications, and medical fraud and incompetence, all of which result in an overall lack of 'uniform quality of care'.[74] Gross and other critics are concerned with how HMOs and managed care have altered medical practice – especially in terms of how healthcare services are organised and delivered.[75]

There is also recognition that some of the pharmaceutical agents and technological therapies of dominant medicine have not delivered all they promised.[76] The above mentioned mortality and side-effects caused by pharmaceutical drugs, and the inability of dominant medicine to cure certain chronic diseases like multiple sclerosis, diabetes, and arthritis, have led some critics to question the image of science-based medicine as a bastion of therapeutic superiority. In the now famous words of Ivan Illich, for some people 'the medical establishment has become a major threat to health'.[77]

Added to these issues are concerns over the fragility of the American biomedical system as a whole – everything from escalating medical costs and diminishing physician salaries to rising medical malpractice law suits, excessive paper work, undue therapeutic constraints, and exceptionally long working hours and occupational stress. The overall effects of these professional troubles have led Jerome P. Kassirer, editor of *The New England Journal of Medicine*, to label the current discontent among medical doctors as a state of 'substantial dismay'.[78] Kassirer further concludes that 'cranky' (irritable) doctors are not likely 'to provide outstanding medical care'.[79]

Barrett is not unaware of these criticisms. One *Quackwatch* reader questioned Barrett's positive 'bias' toward the 'vaunted medical profession' given the current rise in 'malpractice, misdiagnoses, morbidity rates, the number of unnecessary surgical procedures such as hysterectomies, the accidental surgical removal of the wrong limb, and the like'.[80] Barrett's response is telling: 'We [meaning his team promoting anti-quackery discourse] emphasise practices that are related to bad science rather than to poor medical practice'.[81] In other words, quackery for Barrett entails the use of therapeutic practices not 'consistent with established scientific concepts'.[82] In contrast, Barrett maintains that the facts, logic, and testable observations and hypotheses of science are 'equally applicable to health-related issues'.[83] From such statements, it appears that Barrett's concern is for what constitutes good science, not for what works or does not work for patients. Viewed this way, Barrett seems to assume that the approach to medical science he promotes is independent of human flaws, foibles, and desires and devoid of social, institutional, and economic considerations. As will be highlighted below, from an alternative health perspective, healing is not physics. By limiting medical legitimacy to therapeutic practice that conforms to abstract, scientific standards, Barrett seems to overlook important considerations of how and why people get healed. Put another way, for many medical patients and practitioners, the art of healing entails more than correspondence to 'scientific' truth.

Therapeutic disenchantment

The increasing use of expensive hi-tech equipment, busy schedules, and the need to cut costs sometimes leads to the perception that M.D.s no longer have time to listen and treat a patient as a person.[84] Joe Collier, senior lecturer and honorary consultant in clinical medicine at England's St George's Medical School, observes that, in contrast to what some consider to be the impersonal and hurried practice of biomedicine, complementary and alternative therapies often entail a 'rather close physical and/or emotional "caring" relationship between the patient and therapist which often involves "personal touching and longer periods of contact time"'.[85]

Other factors that lead some patients to seek out alternative medicine include the recognition that dominant medicine cannot cure many important chronic and degenerative diseases such as allergies, asthma, arthritis, high blood pressure, diabetes, lower back pain, and the ever widening occurrence of auto-immune diseases such as lupus, chronic fatigue, and AIDS.[86] Robert Hass succinctly summarises this view when he observes that 'although modern medicine excels in managing medical emergencies, fighting infectious diseases, and developing life-saving surgical techniques', it has been far less successful in the 'prevention, management, and reversal of the chronic diseases that account for 85 per cent of our national health-care bill'.[87]

A number of other forces are leading some medical doctors to be more open to alternative and complementary medicine, including rising medical malpractice law suits and the loss of autonomy in their therapeutic practice. Although American medical celebrity doctors like Deepak Chopra, Bernie Siegel and Andrew Weil are responsible for drawing public attention to this trend, this move is not limited to the orthodox fringe. A recent article in *The Journal of the American Medical Association* reveals that well over half (64 per cent) of the 125 medical schools surveyed in the United States are now offering courses in alternative medicine.[88] This openness has resulted in the increasing use of some of the 'alternative' therapies that Barrett rejects such as homoeopathy, Chinese traditional medicine, herbal medicine, acupuncture and nutritional supplements.

Having done his homework, Barrett is cognisant of such issues. *Quackwatch* contributor William T. Jarvis offers psychological insight into why individuals 'trained in the health sciences' turn to promoting quackery.[89] Such reasons include 'boredom', 'low professional esteem', 'paranoid mental state(s)', the corrupting influence of 'religious' and 'philosophical values' which 'distort scientific diagnostic, prescriptive or therapeutic procedures', and the 'profit' and 'prophet' motives.[90] However, by reducing 'conversions' to alternative medicine to states of psychological imbalance and unethical motives Barrett and his *Quackwatch* team again miss some of the subtler reasons physicians and patients embrace unorthodox medical practices.

Questionable medical science

One of the underlying themes of Barrett's *Quackwatch* discourse is that medical science is superior because the 'scientific method offers an objective way to evaluate information to determine what is false'.[91] Barrett posits that science offers unbiased descriptions and explanations of naturally occurring phenomena and that such explications are grounded in a supportable logic based on testable observations and hypotheses.[92] Inherent within Barrett's premise is the assumption that such an ideal is automatically translatable to the medical sphere. For some critics this assumption appears questionable.

Medical critic Thomas Moore draws attention to the way institutional leaders of medical science often define sickness in ways that include large numbers of people in order to 'require expensive programs of medical treatment'.[93] Moore offers evidence that medical establishment leaders sometimes skew the interpretation of medical studies and data to fit organisational needs and agendas.[94] For example, current public health campaigns and warnings by medical authorities against the 'three big risk factors' of obesity, high blood pressure and elevated cholesterol have little basis in scientific fact.[95] Moore also makes the case that such campaigns have economic motives, that is, they are orchestrated by a 'strange partnership of government, medicine and private enterprise'[96] which are 'quietly bankrolled by food companies and drug companies'.[97] Moore also reveals the political machinations operating in the US National Institutes of Health whose leaders use the fear of punishment to induce conformity to their public policy positions on obesity, high cholesterol, etc.[98] He also highlights the way drug companies 'cultivate' the friendship of both 'practicing physicians and the academic elite with great care'.[99] Such cultivations include collusions between federal medical agencies – including the National Institutes of Health and Federal Drug Agency – and the pharmaceutical industry that sometimes results in the misrepresentation or manipulation of clinical drug trial data.[100] In short, science in the laboratory is sometimes far removed from some of the economic and political realities taking place in medical science.

In addition to Moore, a number of alternative healthcare advocates have used the internet to promote their view that dominant medicine is not free from using science in a hegemonic way.[101] The shrill language of Marijah McCain is indicative of the passion many alternative health proponents feel when she writes, 'I cannot tell you how disgusted I am with the conventional healing system in this country and I know a great many of you feel the same way. The Feds closed my clinic 2 years ago, Arkansas outlawed the title Doctor for naturopaths and they continue to kill people everyday with poisonous drugs!'[102]

Though McCain's views are extreme, other alternative health advocates, like Ralph Moss, have exerted influence on some key US government decision makers.[103] Moss authors the internet-based 'Cancer Chronicles' – a website that highlights anti-medical establishment political activity. Moss notes that the alternative health business is growing rapidly and although it does not approach the economic power of medical and pharmaceutical companies, it is winning the support of a 'good portion of the population' in America.[104] Because of this, it is beginning to flex some political muscle as evidenced by the recently formed National Center for Complementary and Alternative Medicine (NCCAM) at the National Institutes of Health (NIH).[105] According to a NIH press release, NCCAM 'will provide greater autonomy to initiate research projects at a time when the public is increasingly interested in CAM [complementary and alternative medicine] therapies,' and will conduct basic and applied research, research training, and disseminate health information and other programs with respect to identifying, investigating, and validating CAM diagnostic, treatment and prevention protocols.[106] Although the research projects carried out by NCCAM are, like dominant medicine, rigorously scientific in nature, the fact that a major US government agency is working with unconventional therapies is indicative of a mood change among some within the medical establishment.

The implications of these cultural expressions indicate that Barrett's drive to limit the right to alternative therapies seems to overlook a number of complex institutional, political, and economic issues at play in contemporary American society. It also appears to disregard recent scientific insights into less mechanistic operations at work in the healing process.

The complexity of healing phenomena

Beginning with Walter B. Cannon's explanation of 'voodoo' death and the often cited research of Henry Beecher, a bevy of scientific studies[107] have explored how mental and emotional states affect our physiology.[108] In addition, neurobiologists have found a direct physiological connection between brain response and the immune system.[109]

According to medical researcher Herbert Benson, there is a direct correlation between the expectation of a good outcome by both patient and physician and the success rate of a healing protocol.[110] Benson's research, and that of other neuro-physiologists, has found that sensory and 'mental' perceptions, such as thoughts and emotions, stimulate a cascade of chemical reactions in the brain that affect the body. This research into what is often referred to as 'mind/body' medicine also lends insight into why persuasive and positive words, actions, and beliefs elicit healthful physiological responses in the body.[111] Benson and others have found that the stimulation that results from belief and expectancy creates neurosignatures, or ingrained patterns of nerve cell activity, that can profoundly affect our health and wellbeing.[112] That is, emotional and cognitive elements such as expectation and belief alter human immuno-physiological response via neuro-chemical connections and stimulation between regions of the cortex and the limbic system, hypothalamus and pituitary-adrenal glands. In particular, research has shown that positive and proactive words of health and activity induce the body to 'reconfigure' its 'image of itself'.[113] Neurobiological researcher David Felten further points out that one of the main factors that affect immune response is whether or not the individual has control over a situation – a key component in many alternative health therapies.[114]

The implications of this research are important. Such findings help argue that the current cultural move toward greater acceptance of alternative medicine is more than a matter of the adroit skills of self-promotion that Barrett blames for the contemporary growth of quackery. Much of the 'hype' Barrett attributes to quackery could also be viewed as a type of enthusiastic, hopeful and optimistic persuasion that helps stimulate positive or healthful physiological changes in the body – what medical surgeon Bernie S. Siegel calls 'self-induced healing'.[115] When Barrett avers that 'the trickiest misconception about quackery is that personal experience is the best way to tell whether something works' and that we cannot trust anecdotal self-reports from those who say they feel better after using a product or procedure because most ailments are 'self-limiting, and even incurable conditions can have sufficient day-to-day variation to enable bogus methods to gain large followings',[116] he overlooks the important role subjectivistic and non-mechanical actions play in the healing process.[117]

The placebo effect also draws attention to another potential problem for Barrett's scientism. For some researchers, the pharmacological method of science-based, double blind studies that seek to maximise experimental control delivers a limited type of medical truth and discovery – one that disregards a multiplicity of other variables at play in the healing process. As Goodwin and Goodwin point out, many 'efficacious' treatments for certain diseases are 'ignored or rejected' because they do 'not make sense in the light of accepted theories of disease mechanism and drug action'.[118] Goodwin and Goodwin have deemed this phenomenon the 'tomato effect', by which they mean, established medical and scientific models often blind researchers to potentially beneficial therapies. They cite the example that Americans, until 1820, did not eat tomatoes because they were members of the deadly nightshade family and thus, according to botanical beliefs of the era, they must be poisonous.[119] This, despite the fact that they knew Europeans to be eating tomatoes with no toxic effects. For the Goodwins, the lesson is instructive. Sometimes, *a priori* conceptions lead researchers to overlook, or not accept, evidence simply because it does not fit prevailing conceptual models and criteria. To restrict all of medical truth to the epistemological constraints of the pharmaceutical model that seeks to isolate specific drug activities might force medical researchers to overlook more complicated activities at play in the therapeutic process.

Quackery reconsidered

In the eyes of some adherents of unorthodox therapies, rationality oriented medical scientism neglects psycho-social components at play in many therapeutic situations. Viewed this way, the cultural shift toward alternative medicine is a sign that dominant, science-based medicine is not meeting important patient needs – whether physical, emotional, spiritual or social in origin. Thus, when anti-quackery leaders like Barrett discredit the efficacy of alternative therapies such as homoeopathy, herbal remedies, aromatherapy and chiropractic care by focusing on their question-able scientific status, they overlook the important point that faith, persuasion, spirituality and cognition can be potent forces in the treatment process.[120]

However, in making this observation, I do not mean to imply that Barrett's concern for unsubstantiated promotion and hype is remiss. Barrett's concern for fraudulent and potentially dangerous medical practices is important. However, it can also be argued that Barrett's tendency to lump all forms of alternative medicine under the rubric of quackery is unjustified. Especially when he applies the term of quackery to procedures that many consumers and health professionals find beneficial. Stated another way, Barrett weakens his medical argument when he ignores the fact that both the art of medicine and the process of healing entail a complex nexus of genetic, physiological, psychological, spiritual, social, and environ-mental elements that cannot be reduced to mere mechanistic factors. As Roger

Cooter notes, the rise in interest in alternative medicine often results from an 'aversion to the fragmented gaze of medical specialists' and the desire by patients to gain control over their health destiny without being limited by medical models that discount important aspects of the healing process.[121] In light of this, Inglis observes that the 'quack who sold coloured water to unsuspecting clients (who believed in its medicinal efficacy) had not been such a rogue after all'.[122]

Inglis' insight harbours weighty implications. Given the radical questioning of disciplinary and conceptual boundaries that mark the present day 'postmodern' mood, formerly convenient notions like quackery become less certain.[123] In the eyes of some critics, Barrett's anti-quackery crusade reflects modernity's hegemonic tendency to justify science's credibility to adjudicate truth claims. Such a tendency has its conceptual roots in modernism which many commentators claim often gives rise to an epistemological certainty and a logic of mastery and control that seeks to reduce or assimilate the 'other' to the 'same'.[124] This insight helps to partially explain why Barrett labours to limit medical pluralism. That is, when the science-based biomedical model becomes the only legitimate form of medical praxis and understanding it appears to grant the right to limit healthcare to that which fits its parameters. Barrett's presupposition that medical knowledge can be separated from psycho-social forces fosters the form of paternalism manifested in the aphorism that 'only' medical doctors know what is best for a patient. It is also this attitude that leads some proponents of the dominant medical community like Barrett (and Flexner) to a form of therapeutic elitism that dismisses those healers who do not have the proper, science-based education and training.

A number of authors in this volume, including Maarten Bode, Kate Reed and Volker Scheid draw attention to the important role issues of local medicine, globalisation, subalternisation, cultural identity, and ethnicity play in the therapeutic process.[125] When Barrett states that traditional Chinese medicine (TCM) 'encompasses a vast array of folk medical practices based on mysticism', or that Ayurvedic medicine is 'mumbo jumbo', his medical epistemology prevents him not only from assessing other modes of healing on the basis of their own epistemological claims, but also leads him to overlook the patient's role in the healing process.[126] Of importance, too, is the function hybridisation and syncrecy play in helping patients obtain healing. Bode, Liebeskind, Reed, Reis, and Scheid each paint detailed views of how therapeutic practice becomes enriched when Western biomedicine and traditional and indigenous forms of medical practice mix.[127] Each of these authors in their own way draws attention to how the healing process is mediated through a complex web of emotions, beliefs, and a variety of other non-mechanistic personal, social and environmental factors. Viewed this way, medical diversity becomes a vital aspect of medical care. If this is true, then Barrett's medical monism and hegemonic crusade to undermine belief in traditional and alternative forms of medicine actually undercuts a potentially potent aspect of healthcare. As such, Barrett's well-intentioned concern to protect the gullible public from quackery undermines his aim. In reducing the alternative 'other' to the biomedical 'same', Barrett ironically might be doing therapeutic harm like the quacks he warns against.

Conclusion

This chapter has explored how the idea of quackery has been employed by some proponents of dominant medicine to discredit and limit unorthodox medical practices. In doing so, I have explored several lines of thought that reveal that medical science cannot be separated from human complexity. Included among them is the way an over-zealous application of medical scientism can sometimes blind its proponents to some of the good that alternative medicine can provide. I have also drawn attention to how the limited viewpoint medical scientism fosters can have potential harmful effects on patients when it becomes the only mode of medical understanding and praxis. As such, medical scientism becomes an exclusionary tactic that limits how medicine is practised, and its mechanistic epistemology sometimes undermines the role non-material factors can play in therapeutic success.

Contemporary online and self-described 'quack-buster' Dr Stephen Barrett devotes a sizeable amount of energy to defend science-based, dominant medicine from what he considers to be the fraudulent promotion of alternative medicine. To some extent, Barrett continues a rich tradition in American medicine that seeks to advance the assumed epistemological and professional superiority of science-based medicine at the expense of heterodox medicine. In doing so, Barrett is well intentioned in his drive to educate consumers about the potential for fraud, commercial self-interest and harm in the alternative health marketplace. It is not difficult to find unorthodox therapies and diagnostic tools that stretch both credibility and ethical standards beyond repair.

However, Barrett's anti-quackery discourse can also be seen as problematic. Crusaders like Barrett often justify the hegemonic imposition of power and authority by appealing to science and by emphasising the possibility for abuse and personal harm if untested and unorthodox therapeutic practices go unregulated. However, to date no research has uncovered that alternative medical practices kill or harm people to anything approaching the degree of biomedicine. According to the US National Academy of Sciences' Institute of Medicine 'more people die from medical mistakes each year than from highway accidents, breast cancer, or AIDS'.[128] In addition, despite amazing technological and scientific developments, in many instances, orthodox medicine has remained less effective in treating a number of common degenerative diseases. Given these facts, many in the alternative health care field view the hegemonic impulse of dominant medicine as less than justified.

From an alternative health perspective, the institutional drive for medical scientism, spurred in the USA by Abraham Flexner at the turn of the twentieth century, has resulted in an overly constraining approach to health and healing that does not address the fundamental needs of many patients. Advocates of rational and scientific medicine like Flexner and Barrett often fail to realise Foucault's insight that the experience of pain is 'not conjured away by means of a body of neutralised knowledge'.[129] Put another way, illness entails a number of complex social and psycho-physical factors that often elude the 'reductive discourse of the doctor' and require 'non-scientific' means of cure.[130] Or as Campion observes, 'for such subjective responses as pain and fatigue, about a third of the people will respond to any placebo'.[131] In light of this, Barrett cannot take for granted that scientific medicine and the objectivity it claims are inherently superior to the allegedly metaphoric descriptions and false treatments of sickness that alternative medicine advances.[132] The considerable popularity of alternative medicine, as evidenced by surveys conducted by Barrett's biomedical peers, seems to indicate there is a fundamental social need in American culture for medical diversity.[133] In the words of Cooter, the 'intimate nature of our relations with our bodies stimulates the desire to shop around for the most effective and satisfying means to well-being'.[134]

Medical pluralism also takes on important dimensions when viewed in light of current insights into psychoneuroimmunology, or mind/body medical research, which reveals the way belief – whether or not it conforms to scientific reality – can contribute to healing. For even if alternative therapies are merely placebo in their effect, they can have something important to offer in the complex processes involved in the experience of human health and healing.[135]

At the same time, Barrett's campaign draws attention to a knotty social problem. The issue of consumer protection entails no easy answers as we wrestle with how to shield people from potential medical harm while allowing them the freedom to try unorthodox therapies. The thoroughness of Barrett's research and the care he extends to guard people from hucksterism and harm are admirable. At the same time, Barrett's zeal sometimes blinds him to the good that is taking place as people explore new and traditional forms of healthcare and healing. By seeking to suppress such possibilities, Barrett is missing an important message that adherents of alternative medicine are delivering to the dominant medical establishment – that the road to health and healing is far more complex than any one medical theory or therapy can entail.

In conclusion, we may need both the vigilance of Barrett and the pioneering spirit of those who expand the boundaries of medical understanding. Both scientific and heterodox medicine have their place. The growing dissatisfaction with dominant medical practice is both a wake-up call and a challenge for those truly interested in what is best for patients and clients. Viewed this way, Barrett's *Quackwatch* website generates a number of problems that merit further investigation.

Notes

1 According to the *Quackwatch* homepage, as of January 2001, over 1.5 million 'visitors' have contacted its site. As of January 2001, the *Quackwatch* homepage, 'launched in December 1996', can be found at <http://www.quackwatch.com>. All sites will be referenced as they appeared under topic headings contained on the *Quackwatch* homepage between September 1999 and January 2001.

2 In the interest of simplicity, I will use the term 'alternative' to encompass the diverse range of therapeutic products, treatments, and beliefs that fall under these labels. In doing so, the term alternative will stand in contrast to what is often referred to as dominant, scientific-based biomedicine. Or as Eisenberg notes 'alternative medical therapies' are 'functionally defined as interventions neither taught widely in medical schools nor generally available in US hospitals', D. Eisenberg *et al.*, 'Trends in alternative medicine use in the United States, 1990–1997', *Journal of the American Medical Association*, 280, 11 (1998): 1569.

3 Some of Barrett's works include *Dubious Cancer Treatment*, published by the Florida Division of
   the American Cancer Society; *Health Schemes, Scams, and Frauds*, published by Consumer Reports
   Books; *The Vitamin Pushers: How the 'Health Food' Industry Is Selling America a Bill of Goods*, published
   by Prometheus Books; and *Reader's Guide to Alternative Health Methods*, published by the American
   Medical Association. S. Barrett, 'Biographical Sketch and Contact Information', <http://
   www.Quackwatch.com/10Bio/bio.html>, 10 January 2001.
4 According to other biographical information contained on his website, in 1984, Barrett received
   an FDA Commissioner's Special Citation Award for Public Service in fighting nutrition quackery.
   In 1986, he was awarded honorary membership in the American Dietetic Association and he
   has taught health education at The Pennsylvania State University. S. Barrett, 'Biographical
   sketch and contact information', <http://www.Quackwatch.com/10Bio/bio.html>.
5 Though my focus in this chapter is on Barrett's attack against alternative and complementary
   medicine, it is important to note that issues of institutional and professional health fraud are
   also addressed on Barrett's *Quackwatch* site. See S.R. Slades' 'Health care fraud: how far does the
   False Claims Act reach?' which address this important issue, <http://www.quackwatch.com/
   02ConsumerProtection/fca.html>.
6 The 'Mission Statement' also states that the umbrella organisation *Quackwatch* Inc. is a member
   of the Consumer Federation of America and that it was founded in 1969 in Pennsylvania by
   Barrett – when it was known as the Lehigh Valley Committee Against Health Fraud. *Quackwatch*
   Inc. was incorporated in 1970 and assumed its current name in 1997, <http://www.Quackwatch.
   com/00AboutQuackwatch/mission.html>, 11 January 2001.
7 During a telephone conversation, Barret told me his friends refer to him as the world's best
   'crap detector', which, as Barrett explained, means he is good at finding 'internal inconsistencies'
   whether they are 'something big' or 'subtle'.
8 It is ironic that Barrett, a retired psychiatrist, attacks the non-scientific aspects of alternative
   medicine when, as medical philosopher Arthur Kleinman points out, psychiatry is 'regarded as
   marginal by the rest of biomedicine'. Kleinman, *Writing at the Margin: Discourse Between Anthropology
   and Medicine*, Berkeley, University of California Press, 1995, p. 2. That is, some in the scientific
   community find some of psychoanalytic theory more closely akin to pseudo science and quackery
   than hard medical science. As will be seen below, it is also ironical that, as a psychiatrist, Barrett
   fails to take into consideration many of the mental and cognitive elements operating in the
   healing process.
9 D. Eisenberg, *et al.*, 'Trends in alternative medicine use in the United States, 1990–1997', *Journal
   of the American Medical Association* 280, 11 (1998): 1569–75. Eisenberg's study was a follow up to
   a prior national survey conducted in 1990. See D. Eisenberg *et al.*, 'Unconventional medicine in
   the United States: prevalence, costs, and patterns of use', *The New England Journal of Medicine*
   328, 28 (1993): 246–52.
10 See Barrett's 'warnings' on his links to 'Interesting Websites', <http://www.quackwatch.com/
   05Links/othersites.html>, 10 January 2001.
11 As of 11 January 2001, other websites related to medical and health quackery include *The American
   Council on Science and Health, Inc.* <http://www.acsh.org>, *Better Business Bureau Health Quackery*,
   <http://www.bosbbb.org/lit/0011.htm>, *Canadian Quackery Watch* <www.healthwatcher.net/
   Quackerywatch/index.html>, the *Committee for the Scientific Investigation of Claims of the Paranormal*
   <http://www.csicop.org/>, *Health Frontiers Center for Quackery Control, Inc.* <http://www.
   netasia.net/users/truehealth/index.htm>, *Healthcare Reality Check* <http://www.hcrc.org/
   index.html>, *Museum of Questionable Medical Devices* <http://www.mtn.org/quack>, *The National
   Council Against Health Fraud* <http://www.ncahf.org>, *Pictures of Health* <http://
   www.tld.jcu.edu.au/hist/quack/index.html>, *Qakatak* – Australian Skeptics <http://
   www.skeptics.com.au/features/qakatak/qakatak.htm>, and *The Skeptics Dictionary – Alternative
   Medicine* <http://www.dcn.davis.ca.us/~btcarrol/skeptic/tialtmed.html>. See the *Quackwatch*
   Skeptical information sources for links to local groups <http://www.quackwatch.com/05Links/
   skepticsites.html>.
12 Since I began a study of Barrett in February 1998, Barrett has added three other websites to his
   anti-quackery campaign. In October 1998, Barrett inaugurated *Chirobase*, a 'skeptical guide to

chiropractic history, theories, and current practices' <http://www.chirobase.org>. *Chirobase* is co-sponsored by the National Council Against Health Fraud, Inc. and Victims of Chiropractic'; and in January 1999 Barrett launched *MLM Watch*, 'a skeptical guide to multilevel marketing' <http://www.mlmwatch.org>. In February 2000 Barrett, 'with help from Manfred Kroger, PhD' began *NutriWatch*, a project of *Quackwatch* which provides an 'analysis of health claims made for nutrition-related products', 'warnings about inappropriate claims', 'reporting illegal claims for products to regulatory agencies' and 'helping people seek legal redress against dietary supplement companies', S. Barrett, '*NutriWatch* Mission Statement', 10 January 2001 <http://www.nutriwatch.org/00AboutNutriwatch/mission.html>.

13 According to Barrett's definition, a cursory read of most American medical journals would seem to qualify pharmaceutical drugs – a central biomedical therapy – as quackery, given the enormous amount of money spent on promotion and the excessive marketing and pitching activities of pharmaceutical sales reps.

14 Multi-level marketing (MLM) – also commonly known as 'network' marketing – involves the direct sale, marketing and distribution of goods, services, and products through a chain of 'downlines', or vertical payout groups by independent distributors or sales associates. Individuals are rewarded and compensated with money, trips, automobiles and prizes according to how many members they can recruit into their downline organisation. This drive to recruit helps account for much of the product hype and sales pressure that Barrett criticises.

15 See Barrett's 'The mirage of multilevel marketing', <http://www.quackwatch.com/01QuackeryRelatedTopics/mlm.html>, for a list of such claims and his critique of using personal experience as a measure of therapeutic value – a theme to be pursued later in this article.

16 Hardey, 'Health for sale', (Chapter 12) in this volume, draws further attention to this potential problem.

17 <http://www.quackwatch.com/01QuackeryRelatedTopics/harmquack.html>.

18 Several writers in this volume draw attention to the complex role psycho-cultural and spiritual forces play in the healing process including Reis, 'Medical pluralism' (Chapter 6) and Laing, 'Spirituality, belief and knowledge' (Chapter 9).

19 By employing the term 'crusade' to characterise Barrett's internet campaign, I capitalise upon the implications embodied within this word. According to *Webster's Dictionary*, 1977, a 'crusade' is both a 'war or expedition having a religious object' and an 'enterprise projected in a spirit of enthusiasm and conducted with earnestness for some idea or cause, or against some social or economic wrong'. That Barrett conceives of most alternative medicine as a socio-economic wrong and that he is conducting a 'cause' will become apparent throughout this chapter.

20 Barrett pays homage to this understanding of *quack*ery by placing the image of a 'Sherlock Holmes'-like cartoon duck character at the top of his homepage. As will be seen, I distinguish quackery as the pejorative labelling of competing schools, systems and techniques of medical practice which do not conform to the standards of dominant biomedicine from the European mountebank and American medicine show hucksters, 'snake oil sellers' and others who unscrupulously and intentionally sell worthless nostrums and techniques to bilk people of their money. However, this is not to imply that all itinerant merchants were snake oil artists. See Fowler, *Mystic Healers and Medicine Shows: Blazing Trails to Wellness in the Old West and Beyond*, Santa Fe, Ancient City, 1997 and McNamara, *Step in the Right Direction*, Jackson, University of Mississippi Press, 1995 for studies of the travelling medicine show – a unique American mixture of health information, medicine and frontier entertainment.

21 Gevitz, 'Three Perspectives on Unorthodox', in Norman Gevitz (ed.), *Other Healers: Unorthodox Medicine in America*, Baltimore, Johns Hopkins University Press, 1988, p. 2. See also C.J.S Thompson's *The Quacks of Old London*, New York, Brentano's, 1928, which offers a historical perspective on the notion of quacks and quackery, chronicling their rise and development in sixteenth-century England.

22 Loudon offers a brief summary of the number of notions the term quack has signified in Western history – everything from someone who practised medicine but lacked formal education in classical Greece to rapacious, modern itinerant 'snake oil' artists who exploit and fleece people,

'The vile race of quacks with which this country is infected', in W.F. Bynum and Roy Porter (eds), *Medical Fringe and Medical Orthodoxy 1750–1850*, London, Croom Helm, 1987, pp. 106–28.

23 P.S. Brown, 'Social context and medical theory in the demarcation of nineteenth-century boundaries', in W.F. Bynum and Roy Porter (eds), *Medical Fringe and Medical Orthodoxy 1750– 1850*, London, Croom Helm, 1987, pp. 216–33.

24 B. Inglis, *The Case For Unorthodox Medicine*, New York, G.P. Putnam, 1965, p. 9.

25 See P. Starr for a detailed chronicling of the battle for medical dominance during the nineteenth century between orthodox and irregular medical practitioners, *The Social Transformation of American Medicine: The Rise of a Sovereign Profession and the Making of a Vast Industry*, New York, Basic, 1982, pp. 9–29 and pp. 79–144.

26 See also Gevitz 'Three perspectives', op. cit., pp. 9–10, for a succinct summary of the AMA's involvement in the legal repression of patent medicines. However, as Brown, 'Social context', op. cit., pp. 216–9 reveals, it was not only quacks who peddled patent medicines. Many allopathic practitioners of the time also used proprietary formulas in their practice.

27 J.H. Young, *The Medical Messiahs: A Social History of Health Quackery in Twentieth-Century America*, Princeton, NJ, Princeton University Press, 1967, pp. 360–89, vividly re-tells the celebrated 1950's Harry Hoxsey case and how local and federal authorities were tireless in their efforts to stop his cancer cure. Young's description of Hoxsey's fraudulence and medical quackery appears solid in its dismissal of Hoxsey's formula. However, P.S. Ward, in a study commissioned by the Office of Technology Assessment of the United States Congress, 'History of Hoxsey', <http:// biomedical.hypermart.net/ward.html>, reveals how recent scientific studies have shown that many of the herbs used in Hoxsey's formula do have anti-tumour properties. She also highlights the way the medical authorities of the time did not test Hoxsey's formula. See also the *Quackwatch* reprint of the 1990 US Office of Technology Assessment: Unconventional Cancer Treatments document which addresses the medical politics entailed in the Hoxsey case, Ch. 4, <http:// www.quackwatch.com/01QuackeryRelatedTopics/OTA/ota04.html>.

28 In essence, Barrett follows the biomedical convention of grounding the criteria for quackery in a scientific perspective, e.g. 'quackery entails the use of methods that are not scientifically accepted', 'Quackery: how should it be defined?', 22 January 2001, <http://www.Quackwatch. com/01QuackeryRelatedTopics/quackdef.html>.

29 Just as the Jacksonian era (c.1828–48) had unleashed a populist drive toward medical freedom and individual autonomy that led to a proliferation of medical sects, practices and products, so the Progressive era released a drive to 'cleanse' American institutions of fraud, corruption and unbridled self-interest. Such reform coalesced into public policy that restricted the selling of untested and non-efficacious patent medicines. The spirit behind the Progressive movement, coupled with the increasing sophistication of chemical and scientific analysis to confirm test results on questionable food and drug products, gave rise to the large number of quack-busters during this period. See J.G. Burrow, *Organized Medicine in the Progressive Era: The Move Toward Monopoly*, Baltimore: Johns Hopkins University Press, 1977; J.H. Young, *The Toadstool Millionaires: A Social History of Patent Medicines in America Before Federal Regulation*, Princeton, NJ, Princeton University Press, 1961; and *Medical Messiahs*, op. cit., for detailed insights into this era.

30 See Young, *Medical Messiahs*, ibid., pp. 28–35, for an in-depth look at this period and the type of anti-quackery and anti-nostrum muckraking that led to the enactment of the 1906 Pure Food and Drug Act.

31 See also L.S. Reed, *The Healing Cults: A Study of Sectarian Medical Practice: Its Extent, Causes, and Control*, Chicago, University of Chicago Press, 1932, for further insight into the drive to control medical sects.

32 In 1906, the Pure Food and Drug Act was enacted to protect the public's health and welfare from mislabelled and adulterated foods, drinks and drugs, as well as cure-all claims and unproven and harmful nostrums and elixirs. In 1911, the Sherley Amendment was passed which prohibited labelling medicines with what were perceived to be false therapeutic claims. Though the 1938 Food, Drug and Cosmetic Act eliminated the Sherley Amendment, it, among other things, set strict guidelines requiring that new drugs be shown safe before they are marketed to the public. In order to enforce these laws the US Congress, in 1927, created the Food, Drug and Insecticide

Administration, which in 1930 became the Food and Drug Administration (FDA). See Young, *Medical Messiahs*, op. cit., for a detailed history of the medicinal laws passed during the first half of the twentieth century. See also the *US Food and Drug Association's Center for Food Safety and Applied Nutrition*, website, <http://vm.cfsan.fda.gov/mileston.html>, for a succinct history of the 'Milestones in U.S. food and drug law history'. See also P.S. Brown, for a brief description of the medical laws that extended the reach of 'orthodox medicine's monopoly' in England during the first half of the twentieth-century, 'The vicissitudes of herbalism in late nineteenth- and early twentieth-century Britain', *Medical History*, 1985, pp. 87–8.

33 'Quackery: how should it be defined?', <http://www.Quackwatch.com/01QuackeryRelated Topics/quackdef.html>.

34 Ibid.

35 Ibid.

36 I use the phrase 'scientific thinking' instead of 'scientific revolution' (*c.*1550–1700) to characterise the empirical and mechanistic orientation that marks modern science. I do this because, as a number of historians observe, contemporary insight into sixteenth- and seventeenth-century understanding of science makes such notion of a scientific revolution (*c.*1550–1700) problematic at best. See S. Shapin, *The Scientific Revolution*, Chicago, University of Chicago Press, 1996, and D.C. Lindberg and R.S. Westman, *Reappraisals of the Scientific Revolution*, Cambridge, Cambridge University Press, 1990, for further insight into contested notions of radical conceptual breaks, 'autonomous ideas' and 'disembodied mentalities' that have traditionally been attached to the notion of scientific revolution.

37 In addition to Barrett, authors who have been influenced by Cramp and Fishbein and the spirit that underlies their work include: E. Jameson, *The Natural History of Quackery*, London, Michael Joseph, 1961, who presents a historical overview of the role quacks and their nostrums have played in the course of Western history from the ancient Greeks to the present; Young, *Toadstool Millionaires*, and *Medical Messiahs*, op. cit., who offers a detailed anti-quackery survey of the social history of pre-federal and post federal regulation of patent medicines; S.H. Holbrook, *The Golden Age of Quackery*, New York, Macmillan, 1959, who chronicles the origins of the 1907 Federal Pure Food and Drug Act and, like Young, highlights many of the colourful personalities involved with this period; G. Carson, *One For a Man, Two For a Horse*, Garden City, Doubleday, 1961, who presents a light spirited-attack against the 'proprietary sharpshooters' who have sent 'secret remedies, gurgling down the American gullet in a brown, bitter flood', p. 7; A. Bender, *Health or Hoax: The Truth About Health Foods and Diets*, New York, Prometheus, 1986, who promotes the assumption that there is 'no such thing as a health food', and that the health food industry is a fraudulent (non-science-based) enterprise that seeks, through slick 'salesmanship', to take advantage of consumer gullibility and fear in order to make money. R.M. Deutsch, *The Nuts Among the Berries*, New York, Ballantine, 1961; and F.J. Stare, *Eating for Good Health*, New York, 1964, are earlier versions of Bender's work. Deutsch's work is derisive in tone as it seeks to offer 'informative glimpses into that dizzying and overpopulated pageant' of medical and dietary quacks and faddists, op. cit., p. 11. Stare, in turn, seeks to dispel the 'tons of nonsense' fed to the public by 'food faddists masquerading as ministers of good health', op. cit., p. 2. However, it is worth noting that some of the assertions made by anti-quackery writers like Bender, Deutsch and Stare have been contradicted by later molecular-chemistry and bio-nutritional research, e.g. their claim that whole wheat bread and thoroughly chewing your food are not good for you.

38 In focusing on Abraham Flexner and his famous 'report' I do not mean to imply this was the only, or main, contributory force in the cultural ascendancy of scientific medicine during the early part of the twentieth century. J.G. Burrow highlights the enormous contribution Joseph N. McCormack made in helping the AMA achieve 'mastery of the techniques' of 'mass appeal' and 'political leverage' in 'mingling public interest with its own', *Organized Medicine*, op. cit., p. 16. I focus on the 'Flexner Report' because of its explicit contribution to the undermining and marginalising of competing medical systems.

39 The Flexner Report was underwritten by a large grant given by the Carnegie Foundation and sought to stem what Henry S. Prichett, president of the Carnegie Foundation for the Advancement of Teaching, said was the 'enormous over-production of uneducated and ill-trained medical

practitioners' that the medical schools of the time were churning out, Pritchett, Introduction, *Medical Education in the United States and Canada: A Report To The Carnegie Foundation For the Advancement of Teaching*, by Abraham Flexner, New York: n.p., 1910, x. See Burrow, *Organized Medicine*, op. cit., and S.C. Wheatley, *The Politics of Philanthropy: Abraham Flexner and Medical Education*, Madison, University of Wisconsin Press, 1988, for a more detailed narrative of Flexner's report and the cultural factors that led to it.

40   Flexner's critique, like some of Barrett's rhetoric, was blunt in tone. Representative examples of Flexner's direct style include his denunciation of the Georgia College of Eclectic Medicine and Surgery of which he said 'nothing more disgraceful calling itself a medical school can be found anywhere', A. Flexner, *Medical Education in the United States and Canada: A Report To The Carnegie Foundation For the Advancement of Teaching*, New York, n.p., 1910, p. 205. See also his statement that the Missouri medical schools were 'utterly wretched' and 'without promise', ibid., p. 258.

41   Ibid., p. 24

42   Ibid., p. 25.

43   J.A. Lee, 'Social change and marginal therapeutic systems', in Roy Wallis and Peter Morley, (eds), *Marginal Medicine*, New York, Free Press, 1976, 25.

44   Flexner, op. cit., 24–5. In further support of this view, Flexner quotes a Dr Osler who claims that 'a new school of practitioners has arisen, which cares nothing for homoeopathy and less for so-called 'allopathy'. It seeks to study rationally and scientifically, the action of drugs, old and new'. Ibid., p. 162.

45   S. Shapin, op. cit., p. 44.

46   Flexner, op. cit., p. 158.

47   See Reed for a later application of Flexner's approach to medical sects during the 1930s. Reed, despite his claim 'to be objective and without bias', follows Flexner's perspective so closely, it could make a case for plagiarism. See also Reed's cutting condemnation of chiropractors, op. cit., pp. 108–9. Dominant medicine's antipathy toward chiropractic medicine continues today, as evidenced by a recent *New England Journal of Medicine* article, Cherkin, *et al.*, 'A Comparison of Physical Therapy', 1998, pp. 1021–8.

48   Despite appeals to 'professional patriotism' and the non commercial nature of the medical profession, Flexner's report was quite explicit in its claim that the 'interests of the social order will be served best when the number of physicians entering a given profession reaches and does not exceed a certain ratio', Pritchett, op. cit., p. xiv, and that the way to get 'better doctors' is to 'produce fewer', Flexner, *Medical Education*, 1910, p. 17. See Burrow for a sample of contemporary criticism aimed at Flexner and his report, including the hasty and prejudicial way it was conducted, Burrow, op. cit., pp. 43–7.

49   Barrett is especially critical of chiropractic care. He not only offers more than ten anti-chiropractic articles in his *Quackwatch* website but he has added a website dedicated to anti-chiropractic discourse called *Chirobas*, which Barrett bills as a 'Skeptical guide to chiropractic history, theories, and current practices', <http://www.chirobase.org>.

50   Most of the criteria Flexner uses to measure if medical schools meet his standard are based upon the knowledge and equipment used in the sciences of 'physiology, pathology, chemistry, (and) microscopy', Flexner, op.cit., 164. In doing so, Flexner helped promote the basic tenets of medical scientism, e.g. the universal and homogenous application of the methodological procedures of natural science, the desire to formulate 'standards of exactness and certainty' and law-like medical statements and a drive to establish objective and technical results. (I am grateful to R. Dingle for insights into scientism, *Aspects of Illness*, New York, St Martin's Press, 1976, p. 15.) However, it is also important to point out, as Wheatley reminds us in his *Politics of Philanthropy*, op.cit., that Flexner did not initiate the development of modern science in medicine. This momentum had started long before him. Flexner's skill lay in his ability to control, shape and manage the institutional destination to where the scientific path led.

51   'Be wary of "alternative" health methods'. <http://www.Quackwatch.com/01QuackeryRelated Topics/altwary.html>.

52   See Barrett and Victor Herbert's 'twenty-five ways to spot quacks and vitamin pushers' (especially No. 23) – 'They claim they are being persecuted by orthodox medicine and that their work is

being suppressed because it's controversial', <http://www.familyinternet.com/quackwatch/01QuackeryRelatedTopics/spotquack.html>, as another example of how Barrett is aware of the socio-rhetorical strategies his opponents employ.

53 Barrett's determination to stop what he considers health-oriented 'consumer fraud' has led him to 'set up a clearinghouse' to help 'potential plaintiffs' find attorneys who can help them prosecute violations of 'consumer protection lawsuits', S. Barrett, 'Plaintiffs wanted', <http://www.Quackwatch.com/02ConsumerProtection/suits.html>. In addition, Barrett has approximately twenty lawyers on his 'Legal Advisory Board' – many of whom are 'interested in filing lawsuits on behalf of quackery victims', '*Quackwatch* Legal Advisory Board', <http://www.Quackwatch.com/09Advisors/legal.html>.

54 'A few thoughts on *Ayurvedic* mumbo-jumbo', <http://www.Quackwatch.com/04Consumer Education/chopra.html>.

55 'The mercury amalgam scam', <http://www.Quackwatch.com/01QuackeryRelatedTopics/mercury.html>.

56 'Steer clear of "chiropractic nutrition"', <http://www.Quackwatch.com/01QuackeryRelated Topics/chironutr.html>.

57 The Bates Method is a technique of eye correction based on exercises employing relaxation and special movement. It was developed by American ophthalmologist W.H. Bates (1865–1931). See the Bates Association for Vision Correction website for more information http://www.seeing.org. 'Eye-related quackery', <http://www.Quackwatch.com/01QuackeryRelated Topics/eyequack.html>.

58 <http://quasar.as.utexas.edu/BillInfo/Quack.html>, 19 April 2000

59 'A proposal to combat quackery and health fraud in California', <http://www.Quackwatch.com/02ConsumerProtection/calif.html>.

60 Ibid.

61 'Plaintiffs wanted for consumer protection suits!', <http://www.Quackwatch.com/02Consumer Protection/suits.html>.

62 Authors who highlight the larger socio-political factors involved in the suppression of medical plurality include D. Arnold (ed.), Introduction, *Imperial Medicine and Indigenous Societies* Manchester, Manchester University Press, 1988, pp. 1–26; H. Berliner, 'Medical Modes of Production', *The Problem of Medical Knowledge: Examining the Social Construction of Medicine*, Edinburgh: Edinburgh University Press, 1982, pp. 162–73; H.S. Berliner and J.W. Salmon, 'The holistic health movement and scientific medicine: the naked and the dead', *Socialist Review* 43 (1979): 31–52; S. Cant and U. Sharma, *Complementary and Alternative Medicines: Knowledge in Practice*, London, Free Association Books, 1996; B. Good, *Medicine, Rationality, and Experience: An Anthropological Perspective*, New York, Cambridge University Press, 1994; E.A. Krause, *Power and Illness: The Political Sociology of Health and Medical Care*, New York, Elsevier, 1977; R. Wallis, Introduction, in Roy Wallis (ed.), *On the Margins of Science: The Social Construction of Rejected Knowledge*, Keele, UK, University of Keele, 1979, pp. 5–8; and B. Wynne, 'Between Orthodoxy and Oblivion: The Normalization of Deviance Science', in Roy Wallis (ed.), *On the Margins of Science: The Social Construction of Rejected Knowledge*, Keele, UK, University of Keele, 1979, pp. 67–84. In addition, D. Smith, *Nutrition in Britain*, London, Routledge, 1996, reveals how medical marginalisation and social control have been at play in the production and application of nutritional scientific knowledge in England, and P. Bartip, 'Themselves Writ Large: The British Medical Association 1832–1966', London, *BMJ*, 1996, offers insight into the way 'medical politics' played a role in the suppression of 'quacks' during the formative days of the British Medical Association – a process that was followed later in the USA. For a Continental perspective of socio-medical politics, see M.H. Gijswit-Hofstra, H. Marland and H. de Waardt, Introduction, in Marijke Gijswijt-Hofstra, Hilary Marland and Hans de Waardt, (eds), *Illness and Healing Alternatives in Western Europe*, London, Roultledge, 1997, pp. 1–13.

63 Starr, op. cit., p. 24.

64 S. Aronowitz, *Science as Power: Discourse and Ideology in Modern Society*, Minneapolis, University of Minnesota Press, 1988, p. 107.

65   Although the creation of the FDA can be interpreted as a way to protect the public and the consumer from the forces of big business that seeks to take advantage of them (see Young, *Medical Messiahs*, op. cit., p. 98) for some in the contemporary alternative health field the FDA is also construed as a way to shore up monopolistic control over healthcare by allowing dominant medicine and large pharmaceutical conglomerates to weed out competition within the medicinal marketplace. See McCain's website as an example of an outspoken internet proponent of this view, <http://www.herbalhealer.com>.

66   E. Campion, 'Why unconventional medicine', *New England Journal of Medicine* 328, 28 (1993): 283.

67   In drawing this distinction, I do not mean to undermine the legitimate concern over medical hucksters, charlatans and cranks who harm people by promoting products of worthless or dangerous medicinal value.

68   B. Starfield, 'Is US health really the best in the world', *The Journal of the American Medical Association* 284 (2000): 483–5.

69   Other reports have revealed the high number of iatrogenic or 'treatment induced' deaths and complications occurring in mainstream hospitals. See J. Lazarou, *et al.*, 'Incidence of adverse drug reactions in hospitalized patients', *The Journal of the American Medical Association* 279 (1998): 1200–5; R. Voelker, '"Treat systems, not errors", experts say', *The Journal of the American Medical Association* (20 November 1996); and T. Wieland, 'Iatrogenic complications and quality improvement in everyday medical practice', *Schweiz Med Wochenschr* 126 (1996): 517–21, as representative examples. Lazarou cites the unsettling fact that in 1994 approximately 106,000 American hospital patients died from ADR, 'adverse drug reactions' op. cit. p. 1204. Inglis further chronicles other incidents that have disillusioned some medical practitioners and led many patients away from biomedicine as their first medical response. Inglis, *The Case for Unorthodox Medicine*, New York, G.P. Putnam, 1965, pp. 15–64.

70   'Doing what counts for patient safety: federal actions to reduce medical errors and their impact' <http://www.quic.gov/report>, February 2000.

71   Ibid.

72   B. Starfield, op. cit., p. 483–4.

73   Ibid., p. 484.

74   M.L. Gross, *The Medical Racket: How Doctors, HMOs, and Hospitals Are Failing the American Patient*, New York, Avon, 1998, p. 232.

75   In essence, the for-profit HMO system has replaced the traditional fee-for-service and insurance indemnity plans that once ruled the medical industry. In the view of some, this has not been in the best interest of patients given that the financially minded 'gatekeepers' of HMOs, rather than physicians, are increasingly the ones who determine if a specialist should be consulted or what treatment should be given. See the Agency for Healthcare Research and Quality webpage on 'Managed Care', <http://www.ahcpr.gov/research/managix.htm>, 12 January 2001, for further insight into the effects on medical care this new system has had.

76   Again my intent is not to undercut the stunning accomplishments medical science frequently accomplishes with its highly developed pharmaceutical and technological therapies.

77   I. Illich, *Medical Nemesis: The Expropriation of Health*, New York, Pantheon, 1976, p. 1. Illich's detailed, seminal critique of the medical establishment and its 'iatrogenesis' – doctor induced illnesses – and 'medicalization of life' was so cogent that some of his ardent critics, such as David F. Horrobin, had to admit that Illich was often 'right' and even 'constructively critical' in his controversial views, ibid., p. 2.

78   J.P. Kassirer readily admits that something has to be done given that 'disgruntled, cranky doctors are not likely to provide outstanding medical care' Kassirer, 'Doctor Discontent', *The New England Journal of Medicine* 339 (1998): 544.

79   Ibid., p. 1543.

80   S. Barrett, 'Comments from *Quackwatch* visitors' <http://www.familyinternet.com/quackwatch/00AboutQuackwatch/comments.html#anchor129310273632>.

81   Ibid.

82 S. Barrett, 'Quackery: how should it be defined?', <http://www.quackwatch.com/01Quackery RelatedTopics/quackdef.html>.

83 S. Barrett, 'Some notes on the nature of science', <http://www.quackwatch.com/01Quackery RelatedTopics/scinotes.html> 12 January 2001.

84 See Beckman, H.B. and Frankel, R.M. 'The Effect of Physician Behavior on the Collection of Data', *Annals of Internal Medicine* 101 (1984): 692–6, and K. Marvel, 'Soliciting the Patient's Agenda: Have We Improved?' *The Journal of the American Medical Association* 281 (1999): 283–7, who reveal the way medical physicians 'interrupt' and 'redirect' patients, on average, after only eighteen seconds of listening.

85 J. Collier, 'Time and touch – what set alternative medicines apart', *The Listener* 3 (1986): 14. As will be noted below, scientific research is beginning to confirm that such acts of caring significantly affect beneficial responses in the healing process.

86 See R.W. Moss, 'The Cancer chronicles', 15 Oct, 1999, <http://ralphmoss.com/events2.html>, for the view that dominant medicine's record on cancer has not fulfilled its promise – especially given the billions of dollars spent on the 'war on cancer' and the toxic side-effects of many pharmaceutical based anti-cancer agents.

87 R. Hass, *Permanent Remissions: Life-Extending Diet Strategies That Can Help Prevent and Reverse, Cancer, Heart Disease, Diabetes, and Osteoporosis*, New York, Pocket, 1997, p. 27.

88 M.S. Wetzel, D.M. Eisenberg and T.J. Kaptchuk, 'Courses involving complementary and alternative medicine at US Medical Schools', *Journal of the American Medical Association* 280 (1998): 784–7. For more on this trend, see the *Boston Globe* article 'Alternative medicine takes hold in schools', 1998, A11.

89 'Why health professionals become quacks'. <http://www.familyinternet.com/quackwatch/ 01QuackeryRelatedTopics/quackpro.html>, 22 January 2001.

90 Ibid., Jarvis' implied belittlement of 'religion' and 'philosophy' is also a trait of scientism.

91 S. Barrett, 'Some notes on the nature of science'. <http://www.familyinternet.com/quackwatch/ 01QuackeryRelatedTopics/scinotes.html>.

92 Ibid.

93 T. Moore, *Life Span: New Perspectives on Extending Human Longevity*, New York, Simon and Schuster, 1993, p. 131.

94 Ibid., p. 154.

95 Although Moore's case against 'excessive weight, elevated cholesterol and high blood pressure' might seem scientifically heretical, he offers cogent scientific data that there is no evidence to back the claims of the dominant medical establishment. See Moore, ibid., pp. 129–204.

96 Ibid., p. 152.

97 Ibid., p. 129.

98 Ibid., p. 144.

99 Ibid., p. 170.

100 Ibid., p. 184.

101 See A.R. Hale, *These Cults: An Analysis of the Foibles of Dr Morris Fishbein's 'Medical Follies' and an Indictment of Medical Practice in General, With a Non-Partisan Presentation of the Case for Drugless Schools of Healing*, New York, National Health Foundation, 1926, who in the 1920s mounted an oppositional campaign against Morris Fishbein and his *Medical Follies* in particular and the oppressive ways of dominant medicine in general. Hale represents an early twentieth-century strain of counter-discourse by heterodox healthcare advocates against those whom they consider to be unnecessarily restrictive of medical pluralism and freedom.

102 'Herbal Healer Academy news update July 1999' <http://www.herbalhealer.com/newsletters/ n0799.html>. See M. McCain's *Herbal Healer Academy* website for other examples of strong anti-medical political sentiments – what she calls 'rants', 'Past newsletters' <http://www.herbalhealer. com/news.html>.

103 Moss, a prolific writer about alternative cancer therapies, mentions how he was instrumental in getting Rick Klausner, director of the American National Cancer Institute (NCI), to 'remove its derogatory statements about non-conventional (cancer) treatments from its website'. L.G. Casura, 'Rooting for the roots: a conversation with Ralph Moss, PhD', *Townsend Letter for Doctors and*

Patients, January 1999, p. 38. He also states that the NCI has 'gone from being the sworn enemy of alternative treatments to a potential partner in evaluating such treatments'. Ibid., p. 39.

104   Ibid., p. 41.

105   See the 'Government resources: alternative medicine resources' homepage, <http://www.pitt.edu/~cbw/gov.html>, for an extensive listing of US state and federal agencies dedicated to alternative and complimentary medicine.

106   'Appropriations Bill establishes the National Center for Complementary and Alternative Medicine' 13 August 1999, <http://nccam.nih.gov/nccam/news-events/press-releases/110398.shtml>. The National Center for Complementary and Alternative Medicine was formerly known as the Office of Alternative Medicine (OAM), which was originally established by a congressional mandate in 1991 to 'place greater research emphasis on the rigorous scientific evaluation of complementary and alternative medicine (CAM) treatments, develop a solid infrastructure to coordinate and conduct research at the NIH, and establish a clearinghouse to provide information to the public'. Ibid.

107   A number of researchers and clinical studies have drawn attention to the connection between emotional states and healing, including medical physicians C.A. Hammerschlag, and H.D. Silverman, *Healing Ceremonies: Creating Personal Rituals for Spiritual, Emotional, Physical and Mental Health,* Phoenix, Turtle Island Press, 1998, who explore the psychoneuroimmunologic, or what they call the mind/body/spirit, implications of personalised healing rituals; B. Justice, *Who Gets Sick: How Beliefs, Moods, and Thoughts Affect Your Health,* Los Angeles, J.P. Tarcher, 1988, who offers a number of case studies revealing the role thoughts and emotions play in disease and health; C. Myss and C. Norman Shealy, *The Creation of Health: The Emotional, Psychological, and Spiritual Responses That Promote Health and Healing,* New York, Three Rivers, 1998, who disclose the way dysfunction emotions and negative attitudes affect health; as well as H. Benson and M. Stark, *Timeless Healing: The Power and Biology of Belief,* New York, Scribner, 1996; J. Borysenko, *Minding the Body, Mending the Mind,* New York, Bantam Doubleday, 1993; J. Borysenko, *Minding the Body,* 1993; and S.R. Maddi and S.C. Kobasa, *The Hardy Executive: Health Under Stress,* Homewood, Dow Johannes-Irwin, 1984, who affirm a physiological link between belief and the healing process.

108   Barrett is aware of the placebo effect. He posts an essay by Barry Beyerstein that acknowledges this force might be at work in alternative therapies. Ironically Beyerstein admits that 'some placebo responses produce actual changes in the physical condition; others are subjective changes that make patients feel better even though there has been no objective change in the underlying pathology', 'Why bogus therapies often seem to work'. <http://www.familyinternet.com/quackwatch/01QuackeryRelatedTopics/altbelief.html>.

109   See M. Kemeny, 'Emotions and the Immune System', *Healing and the Mind,* Bill Moyers (ed.), New York, Doubleday, 1993, pp. 195–211. It is also noteworthy that the prevailing view of the immune system as 'an entirely autonomous, self-regulating system' prevented earlier scientists from seeing that the brain is connected to immunological response and that 'hormones and neurotransmitters can influence the activities of the immune system', D. Felten, 'The brain and the immune system', *Healing and the Mind,* Bill Moyers (ed.), New York, Doubleday, 1993, pp. 215.

110   H. Benson and M. Stark, *Timeless Healing: The Power and Biology of Belief,* New York, Scribner, 1996, pp. 32–4. Benson has also been acting director of the Mind/Body Medical Institute, a Division of Behavioral Medicine, at the New England Deaconess Hospital.

111   Benson, and others, who have studied the placebo effect – the ability of inert substances to produce a cure – have found that beliefs, emotions and attitudes have a profound effect upon the body and the healing process. The placebo effect is so strong that Benson cites a study where pregnant women suffering from persistent vomiting and nausea were given a drug they were told would 'cure the problem'. In fact they were given – syrup of ipecac – a drug that causes vomiting. However, test results revealed that the nausea and vomiting ceased in the women taking syrup of ipecac. What was interesting for the researchers was that belief in the power of the medication 'reversed the proven action of a powerful drug', ibid., p. 32.

112   Benson also draws attention to the way most health professionals and patients are 'eager to please one another, the former by being friendly, hopeful, and confident in the therapies being

recommended, and the latter by getting better, by reporting improvements in health or by complying with instructions', ibid., p. 35. Benson has also found that there are three components in the way belief, or the 'expectation of a good outcome can have formidable restorative power', ibid., p. 32. They include: 1. belief and expectancy on the part of the patient and the caregiver for a positive outcome, 2. the quality of the relationship between the patient and health practitioner, and 3. that there is a direct correlation between the enthusiasm conveyed by the physician and success rates, ibid., 34. This insight helps shed light on why some alternative healers appear to be successful despite lack of formal training.

113 Ibid., p. 61. The opposite is also true. As Benson points out, when the body is 'fed images of disability and despair', it is 'wired to accept these limitations as truthful and to respond with impairment', ibid., p. 60. It appears Barrett is cognisant of this research given that his daughter has posted a web article that addresses emotional and mental ways to overcome chronic pain. See D. Barrett, 'Maintaining a positive attitude: ten strategies', <http://www.quackwatch.com/03HealthPromotion/fibromyalgia/fms05.html>, 12 January 2001. It is also interesting to note that Barrett's use of mind/body medicine centers on fibromyalgia – a disease biomedicine cannot cure.

114 D. Felten, op. cit., p. 216.

115 E. Padus, *The Complete Guide to Your Emotions and Your Health: New Dimensions in Mind/Body Healing*, Emmaus, Rodale, 1986, p. 528. Barrett admits that such mind/body and placebo phenomenon are real when he cites several studies that have shown that health problems patients attribute to amalgam dental fillings are 'psychosomatic in nature and have been exacerbated greatly by information from the media or from a dentist', 'The mercury amalgam scam' <http://www.Quackwatch.com/01QuackeryRelatedTopics/mercury.html>.

116 'The mirage of multi level marketing' <http://www.quackwatch.com/01QuackeryRelatedTopics/mlm.html>.

117 Barrett's disavowal of personal testimonials that many proponents of alternative medicine employ to bolster their case has conceptual roots in the quack-busters who preceded him. Young notes that Cramp would visit schools, fairs and other venues where he spoke and hang a sign that read 'Testimonials are worthless', Young, *Medical Messiahs*, op. cit., p. 131.

118 J.S. Goodwin and J.M. Goodwin, 'The tomato effect: rejection of highly efficacious therapies', *Journal of the American Medical Association*, 251 (1984): 2387.

119 I am grateful to Robert Shellenberger and Judith Green for drawing my attention to the 'tomato effect'. An online reprint of their book *From The Ghost in the Box To Successful Biofeedback Training*, (originally published by Health Psychology Publications, Greeley, Co, 1986), is available <http://www.incontinet.com/ghost.htm> 17 January 2001. Chapter Five, 'The tomato effect, the placebo effect, and science', <http://www.incontinet.com/ghost5.htm> is particularly insightful regarding the limitations of the 'one, active ingredient, one independent variable', pharmaceutical methodology when it is applied to biofeedback.

120 See Benson and Stark, *Timeless Healing*, op. cit., p. 51.

121 R. Cooter, 'Introduction: the alternations of past and present', in Roger Cooter (ed.), *Studies in the History of Alternative Medicine*, New York, St. Martin, 1988, p. xi.

122 B. Inglis, *The Case*, op. cit., p. 39.

123 See R.J. Bernstein, *The New Constellation: The Ethical-Political Horizons of Modernity/Postmodernity*, Cambridge, MIT Press, 1992, for insights into the socio-political ramifications of key 'post-modern' ideas.

124 Ibid., pp. 69–71.

125 See Bode, 'Indian indigenous pharmaceuticals' (Chapter 11); Reed, 'Local–global spaces' (Chapter 10); Scheid, '*Kexue*, and *Guanxixue*' (Chapter 8) in this volume.

126 S. Barrett, 'Acupuncture, Qigong, and 'Chinese medicine', <http://www.quackwatch.com/01QuackeryRelatedTopics/acu.html>, 'A few thoughts on Ayurvedic mumbo-jumbo', <http://www.quackwatch.com/04ConsumerEducation/chopra.html>, 12 January 2001.

127 See Bode, 'Indian indigenous pharmaceuticals' (Chapter 11); Liebeskind, 'Arguing science' (Chapter 4); Reed, 'Local–global spaces' (Chapter 10); Reis, 'Medical pluralism' (Chapter 6); Scheid, '*Kexue* and *Guanxixue*' (Chapter 8) in this volume.

128   National Academy of Sciences, Institute of Medicine, 'Preventing death and injury from medical errors requires dramatic, system-wide changes'. http://www4.nationalacademies.org/news.nsf/0a254cd9b53e0bc585256777004e74d3/e337b783cfa1b87c85256838007328eb?Open Document, 29 November 1999.

129   M. Foucault, Preface, *The Birth of the Clinic: An Archaeology of Medical Perception*, Trans. A.M. Sheridan Smith, 1973, New York, Vintage, 1994, p. xi.

130   See Olness' research on the use of relaxation imagery and other self-regulating strategies to control migraine headaches, K. Olness, 'Self-regulation and conditioning', in Bill Moyers, (ed.), *Healing and the Mind*, New York, Doubleday, 1993, p. 72.

131   E. Campion, 'Why unconventional medicine', *New England Journal of Medicine* 328, 28 (1993): 282–3. Campion cites H. Beecher, 'The Powerful Placebo Effect', *Journal of the American Medical Association* 159 (1955): 1602–6, to support his claim.

132   At the same time, openness to phenomena that do not fit current scientific models does not mean that medical science needs to abandon its verifying standards and criteria. Science is a cogent heuristic lens that uncovers and verifies many important phenomena. Yet medical science needs to explore the way its current conceptual grid might foster a limited epistemic reach that fails to account for many important components in the healing process. Biomedical advocate Louis Reed offers multifactorial insight why this is important. In the early 1930s, Reed listed several key reasons why people turn to what he calls medical 'delusions' or 'cults' – what today is deemed alternative or complementary therapy. They include patient ignorance, gullibility, superstition, and deficiencies in scientific knowledge, the medical profession's impotence to cure certain diseases; as well as the physicians' disregard of mental, nervous, and emotional factors and their influence upon the health of the body, and the lack of a doctor's willingness to investigate obscure illnesses rather than 'change medication again'. Reed, *Healing Cults*, op. cit., pp. 110–15. In other words, Reed, a staunch enemy of medical 'cults' and an ardent defender of scientific medicine, presciently saw how medical 'specialism' has divided the human body into a 'multiplicity of departments' and thereby lost its 'soul and spirit to the tyranny of materialism', ibid., pp. 113–4. In effect, as Robert Ader reminds us, the 'compartmentalised and bureau-craticised' divisions of medical science into the separate fields of immunology, cardiology, histology, etc. have no bearing on the way life operates because biology doesn't recognise such divisions. R. Ader, 'Conditioned responses', in Bill Moyers (ed.), *Healing and the Mind*, New York, Doubleday, 1993, p. 245.

133   According to a 1997 survey, total 'out-of-pocket expenditures relating to alternative therapies', estimated at US $27.0 billion, is comparable to the 1997 out-of-pocket expenditures for 'all US physician services'. D. Eisenberg, *et al.*, 'Trends in alternative medicine use in the United States, 1990–1997', *Journal of the American Medical Association* 280, 11 (1998): 1569.

134   Cooter, 'Introduction', op. cit., p. x.

135   This also implies that diagnostic labels must be used with caution given that, as Benson points out, they shape a patient's 'psyche' and can affect the way a patient responds to treatment. Benson and Stark, *Timeless Healing*, op. cit., p. 18. By way of example, Benson mentions how one doctor used fear to encourage a woman to get a calcium deposit removed from her breast, 'just in case'. The emotional distress the woman felt from the operation over what she perceived to be a deformity in her breast led to far greater damage than the initial surgery, ibid., p. 18.

Index